D0674177

The **Smaller Perennials**

The **Smaller Perennials**

Jack Elliott

B.T. Batsford Ltd, London

Acknowledgements

I am indebted to Elizabeth Strangman and Graeme Gough for letting me study and in some instances photograph plants in their fine collection at Washfield Nursery.

I am especially grateful to my wife Jean for putting up patiently with all the hours of computer widowhood, and for her invaluable proof-reading and encouragement.

First published in Great Britain 1997

All photographs are by the author.

A CIP catalogue record for this book is available from the British Library.

ISBN 0 7134 7799 7

Printed in Hong Kong

For the Publishers

B.T. Batsford Ltd
583 Fulham Road
London SW6 5BY

Contents

Photographic plates

Chapter 1

Chapter 2

Chapter 1

What are Smaller Perennials

In defining small perennials I am including plants up to a maximum height of about 75 cm (2.5 ft), bearing in mind that their height varies greatly from garden to garden and from season to season, according to rainfall and nutrient levels, and I am relying mainly on experience in my own garden. Where foliage is their most important feature I have included a few plants that may be somewhat taller when they are in flower.

I have not set a minimum size, and in drawing a line between 'alpines' or 'rock plants' and 'small perennials' my choice has been governed by ease of cultivation, vigour, and ultimate spread. Also I have only included plants which are sufficiently robust for use in the front of a herbaceous or mixed border, or among shrubs in woodland or in a shady bed, and which would be out of place in the average-sized rock garden. There are many genera mainly composed of plants which are of the right height for the rock garden but which are altogether too strong-growing, for example *Epimedium*, *Lamium*, and *Ajuga*, and a large proportion of *Geranium*.

I have excluded plants normally accepted as shrubs, and also all bulbous- and tuberous-rooted plants, although some rhizomatous plants will be found. I have also omitted culinary herbs, unless they possess some merit as flowering plants, and aquatic plants.

Small Plants for Small Gardens

Most gardening enthusiasts eventually suffer from (or perhaps enjoy) a desire to grow as many plants as possible, whether they garden in a plot of a few square metres or of several acres. Choosing smaller perennials makes it possible to grow a larger collection in a restricted space, while maintaining the scale of the garden. The usual design of a border need not be affected, with a gradient from taller plants at the back to prostrate plants in the front – and even some extra tall 'dot plants' for special effect – but with the whole scale reduced to half or less, with the tallest plants only 1–1.5 m (3–5 ft) high.

1 *Veronica austriaca* 'Crater Lake Blue' with a Dianthus seedling, and a white Helianthemum

Foreground Planting

In many gardens with herbaceous or mixed borders, the area between the path or lawn and the main plant groups is left bare or sparsely planted. This is an ideal position for low-growing plants. These can be used to give added colour in front of the main flowering masses, or to provide bloom before the main display has started. Good examples of low-growing, spring- or early summer-flowering plants are phlox, pulmonarias, dianthus, *Arenaria montana*, or *Veronica peduncularis*, while at the end of the season sedums, zauschnerias, origanums and other late-flowerers may be used.

Some care is needed in the choice and positioning of plants if the bed abuts on a lawn in order to avoid plants flopping across the grass too much. However, alongside a path or an edging of paving slabs, the plants can be closer to the edge and allowed to spread across and soften the outline. The low-growing campanulas, dianthus, diascias, smaller geraniums, and violas are ideal for this purpose.

Interplanting Shrubs

In beds planted with shrubs with proper regard to their eventual spread, large areas of soil between them are often left bare. These can be planted with perennials to give a colourful undercarpet. The opposite extreme is seen in gardens devoted to the popular conception of labour-saving with shrubs and ground cover. The shrubs are underplanted with rapidly spreading plants such as *Lamium galeobdolon*, *Geranium procurrens*, *Vinca major*, or ivies. This type of gardening may achieve its aim as long as perennial weeds have been cleared before planting. The problems start if the gardener becomes bored with the limitations of his ground cover and decides to replace it with more interesting plants.

Ground cover is easier to establish than to remove. A lot of hard work or even use of weed-killers may be necessary to recover some bare soil which will need improving with compost or manure before more exciting plants can be installed. The moral is that unless you want a garden in which large areas are furnished with a few trouble-free plants, it is better to choose more interesting slower-growing perennials, which will take longer to establish, but will give a lot more pleasure over the years.

Planting in Shade

There is a tremendous variety of small plants which enjoy shady conditions, and these can be planted among trees and shrubs, or in beds shaded by walls, fences, or buildings. There they can be associated with shade-loving bulbs, such as trilliums, erythroniums, *Anemone nemorosa* and *A. raunnculoides* forms, or with larger perennials such as meconopsis, polygonatums, hostas, cardiocrinums etc.

Dry shade presents special problems as the dryness is often associated with the proximity of a wall or with tree roots. Soil preparation is discussed below and some suggestions for possible plants for this difficult type of site are made in the alphabetical list. Appendix 1 lists the main genera of shade-loving plants.

Tender Plants

Although I have excluded greenhouse plants, I have described many semi-hardy plants that can be grown rapidly from overwintered cuttings and which will flower continuously from early summer until the frosts of autumn. These are enjoying a well-deserved vogue, both as plants for ornamental containers and for filling in gaps in the border. Many of them, for example, osteospermums and verbenas, will survive our milder winters if left in the garden, and they are hardy in gardens in parts of the USA and in warmer countries elsewhere.

In cold gardens cuttings of these plants should be taken in late summer, when they will root quickly, and the young potted plants overwintered in a frost-free greenhouse for planting in the garden when the danger of frosts is over in late spring.

Soil Preparation

Most of the plants described are easy to grow, but suitable soil preparation can make all the difference between happy plants of full size, which increase freely, and stunted plants which fail to thrive. Much depends on the natural soil of the garden and if this is a good, reasonably well-drained loam, little preparation will be needed other than appropriate use of fertilisers if nutrients are low.

Light sandy soils are a joy to work with, but the plants tend to exhaust their nourishment quickly, unless regular steps are taken to improve the ground by incorporating manure, compost, or leafmould whenever possible.

Clay soils are much more difficult to cope with, but once they have been improved many plants will thrive better on them and will persist longer. Drainage is the main problem and this can often be improved by digging in coarse, crushed grit in the beds before planting. A size of 6 mm diameter down to sand is ideal for this. Humus may help to a lesser degree in the form of manure, compost, peat, or peat substitute, dug in whenever the ground is workable.

Shade-loving plants are also lovers of humus-rich soil and moisture. They benefit from the incorporation of as much peat, leaf mould or compost as possible, reducing the need for irrigation. Many of them need acid soil, and care should be taken not to alter the pH if it is already acid. Certain types of leaves, notably beech, along with bone-meal and mushroom compost are usually alkaline, and should be avoided where lime-haters are to be grown. Manure may also raise the pH appreciably unless it is mixed with peat.

Plant Associations

Some suggestions for associations with other perennials, shrubs, and bulbs, have been included in the plant descriptions and are shown in some of the photographs, but exigencies of space have prevented me from dealing with this subject as fully as I would like. I hope that the descriptions of the plants will give sufficient information for the reader to plan his own associations, be they gentle combinations of pastel shades or startling contrasts of hot reds and yellows.

2 *Cuphea caeciliae*, Arctotis 'Flame' and *Bidens ferulifolia* in containers

Propagation

I have indicated for most genera the best methods of propagation, but I would refer those who are uncertain of the techniques involved to the many books covering the subject. See the Appendix on Further Reading.

Award of Garden Merit 🏆

This award is given by the Royal Horticultural Society to those plants considered to be of the greatest value as easily-grown and readily available garden plants. The AGM list is produced after a great deal of discussion by the various specialist committees involved, and although it will be constantly updated, I think the present list is of great value. I have put the AGM symbol 🏆 after the names of those plants mentioned which have received the Award.

✸ – This symbol is used to indicate plants of special merit for their flowers, apart from those which have received the 🏆. It is a personal choice with a slight bias towards the charm of natural species rather than to man-made hybrids.

✪ – This symbol denotes a similar personal choice of plants with outstanding foliage which have not received the 🏆.

Chapter 2

Acaena (*Rosaceae*)

A genus of some 100 species, mainly from C. and S. America, and New Zealand. Creeping, usually evergreen perennials, rooting down as they spread, making low carpets of attractive, fern-like leaves, light green or tinged with blue or bronze, with insignificant flowers and burr-like fruits. Easy in any but the heaviest soils in sun or light shade, many species are invasive, and their burrs can be very troublesome to domestic animals, so that 'new' unknown species should be treated cautiously. They are really too vigorous for the rock garden, or for 'covering' small bulbs, but can be grown in paving cracks, or as ground cover among shrubs or larger perennials. Those described are the commonest (and safest) in cultivation. Easily propagated by division in spring or by cuttings during summer. From New Zealand unless stated.

A. affinis (syn. *A. adscendens*) Mat with blue-green leaves and red fruits, not rooting down too freely. S. Am.

A. anserinifolia Robust-rooting carpet, leaves pinnate, 8 cm (3 in) long, brown-tinged, burrs yellowish to brown.

A. 'Blue Haze' (syn. *'Pewter'*) ☼ Spreading widely without rooting, leaves to 10 cm (4 in), pinnate, pale grey-blue, burrs reddish on 15 cm (6 in) red stems. Of uncertain origin but one of the most valuable and ornamental.

A. buchananii Very vigorous carpet, leaves green, fruits brown. A spreader and a menace to cats.

A. caesiiglauca Vigorous, low, mat-forming, leaves beautiful glaucous blue, pinnate, to 5 cm (2 in), burrs pale brownish on 12 cm (4.7 in) stems in autumn.

A. inermis (syn. *A.microphylla* var. *inermis*) Differs from *A. microphylla* in its longer leaves, and spineless, reddish burrs.

A. magellanica (syn. *A. anserinifolia* hort) Variable, not rooting down freely, leaves 5 cm (2 in), fern-like, blue-green, burrs brownish on 12–15 cm (4.7–6 in) stems.

A. microphylla Creeping, rooting mat, leaves 3 cm (1.2 in), pinnate, green, or bronze-tinged, burrs conspicuously red-spined. Probably the most ornamental in fruit. 'Kupferteppich' copper-coloured leaves, 'Robusta' more vigorous.

A. myriophylla Vigorous, sparsely-rooting species, leaves 10 cm (4 in), fern-like, hairy, fruits insignificant. S. Am.

A. novae-zelandiae Carpeting, leaves 10 cm (4 in), green, fruits striking, reddish-purple, spiny.

A. pinnatifida Over-vigorous carpeter with excessively spiny fruits. S. Am.

A. sericea Very good foliage plant, leaves to 8 cm (3 in), silky-hairy, silver or pale yellowish. S. Am.

Acanthus (*Acanthaceae*)

About 20 species, mainly Mediterranean, of hardy, clump-forming perennials with thick, fleshy roots. The widely grown and majestic species *A. mollis*, *A. spinosa*, and *A. hungarica* (*A. balcanicus*) are too big to consider here, but there are some less common species which have the same air of importance on a smaller scale, with dark, glossy-green, deeply cut or lobed leaves, and fascinating spiny spires of hooded flowers. They are easily grown in a sunny or slightly shaded border in rich soil, and are less invasive, at least for a while, than their larger brethren. All can be increased from root cuttings, and they may also be raised from seed. Self-sown seedlings can become a nuisance if they are not dead-headed.

A. caroli-alexandrae Possibly a dwarf form of *A. hungarica*, 60 cm (2 ft), with white flowers with dark purplish bracts. It does not spread quite so quickly. Rarely offered.

A. dioscoridis Smaller with pink flowers beneath grey-green bracts, leaves simple and lanceolate in var. *dioscoridis*, deeply cut and spiny in var. *perringii*. Var. *brevicaulis* only 18 cm (7 in) high. S. Am.

A. hirsutus Uncommon, with deeply lobed, pale green leaves and hairy stems, flowers yellowish with green bracts.

A. spinosissimus ☼ A striking, hedgehog-like foliage plant, with deeply divided leaves, abundantly furnished with silvery spines. Tall if it produces its slender spikes of flowers.

A. syriacus (syn. *A. hirsutus* subsp. *syriacus*) Similar to *A. caroli-alexandri*, but shorter, leaves very spiny, flower spikes more compact.

Achillea (*Compositae*)

A popular and widely grown genus of clump-forming perennials, mainly from S. Europe, many of them at the upper limit of our height range, and a few over. Most have attractive, finely divided grey or green leaves, and the typical, dense flat-heads of tiny, daisy flowers in shades from white to deep yellow, with a few newer hybrids in pinks and reds, in mid- to late summer. They are easily grown in any sunny border, but the taller may need staking. All tend to to turn to an ugly brown as they fade, and are better dead-headed. They can be propagated by division or by cuttings of the young shoots. Most benefit from frequent division and replanting.

I have excluded those usually over 70 cm (28 in), and several small species under 15 cm (6 in), which do best in a well-drained rock garden.

A. abrotanoides 20–35 cm (8–14 in) leaves pale green, ferny, flowers small white in loose heads. Not among the best.

A. ageratum (syn. *A. decolorans*) Usually seen in the form of 'W.B. Child', possibly a hybrid of *A. ptarmica*. 60–70 cm (24–28 in), leaves dark green, finely cut, flowers white with yellowish centres, in good loose heads.

A. cartilaginea Resembles *A. ptarmica*, leaves larger, flowers smaller.

A. clypeolata To 60 cm (2 ft), fine leaves, silvery feather-like, flowers, bright yellow in flat heads.
A.* x *lewisii 'King Edward' 🏆 Mats of simple grey-green, toothed leaves, flowers in fine lemon-yellow heads, paling with age. A beautiful dwarf species good in front of the border.
A. millefolium (Yarrow) An invasive weed, with several better, more easily controlled forms, for the front of the border with finely divided, dark green leaves, and small flowers in broad flat-heads, pink in 'Borealis', deeper pink in 'Cerise Queen', dark red in 'Sammetreise', and 'Red Beauty', even darker in 'Summer Wine'. Various other names may appear. Seedlings have a tendency to revert and should be removed promptly.
A. ptarmica (Sneezewort) Creeping to 60 cm (2 ft), leaves simple lanceolate, green, flowers muddy-white in loose heads. Scarcely worth growing but with better pure white double-flowered forms – 'Perry's White' and 'The Pearl', 'Nana Compacta', a good dwarf semi-double.
A.* x *taygetae (***A. millefolium*** x ***A. clypeolata***) An attractive hybrid with ferny green leaves and flat-heads of cream flowers, to 50 cm (20 in) high.
A. tomentosa 🏆 An excellent dwarf species, making a low spreading carpet of silvery-grey hairy leaves, with 20 cm (8 in) stems bearing flat-heads of bright yellow flowers.

Other Hybrids: There are several other excellent hybrids and cultivars to 60 cm (2 ft) high, mainly of *A. tomentosa* and *A. taygetae*; Alabaster, Leaves grey, ferny, flowers pale yellow, fading white; Anthea, ✱ leaves silvery, cream; Apfelblute (Appleblossom), tall, pink; 'Coronation Gold' 🏆 leaves grey-green ferny, deep gold; Fanal (The Beacon), red; Hartington White, leaves grey-green, ferny, white; Hoffnung, pale yellow; Lachsschonheit (Salmon Beauty); salmon fading cream; Martina, leaves ferny green, pale yellow. Moonshine, 🏆 leaves grey-green, ferny; Paprika, red; Schwefelblute, leaves grey, feathery, sulphur-yellow; Schwellenberg, lemon yellow; Wesersandstein, leaves green, feathery, deep salmon fading to pale yellow.

3 *Achillea* 'Coronation Gold'

Aciphylla ☼

An interesting genus from Australasia, which presents some problems in the context of this book as the largest species will become well over 60 cm (2 ft) high in time; the smaller species are best grown in the alpine house or rock garden.

All form remarkable rosettes of dangerously pointed, needle-like leaves, gold or blue in colour, eventually with tall,spiny flower spikes of insignificant flowers. The only larger species in general cultivation are *A. aurea*, with golden rosettes up to 1 m (3 ft) wide, *A. glaucescens* and *A. scott-thompsonii*, with even larger rosettes of glaucous blue leaves, and *A. subflabellata*, with greyish-brown rosettes not more than 60 cm (2 ft) wide, all of which will take several years to exceed our limits, and meanwhile are intriguing foliage plants. Although fascinating they are impossible to weed around, and are genuinely dangerous to children.

Aconitum (Monkshood)

A large genus of very worthwhile plants for good soil in semi-shade or sun. The small species are not currently available from trade sources in Britain, and in good conditions the remainder should usually attain 1 m (3 ft). In my experience one or two are often shorter, notably *A. lycoctonum* ssp *vulparia*, with the typical palmately divided leaves of the genus, and hooded flowers of a pleasing, pale creamy-yellow in mid- to late summer. 'Ivorine' probably a form of the blue-flowered and generally larger *A. lycoctonum* ssp. *lycoctonum*, has green-tinged white flowers, and also barely reaches 60 mm in my dry soil.

Adenophora (*Campanulaceae*)

A neglected genus closely resembling *Campanula*, which may become more popular with the recent introduction of several new species from China and Japan. All are most attractive, clump-forming perennials, less invasive than many campanulas, with nodding, bell-shaped flowers in shades of pale blue to deep violet, in mid- to late summer, easily grown in rich, preferably well-drained soil in sun or partial shade. Propagate from seed, which germinates quickly if sown soon after collection.
A. bulleyana, A. confusa, A. divaricata, A. polyantha, and ***A. stricta,*** probably too tall for inclusion, attaining 1 m (3 ft) in good soils.
A. forrestii Upright to 30 cm (1 ft), leaves in rosettes 5 cm (2 in), lanceolate, flowers in loose sprays on slender branching stems, deep violet-blue. A promising plant.
A. liliifolia Upright, 40 cm (16 in), leaves coarsely toothed, ovate-lanceolate to 7 cm (2.8 in), spires of widely bell-shaped pale blue flowers.
A. nikoensis Smaller, 20–30 cm (8–12 in), leaves narrowly lanceolate to 8 cm (3 in), loose spikes of pale blue bells. Var. *stenophylla* (syn. *A nipponica*) similar but with broader untoothed calyx lobes.
A. pereskiifolia 40 cm (16 in), leaves whorled, ovate,

pointed with deeply toothed margins, flowers in abundant racemes, often branching, mid-blue, occasionally white. Var. *heterotricha* taller with denser racemes.

A. potaninii Taller with floppy stems, leaves 5 cm (2 in) wide, usually toothed, flowers in loose heads, widely bell-shaped, nodding, violet.

A. stricta To 80 cm (30 in), branching stems, lower leaves kidney-shaped, upper ovate, toothed, flowers large, nodding, violet, on short petioles, in short dense spikes. A good late-flowering species. Var. *sessilifolia* in my garden is shorter, with sessile flowers.

A. takedae Variable to 60 cm (2 ft), leaves long, narrow on arching stems, leafy few-flowered spikes of pale violet flowers. Var. *howozana* is a dwarf, high alpine form, 15 cm (6 in), with smaller flowers.

A. tashiroi Low growing with semi-prostrate stems, leaves alternate, small, ovate, toothed, flowers few, violet in a short terminal spike.

A. triphylla Variable to 80 cm (30 in), in my experience much shorter, leaves ovate in whorls, flowers pale blue, broadly bell-shaped, in short, upright, branching spikes. Var. *japonica* flowers larger.

Adonis (*Ranunculaceae*)

A small genus of exquisitely beautiful plants, with finely dissected leaves, and proportionately large, buttercup-like flowers in spring. Only two perennial species are commonly in cultivation, and none seem very easy to please. They do best in humus-rich, well-drained soil that never dries out, in sun or partial shade, at the front of a border or among shrubs. They associate well with bulbs such as dwarf narcissi, scillas, chionodoxas, and crocus species. Propagation is best by seed sown immediately after collection.

A. amurensis ✱ Clump-forming, leaves 15 cm (6 in), pale green, beautifully feathery, finely cut, flowers solitary, pure yellow, bowl-shaped to 5 cm (2 in) wide, in early spring. Japan. Many cultivars in Japan, but only the double-flowered 'Flore Pleno' and 'Fukujakai' are readily available elsewhere. The latter has larger semi-double flowers and may prove more robust.

A. pyrenaica More scarce, differs mainly in having basal as well as stem leaves.

A. vernalis Similar to *A. amurensis*, but with shorter and broader, even more finely dissected leaves, and flowering a little later. Europe.

Agapanthus (*Liliaceae*)

A superb genus from S. Africa, much hardier than gardeners expect, especially the deciduous species and hybrids. Densely clump-forming, with glossy, strap-like leaves, and fine, rounded heads of bright blue or white flowers on stiff upright stems in late summer. They thrive in rich soil in sun, and build up into crowded colonies. Overcrowding suits them; they flower better, and can be left undisturbed for many years. Increase by division. Mostly too big to describe here, but 'Headbourne Hybrids' ✱ are 50–100 cm (20–40 in), in shades of blue or pure white. 'Lilliput' a delightful new miniature, dark blue flowers on stems of 30 cm (1 ft) or less, has proved hardy for a few winters.

Agastache (*Labiatae*) (Mexican Hyssop)

An interesting N. American genus, many of which have only recently appeared in gardens, mainly thanks to seed collections in the USA. Most of the species are upright perennials with branching stems and long-lasting dense spikes of tubular, 2-lipped flowers in mid- to late summer. They are easily raised from seed, or can be divided when established. They do best in warm, sunny positions in the border. They may not be long-lived, but they are easily propagated by seed sown in autumn or by cuttings of young shoots in early summer. The smaller species described here are considered to be the least tender and they have survived to -6 °C (21 °F) in Kent.

A. barberi Only in cultivation as the very striking cultivar 'Firebird' ✱ 40 cm (16 in), basal leaves ovate with crenate margins, stems upright, branching, leaves simple, oval-lanceolate, grey-green, flowers tubular 2.5 cm (1 in), bright pinkish-orange, in terminal spikes, late summer. It combines well with the salmon shades of some diascias.

4 *Agastache* 'Firebird'

A. cana Similar to the last but with deep rose-pink flowers. Slightly more tender.

A. foeniculum Erect with unbranched stems, sometimes taller than the above, leaves larger, toothed, ovate, whitish beneath, scented, flowers smaller, violet-coloured in short spikes. Two cultivars available, 'Alabaster' and 'Alba', both white. They may be identical.

A. mexicana (syn *Cedronella mexicana*) A better-known species, similar to *A. cana*, slender spikes of flowers varying in colour, most commonly a dark reddish-pink. Three

cultivars reflect some of the colour range, 'Carille Carmine', 'Champagne', and 'Mauve Beauty'.
A. pallidiflora Uncommon in cultivation, 60–100 cm (24–40 in), flowers white or pale pink.

Ajuga (*Labiatae*) (Bugle)

Vigorous, very hardy, carpet-forming, stoloniferous, evergreen perennials, those listed mainly from Europe, useful as ground cover in difficult conditions of dry shade or poor soil but, with a few exceptions; too invasive in good garden soil. Many cultivars are listed with attractive variations in leaf colour. The whorls of 2-lipped tubular flowers in early summer tend to be obscured by leafy bracts, but are worthwhile in some plants. They are easily propagated by division.
A. genevensis Rarely grown species, leaves long-petiolate, obovate, stems hairy to 20 cm (8 in), flowers in terminal whorls, good deep blue, not concealed by bracts, with broad lower lips. Not so invasive and prefers more sun than the others.
A. pyramidalis Common, similar to *A. genevensis*, rosettes of dark green leaves and blue flowers in dense pyramidal spikes, leafy bracts longer than the flowers. 'Metallica Crispa' similar but the leaves have a bronze sheen and crinkled margins. Less vigorous and usually non-invasive.
A. reptans Stoloniferous, rooting at the nodes and spreading very freely, to 15 cm (6 in). Leaves in rosettes, oval to rounded, long petioles, varying greatly in colour, short dense spikes of flowers, in shades of blue, pink, or white. The following cultivars are readily available, with blue flowers except where stated: 'Alba', Leaves dark green, flowers white, 'Atropurpurea', Leaves dark purple, 'Braunherz', Leaves dark purple, glossy, 'Burgundy Glow', Leaves pale green centre, cream edge, purple shading, 'Catlin's Giant', ✪ Leaves very large, bownish purple, a striking plant in good soil, 'Delight', Leaves bronze-tinged, with pink and cream streaks, 'Julia', Leaves green, good purplish-pink flowers, 'Jungle Beauty' Leaves very large, bronze in winter, flowers deep blue, 'Multicolor' ('Tricolor', 'Rainbow') Leaves bronze, streaked with yellow and pink, 'Pink Elf', Leaves green, good pink flowers, 'Pink Surprise', Leaves dark purple, flowers reddish-pink, 'Silver Carpet', Leaves silvery, 'Silver Shadow', Leaves pale grey-green, 'Variegata' Leaves grey-green, edged white, pink-tinged in winter.

Alchemilla (*Rosaceae*)

Charming plants, especially to the lover of 'greenery', with beautiful leaves, and clusters of green or yellowish-green flowers, which stay in fine condition over a long period in early to mid-summer. *Alchemilla mollis* is one of the most popular of all plants with large, downy, pale green, palmate leaves, often retaining raindrops in their centres, and loose sprays of abundant tiny yellow-green flowers to about 60 cm (2 ft). Easily grown in sun or part shade, it can become a menace if the old flower stems are left to scatter their seed around the garden. Perhaps at its best when it self-seeds into a paving crack. Most other species give a similar effect on a much smaller scale, and although suitable for the rock garden, they can make a good border edging in front of other perennials or shrubs. Propagate by seed, or by division of the creeping species. Those described are mainly European.
A. abyssinica Mat-forming, leaves pale green, 6–7–lobed, sparsely hairy, to 4 cm (1.6 in) wide, flowers in small green heads. N. Africa, possibly not hardy below -8 °C (18 °F).
A. alpina Clump former, leaves rounded, deeply divided, hairy, with silvery backs, flowers yellowish-green. An appealing small, silvery foliage plant.
A. conjuncta Similar to *A. alpina*, leaves less deeply cleft, grey-green, silver-hairy on the back and margins.
A. elisabethae Similar to *A. erythropoda*, flower stems taller, leaves 7-lobed.
A. ellenbeckii Low carpeter from Africa, surprisingly hardy, freely rooting, prostrate reddish stems, leaves 2–2.5 cm (0.8–1 in), hairy, palmate, flowers in little, rounded clusters among the leaves. Good low ground cover in sun or partial shade
A. erythropoda 🏆 Small, clump-forming, 20 cm (8 in), leaves very hairy, bluish, flowers yellowish-green in small clusters.
A. faeroensis Clump-forming, 25 cm (10 in), leaves deeply cleft, 7-lobed, silver-hairy beneath, flowers in small clusters. *A. lapeyrousii* (syn. *A. hybrida*) similar, leaves reniform, uniformly hairy.
A. mollis 🏆 The splendid large species described above. 'Robusta' is doubtfully distinct.
A splendens Clump-forming, leaves shallowly lobed, sparsely hairy, flowers yellow-green in multiple small heads on wiry stems.
A. xanthochlora (*A. vulgaris*) Like *A. mollis*, less effective, flower heads smaller, less yellow, leaves less hairy.

Alonsoa (*Scrophulariaceae*)

Small genus of tender, upright perennials from S. America, with masses of flat-faced flowers, closely resembling those of diascias. They are easily grown from seed; treated as annuals in cold areas. They are useful for their very long flowering season through the summer, as container plants or as 'fillers' in the border. They may also be grown from cuttings, and these overwintered in a frost-free house.
A. meridionalis Similar to *A. warscewiczii*, but flowers very small, orange, in loose terminal spikes, obscured by the leaves.
A. warscewiczii 🏆 Upright clump of loosely branching stems, leaves small-toothed, flowers abundant, brilliant orange-scarlet for many weeks, the best species. 'Peachy Keen' ✸ is a less startling colour, a pleasing soft salmon-pink, and possibly even more floriferous.

Alstroemeria (*Liliaceae*/*Alstroemeriaceae*)

A spectacular genus of S. American tuberous-rooted perennials, which have been popular for many years, mainly in the form of *A. aurea* (syn *A. aurantiaca*), and the 'Ligtu

Hybrids'. Recently a magnificent race of hybrids has been developed for the cut-flower market, and they are proving reasonably hardy in the garden. All are too tall for consideration here when well-grown. During the last few years an increasing number of new species have been introduced, many of them still relatively untried. Their size varies, depending on the area of their collection and on their method of cultivation; some of those mentioned may attain more than 60 cm (2 ft).

Although slow to establish, some species can become invasive, and this should be considered when choosing a site for them. Generally they thrive in a warm, sunny border with excellent drainage, but will tolerate some shade. They strongly resent disturbance once established and although they can be divided with care, propagation is safer from seed. This germinates best if the seed pans are kept in bottom heat for six weeks, and then kept cool in the open or in a cold frame until germination. A few may germinate while in the heat.

A. hookeri A beautiful dwarf to 12 cm (4.7 in), usually grown in the cold greenhouse, but worth trying in mild areas. Leaves glaucous, blue-green, narrow and twisted, shorter and broader on flowering shoots. Flowers in large umbels, funnel-shaped, clear pink spotted with red.

A. ligtu The parent of the 'Ligtu Hybrids', recently re-collected with some smaller forms. All have narrowly ovate to lanceolate glaucous, or green leaves, and large, tubular flowers with the upper petals much longer than the lower, varying in colour but with darker stripes. Subsp. *ligtu*, very variable in size, has pale to deep pink, or soft orange flowers, with darker streaking. Subsp. *simsii* (syn. *A. haemantha*) usually taller, with long, narrow, deep reddish-orange flowers, streaked orange. Subsp. *incarnata* (syn. var. *andina*) is shorter, with pink flowers with brownish markings. All are good garden plants, but can spread widely.

A. pallida Relatively untried, usually to 30 cm (1 ft), leaves narrow, twisted; fine flowers very broad white to deep pink, in large umbels.

A. pelegrina ✱ 15–25 cm (6–10 in) Leaves thick, glaucous, twisted, flowers very large, open-faced, pale pink, with a deep rose centre to each petal, marked brown and yellow towards the base of the upper petals. It is a very beautiful species which I find somewhat tender; has survived recent mild winters outside. Var. 'Alba' is similar, flowers pure greenish-white, with dark green markings on a yellowish base on the upper petals.

5 *Alstroemeria pelegrina* in front of a south wall

A. psittacina (syn. *A. pulchella*) 80–100 cm (30–40 in), leaves green and twisted, flowers a fascinating combination of deep crimson with heavy brown spotting and streaking, and prominent green tips. It seems remarkably hardy. 'Variegata' leaves edged pale cream, shorter-growing.

A. revoluta Medium height, leaves glaucous, twisted, flowers pink with markedly recurved petals, in tight umbels, the upper with red speckling on a yellow band. It seems reasonably hardy.

A. spathulata Recently introduced, leaves fleshy, glaucous, spathulate, flowers narrow pink with red markings in the throat, in umbels. It becomes drawn under glass but may be sufficiently hardy for the garden.

A. violacea (syn. *A. paupercula*) A most beautiful species which sadly seems to need glass protection in southern England. The leaves are green with wavy margins, the flowers large, widely open, rich violet with darker violet spotting, sometimes paler and sometimes with a white band on the upper petals.

Alyssoides (*Cruciferae*)

A. utriculatum The only species in general cultivation; an easily grown, hardy shrublet from S. Europe, with branching stems bearing rosettes of long, spathulate-oblong leaves and racemes of bright yellow crucifer flowers to 30 cm (1 ft) high, in late spring and early summer. The flowers are followed by spires of very attractive spherical, grey-green seed capsules, the plants best feature. It is an interesting plant for the border edge in well-drained soil; not long-lived but seeding around without becoming a nuisance.

Alyssum (*Cruciferae*)

Mainly suitable for the rock garden or dry wall, but with a few larger species which can be used in the front of the border, or on sunny banks. They are characteristically sun-loving, semi-shrubby perennials from S. Europe and W. Asia, forming mounds or carpets with an abundance of flowers, mainly in shades of yellow, in spring and early summer. They may be propagated from seed or by cuttings of young shoots in early summer.

A. markgraffii Rounded shrubby mounds to 30 cm (1 ft), stems branching, leaves tiny, grey-green, myriads of small, bright yellow flowers in early summer. An uncommon species that self-seeds freely in any sunny spot.

A. montanum Low spreading mounds, leaves greyish, abundant, small, dense heads of yellow flowers The most widely grown species, good in walls with aubrietas and similar rock plants, but suitable for a border edging. 'Berggold' similar but flowers paler.

A. moellendorfii Darker orange-yellow flowers and leaves with longer petioles.

A. saxatile See ***Aurinia***

6 *Alyssum markgrafii* with *Astrantia major* behind it

A. tortuosum Low mats of tiny, silver leaves, flowers deep yellow in small clusters; late spring. Uncommon in the garden, but well worth growing, self-sowing freely.

Amsonia (*Apocynaceae*)

Upright-growing perennials to 60 cm (2 ft), now including *Rhazya*, with long, narrow, alternate stem leaves with conspicuous veins and terminal clusters of good blue flowers over a long period in summer; thriving in good moist soil in sun or light shade. They may be propagated by division or by cuttings of the new growths in early summer.

A. ciliata 40 cm (16 in), leaves very narrow, flowers pale blue. The least common. S. USA.

A. orientalis (syn. *Rhazya orientalis*) 🏆 Upright stems from a dense, woody rootstock to 60 cm (2 ft), leaves glossy lanceolate, flowers clear blue, long-tubed, in loose heads. Excellent for the border. E. Europe–Caucasus.

A. tabernaemontana Very similar but not quite as effective as *A. orientalis*. being slightly shorter with less conspicuously veined leaves and paler flowers. S.E. USA.

Anaphalis (*Compositae*)

These are generally vigorous, spreading, clump-formers from Asia with very white, woolly leaves, and dense clusters of white 'everlasting' flowers. None are tall and they are excellent for providing a grey edging to a border, in sun or shade, even growing well in poor soils. They are easily increased by division or may be raised from seed sown in autumn and kept cool. The flowers of all the species dry well for flower arrangements.

A. margaritacea (syn *A. cinnamonia*) Spreading, rhizomatous, upright stems to 60 cm (2 ft) or slightly more, leaves grey-green above, whitish beneath, flowers small, white with brownish centres, in loose heads in mid- to late summer. Var. *yedoensis* 🏆 similar but even whiter.

A. nepalensis (syn *A. triplinervis* var. *intermedia*) More compact, usually less than 30 cm (1 ft), leaves very white-woolly, lanceolate, flowers pure white in small clusters.

A. sinica 30 cm (1 ft), leaves 4–6 cm (1.6–2.3 in) long, greyish-green, flowers white in dense rounded heads, less widely grown. Var. *morii* is more compact with smaller flowers heads.

A. trinervis To 60 cm (2 ft), slender stems, leaves grey-green, white-backed, white flowers in loose heads. A rare species.

A. triplinervis 🏆 Robust to 60 cm (2 ft), leaves oval, silver-grey, flowers large, shining white. *A. t. intermedia see A. nepalensis. A. t. var. monocephala* (syn. *A. nubigena*) smaller growing with larger flower heads. 'Summer Snow' 🏆 is a particularly fine cultivar.

Anchusa (*Boraginaceae*)

A genus of excellent, mainly herbaceous perennials, the majority tall and upright-growing with branching heads of truly blue flowers. They contrast well in the border with the various yellow 'daisies' of summer.

A. azurea Fine genuinely blue perennials, too tall except 'Little John', an upright 40 cm (16 in) clump-former, leaves coarsely hairy, lanceolate, flowers bright blue, funnel-shaped in branching heads. It should not need staking.

A. leptophylla Upright-growing to 40 cm (16 in), flowers azure in loose sprays. Once confused with the typically alpine *A. caespitosa*, this is a beautiful species, usually short-lived, but very easy to raise from seed.

Anemone (*Ranunculaceae*)

A very important genus of perennials, varying greatly in habit and in type of rootstock. Many are typical small alpines, and many are tuberous-rooted; I have excluded most of these, with the exception of *Anemone nemorosa* cultivars, which can cover a substantial area in shady or woodland conditions and make considerable impact. Most of those described are herbaceous, with spreading rhizomes, palmate or deeply divided leaves, and large, usually saucer-shaped flowers, solitary or in umbels, often on branching stems.

In general they do best in humus-rich soil in partial shade, but will tolerate full sun if the soil is reasonably moist, and in good conditions many can become slightly invasive; a glorious sight in the right place. Propagation is usually by division, essential for the cultivars, or by seed, which should be sown as soon as possible after collection and kept cool.

A. altaica Very similar to *A. nemorosa* but rhizomes thicker, and flowers with blue veining on the inside of the segments. Russia.

A. baicalensis Rhizomatous, with single white flowers on 20 cm (8 in) stems in late spring. Uncommon, not very floriferous, and capable of covering a lot of ground. E. Asia.
A. canadensis (syn. *A. pennsylvanica*) 20-50 cm (8–20 in), vigorous, spreading plant, leaves 5-lobed. Lobes divided and toothed, flowers starry-white in a branching head in early summer. The true plant described is a useful woodlander, but I have seen *A. multifida* under this name. N. Am.
A. cylindrica Over-leafy, large plant, with very small flowers in summer, resembling *A. canadensis*. N. Am.
A. hupehensis To 60 cm (2 ft), leaves 3-lobed, deeply toothed, flowers white, pale pink, or deep pink, to 6 cm (2.3 in) wide, the reverse of the petals much darker, in splendid branching heads. China. Var. *japonica* differs in having up to 20 narrow, clear pink segments, flowering later. Usually the earliest and most compact of the large 'Japanese Anemone' group, which are among the best plants for providing colour late in the season in shady, humus-rich beds, where they combine well with the few other tall and late-flowering shade-lovers, *Aconitum* and *Cimicifuga* species for example, and with autumn-flowering gentians in front of them. They can be grown in the sun with adequate moisture. Once established they spread widely by their rhizomes, so that care is needed in their placing. They all approach our upper size limit, but *A. hupehensis* and its cultivars tend to be smaller than the forms of *A.* x *hybridum.*

Several cultivars of *A. hupehensis* and var. *japonica* have been named though they are not always clearly distinguishable from those of *A.* x *hybridum.* Some may exceed 60 cm (2 ft) in good soils. 'Bowles Pink', taller, deep purplish-pink; 'Hadspen Abundance', 🏆 60 cm (2 ft), very dark purplish-pink, a splendid new cultivar; 'Elegans', a little taller, soft pale pink; 'Praecox', deep rose, early flowering; 'September Charm', 🏆 silvery-pink flowers with darker reverse, taller, very free-flowering; 'Prince Heinrich', 🏆 flowers very deep coloured, segments unusually long, tall; 'Bressingham Glow', semi-double, more compact; 'Rosenschale', flowers very large, single, deep pink; 'Whirlwind' is a little taller with semi-double white flowers.
A.* x *hybrida (*A. hupehesis japonica* x *A. vitifolia*) Most of these magnificent late-flowering perennials are too tall for consideration here, and as the shorter ones are usually to be found under *A. hupehensis* I have described them above. *A. tomentosa* (*A. vitifolia* hort.) is also too tall.
A* x *lesseri (*A. multifida* x *A. sylvestris*) Clumps 20 cm (8 in), leaves palmate, the lobes further divided and toothed; flowers 2 cm (0.8 in) wide, deep purplish-pink in early summer. An attractive hybrid for the front of the border. It usually comes true from seed.
A. leveillii A very rare species which I have grown for a year only. It resembles an improved *A. rivularis*, with larger white flowers flushed with purple on the reverse. China.
A.* x *lipsiensis (syn. *A. seemanii*) *A. nemorosa* x *A. ranunculoides*. ✱ A very fine woodland anemone, between its parents in habit and appearance; flowers quite large, pale primrose over several weeks in spring. (See *A. nemorosa*)
A. multifida (*A. magellanica*) A very variable plant, liable to appear under various incorrect names in catalogues, e.g. *A. baldensis*, *A. canadensis*, *A. demissa*, and others. Clumps of finely divided 3-lobed leaves, with clusters of 1–5 flowers on upright stems, greenish, off -white, or pale to deeper yellow, from squinny to 2 cm (0.8 in) wide. Easily raised from seed, they self-seed freely in sunny sites in well-drained soils, so it is important to acquire good forms. N., S. Am. *A. m.* 'Major' (*A. magellanica* 'Major') ✱ An excellent plant to 20 cm (8 in), several large pale yellow flowers to a stem, thriving in any good soil.

7 *Anemone multifida* 'Major'

A. narcissiflora Clump-forming, 30–40 cm (12–16 in), leaves long-petioled, palmate with further divided lobes, a whorl of similar stem leaves beneath the flowers; flowers white, 3 cm (1.2 in) wide, usually flushed pink on the outside, with a cluster of yellow anthers, in umbels of 3–9. A beautiful species not always easy to please, needing humus-rich, well-drained soil, in partial shade, which never dries out. C., S. Europe.

A. nemorosa (Wood Anemone) 🏆 This species and its numerous cultivars are among the most beautiful of all early spring-flowering perennials for woodland or shady beds; in moist humus-rich soil, making spreading carpets of bloom, to accompany shade-loving bulbs such as erythroniums, trilliums, and some of the narcissus species, beneath the earliest ericaceous shrubs, camellias, rhododendrons etc. All have thin, branching rhizomes that quicky form a colony, with long-stalked, 3-lobed leaves, further deeply divided, the basal leaves often developing after the flowers. Flowers solitary, 1.5–4 cm (0.6–1.6 in) across, single or double, in many shades from white through blue to purple. Europe.

The flowers of most of the cultivars are described below: 'Alba Plena', double white, smaller than 'Vestal'; 'Allenii' 🏆 largest lavender-blue, reverse lilac; 'Atrocaerulea', dark blue; 'Blue Beauty', large pale blue, reverse cream; 'Blue Bonnet', azure-blue, greyish-blue reverse, late; 'Bracteata Pleniflora', full double with narrow petals, the outermost green; 'Grandiflora', large white; 'Green Fingers', white, tinged green; 'Leeds Variety' 🏆 very large to 6 cm (2.3 in) only flushed pink with age, early; 'Lychette', large white; 'Monstrosa', segments divided, outer green; 'Pentre Pink', white, faintly flushed pink, becoming very deep pink; 'Robinsoniana' 🏆 deep lavender, with grey reverse; 'Rosea' variable pink flush increasing with age; 'Royal Blue', deep rich blue; 'Vestal' 🏆 pure white with a dense centre of tiny petals; 'Virescens', segments replaced by ferny green bracts; 'Wilks White', similar (identical?) to 'Leed's Variety'.

8 *Anemone nemorosa* 'Robinsoniana'

A. ranunculoides 🏆 (See plate 22) Similar to *A. nemorosa*, but leaves usually smaller, flowers deep yellow. A fine plant bringing yellow to the wood anemones. Europe. A good double form 'Pleniflora' is occasionally grown. There is a much larger plant in cultivation, which is twice as tall with much bigger leaves and flowers, but is said to fall within the normal variation.

A. rivularis 60 cm (2 ft) Stems, leaves long-stalked, deeply divided, 3-lobed in whorls, flowers small, white flushed with blue on the reverse, in loose umbels. Quite pleasing in woodland, but not in the top rank. Himalayas. China.

A. rupicola 5–20 cm (2–8 in) Stems, 3-lobed leaves, variable in their degree of dissection, solitary, large white flowers to 5 cm (2 in) wide, sometimes faintly flushed pink on their backs. A delightful species in its best forms, but I have not found it easy. Himalayas. China.

A. sylvestris Basal clump of palmately lobed leaves and stems to 50 cm (20 in) with a single whorl of leaves and fine white flowers to 6 cm (2.3 in) in diameter, usually solitary. E. Europe, W. Asia.

A. trifolia Like *A. nemorosa*, with sharply toothed leaflets, flowers solitary, white flushed with blue on the reverse, with conspicuous blue anthers. Very attractive. S. Europe.

A. vitifolia The true plant sometimes appears from recent seed collections. Very variable, 30–80 cm (12–30 in), leaves large, vine-like, untoothed, flowers large, pure white in loose branching heads. Another of the 'Japanese' anemones. E. Asia.

Anemonopsis (*Ranunculaceae*)

The solitary species is a most beautiful woodlander from Japan, suitable for a shady bed in humus-rich soil, where it can be left undisturbed. It can be raised from seed sown as soon as ripe and kept cool.

A. macrophylla ✸ 60 cm (2 ft) Clump-forming, herbaceous perennial, leaves 3-lobed, toothed, on purplish stems, flowers pendant, cup-shaped, anemone-like, reddish-purple fading to white in the centre, in loose heads.

Antennaria (*Compositae*)

Low, mat-forming perennials, with grey-green, usually white-backed leaves, and tight heads of small flowers, usually white or pink. *A. dioica* and its various forms will tolerate the ordinary soil of a border edge but they are scarcely effective enough.

Anthemis (*Compositae*)

Among the best of smaller daisies for the border. They are moderately hardy perennials, mainly from S. Europe, with attractive, finely cut leaves, often silvery, and large daisy flowers in shades of white or yellow in summer. The larger species and their cultivars are excellent for cutting. These are often short-lived unless cut back hard after flowering. The mat and cushion-forming species can be grown in the front of other perennials in the border. All grow best in full sun in well-drained soil. Propagate by division in spring or autumn, or by cuttings of young shoots in spring.

A. carpatica Cushion-forming, woody, 20–25 cm (8–10 in), leaves finely cut, grey-green or white-hairy, flowers solitary, large white daisies with yellow centres.

A. cretica Similar to *A. carpatica*, but leaves whiter and more hairy.

A. marschalliana Similar with very white leaves and deep yellow flowers.
A. punctata The subsp. *cupaniana* (syn. *A. cupaniana*) 🏆 is usually grown, a low mat-former, leaves very silky-white, flowers large white, yellow-centred. The type species is more tender.
A. sancto-johannis Upright, similar to *A. tinctoria*, more compact, fine ferny leaves and bright orange-yellow flowers.
A. tinctoria Widely grown with its cultivars and hybrids, for colour in the garden and for cutting. The species has finely cut leaves, deep green above and greyish below, and abundant deep yellow flowers on 60 cm (2 ft) branching stems. The following are common cultivars, all with yellow centres: 'Alba', white, low-growing, leaves dark green; 'E.C. Buxton', with *A. tinctoria* pale yellow, leaves dark, very compact; 'Grallach Gold (syn. 'Beauty of Grallach'), deep yellow, leaves dark green, one of the tallest; 'Sauce Hollandaise', very pale yellow changing to cream, compact; 'Tetworth' (*A. tinctoria* x *A. cupaniana*), pure white, semi-double, leaves finely cut grey; 'Wargrave Variety', mid-yellow, dark leaves.

9 *Anthemis tinctoria* & 'A.E.C. Buxton'

A. tuberculata Spreading cushion, 15 cm (6 in) stems, leaves finely divided, hairy, flowers large white.

Anthericum (*Liliaceae*)

Beautiful clump-forming plants, mainly European, with long grass-like leaves and upright spikes of white flowers in summer. They do well in a sunny, well-drained border. They are easily raised from seed; *A. ramosum* self-sows readily without becoming a nuisance.
A. liliago 🏆 Stems usually unbranched, 50 cm (20 in), flowers white, 3 cm (1.2 in) long, lily-like, in loose spikes of up to ten. Var. 'Major' to 90 cm (3 ft), flowers slightly larger.
A. ramosum ✸ Dense clump of long, glossy leaves, branched stems to 60 cm (2 ft), flowers 1.5 cm (0.6 in) wide, white, open-faced, prolific for several weeks. Long-lived.

10 *Anthericum ramosum*

Anthriscus (*Umbelliferae*)

A. sylvestris (Cow Parsley) *A. s.* 'Raven's Wing' is a pleasant foliage plant with white flowers similar to those of Cow Parsley, but leaves heavily tinged with purple, especially in spring. It may be a little tall when established.

Antirrhinum

The perennial antirrhinums include some attractive, but often short-lived, S.W. European plants for a warm, sunny bed, varying in habit but all with typical 2-lipped flowers in various colours. They tend to self-seed freely and also to hybridize, so that unless they are raised from cuttings, an easy procedure, the border becomes full of a strange mixture of intermediate seedlings. They are moderately hardy in well-drained soil but it is advisable to take cuttings regularly.
A. braun-blanquetii Upright, shrubby, to 50 cm (20 in) or more, leaves small, lanceolate, flowers 2–5 cm (0.8–2 in) (0.8–2 in) pale yellow, deeper in the throat, in loose spikes in summer. It is short-lived and liable to become swamped with seedlings which rarely come true.
A. hispanicum Mound-forming to 25 cm (10 in), leaves hairy, oval-lanceolate, abundant flowers yellow or occasionally pink with yellow throats. Subsp. *hispanicum* (syn. *A. glutinosum*) is the form usually grown.
A. majus subsp. *linkianum* Perennial subspecies, a low-spreading mat of branching stems, leaves small, glabrous, flowers pink, white in the throat. Somewhat leafy for the amount of flower.
A. majus (Taff's White) Upright-growing plant, leaves variegated, bordered with clear creamy-yellow, spikes of large

white flowers, tinged with green at the base. An outstanding foliage plant, easily propagated from cuttings. It has survived recent mild winters outside.
A. molle Spreading mound to 20 cm (8 in), leaves oval, very hairy, bluish-green, flowers quite large, pale pink, usually with some yellow in the throat. An effective low edging to a border. It hybridizes freely and the progeny may be taller and vary in colour.

11 *Antirrhinum molle*

Aphyllanthes (*Liliaceae*)

A. monspeliensis The only species, small, clump-forming, with linear, rush-like stems 10–20 cm (4–8 in) high, flowers rich blue, funnel-shaped with spreading segments, from a dense cluster of reddish bracts in summer. It needs very well-drained soil in a sunny spot. S.W. Europe.

Aquilegia (*Ranunculaceae*)

The columbines must be among every gardener's favourite plants, with their attractive divided leaves and multicoloured flowers. The leaves, in shades of green or often glaucous-blue, are usually 2- or 3-ternate, with each leaflet further lobed or divided into 2 or 3. The flowers are composed of a ring of five petal-like sepals, with a conspicuous wide central tube, composed of five petals joined and extended back into spurs of variable length and shape.

Most of the species come within our height range and can be grown in any reasonably well-drained soil in sun or light shade, although some are short-lived. I have excluded the smaller species, under 15 cm (6 in), which are best grown on the rock garden among other small plants. They are very easily raised from seed and often self-sow around, but unfortunately only a few come true from seed if several species are grown together. Wild collected seed, which is often available from specialist societies, is the best source of plants reliably true to name. It is possible to divide established plants but the divisions take some time to recover.
A. alpina 20-50 cm (8–20 in) Flowers 1–3 on a stem, 3–5 cm (1.2–2 in) long, nodding, uniformly blue, with 2.5 cm (1 in) spurs. An attractive species rarely obtainable true, some form of *A. vulgaris* or a hybrid, taking its place. It. Alps.
'Hensol Harebell' 🏆 a good compact cultivar with pure blue flowers.
A. amaliae 20–40 cm (8–16 in) Flowers 3 cm (1.2 in), nodding, pale violet, tubes white, spurs 1 cm (0.4 in) (0.4 in), hooked. Uncommon, best in partial shade. Balkans.
A. atrata 60 cm (2 ft) Flowers several on a stem, deep purple to chocolate, 3–4 cm (1.2–1.6 in) long, nodding. One of the darkest of all, it makes a spectacular group, planted in front of a taller yellow perennial like *Thermopsis mollis*. It comes reasonably true to colour from seed. Alps.
A. aurea Height 10-40 cm (8–16 in), flowers 3–5 cm (1.2–2 in) long, deep golden-yellow, upward- or outward-facing, spur short, hooked. Uncommon but said to come true from seed. Balkans.
A. buergeriana 30-60 cm (1–2 ft), leaves bluish, flowers nodding, sepals yellow or brownish-yellow, tube yellow, spurs straight, purplish. Japan.
A. caerulea 🏆 To 60 cm (2 ft), leaves very glaucous blue, flowers large, clear blue with white tubes and long straight spurs. A wonderful species in the aspen woods of the Rocky Mountains, and a parent of some good long-spurred hybrids; not widely obtainable true. Prefers cool, moist conditions. W.C. USA.
A. canadensis 🏆 To 40 cm (16 in), flowers 3 cm (1.2 in) long with red sepals, yellow tube, and 2–5 cm (0.8–2 in) (0.8–2 in) long straight spurs, several on branching stems. One of several species with similar red and yellow flowers, they look good in front of pale variegated foliage, or with silver artemisias, or mixed with other yellow-flowered perennials. E., N. Am.
A. chrysantha To 1 m (3 ft), flowers pure yellow, outward-facing, 2.5 cm (1 in) long, spurs to 5 cm (2 in), curving outwards. Parent with *A. longissima* of some yellow 'Long-spurred Hybrids.' Thrives in partial shade. S. USA. Var. *chaplinii* (*A. chaplinii*) A small form only growing to 30 cm (1 ft). S. USA, Mexico. 'Yellow Queen', very tall and vigorous cultivar.
A. discolor Very similar to *A. alpina*, smaller with white petals. Spain.
A. einseliana To 40 cm (16 in), flowers nodding, 2 cm (0.8 in), bluish-violet, spurs straight, 1 cm (0.4 in). Generally true from seed. S.E. Alps.
A. elegantula Like *A. canadense*, but smaller, tube unusually long. C. USA.
A. eximia (syn. *A. formosa* var. *truncata*.) Like a tall *A. canadense* with shorter tube; a long-lived perennial in my garden making a striking feature planted in partial shade in front of the pale *Philadelphus coronarius* 'Variegatus'.
A. flavescens Resembling *A. canadensis*, but flowers pure yellow, spurs short, hooked. Good in shade or sun. W.C. USA.
A. formosa Taller, vigorous *A. canadense* look-alike. Var. *truncata* similar with shorter petals. W.N. Am.

12 *Aquilegia eximia* in front of *Philadelphus coronarius* 'Variegatus'

A. fragrans ✱ 15-50 cm (6–20 in) Leaves very glaucous, flowers nodding, soft, creamy-yellow, rarely flushed with blue, beautifully scented, 3–5 cm (1.2–2 in) with 2 cm (0.8 in) hooked or curved spurs. A delightful Himalayan species of which there have been several recent collections. It seems to grow best in humus-rich soil in partial shade. Often true from seed, but the dwarfer forms tend to become taller. Himalayas.
A. glandulosa 40 cm (16 in) Easily-grown, 1–3 large nodding flowers, deep blue throughout or tube white, spurs short, hooked. USSR. Var. *jucunda* differs in its broader white tube.
A. grata 50 cm (20 in) Flowers several, nodding, very dark purplish-blue, tube tipped white, long straight spurs. Balkans.
A. longissima Easy but usually short-lived, tall, flowers clear yellow, erect, spurs 1-5 cm (0.4–2 in). S. USA, Mex.
A. micrantha 30-60 cm (1–2 ft) Flowers several, medium-sized, upward-facing, variable in colour, petals white, pale yellow, or pale blue, sepals generally white, spurs to 2 cm (0.8 in), straight. S. USA.
A. moorcroftiana 20–40 cm (8–16 in) Glaucous leaflets, flowers deep purplish-blue, 3 cm (1.2 in), sepals whitish-tipped, spurs straight, 2 cm (0.8 in). Available from recent seed collections. Probably best in partial shade in gritty soil rich in leaf mould. Himalayas.
A. olympica 30-60 cm (1–2 ft) Flowers 3 cm (1.2 in), reddish-purple, tubes white, spurs very hooked. Cauc.
A. ottonis Very similar to *A. amaliae*, but taller with longer tube. It, Gr.
A. oxysepala Very similar to *A. buergeriana*, but taller with sepals yellowish-purple. E. Siberia.
A. pubiflora Very similar to *A. moorcroftiana*, flowers a little smaller, spur hooked. Himalayas.
A. pyrenaica Like a small *A. alpina*, 30 cm (1 ft) or less, deep blue flowers. Pyr.
A. shockleyi Among the smallest of the yellow and red group, best on the rock garden. W. USA.
A. sibirica To 70 cm (28 in), stems branching, many-flowered, nodding, pale lavender-blue, tube white, spurs 2 cm (0.8 in), hooked. Siberia.
A. skinneri Tall with nodding flowers, sepals greenish-yellow, petals and spurs reddish-orange. It needs a sunny position. S. USA.
A. thalictrifolia Very similar to *A. einseliana* but taller with larger flowers. N. Italy.
A. triternata Very similar to *A. elegantula* but leaves triternate (biternate in *A. elegantula*). S.W. USA.
A. viridiflora To 40 cm (16 in), nodding flowers 2–3 cm (0.8–1.2 in) long, several to a stem, sepals green, petals green suffused with purple to the extent that they may appear almost black, the spurs long and straight. An intriguing plant that grows well in shade and usually comes true from seed. W. China.
A. vulgaris (Granny's Bonnets, Columbine) A very variable tall species which hybridizes freely with most other species and self-sows all over the garden unless dead-headed. This effect can be useful in the wild garden, when the various colour forms mingle. The flowers are generally nodding, with hooked spurs to 2 cm (0.8 in) long, but sometimes spurless, in many shades of blue, white, or reddish. Europe. Var. ***stellata*** A group of spurless plants of which the best known is more frequently offered as *A. clematiflora*, ✱ an excellent 'strain', height 20–40 cm (8–16 in), reasonably true from seed, flowers spurless in an appealing deep shade of reddish-purple.

A. vulgaris cultivars and hybrids

Many cultivars and hybrids of *A. vulgaris* have been named. A few may be in the last section. 'Adelaide Addison', blue with a double white centre, edged with blue; 'Nivea' (syn. 'Alba, 'Munstead'), 🏆 pure white, spurred, usually true from seed; 'Clematiflora Alba', greenish-white, spurless, seeds true; 'Nora Barlow', 🏆 ever-popular, very double pink and green, usually true from seed; 'Gisella Powell', deep orange-yellow; 'Tom Fairhurst', pale pink with a red tube; 'Red Star', striking true-breeding cultivar, deep red with a white tube; 'Verveana Group', conspicuously yellow-variegated leaves, wide a range of flower colours.
A. yabeana Variable, usually to 50 cm (20 in), with purplish-blue flowers.

Other *Aquilegia* Cultivars

The following list includes most of those commonly offered

by nurseries but is not comprehensive. Biedermeier Mixed, a strain of very dwarf cultivars in a wide range of colours for the front of the border; 'Celestial Blue', vivid blue, to 60 cm (2 ft); Dragonfly hybrids, mixed collection of intermediate size in a wide range of colours; McKenna hybrids, among the largest and most floriferous long-spurred hybrids; Mrs Scott-Elliot hybrids, similar with generally paler colours; Music Hybrids 🏆 neat plants to 45 cm (1.5 ft), very long spurs, a good mixture of bright colours; 'Schneekoningin' (syn 'Snow Queen') pure white, long-spurred.

Arabis (*Cruciferae*)

The Arabis species are popular plants for the rock garden, and make a great show planted in retaining walls. The largest of them are also sufficiently vigorous to be used as a border edging in any reasonably well-drained soil. Only these will be considered here. They form extensive mounds of foliage which are smothered in late spring with white flowers of typical crucifer shape. They should be cut back hard after flowering to keep them tidy. They may be propagated from cuttings in early summer, or from seed sown in autumn.

A. alpina Extensive mats, small green leaves, flower stems to 20 cm (8 in). Often confused with *A. caucasica* which is included in it as a subspecies by some authorities. Europe.

A.* x *arendsii (*A. alpina* 'Arendsii Group') *A. aubretioides* x *A. caucasica.* Similar in habit to its parents, with pink flowers. 'Rosabella' and 'Compinkie' are probably the best cultivars.

A. blepharophylla Leaves green and flowers a deep reddish-pink in early summer. A superior more slow-growing species, unfortunately a little tender, for very well-drained soil. It is easily raised from seed. 'Fruhlingzauber' (syn. 'Spring Charm') 🏆 is the best cultivar W. USA.

A. caucasica (syn. *A. alpina* subsp. *caucasica*) Large mats of downy grey-green leaves, a mass of white flowers in late spring. The most widely grown species. W. Asia. *A. c.* 'Flore Pleno' has fully double flowers carried well above the foliage. 'Snowcap' 🏆 is a good low-growing carpeter. 'Variegata' has the added asset of attractive yellow margins to the leaves, and is worthwhile as a foliage plant for the border.

A. ferdinandi-coburgi A very low mat of dark green leaves, with short spikes of very small white flowers. It has less impact in a border than the larger species, but the attractive 'Variegata' is worth growing as a foliage plant, with the leaves white-bordered. It has an unfortunate tendency to revert to green. Balkans.

Arctotis (*Compositae*)

An invaluable genus of S. African tender plants for containers or as gap-fillers in a sunny border; flowering non-stop throughout the summer, from cuttings rooted in late summer and early autumn and kept under glass until spring. There is a tendency for every shoot to flower but even flowering shoots will make good plants if the buds are removed. It is important to keep the plants dead-headed to ensure continuous flowering. In frost-free gardens they are perennial, and will need cutting back at the end of their season to keep them tidy.

Some sixteen named cultivars of *Arctotis* x *hybrida* (*Venidio-Arctotis* Hybrids) are available in shades of white, yellow, orange, pink to purple, and brownish. Most have narrow, toothed, felted, silvery-grey leaves and solitary daisy flowers to 7 cm (2.8 in) (2.8 in) in diameter, with very dark blackish centres, on 10–15 cm (4–6 in) stems. Although the flowers close when the sun goes in, they are surprisingly effective as cut flowers for a day or two.

Among the most successful in my experience, being easy to propagate and continuous-flowering if dead-headed, are the orange-brown 'Flame' (see plate 2) and the darker 'Mahogany', 'Rosita', 'Wine' and 'China Rose', all in shades of silvery-purplish-pink. The appropriately named 'Apricot', a beautiful soft shade, and 'White' have broader stems and leaves, and larger but slightly less profuse flowers. Other cultivars available are 'Bacchus', orange-red, 'Champagne', similar to or the same as 'White', and 'Rasberry', and 'Yellow', both self-explanatory.

13 *Arctotis* 'Rosita'

Argemone (*Papaveraceae*)

It is remarkable that these fascinating, mainly N. American poppies are not more widely grown, and that only two are commonly obtainable from trade sources. Others are available to enthusiasts from seed lists of specialist societies. They all combine robust, very thorny stems to 60 cm (2 ft), with attractive, lobed, thorny leaves with pale veins and margins, and large, silky poppy flowers of the utmost delicacy, usually white or yellow, with purple stigmas. They do best in a very sunny site in well-drained soil. They are short-lived, often behaving as annuals or biennials, but they set seed and are easily raised, and will often sow themselves around close to the original plants so that the group appears perennial. The seed capsules are very spiny and gloves will be required when dealing with them. Sow seed in autumn and plant the young seedlings out as soon as possible as they resent disturbance.

A. albiflora Usually biennial or annual, tall with branching, prickly stems, leaves green or grey-green, pinnately lobed with spiny margins and veins, spiny beneath, flowers 5-10 cm (2–4 in) wide, pure white, anthers and filaments yellow, stigmas purple. *A. polyanthemos* differs only in having a longer spine on the end of the sepal, and narrower seed capsules.

A. grandiflora Annual or short-lived perennial, flowers similar to the last, but stems red-tinged and smooth, leaves with more prominent white veins, and marginal spines only.

A. mexicana White-veined, glaucous leaves, flowers bright yellow, to 4 cm (1.6 in) wide. Definitely an annual, so strictly outside the scope of this book, but very similar to the others with a gift for establishing itself in colonies, which at least look perennial.

A. munita Often perennial in well-drained soils, this has very prickly bluish stems, leaves and buds, and very large white flowers to 10 cm (4 in) wide.

A. ochroleuca Very close to *A. mexicana*, and equally easy to grow, this differs in having pale creamy-yellow flowers.

A. platyceras Foliage distinct with few softer spines except on the very prickly seed capsules; flowers the largest of all. The biggest and best of the white-flowered species, but a little tall.

A. sanguinea A rarity, included here because it is occasionally offered in seed lists and would offer a colour break, the flowers being pale lavender in some forms.

Aristea (*Iridaceae*)

A small genus of uncommonly grown plants mainly from S. Africa, of borderline hardiness, they will tolerate a degree or two of frost, and are worth trying in mild gardens. They grow best in rich, well-drained soil. They are easily raised from seed under cold glass. The two species usually available have iris-like leaves and short heads of bright true-blue flowers in summer.

A. ecklonii 30–50 cm (12–20 in) Leaves arching to 30 cm (1 ft), flowers clear deep blue in a 2 cm (0.8 in) wide loose head on wiry stems.

A. ensifolia Shorter, leaves narrower, paler green, loose heads of small bright blue flowers.

Armeria (*Plumbaginaceae*) (Thrift, Sea Pink)

Dense cushions of grass-like leaves above which the tight, rounded heads of pink or white flowers are borne on stiff, upright stems in summer. *A. maritima* looks very fine decorating our shores and cliffs, but generally the species are not spectacular. The smallest are good for the rock garden, and only the larger species are considered here. They are useful for retaining walls and can be used as an edging to the border, their pink flowers mingling well with the blue of campanulas and violas. Those with long stems can be used for cutting. Individual rosettes can be rooted as cuttings, or they can be raised from seed.

A. alliacea (syn. *A. arenaria*, *A. plantaginea*) To 40 cm (16 in), cushions of 5–10 cm (2–4 in) long linear leaves, flowers reddish-purple or white to 2.5 cm (1 in) wide in dense heads. W. Europe. Var. *leucantha* has white flowers. 'Formosa Hybrids', flowers varying in shade from white to very deep pink.

A. leucocephala Very similar to *A. maritima*, with white flowers, sometimes confused with that species. Corsica.

A. maritima Cushions of grassy leaves, 20 cm (8 in) upright stems, carrying typical 1.5–2.5 cm (0.6–1 in) wide flower heads. An extremely variable plant with a number of named cultivars. N. hemisphere. The following are some of the best known: 'Alba', white, 'Bloodstone', deep red, 'Dusseldorf Pride', dark crimson, 'Glory of Holland', a vigorous plant with large pink heads, 'Laucheana', deep pink, 'Ruby Glow', glowing red, 'Splendens', deep red, 'Vindictive' 🏆 deep rose-pink.

A. welwitschii Shrub-like hummocks of linear-spathulate leaves, 2.5-3 cm (1–1.2 in) wide flower heads, pale pink or white. Rather tender. Portugal.

Arnebia (*Boraginaceae*)

A. pulchra (syn. *A. echioides*) The only species in general cultivation. A clump of 10–15 cm (4–6 in) long lanceolate leaves, upright unbranched stems, flowers soft yellow, 2 cm (0.8 in) wide in clusters. The fascinating feature of this plant is that each petal has a dark brown spot at the base for a day or two, which then fades away completely. Although usually seen on the rock garden it has sufficient height and vigour for a sunny border in well-drained soil. It can be propagated from cuttings of young shoots in early summer. W. Asia.

Arnica (*Compositae*)

A small genus of moderate-sized, clump-forming, herbaceous perennials, with usually simple, opposite leaves and large yellow daisy flowers, single or in heads, in summer. They are easily grown in any reasonably moist but well-drained soil at the front of sunny borders, where their rather harsh yellows combine well with the lilac-blue of many campanulas or *Viola cornuta* forms. They can be propagated by division. Four species are regularly obtainable.

A. angustifolia (syn. *A. alpina*) Clump-forming, 30–40 cm (12–16 in), leaves downy, 12 cm (4.7 in), narrowly elliptic, flowers bright yellow to 5 cm (2 in), usually solitary. Subsp. *iljinii* taller with more leafy stems with 3–4 pairs of leaves, instead of 2–3. Arctic.

A. chamissonis 60 cm (2 ft) Differs from *A. angustifolia* in toothed leaves, several paler yellow flowers of similar size. W., N. Am.
A. montana Dense clump of almost stemless basal leaves, solitary flowers even larger, deeper orange-yellow. It does best in acid soils. Europe.
A. sachalinensis (syn. *A. chamissonis* subsp. *sachalinensis*) Taller spreading clump, leaves lanceolate, flowers 4–5, mid-yellow, drooping. Japan.

Artemisia (*Compositae*)

A large genus of plants mainly from S. Europe grown, with very few exceptions, for the unequalled beauty of their silver foliage, the flowers being insignificant. They vary enormously from 4 cm (1.6 in) high mats to 2m (7 ft) upright perennials, and from difficult-to-grow alpines to invasive ground cover. Their silver foliage is invaluable in a sunny border, to separate clashing colours, or to combine elegantly with more pastel shades, or with purple leaves, or as part of a white scheme. Several of the larger species may tempt one with their very attractive foliage and then quickly overwhelm the neighbouring plants with which they are intended to combine.

All thrive in very well-drained soils in full sun, and benefit from being cut back hard after flowering, especially if they become woody and straggly. They can be propagated from cuttings in early summer. The following list includes most of the species of intermediate size; I have excluded the smallest species more suited to the rock garden or alpine house. Mainly native to S. Europe and W. Asia.
A. absinthium Tall, but 'Lambrook Silver' 🏆 is usually under 80 cm (30 in), beautiful, finely divided 10 cm (4 in) long silvery-grey leaves, tall grey flowers, spikes on branching stems. An outstanding 'silver'.
A. alba Grown usually as *A. a.* 'Canescens' (syn. *A. canescens, A. glabrescens*) 🏆 (see photo 58), perhaps the finest of the lower-growing species, a 15–20 cm (6–8 in) mound of delicate silver filigree; insignificant flowers. It looks well with the magenta of *G. cinereum* 'Subcaulescens' or with the softer shades of diascias or low campanulas.
A. arborescens A tall shrub of spectacular beauty, but more tender than most. A. a. 'Powis Castle' 🏆 hardier, more compact, with similar finely divided, gleaming, silver foliage which responds well to cutting back hard when it becomes leggy.
A. campestris Variable, 30-80 cm (12–30 in), shrubby, lower leaves finely divided, grey-green with silky hairs, flowers in small yellow heads on upright stems.
A. caucasica (*A. pedemontana*) 🏆 Low-growing, tufted, to 25 cm (10 in), leaves very silver, finely cut flowers insignificant. An excellent plant needing very good drainage.
A. frigida 🏆 Tufted,10-40 cm (4–16 in), leaves very finely divided, silver-hairy.
A. ludoviciana Rhizomatous, stems to 1 m (3 ft), leaves silver-grey, lanceolate, usually only shallowly lobed. A splendid perennial but spreads too quickly for most situations. W. USA, Mex. *A. l.* 'Valerie Finnis' 🏆 and 'Silver queen' 🏆 are excellent 'silvers' with leaves less deeply toothed, spreading and usually within our height limits.
A. pontica 🏆 Spreading rhizomatous species, leaves deeply divided grey hairy. Can be very invasive.
A. schmidtiana 🏆 Creeping, to 30 cm (1 ft), leaves intensely silver, doubly palmately lobed, good for a border edging in well-drained soil, in the same way as *A. alba*. Japan. *A.s.* 'Nana' 🏆 only half as high, perhaps better on the rock garden.
A. splendens A hummock of finely divided silvery leaves to 30 cm (1 ft).
A. stelleriana ✿ Spreading rhizomatous mat, leaves deeply lobed, silvery-white hairy. One of the best in the garden, especially in 'Mori's Form', with more compact growth and even whiter leaves. N. Am. N.E. Asia.
A. vallesiaca Sub-shrubby, with upright branching stems, leaves very finely divided, silvery-white, lanceolate with a few teeth at the apex, flowers insignificant.

Arthropodium (*Liliaceae/Anthericaceae*)

A small but interesting genus of mainly Australasian summer-flowering perennials that are not as widely grown as they deserve. They vary greatly in habit and in hardiness, but are easy in moist but well-drained soil in sun or light shade. All may easily be raised from seed, or division.
A. candidum Clump-forming, leaves narrow, grassy, pale green or bronze, or with brownish spotting, to 15 cm (6 in), flowers small white stars, in loose sprays just above the leaves. A little small for the border but easily grown.
A. cirrhatum Much more robust with broad, arching, lanceolate leaves to 30 cm (1 ft) or more, and panicles of 3 cm (1.2 in) wide; white flowers with recurving petals. Sadly only hardy to about -4 °C (25 °F).
A. milleflorum ✱ Clumps of very glaucous, lanceolate 15 cm (6 in) leaves, wiry, branching, purple-tinged stems to 25 cm (10 in), flowers soft, violet-purple, star-shaped, with a prominent cluster of stamens, the filaments with long white or violet hairs, in loose branching sprays. The most beautiful and hardy species, has survived to -18 °C (-0.4 °F) in my garden.

Asarina (*Scrophulariaceae*)

Only one is grown regularly, closely resembling an antirrhinum in appearance, with typical 2-lipped flowers. It survives mild winters in well-drained soils, and is a useful mat-forming plant for the edge of a border, or for a retaining wall, in full sun. It can be raised from seed sown in spring or by cuttings during summer.
A. procumbens (syn. *Antirrhinum asarina, A. procumbens*) Tufted with long prostrate stems, leaves grey-green, sticky, hairy, kidney-shaped, flowers solitary in the leaf axils, white

with pale yellow lips and deep yellow in the throat. Pyrenees. 'Alba' with white flowers, and a dwarf form are also sometimes offered.

Asarum (*Aristolochiaceae*) (Wild Ginger) ☼

Genus of rhizomatous perennials, growing naturally in deep shade and forming carpets of glossy leaves, beneath which the strange purplish or greenish, cup or urn-shaped flowers are usually hidden at ground level. They consist of 3 calyx lobes joined, at least at the base, and are pollinated by flies; of little merit to the gardener. Their fine leaves, sometimes mottled like cyclamen, usually 8-15 cm (3–6 in) long with elongated petioles, make good low ground cover in deep shade in moist humus-rich soil. Slugs can be a great problem unless precautions are taken. They can be increased by division in spring. N. America except where stated.

A. arifolium Leaves evergreen, triangular-ovate, often marbled, flowers 3 cm (1.2 in) long, constricted at the neck, purplish and hairy inside. One of the more tender.

A. canadense Hardy deciduous mat-former, leaves broad cordate, hairy, flowers purplish to 4 cm (1.6 in).

A. caudatum Hardy evergreen, leaves glossy, hairy, heart-shaped, flowers larger, deep purple. One of the best as ground cover.

A. europaeum Leaves very glossy, deep green, kidney-shaped, flowers short, greenish-purple. Excellent in deep shade. Europe.

A. hartwegii Very similar to *A. caudatum* but leaves attractively marbled like those of cyclamen.

Asclepias (*Asclepiadaceae*) (Butterfly weed)

Mainly clump-forming perennials with upright stems bearing flat-heads of many small, brightly-coloured flowers with reflexing petals, in summer. The hardy species do best in well-drained soils in full sun, but most are too tall to consider here. A few other species are offered occasionally by specialist seed sources. They can be raised from seed, or from division if a large enough clump can be produced. Mainly N. Am.

A. speciosa A rare shrubby species to 70 cm (28 in), leaves grey or white, ovate, flowers purplish or off-white.

A. tuberosa 60–80 cm (24–30 in) Leaves whorled, pale green, narrow, lanceolate, flowers brilliant orange in broad flat-heads. The brightest and most sought-after species, it is a very striking plant but hard to please, probably thriving best in a warm bed of sandy but humus-rich soil. 'Gay Butterflies Group' are easily raised from seed, and vary in colour between orange, gold, red, and pink.

Asphodeline (*Liliaceae*/*Asphodelaceae*)

The asphodels and asphodelines must appeal to any gardener who has seen them growing around the Mediterranean, with good foliage and conspicuous tall spikes of white or yellow flowers, which usually open in the afternoon and evening. They can be equally effective in the garden, needing a warm position in very well-drained soil, and can be raised from seed sown in autumn.

A. brevicaule ✱ To 60 cm (2 ft) or more, clumps of glaucous blue leaves, dense spikes of abundant starry flowers, creamy-yellow, striped brown on the back of each petal, giving an overall golden effect. Easy and hardy. Asia Minor

A. liburnica Similar to *A. brevicaule*, leaves longer and less glaucous, tall spikes of deep yellow flowers with a greenish stripe. S. Europe.

14 *Asphodeline liburnica*

A. lutea Taller and more robust, spikes of deep yellow flowers. The commonest in the garden but less attractive. Med.

Asphodelus (*Liliaceae*/*Asphodelaceae*)

These tend to be much taller than the asphodelines, and only *A. acaulis*, definitely a plant for the rock garden or alpine house, and *A. fistulosus* are under 1 m (3 ft) high.

A. fistulosus Leaves slender to 30 cm (1 ft) long, flowers 2 cm (0.8 in) wide, white, on upright stems to 40 cm (16 in). A short-lived species almost behaving as a biennial, flowering quickly from seed. S. Europe, S.W. Asia.

Astelia (*Liliaceae*/*Asteliaceae*)

A mainly Australasian genus of fine evergreen foliage plants, grown for their handsome clumps of narrow, keeled leaves; often covered with scales or hairy, the flowers hidden among the leaves but followed by attractive orange fruits in the wild, rarely in the garden. They vary in hardiness, but are generally easy to grow in rich but well-drained soil, in sun or light shade, where temperatures do not drop below about -7 °C

(19 °F). They may be raised from seed sown as soon as ripe.
A. banksii Narrow deep green leaves, to 80 cm (30 in) long, with scaly upper surface and white, downy lower, and conspicuous silvery midrib. It is not hardy below -5 °C (23 °F).
A. fragrans Large clumps of leathery leaves to 50 cm (20 in) x 3 cm (1.2 in), with reddish midribs, and greenish flowers, followed by conspicuous orange fruits.
A. graminea Rare species, leaves to 40 (16 in) x 5 cm (2 in), keeled, bronze-tinged above and creamy felted below.
A. nervosa Widely grown, arching leaves to 80 (30 in) x 3 cm (1.2 in), silvery-green above and whitish woolly beneath. It is one of the hardiest and most reliable in the garden. Var. *chathamica* is larger growing but less hardy, with very scaly leaves. 'Silver Spear' ✪ is a very fine cultivar with more silvery leaves.
A. nivicola Low-growing species to 30 cm (1 ft) with leaves green above and heavily reddish-brown felted beneath.
A. solandri Uncommon, with very long linear leaves to 1 m (3 ft) or more, glossy green above, and white-scaly underneath.

Aster (*Compositae*)

A very large genus of mainly herbaceous perennials, with uninteresting, simple alternate leaves, usually lanceolate, and sprays of large daisy flower, usually in shades of blue, pink and white, varying from tiny species for the rock garden to tall upright plants for the back of the border. The various taxa can be in flower from spring to autumn, although the late flowering ones are probably the most useful. Most of those usually seen in the garden are hybrids and cultivars of a few species, raised and grown for their overwhelming flower-power, but there has been more recent interest in the daintier species themselves.

They are generally easy plants for average soils, in full sun, easily increased by division, preferably in early spring. The smaller species and cultivars make an excellent border edging, and the larger can be used throughout. Unfortunately the taller species may need staking, and experience is the only reliable guide to this. I have excluded a large number of species and cultivars including those of *A. cordifolius*, *A. ericoides*, *A. lateriflorus*, *A. novae-angliae*, *A. novae-belgii*, which have very few cultivars that will not exceed 80 cm (30 in) in height, and a few tiny species for the rock garden.
A. alpigenus Uncommon, clump-forming, stems to 30 cm (1 ft), flowers solitary, 3–4 cm (1.2–1.6 in) wide, lilac to purple, late summer. W. USA.
A. alpinus 🏆 Excellent low, mat-forming species for the border edge, to 30 cm (1 ft), flowers to 4 cm (1.6 in), in shades deep blue to violet, with yellow centres. Several named cultivars include 'Albus', white, 'Beechwood', clear blue, 'Dunkle Schone' ('Dark Beauty') purple, 'Happy End', pink, 'Roseus', pale pink, 'Trimix', pink, blue, & white, 'Violet', violet, 'White Beauty', white.
A. amellus All 50-70 cm (20–28 in), varying mainly with soil fertility, 4–5 cm (1.6–2 in) wide flowers with conspicuous yellow centres. Among the best of all late-flowering perennials, combining well with low-growing diascias, dianthus, or asteriscus, and taller yellow daisies like heleniums and helianthus. Cultivars include 'Blue King', deep violet, 'Breslau', violet-blue, 'Brilliant', bright pink, 'Doktor Otto Petschek', lavender-blue, 'Framfieldii', 🏆 'King George', 🏆 deep violet, 'Kobold', violet, 'Lac de Geneve', soft violet, 'Lady Hindlip', deep pink, 'Moorheim Gem', violet, 'Nocturne', lilac, 'Pink Zenith', pink, 'Praecox Junifreude', pale blue, early, 'Rudolph van Goethe', deep violet, 'Sonia', soft pink, 'Sternkugel', pale violet, 'Ultramarine', deep purple, 'Violet Queen' (Veilchenkonigi) 🏆 deep purple.
A. bakerianus Clump-forming, 30 cm (1 ft), flowers solitary, 4 cm (1.6 in) wide, with narrow florets, pale to dark blue or white. Tender. S. Africa.
A. diplostephioides ✱ Clumps to 30 cm (1 ft), leaves hairy, broadly lanceolate, pale green, flowers solitary 5 cm (2 in) wide, with very narrow, recurving ray florets, deep lavender with dark purplish-brown centre. Excellent species which I grew from Chinese seed (as *A. yunnanense*), easy in sun or partial shade. Himalayas, China.

15 *Aster diplostephioides* (? *A. yunnanense*)

A. divaricatus Spreading rhizomatous, flopping stems to 60 cm (2 ft), flowers white with brownish-yellow centres in small sprays. E. USA.
A.* x *frikartii (*A. amellus* x *A. thomsonii*) Upright to 60 cm (2 ft) or a little more, flowers abundant, 4–5 cm (1.6–2 in) in shades of clear lavender-blue. The best of all medium-sized

asters, self-supporting, and disease-free, with a very long-flowering season in late summer. Their colours combine equally well with the bright yellows of many daisies of summer, and with the softer pinks of diascias planted in front of them. Several cultivars have been named. 'Flora's Delight', pale lilac, very compact, 'Jungfrau', deep blue, to 70 cm (28 in), 'Monch' ♡ pure pale lilac-blue, the most popular, very free-flowering, 'Wunder von Stafa' ♡ similar to 'Monch', but a slightly different shade, a little taller and looser growing.

16 *Aster* x *frikartii* with *Diascia vigilis*

A. himalaicus Clump former to 30 cm (1 ft), rhizomatous, flowers solitary, 4 cm (1.6 in) diameter, deep purplish-blue, early summer. Himalayas.
A. linosyris A curiosity, 30–40 cm (12–16 in) clump-forming with linear stem leaves and clusters of ray-less, yellow pom-poms. Europe.
A. ptarmicoides Clump-forming to 60 cm (2 ft), leaves linear, stems branching, flowers small with long, narrow white florets, and white centres, abundant. C.N. USA.
A. sedifolius Vigorous tall plant with a good compact form *A. s.* 'Nanus', bushy to 40 cm (16 in), flowers profuse, narrow-rayed, clear blue over a long period in late summer.
A. thomsonii 'Nanus' ✱ To 30 cm (1 ft) or less, flowers soft lilac in profusion over a very long season. A superb small-growing species with the attributes of *A.* x *frikartii*, on a small scale; a good foreground to yellows or pinks. Himalayas.
A. tongolensis Spreading clump, 30–40 cm (12–16 in), leaves sessile, flowers solitary, large pale blue with broad yellow discs. Useful early summer-flowering species. Himalayas. China. Several good cultivars. 'Berggarten' 40 cm (16 in), flowers lilac, disc orange-yellow, 'Lavender Star', lavender-blue, shorter, 'Napsbury', lower still, flowers dark blue with orange discs, 'Wartburgstern', strong-growing, flowers violet-blue.
A. tripolium Clump-forming to 60 cm (2 ft), stems reddish, flowers small bright lilac-blue in clusters. Short-lived. Europe.
A. vahlii Rhizomatous, 30 cm (1 ft), flowers 1–3, pale purple, to 4 cm (1.6 in) wide. Falklands.
A. yunnanensis See ***A. diplostephioides***

Asteriscus (*Compositae*)

A. maritimus ✱ The only species grown regularly. Doubtfully hardy below -4 °C (25 °F) it is excellent treated as for other 'tender' perennials, taking cuttings in late summer to overwinter, with some chance of its survival in a warm site in well-drained soil. It makes a mound of dark green, ovate-spathulate, very hairy leaves to 15 cm (6 in), and bears an unending succession of large, short-stalked, deep yellow daisy flowers to 5 cm (2 in) wide, from early summer to autumn. Med.

17 *Asteriscus maritimus*

Astilbe (*Saxifragaceae*)

A supremely beautiful genus of densely clump-forming perennials, mainly from E. Asia, with attractive, fern-like leaves, often tinged with purple or bronze especially when young, and long-lasting, elegant, tapering plumes of tiny flowers in shades of white, pink to purple, and reddish, in summer. They are easily grown as long as there is adequate moisture. They will tolerate full sun if the soil is permanently damp and rich in humus, but in dry gardens they do better in partial shade, and will benefit from irrigation when necessary. They look splendid grown in drifts of various cultivars, and will combine beautifully with other moisture-loving perennials like the candelabra primulas, meconopsis, iris and lobelias. The smaller species make a good edging for a damp border.

The species may be grown from seed, preferably sown in early spring in loamless compost, with bottom heat. They can all be propagated by division of established clumps, although they are best left undisturbed for periods of 4–5 years before dividing.

Several of the species, and a large range of hybrids and cultivars, are small enough to include and are tabulated below. The largest group are those of *A.* x *arendsii* which are of complicated parentage and are mainly large. I have selected

Hybrids and Cultivars

Name	Parentage	Height	Flowers	Notes
'Alba'	*simplicifolia* x	40 cm (16 in)	White	
'Aphrodite'	*simplicifolia* x	40 cm (16 in)	Carmine	
'Atrorosea'	*implicifolia* x	50 cm (20 in)	Deep salmon	Arching sprays
'Betsy Cuperus'	*thunbergii* x	50 cm (20 in)	Pale pink	
'Bonn'	*japonica* x	60 cm (2 ft)	Carmine	
'Bridal Veil' (Brautschleier) 🏆	*arendsii* x	70 cm (28 in)	White fading cream	Loose sprays
'Bronce Elegans' (Bronz Elegance)	*simplicifolia* x	30 cm (1 ft)	Pink and cream	Arching sprays, late
'Carnea'	*simplicifolia* x	30 cm (1 ft)	Salmon-pink	
'Deutschland'	*japonica* x	50 cm (20 in)	White	
'Dunkellachs'	*simplicifolia* x	30 cm (1 ft)	Salmon	Bronzed foliage
'Emden'	*japonica* x	50 cm (20 in)	Purplish-pink	
'Europa'	*japonica* x	60 cm (2 ft)	Pale pink	Dense spikes, early
'Fanal' 🏆	*arendsii* x	60 cm (2 ft)	Deep crimson	Short spikes, early
'Finale'	chin*ensis* x	40 cm (16 in)	Bright pink	Compact
'Gloria'	*arendsii* x	60 cm (2 ft)	Deep pink	Early
'Gnom'	*crispa* x	25 cm (10 in)	Rose pink	
'Inshriach Pink'	*simplicifolia* x	35 cm (14 in)	Pink	
'Irrlicht'	*arendsii*	40 cm (16 in)	White	Early
'Koblenz'	*japonica* x	60 cm (2 ft)	Carmine	
'Koln'	*japonica* x	50 cm (20 in)	Deep pink	
'Montgomery'	*japonica* x	70 cm (28 in)	Deep red	
'Obergartner Jurgens'	*arendsii* x	60 cm (2 ft)	Carmine	Early
'Peach Blossom' ('Drayton Glory')	*japonica* x	x 50 cm (20 in)	Pale pink	
'Perkeo' 🏆	*crispa* x	x 30 cm (1 ft)	Deep pink	Bronze young foliage
'Peter Barrow'	*glaberrima* x	x 40 cm (16 in)	White	
'Praecox Alba'	*simplicifolia* x	x 30 cm (1 ft)	White	
'Professor van der Wielen'	*thunbergii* x	x 45 cm (1.5 ft)	Pink	
'Rheinland' 🏆	*japonica* x	x 60 cm (2 ft)	Clear pink	Early
'Rosa Perle' ('Pink Pearl')	*arendsii* x	x 70 cm (28 in)	Coral pink	
'Rosea'	*simplicifolia* x	x 35 cm (14 in)	Rose	
'Serenade'	*chinensis pumila* x	x 45 cm (1.5 ft)	Clear pink	Late
'Snowdrift'		60 cm (2 ft)	White	
'Spatsommer'	*chinensis pumila* x	x 40 cm (16 in)	Pink	
'Spartan'	*arendsii* x	60 cm (2 ft)	Deep red	
'Sprite' 🏆	*simplicifolia* x	45 cm (1.5 ft)	Shell pink	
'Veronica Klose'	*chinensis* x	40 cm (16 in)	Dark pink	
'Washington'	*japonica* x	x 60 cm (2 ft)	White	
'William Buchanan'	*simplicifolia* x	20 cm (8 in)	Pink	

those unlikely to exceed 60–70 cm (24–28 in) in average conditions.

A. chinensis Spreading, rhizomatous clump, leaves 2–3-ternate, leaflets ovate, toothed, flowers pink, stems to 60 cm (2 ft). *A. c.* var. *pumila* 🏆 similar on a smaller scale to 30 cm (1 ft). Several cultivars.

***A.* x crispa** (*A. simplicifolia* x *A. chinensis* var. *pumila*) Clump-forming hybrids, with toothed, crinkly leaflets often with bronze tinges when young and in autumn.

A. glaberrima (syn. *A. japonica* var. *terrestris*) Var. *saxatilis* 🏆 is usually grown, a tiny clump-former to 15 cm (6 in), leaves reddish-tinged, flowers pinkish-mauve tipped with white.

A. japonica Usually tall, but with smaller cultivars. Leaves biternate, leaflets narrow, deeply toothed, small plumes of white flowers.

A. microphylla Uncommon, 30 cm (1 ft) mound of ferny leaves with deeply toothed margins, plumes of flowers pale pink or white.
A. simplicifolia 🏆 Clump, 20–40 cm (8–16 in), leaves single with deeply toothed edges, flowers white in narrow spikes. One of the best small species and parent of some good hybrids.
A. thunbergii Clump-former to 50 cm (20 in), leaves pinnate with ovate, toothed leaflets, flowers white in loose plumes.

Astrantia (*Umbelliferae*)

An invaluable genus of herbaceous perennials from C. and E. Europe, which rely on delicate charm rather than flamboyant colouring for their attraction. They all come within our scope, although *A. major* in its various forms may become a little tall in good conditions. All have palmately divided leaves and sprays of flowers in shades of pink, crimson, or white, often veined and suffused with green. Each 'flower' consists of a tight umbel of tiny true flowers surrounded by a conspicuous ring of coloured bracts, the whole 2–3 cm (0.8–1.2 in) in diameter. They are easily grown anywhere in sun or shade, but thrive best in rich moist soils with plenty of humus. Their only disadvantage is that they seed around prodigiously unless dead-headed, and the seedlings have a gift for firm attachment at an early age. Seedlings are always attractive but named cultivars are superior. These can be propagated by division but it is a slow process.
A. carniolica To 40 cm (16 in), leaves deeply 5-lobed, flowers white, late summer. *A. c.* var. *rubra* is commonly offered, but seems very variable. Correctly to 30 cm (1 ft), with flowers deep purplish-crimson, but the plant now offered frequently resembles *A. major* in size and habit, with dark flowers
A. major (see plate 6) To 70 cm (28 in), leaves long-petioled, palmately divided, margins toothed, sprays of greenish-white true flowers with generally pinkish-white bracts netted and veined with purple and green. Widely grown. Europe. *A.m.* Subsp. *involucrata* has a collar of very long-pointed white bracts. Various excellent cultivars or hybrids between the species have been named. The following are among the best. 'Barrister', fairly compact with large white flowers veined with green, and some white-streaking of the leaves. 'Buckland' ✸ Beautiful, pale pink flowers suffused with green. 'Claret', very dark reddish-purple flowers. 'Hadspen Blood', is similar, and one of the darkest. 'Rosea', more pink suffusion of the flowers and the bracts. 'Rubra', darker still. 'Ruby Wedding' ✸ The finest dark-flowered hybrid raised to date, with purple-tinged stems, as well as exceptionally dark flowers produced over a long period. 'Shaggy', (syn. 'Margery Fish') 🏆 one of the finest, large with exceptionally big flowers with long-pointed bracts. 'Sunningdale Variegated' 🏆 A popular plant with leaves heavily streaked creamy-yellow in spring, a variegation which fades as the season progresses.
A. maxima 🏆 Smaller than *A. major*, leaves more shallowly 3-lobed, flowers a delicious shade of soft pink. It is one of the most beautiful, needing good conditions to thrive; it seeds around much less than *A. major*.
A. minor Probably only for the astrantia addict, like a small edition of *A. major* to 20–30 cm (8–12 in), with sparse white flowers with narrow bracts.

Athamanta (*Umbelliferae*)

A small rarely grown genus of typical umbellifers from S. Europe, resembling miniatures of fennel or cow-parsley. They are quite attractive in a sunny, well-drained border, and can be grown from seed.
A. cretensis 30–40 cm (12–16 in), leaves very finely divided grey-green, flowers white in broad umbels.
A. macedonica Leaves pinnate, flowers similar. *A. m.* subsp. *arachnoidea,* leaves grey, softly downy.
A. turbith Similar to *A. cretensis*, a little taller with a filigree of bright green leaves.

Aurinia (*Cruciferae*)

A. saxatilis (syn. *Alyssum saxatile*) 🏆 The most popular of all the alyssums for making a splash of colour in spring, usually planted on the rock garden or as a wall plant with other colour carpets like aubretias, but excellent in the foreground of a sunny, well-drained border. It makes a spreading mound to 20 cm (8 in) high of downy, grey-green leaves, smothered in late spring in bright yellow flowers. C., S.E. Europe. Several cultivars are available. 'Citrinum' 🏆 lemon-yellow, 'Compactum', densely compact to 10 cm (4 in), 'Dudley Nevill', a pleasing shade of brownish-yellow, seen also in its variegated form, 'Flore Pleno', flowers double, 'Gold Ball', compact, gold, 'Gold Dust', strong grower, gold, 'Golden Queen', more compact, paler yellow, 'Variegata', leaves streaked with cream, but tending to revert.

B

Ballota (*Labiatae*)

Begonia (*Begoniaceae*)

There is one remarkably hardy begonia, a most beautiful foliage plant, which also has pleasing flowers in late summer. It does best in rich soils in partial or full shade, and increases freely by small bulbils, or can be divided.
B. grandis var. ***evansiana*** (*B. evansiana*) ✸ ☼ To 60 cm (2 ft), stems branching reddish-hairy, leaves large, pointed, cordate at the base, reddish-green and hairy above, reddish-purple beneath, flowers in loose sprays, small pale pink or white (var. *alba*), from red buds. I have found it hardy to at least -7 °C (20 °F). E. Asia.

18 *Begonia grandis* ssp. *evansiana*

Belamcanda (*Iridaceae*)

B. chinensis The only species generally grown, rhizomatous, flowers deep yellow, six equal segments spotted dark red towards their base. Well worth trying in the open garden, it seems to be hardy to at least -7 °C (20 °F), grown in very well-drained rich soil. Propagation is easy from seed. E. Asia.

Bergenia (*Saxifragaceae*)

A genus of mat-forming, rhizomatous, evergreen perennials from E. Asia, with large sturdy leaves, which form a dense ground cover, with the added attraction of sprays of pink or white flowers in spring on 20-50 cm (8–20 in) reddish stems. The leaves are often hairy and may develop good red or yellow tints in autumn. They are among the best ground covering perennials, for sun or shade, especially in rather poor soils which they tolerate better than hostas, for example.

Several species are grown, and a large number of hybrids and cultivars derived from them which I will describe together.

B. ciliata ☼ Variable, typically leaves very large, 25 cm (10 in) diameter, hairy, tinted red underneath, stems reddish, flowers clear pink from red buds in broad sprays. One of the finest, although less hardy than most, sometimes losing its leaves during the winter, but renewing them in spring. Var. *lingulata* has marginal hairs only, flowers white.

B. cordifolia Hardy, leaves less hairy, rounded, green, flowers lilac in large heads on tall stems. *B. c.* 'Purpurea', large leaves tinted purple in autumn and winter, flowers vivid magenta. A splendid variety.

B. crassifolia Leaves a little smaller, spathulate, margins recurved, becoming bronzed in winter, flowers deep pink.

B. purpurascens (syn. *B. delavayi*) 🏆 Leaves almost vertical, narrow green, deep beetroot in winter, flowers deep pink. An unusual and spectacular species, especially in winter.

B. stracheyi To 20 cm (8 in), leaves smaller, rounded, flowers comparatively large, pink, white in var. *alba*, in short sprays. A delightful small-growing species.

Hybrids and Cultivars

Name	**Leaves**	**Flowers**	**Comments**
'Abenglocken'	Large, red-tinged	Dark reddish-purple	Tall
'Abendglut'	Rounded, deep maroon in winter	Deep crimson, often semi-double	Compact to 25 cm (10 in)
'Admiral'	Erect, oval, bronze-tinged to red in autumn	Cherry-red	
'Baby Doll'	Green	Clear pink in dense heads	25 cm (10 in) or less
'Ballawley'	Round glossy green, purple in winter	Bright crimson in broad heads	
'Beethoven'	Green	White in large heads	
'Brahms'	Light green	Palest pink	
'Bressingham Bountiful'	Dark green with red border	Rose-pink	Compact
'Bressingham Ruby'	Glossy green, purple in winter	Deep rose	Compact 30 cm (1 ft)
'Bressingham White' 🏆	Large, glossy green	White in large sprays	Very good white
'Distinction'	Light green, crinkly	Clear pink	
'Eric Smith'	Large, crinkled, bronze in winter	Pink	
'Glockenturm (Bell Tower)'	Green	Deep to red, abundant	
'Margery Smith'	Very large green	Reddish-purple	
'Morgenrote (Morning Red)'	Large green	Deep carmine	Often flowers again in June

Name	Leaves	Flowers	Comments
'Profusion'	Green, red in autumn	Pale pink	Only 30 cm (1 ft)
'Pugsley 's Pink'	Green, reddish beneath	Pink	Tall
'Purpurglocken'	Green	Deep purple	Sometimes second flowering
x schmidtii 🏆	Broad green, toothed	Deep reddish-pink in dense heads	*B. ciliata x B. crassifolia* Early
'Schneekissen'	Large green, crinkled	Pale pink	Very tall
'Schneekonigin'	Large green, crinkled	Large, pale pink deepening later	
'Silberlicht' 🏆	Large, toothed	Pure white becoming pinkish	
'Sunningdale'	Red-tinged in autumn, deep red reverse	Deep purplish-red	Vigorous

Bidens (*Compositae*)

A very useful genus of remarkably floriferous tender perennials for containers, for filling gaps in the border, or as a permanent feature of frost-free gardens. They have long, semi-prostrate stems set with tiny leaves, becoming a carpet of single deep yellow daisy flowers from early summer until the first frosts. They look good, and contrast well in habit, with *Cuphea caeciliae* or *Europeyops pectinatus* in pots, or in the border as a low margin in front of other yellow or blue 'daisies'. They are very easy in any well-drained soil, and can be propagated from cuttings at any time, but will not survive more than a degree or two of frost.

B. ferulifolia (See plate 2) The only species widely grown, as described above. S. USA, Mexico.

B. humilis (syn. *B. triplinervia* var. *macrantha*) A recent acquisition from collected seed, very similar, even more robust, more hardy, flowers slightly larger, seeding freely. Mexico, S. Am.

Biscutella (*Cruciferae*)

A typical genus of crucifers, of which only one is grown regularly.

B. frutescens Rhizomatous, stems white-hairy, branching, leaves oval, hairy, flowers 4-petalled, small yellow in branching sprays in summer, followed by flattened seed pods. Thrives in full sun in well-drained soil, easy to raise from seed. Med.

Borago (*Boraginaceae*)

B. laxiflora (syn. *B. pygmaeus*) The only species grown as an ornamental perennial in gardens. Tap-rooted, leaves 10 cm (4 in) wide, coarse, dark green in a rosette, stems to 30 cm (1 ft), flowers nodding, pure azure blue in loose sprays. The colour is fine but the plant itself is rather coarse and liable to seed over-freely. It is useful in poor soils under trees. Corsica, Sardinia.

Boykinia (*Saxifragaceae*)

A small genus of clump-forming, herbaceous perennials, resembling heucheras or saxifrages of the Fortunei persuasion, with good leaves and panicles of tiny flowers. They are unspectacular but have the delicate charm of so many woodlanders, for the front of a shady border in humus-rich soil. They can be propagated by seed sown in autumn or by division in spring. USA.

B. aconitifolia 30–40 cm (12–16 in) high, leaves large rounded. 5-6-lobed, stems hairy, flowers small, creamy with yellow centres, in loose heads, in summer.

B. occidentalis (syn. *B. elata*) Leaves similar, glossy, with toothed margins, flowers white in wide heads.

B. rotundifolia To 80 cm (30 in), leaves less deeply lobed, flowers similar, in a one sided loose spike, generally taller.

Brachycome (*Compositae*)

A genus of neat somewhat tender Australasian annuals, and alpine or subalpine perennials, which have recently become popular as container plants, often as unnamed 'blue daisies', so that nomenclature is problematical. They make up for their small size by being tremendously free-flowering, with blue or white daisies over a long period in summer, and are proving unexpectedly hardy, surviving at least to -5 °C (23 °F), so that they are well worth trying in the front of the border, in well-drained soil in sun, as well as in containers for patios etc., or as cold greenhouse plants. They can be raised from seed but this may not set in cool gardens, and cuttings root very easily during the growing season.

The following named perennial species are occasionally offered, as well as the good unnamed or fancy-named perennial plants from garden centres, which are no more tender and may belong under one of these.

B. rigidula A low spreading mound, leaves tiny bright green, narrow, flowers clear lilac-blue to 2.5 cm (1 in) in diameter, throughout summer.

B. tadgellii (syn. *B. nivalis* var. *alpina*) Leaves usually pinnate with toothed lobes, flowers usually white, occasionally blue.

Brunnera (*Boraginaceae*)

B. macrophylla 🏆 The only commonly grown species, with several interesting varieties. The type plant is a spreading herbaceous perennial with large, rather coarse-looking heart-shaped leaves, which get even bigger after flowering and make useful ground cover in shade, especially in less than the ideal conditions needed for more refined plants. The small flowers are very attractive, in loose sprays of clear forget-me-not blue. Some of the forms with improved leaves and similar flowers are less vigorous and well worthy of good conditions of moist humus-rich soil in partial or full shade. E. Europe. 'Betty Bowring', flowers white, showing up well in a dark corner. Dawson's White (syn. Variegata) ☼ leaves bordered with white, a very fine foliage plant needing good conditions in semi-shade. 'Hadspen Cream' ☼ 🏆 similar, but leaves bordered cream. 'Langtrees', leaves very large, their margins spotted with silver.

Bulbine (syn. *Bulbinopsis*) (*Liliaceae*)

Bulbine bulbosa To 30 cm (1 ft), rosettes of pale yellowish-green succulent leaves, flowers small starry, deep yellow with typical yellow-hairy filaments, in loose spikes, over a long period in summer. It is the only species cultivated regularly. An attractive little plant that will seed prodigiously unless dead-headed, hardy to -7 °C (20 °F) or possibly lower. It seems to do equally well in sun or partial shade. Australia.

Bulbinella (*Liliaceae*)

About ten species, allied to the last but having flowers lacking the hairy filaments, and generally hardier. They are interesting clump-forming perennials with long linear leaves and dense spikes of yellow flowers on stiff upright stems. In reasonably moist and well-drained rich soil they can be grown in sun or partial shade. Planted in a group they are quite striking, reminiscent of miniature kniphofias. They can be raised from seed sown in autumn. NZ.

B. angustifolia To 50 cm (20 in), rosettes of leaves to 30 cm (1 ft) with incurving edges, flowers pale yellow in dense spikes.

B. hookeri Leaves similar, sometimes with a bronze tinge, spikes of flowers deep golden-yellow. The most widely grown.

B. rossii Larger than *B. hookeri*, leaves wider at the base tapering towards their tips, flowers on taller stems.

Buphthalmum (*Compositae*)

A small genus of yellow daisy-flowered spreading perennials, of which the one described is the only species in cultivation of suitable size. It is an elegant plant which will combine well with smaller blue-flowered plants in front of or beside it, for example *C. carpatica* (and other low campanulas), the blue erigerons, or equally well with taller background species, such as *Campanula lactiflora*, *C. latifolia* and the earliest asters. It is easily propagated by division, or by cuttings of young growth.

B. salicifolium Spreading mound to 60 cm (2 ft) of slender often floppy stems, leaves lanceolate, flowers large yellow, in abundance over a long period. It is one of the most beautiful of all the yellow daisies. Europe, W. Asia. Several named cultivars include 'Alpengold', 'Dora', and 'Golden Wonder', varying slightly in colour.

Bupleurum (*Umbelliferae*)

A genus mainly from S. Europe, with a similar appeal to that of the euphorbias, but on a smaller and less striking scale, combining interesting leaves with flowers in shades of greenish-yellow. Apart from some annuals and the fine shrubby *B. fruticosum*, they are mainly clump-forming perennials less than 60 cm (2 ft) high, with simple, often conspicuously veined and glaucous leaves, and compact umbels of tiny flowers surrounded by bracts which create most of the impact, in loose branching heads on upright stems. They are easily grown in well-drained soil in sun or partial shade. They may be propagated by seed sown immediately after collection. They often seem to germinate more freely when self-sown than when the gardener takes a hand.

B. angulosum To 40 cm (16 in), a clump of basal lanceolate glaucous leaves, flowers pale green, surrounded by a bowl of jade-green bracts, in several umbels on upright, branching, leafy stems. It is a beautiful plant for the lover of green flowers. A variety has recently appeared with an overall bronze suffusion to the flowers and leaves.

B. barceloi Rare woody species from the Balearics, 40 cm (16 in) with leafy stems and yellowish-green flowers. Hardiness uncertain.

B. falcatum ✱ To 80 cm (30 in) but usually less. Sparse clusters of lanceolate leaves, branching stems bearing myriads of tiny greenish-yellow flowers in late summer, like a yellow gypsophila. One of the most effective, it seeds freely, rapidly filling a square metre or two. Very effective with the red of *Phygelius* or *Lobelia laxiflorus*.

19 *Bupleurum falcatum* & *Phygelius capensis*

B. longifolium Similar in size to the last, leaves broader, umbels much larger, yellow, in less widely branching heads.

B. spinosum (See plate 55) Dense 30 cm (1 ft) high dome of tiny narrow leaves, a few soft spines eventually becoming

woody with age, a sprinkling in summer of tiny yellow umbels on short stalks. An uncommon but interesting plant that has proved hardy to -7 °C (20 °F).
B. stellatum 30–40 cm (12–16 in) or less, leaves narrow, branching stems, each with a few umbels of yellow flowers with greenish-yellow bracts.

Calamintha (*Labiatae*)

The calamints are a genus of spreading, very aromatic, hardy perennials, suitable for foreground planting in sun or partial shade, in well-drained soil, where they will make a dome of hairy leaves with short leafy spikes of small 2-lipped flowers in mid- to late summer. The flowers tend to be overwhelmed by the leaves, but the plants are very easy to grow. They can be divided in spring, or cuttings of young growth may be rooted in early summer.
C. cretica Sub-shrub, very grey-hairy, leaves oval, flowers small white. Crete.
C. grandiflora Rhizomatous spreading mound, leaves hairy, ovate, grey-green, toothed, flowers larger in plentiful leafy spikes. Widely grown. 'Variegata' leaves marked with creamy-white. S. Europe, Iran.
C. nepeta Lower-growing, leaves hairy, grey-green, flowers purplish-pink in branching clusters. A good carpeter. S. Europe. *C. n.* subsp. *nepeta,* leaves larger, flower spikes with more flowers. 'White Cloud', an effective white-flowered form.
C. sylvatica Uncommon native, to 50 cm (20 in), rounded, toothed, very hairy leaves, flowers pinkish spotted with deep purple.

Calceolaria (*Scrophulariaceae*)

A fascinating genus of annuals and perennials with characteristic pouched flowers, perhaps best known as a range of greenhouse plants with bloated, spotted flowers in a multitude of colours. These give little idea of the possibilities of the genus, which contains many small dainty species for the rock garden, alpine house, or peat bed, and a few of intermediate size and variable hardiness which I will consider here. These are perennials with interesting foliage and pouched flowers in various shapes, sizes, and colours, although the majority are yellow. Recent trips to the Andes have increased the number in cultivation, but some are little tested in the garden. They may only be satisfactory in gardens with less than 3–4 °C of frost. In general they do best in rich but well-drained soil which remains moist, and may be best suited in partial shade, especially in dry areas. They are easily raised from seed which germinates well in bottom heat.
C. arachnoidea 20–40 cm (8–16 in), wiry branching stems, leaves intensely white-woolly, rounded, flowers small, deep violet-purple, in loose sprays. A fascinating species needing very well-drained soil in a mild garden to survive the winter outside. Chile.
C. cana Resembles *C. arachnoidea* but flowers small, pale to deep pink, lightly spotted with deep purple, with a yellow throat. A recent introduction from Chile.
C. ericoides Semi-shrubby, long stems upright at first becoming arching or prostrate, densely covered with heath-like leaves, and small, clear yellow flowers on long peduncles for several weeks in late summer. A striking recent arrival from high elevations in Ecuador, quick growing but apparently needing nearly frost-free conditions.
C. integrifolia Semi-shrubby to 60 cm (2 ft) or more, attractive leaves, grey-green, lanceolate, finely toothed and yellowish on the reverse, flowers bright yellow, to 2 cm (0.8 in) long in terminal clusters. Usually considered a greenhouse plant, but hardy to at least -6 °C (21 °F). Chile.
C. lanata Upright-growing, leaves large, oval, felted, pale creamy grey-green, axillary flowers 2–3 cm (0.8–1.2 in) long, narrow, pale cream with red markings in the throat. Another recent introduction from Ecuador and probably the most tender.

Callirhoe (*Malvaceae*)

C. involucrata ✸ The only species in general cultivation. A mat of long prostrate shoots form a central rootstock, leaves rounded, 3–5-lobed, 5 cm (2 in) wide, flowers shallowly bowl-shaped, vivid deep magenta, in late summer. A striking plant in hot summers, for the front of a border, with a long flowering period, but needs full sun and well-drained soil. It can be propagated from cuttings of young shoots, or by seed when this is set. S. USA.

Caltha (*Ranunculaceae*)

A genus of moisture-loving, clump-forming perennials for marginal planting around ponds and streams. They usually have rounded cordate leaves and abundant heads of large yellow or white buttercup flowers. They are easily grown, apart from one or two small 'alpine' plants, in constantly damp or wet soils, and look splendid with *Lysichiton* and *Primula rosea.* They can be propagated by division, or by seed sown as soon as ripe.
C. leptosepala To 25 cm (10 in), flowers solitary white, with a central boss of yellow stamens. A beautiful compact species. N. Am.
C. palustris 🏆 Robust, rhizomatous, a dense clump of kidney-shaped leaves, flowers deep yellow, to 4 cm (1.6 in) diameter, late spring and early summer. The most widely grown species with a number of varieties. Europe, N. Am. Var. *alba* similar, flowers white, var. *minor* (syn. *Caltha minor*) lower growing, rooting at the nodes, flowers slightly smaller, var. *palustris* (syn. *C. polypetala*) very vigorous, creeping, one or a few larger flowers to a stem, 'Plena', double-flowered, var. *radicans* similar to var. *minor* and possibly included in it, 'Flore Pleno' 🏆 a good double form of the last. 'Tyermannii' vigorous with dark, procumbent stems.

Campanula (*Campanulaceae*)

One of the most important of all genera in the garden, it encompasses everything from tiny treasures for the alpine house to statuesque plants for the back of the border. I have excluded the smaller and trickier species, and the large species, and the many annuals and biennials, but have described some of the more robust of the low growers as they can make fine carpets of colour along the edge of a mixed border.

Most of the campanulas have flowers in shades of lilac-blue, but there are several with white and pink flowers, in a variety of shapes from narrow tubular bells to open stars. Most of those described are easy to grow in a border and their colours combine well with pastel shades of pink and silver, as well as with the harder yellows of the many summer daisies. The species can be raised from seed and the majority of the species and hybrids can also be increased by division. A few species can be invasive and need care in their placing, and these will be mentioned individually.

C. alliariifolia Clump-forming, 40–60 cm (16–24 in), leaves hairy, deltoid, with white reverse, creamy-white pendulous bells from pink-tinged buds in elegant one-sided spikes. Caucasus.

C. barbata To 30 cm (1 ft), rosettes of hairy, lanceolate leaves, one-sided spikes of 2.5 cm (1 in) long pale blue nodding bells with characteristic long white hairs on the petal lobes, on stiff upright stems. A beautiful short-lived 'alpine species', effective in a group of several plants, easily grown from seed. Var. *alba* white-flowered. Alps.

C. betulifolia 🏆 Low mats of broad, toothed leaves, often purple-backed, on pink-tinged stems, flowers large white, often pink flushed, from deep pink buds. Usually grown as an alpine, it is not too difficult in well-drained soil. Turkey.

C. 'Birch Hybrid' 🏆 (*C. portenschlagiana* x *C. poscharskyana*) Intermediate between the parents, substantial low mounds, smothered in deep blue flowers. Excellent for wall planting or in the front of a mixed border.

C. bononiensis To 60 cm (2 ft) or more, clumps of grey-green, ovate, cordate stem leaves, violet-blue pendent bells with spreading lobes in few-flowered spikes. An attractive taller species. Caucasus.

C. 'Burghaltii' 🏆 Possibly *C. latifolia* x *C. punctata*, resembles the latter, upright stems to 60 cm (2 ft), 3 cm (1.2 in) long hanging bells, dark in the bud, opening to soft greyish-blue.

C. carpatica 🏆 To 30 cm (1 ft), leaves cordate, toothed, on long petioles, flowers, generally solitary, upward-facing, broadly bell-shaped to 4 cm (1.6 in) wide, in shades of white, blue and purple. Carpathians. One of the best border-edging plants in its many forms, making sheets of colour over a long period in summer. All the cultivars mix well with other low growers like diascias or pinks, and can be used to separate these from the yellow of Asteriscus or Bidens. There are several cultivars: 'Blaue Clips', sky-blue, true from seed, 'Blue Moonlight', grey-blue, shallow, 'Bressingham White', white, 'Chewton Joy', pale blue, edged darker, 'Queen of Sheba', China-blue, shallow, very large, a tall plant, 'Riverslea', purple-blue, large, flat, 'Weisse Clips', white, true from seed.

C. carpatica var. ***turbinata*** Lower-growing, leaves more pubescent grey-green, flowers blue-violet with more pointed lobes. The following hybrids or cultivars are considered to have been derived from the variety. 'Alba', white, 'Isabel', deep violet-blue, 'Jewel', light blue, 'Karl Foester', deep blue, 'Wheatley Violet', deep violet.

C. collina Spreading clump-former, 30 cm (1 ft), leaves hairy, oval, toothed, bells one to a few, nodding purple, to 3 cm (1.2 in). It spreads freely but may not flower freely. Turkey, Caucasus.

C. elatines Prostrate, central tuft of cordate grey-green leaves, masses of pale blue, occasionally white, starry flowers with spreading lobes, on radiating stems. Good for wall planting, or very well-drained soil. Italy.

C. fenestrellata (syn. *C. garganica* subsp. *fenestrellata*) Resembles a more compact *C. garganica*, leaves doubly toothed, flowers blue-violet. Subp. *istriaca* more hairy, leaves simply toothed. Balkans.

C. garganica 🏆 A spreading mound of prostrate, branching stems, leaves rounded, toothed, flowers abundant, 2 cm (0.8 in) wide, starry, blue with a white centre. Vigorous enough for the border edge, and excellent for wall planting. Italy. 'Blue Diamond', leaves grey-green, flowers pale blue with darker centres. 'Dickson's Gold', leaves flushed with gold, flowers paler blue. 'W.H. Paine', 🏆 more compact, flowers darker.

C. 'G.F. Wilson' 🏆 *C. pulla* x *C. carpatica* var. *turbinata* Resembles the latter, flowers narrower, upward-facing, mid-violet-blue. A good low edging plant.

C. glomerata Variable, 30-60 cm (1–2 ft), spreading colony, leaves broadly lanceolate, hairy, toothed, flowers in dense clusters, in shades of violet-purple, mid- to late summer. The species is very attractive but somewhat invasive. Europe, Asia. Several varieties and cultivars are less invasive and make striking border plants, their dark colours combining well with the many strong yellows of summer; var. *acaulis* an excellent dwarf to 15 cm (6 in), flowers dark violet, var. *alba* white, var. *dahurica* taller, flowers very deep violet, 'Alba nana', only 20 cm (8 in), flowers smaller, white, in very compact heads, 'Joan Elliott', early, flowers very large, deep purple, 'Purple Pixie', 20–30 cm (8–12 in), flowers small in dense heads, deep purple, 'Schneekrone' (syn. 'Crown of Snow') 50 cm (20 in), flowers pure white in broad heads, 'Superba' 🏆 strong-growing to 60 cm (2 ft), flowers dark violet-purple in broad dense heads, 'White Barn', 30 cm (1 ft), flowers deep violet in dense heads.

C. grossekii Clump-forming, erect to 70 cm (28 in), leaves rounded, cordate, flowers mid-blue to violet, single or in small clusters. Hungary.

C. x *haylodgensis* *C. carpatica* x *C. cochlearifolia* Low mound of small toothed leaves, flowers widely open, clear blue, double, mid-summer. Barely big enough for the border but a most attractive floriferous plant. *C. h.* 'Warley White' ✱ a superb, rather more compact plant with identical pure white flowers.

C. isophylla 🏆 Loose mound of branching stems, leaves rounded, toothed, hairy, flowers abundant, pale blue, starry in loose clusters. Considered tender, often offered as a greenhouse plant, it will survive mild winters, especially on its side in a wall. An excellent pot plant, or border perennial in warm gardens. Italy. 'Alba' 🏆 pure white. 'Flore Pleno', similar to the type, flowers double blue. 'Mayi' 🏆 larger flowers leaves downy grey-green. 'Variegata' (syn. 'Balchiniana') leaves splashed with cream.

C. kemulariae Cushion-forming to 30 cm (1 ft), leaves glossy, doubly toothed, ovate-cordate, stems upright or spreading, flowers terminal, deep violet, 2.5 cm (1 in). It is a good wall plant.

***C.* 'Kent Belle'** ✱ Clump-forming, upright to 60 cm (2 ft) when established, leaves lanceolate, very large pendent bells of rich violet-purple. An excellent new hybrid.

C. lactiflora Large border plants thriving in sun or partial shade, with upright stems bearing large panicles of broad bells, with one or two smaller exceptions. 'Pouffe', to 30 cm (1 ft), flowers clear mid-blue. 'White Pouffe', similar but flowers white. 'Pritchard's Variety', slightly taller, flowers deep violet.

C.* 'Lynchmere' *C. elatines x ***C. rotundifolia*** Small clump-forming, flowers, nodding, deep violet-blue.

C. lyrata To 70 cm (28 in), clusters of lyre-shaped leaves, flowers narrow cylindrical, violet-blue in loose heads. Short-lived perennial. Asia Minor.

C. ochroleuca Very like *C. allariifolia* 70 cm (28 in), flowers narrow creamy-white.

C. persicifolia 50-70 cm (20–28 in), leaves lanceolate, toothed, narrowing up the stems, long-petioled flowers open cup-shaped, in a variety of shades, in long spikes. Popular border perennials, at the upper end of our height range, with many cultivars. All make spreading colonies and self-seed freely, a nuisance unless dead-headed. They thrive equally in sun or shade, but the less vigorous doubles do best in moist humus-rich soil. Cultivars: 'Alba', single white, 'Alba Coronata', semi-double white, 'Alba Flore Pleno', fully double white, 'Boule de Neige', larger double white, 'Coerulea Coronata', semi-double blue, 'Coerulea Flore Pleno', double blue, 'Cup in Saucer White' 🏆 'Frances', double, very pale blue with dark edge, 'Grandiflora Alba', large white, 'Grandiflora Coerulea', large blue, 'Hampstead White', single white, 'Moorheimii', semi-double white, 'Porzellan', porcelain blue, 'Pride of Exmouth', small purple-blue, 'Telham Blue', very large blue.

C. persicifolia var. ***nitida*** (syn *C. planiflora*) 15 cm (6 in), leaves crinkly, deep green, flowers very large mid-blue (white in 'Alba') in short spikes. A delightful miniature that sometimes seeds true, the seedlings easily recognized, but it sometimes produces *C. persicifolia* itself; best weeded out early.

C. portenschlagiana (syn. *C.muralis*) 🏆 Wide low clumps, small ivy-like leaves, masses of lilac-blue bells with reflexing lobes in summer. The commonest species on the rock garden, grows in any soils in sun or light shade, a good wall plant or edging to a bed. S. Europe. Var. 'Major', bigger, deeper blue flowers. 'Resholt's Variety', flowers a deeper shade of lavender.

C. poscharskyana Similar to the last, widely spreading habit, flowers open pale blue stars, with prominent styles, equally abundant. Another good wall plant. Yugoslavia. Cultivars: 'Blue Gown', flowers larger, deeper blue, 'E.H. Frost', flowers pale milky-blue, starry, 'Lilacina', flowers bluish-pink, 'Lisduggan's variety', the flowers larger, more pink, 'Rosea', the deepest shade of pink, 'Stella', flowers bright violet, star-shaped.

C. punctata Rhizomatous, 40 cm (16 in), leaves pointed, cordate, toothed, bells 5 cm (2 in) long, pendent, pink, heavily spotted with deeper purple, or often creamy-white spotted with deep pink in *f. albiflora.* Very attractive, but somewhat invasive. Japan. Var. *hondoensis,* fewer deeper pink flowers. 'Nana Alba', dwarf white. 'Rosea', pale pink, 'Rubriflora', darker than the type.

C. raddeana Tufted, rosettes of glossy cordate toothed leaves, spikes of broad deep violet pendent bells. Caucasus.

C. rapunculoides Be warned. Dangerously invasive and unfit for any part of the garden except a wilderness. One-sided spikes of violet-purple flowers. Europe.

C. rotundifolia Spreading colony, to 40 cm (16 in), rounded basal, narrow lanceolate stem leaves, loose sprays of nodding, or outward facing, dainty lavender bells on slender stems in summer. Our beautiful native harebell, not widely grown. Europe. Several named cultivars are available. Var. *albiflora* ✱ very beautiful, more clump-forming, pure white, 'Flore Pleno', double, probably a hybrid of *C.* x *haylodgensis.* 'Olympica', leaves dark green, serrate.

20 *Campanula rotundifolia alba*

C. sarmatica ✱ Spreading mound, to 40 cm (16 in), stems prostrate and semi-upright, leaves pale grey-green, pointed, toothed, flowers pale grey-blue, in many loose sprays for several weeks in summer. One of the best species for the border front. Caucasus.

C. scheuchzeri (syn. *C. linifolia*, *C. carnica*) Spreading, very similar to *C. rotundifolia*, less vigorous, flowers deeper violet-blue.

C. speciosa Rosettes of narrow leaves, to 30 cm (1 ft), flowers 3 cm (1.2 in) long, narrow, purplish-blue, occasionally white, in pyramids resembling a 'Canterbury Bell', sometimes proving perennial. S. France, Spain.

C. takesimana Very similar to *C. punctata*, flowers large white, purple-flecked. A first-class plant, probably more invasive; care should be taken to keep both species away from more delicate plants. Korea.

C. topaliana Clump-forming, rosettes of hairy lyre-shaped leaves, heads of flowers 1 cm (0.4 in) long, lavender. An uncommon Greek species. Subsp. *cordifolia*, leaves grey-green, very hairy, cordate, flowers larger.

C. trachelium Nettle-like leaves, spikes of large flowers, lilac with hairy lobes, in the leaf axils, summer. Resembles *C. raponticoides* but much better behaved, although it can spread quite widely, and become naturalized in semi-shade or in sun. Var. *alba*, white, 'Alba Flore Pleno', double white, 'Bernice', double blue.

C.* x *tymonsii *C. carpatica* x *C. pyramidalis* a pleasing dwarf form of *C. pyramidalis*, 20 cm (8 in), flowers violet-blue.

***C.* 'Van Houttei'** Possibly a hybrid of *C. punctata*, sparse spikes of very large, pendent, dark purple, bell-shaped flowers. Grows well in partial shade.

C. versicolor ✱ To 40 cm (16 in), rosettes of dark green cordate leaves, with good-sized flowers with widely spreading lobes, white, deep violet in the centre with a pale violet band at the edge, in long loose branching spikes. Uncommon but very attractive.

21 *Campanula versicolor*

Cardamine (Syn. Dentaria) (Cruciferae)

These shade-loving plants should be more popular in gardens. They are easily-grown, usually deciduous, and flower very early in spring when there are few other perennials to enjoy. The larger species have underground spreading rhizomes and are best planted among shrubs in humus-rich soil where they cannot overwhelm any small shade-loving plants. The less vigorous clump-forming species associate well with groups of bulbs like trilliums and erythroniums, or can be used to edge a shady border.

The species described are mainly European woodlanders. They usually have lobed or deeply divided leaves and loose clusters of typical crucifer flowers in shades of white, creamy-yellow or pink to purple on upright stems. They are easily propagated by division in early spring or autumn, or by seed sown in autumn, and kept cool until germination. One or two need an alpine house.

C. asarifolia (*C. a.* hort = *Pachyphragma macrophyllum*) Stoloniferous, to 30 cm (1 ft), leaves simple, wavy-edged, with long petioles, flowers white, occasionally flushed pink. Uncommon.

C. bulbifera (See plate 87) 20–40 cm (8–16 in) Upright leafy stems, leaves with 5–7 leaflets, toothed, flowers small rosy-purple, in clusters of up to 20. Attractive, but runs underground and develops prolific bulbils in the leaf axils, which drop off at a touch. It will tolerate fairly dry conditions so that it is useful for a shady part of the wild garden.

C. diphylla Rhizomatous, 30 cm (1 ft), leaves 3-lobed, toothed, flowers, comparatively large, white. Little tried in gardens. N. Am.

C. enneaphyllos ✱ Clump-forming, 20–30 cm (8–12 in), leaves 3–5-lobed, flowers nodding, creamy-yellow, in large heads. One of the most beautiful but only spreads slowly, needing good humus-rich soil to thrive.

C. hexaphylla (syn. *C. pinnata*, *Dentaria pinnata*) ✱ Vigorous runner, 20–30 cm (8–12 in), leaves large, pinnate, leaflets broad, usually 7, sparsely toothed and 1.5 cm (0.6 in) wide, flowers 4-petalled, usually white with a faint pink flush, or purplish-pink, in flattish terminal clusters of 15–20 in early spring. It needs room to spread but its early flowering makes it a fine plant for woodland or a large bed.

22 *Cardamine hexaphylla & Anemone ranunculoides*

C. kitaibelii (syn. *C. polyphylla*) Clump-forming, 15–20 cm (6–8 in), leaves divided, 5–12 lanceolate leaflets, flowers large pale yellow. Very attractive but uncommon. S. Europe.
C. macrophylla An attractive tall species to 75 cm (2.5 ft) high with pinnate leaves and quite dense clusters of deep pink flowers. A plant for the future. I have admired it growing in Sichuan and it has now been introduced to cultivation.
C. pentaphyllos ✱ Similar to *C. heptaphylla* but a denser clump, leaves digitate, leaflets narrow, deeply toothed, flowers deep pinkish-lavender in early spring, more nodding in a denser cluster, spreads more slowly.

23 *Cardamine pentaphyllos & Pulmonaria angustifolia*

C. pratensis 'Lady's Smock' Common native species, only suitable for naturalizing in the wild garden, but several less vigorous named clones are sometimes on offer. 'Edith' and 'Flore Pleno' 🏆 both double-flowered, the former white from pink buds, the latter purple fading to lilac; 'Improperly Dressed' a curiosity with apetalous flowers; 'William' a good deep lilac colour.
C. quinquefolia 20 cm (8 in), spreading, flowers bright pinkish-mauve, early spring.
C. raphanifolia (syn *C. latifolia*) Vigorous clump-forming species resembling *C. pentaphyllos*, but taller, leaves pinnate, leaflets more rounded, the terminal one large and kidney-shaped, flowers violet-purple.
C. trifolia Dense evergreen hummocks, leaves dark green, ternate on purple stems, leaflets rounded, sparsely toothed, flowers small, pure white, in 10–15 cm (4–6 in) spikes. Attractive easy species that can be used as a non-invasive, dense perennial edging to a shady bed.
C. waldsteinii ✿ Leaves several, ternate, bluntly-toothed, flowers pure white, with dark greyish-brown anthers, in clusters of up to 8, individually among the largest of the genus. Another beautiful, small, early-flowering species.

Carlina (*Compositae*)

Rosette-forming, thistle-like plants which are easily grown in a sunny bed of ordinary, not over-rich, soil. Thistles, when well-behaved like these, have considerable appeal in the garden, and this species in general cultivation is outstanding in the size of its rosettes and flowers, but the sessile forms need to be placed in front of other plants. They may be increased readily from seed sown in autumn.
Carlina acaulis Rosettes of deeply divided, very spiny, pinnate leaves, flower head 8–10 cm (3–4 in) wide, silvery-white or pinkish, sessile. The large sessile flowers are a striking feature, but the stems tend to lengthen in rich soil or in partial shade which should be avoided. Often short-lived or monocarpic. S. Europe, Russia.
C. acaulis subsp. *simplex* (syn. var. *alpina*, var. *caulescens*) Branching stem to 50 cm (20 in) with 2–5 flower heads, usually a little smaller. The cultivar 'Bronze' (syn. 'Bronce'), leaf rosettes attractively bronze-tinged.

Catananche (*Compositae*) (Cupid's Dart)

C. coerulea The only species of this Mediterranean genus for general cultivation. Clumps to 50 cm (20 in) of grey-green, linear, toothed leaves, flowers on wiry stems, solitary, 3.5 cm (1.4 in) wide lilac-blue, with narrow ray-florets, and dark violet centres, opening from a conspicuous cluster of glossy silver bracts. Several cultivars available. *C. c.* 'Major' 🏆 more robust, flowers larger, deeply coloured. 'Alba', a good pure white, 'Bicolor', white with a deep blue centre. Although not usually long-lived, they are colourful plants for near the front of a sunny border, and associate well with silver foliage or with the pink of diascias. They are also useful for cutting. They are most easily propagated from root cuttings, but mixed batches can be raised from seed.

Cautleya (*Zinziberaceae*)

A fascinating genus of a few rhizomatous perennials resembling small cannas, but more hardy, with deep yellow-hooded flowers with a deeply 2-lobed lip, similar to those of roscoeas, arising from bright red or purple bracts. They need humus-rich but well-drained soil, which never dries out, and usually do better in some shade. They seem to be hardy to about -7 °C (20 °F). They may be raised from seed preferably sown in heat in early spring.
C. gracilis (syn. *C. lutea*) 40 cm (16 in) Leaves pale green, sessile, to 20 cm (8 in), with yellowish edges and often some pink shading beneath; flowers golden-yellow amid brownish-red bracts, in short spikes on slender stems. Uncommon in gardens. Himalayas.
C. spicata Similar to *C. gracilis* but leaves petioled, flower spikes shorter, bracts shorter, brighter red. 'Var. Robusta' strong-growing, flowers deeper yellow, bracts deep maroon. The most widely grown species.

Celmisia (*Compositae*)

Most of these fascinating plants with their superb foliage are too small for consideration here, but the two species described are large enough to make magnificent foliage plants, as well as having striking white daisy flowers. The genus grows well in cool, moist gardens in humus rich soils, preferably well-drained, but suffers in dry conditions, losses being much more frequent from drought in summer than from cold in winter. They need shade in warm gardens but will thrive in sun, given sufficient humidity. If good seed is set it should be sown immediately after collection, as its viability seems very short, and stored seed nearly always fails.

C. semicordata (syn. *C. coriacea*) ✿ Clumps 30–40 cm (12–16 in), leaves glossy, leathery, 20–40 cm (8–16 in) long, with recurving margins and densely white-felted backs, flowers white 5–6 cm (2–2.3 in) diameter with yellow centres, on white stems. The largest species, a magnificent foliage plant in good conditions, contrasts well with ericaceous shrubs or with moisture-loving primulas, and low carpeting shade-lovers. Subsp. *aurigens* ✿ leaves are felted with golden hairs, even more striking.

C. spectabilis ✿ Very similar, 20–25 cm (8–10 in), but the leaves not quite so long and usually buff rather than white on the reverse.

Centaurea (*Compositae*)

A large genus, mainly of hardy perennials with very ornamental, thistle-like flowers enclosed in papery bracts in summer, some with interesting foliage. Many are too large to consider here, but some of the smallest are included as they make sufficient impact to be useful in front of a border, as well as on the larger rock garden. They are easy to grow in full sun, in well-drained soils, and they often have a long flowering season, especially if they are dead-headed after their first flush. They can be propagated by division or by cuttings of new shoots in early summer.

C. bella Low carpeter, 20 cm (8 in), leaves grey, pinnatifid, with elliptic lobes with white-tomentose backs, flowers solitary, dainty, pinkish-mauve, over a long season in summer. Worth growing for its beautiful foliage alone. Caucasus.

***C.* 'Blue Dreams'** Of doubtful origin, a runner like *C. montana*, 30–40 cm (12–16 in), leaves narrow grey-green, flowers solitary, large, soft pinkish blue.

C. cheiranthifolia Usually grown as var. *purpurascens*, similar in habit to *C. montana*, leaves larger, grey-green, flowers solitary, large, cream flushed with pale purple.

C. cineraria (syn. *C. candidissima*) 🏆 Rosettes of large leaves finely divided, unifomly velvety white, typical cornflowers purple, generally hidden among the leaves, and no great addition to the plant's beauty. Grown mainly for its magnificent foliage, it is only suitable for permanent planting in a border in nearly frost-free gardens. In cooler situations it can be used as an annual or short-lived 'filler', or as an excellent container plant overwintered under glass. Italy.

C. dealbata 60–90 cm (2–3 ft) Large clumps of branching stems, leaves green, grey-backed, flowers bright pink, solitary or a few, over a long period if dead-headed. A little tall in good soils especially if it is staked rather than allowed to flop. Caucasus. 'Steenbergii', similar in leaf, flowers deeper purplish-pink; tends to be more invasive.

C. hypoleuca Similar to *C. dealbata*, lower, leaves deeply lobed, white-backed, fine flowers deep rosy-purple in early summer, surrounded by silver papery bracts which persist on the attractive seed heads. Asia Minor. 'John Coutts' is the selection usually grown. It combines well with the lavender-blues of the taller early campanulas.

C. montana A runner, leaves green with whitish backs, flowers 5 cm (2 in) wide, blue with a purplish centre in the type, in a range of colours in its various cultivars, over a long season in early summer. It tends to flop and needs staking in tidy gardens, but it is effective unstaked at its first flowering, and can be cut back hard afterwards. Europe. *C. m. alba* ✸ (see plate 110) excellent pure white, invaluable in the early border. *C. m. carnea* (syn. *rosea*) soft purplish-pink. 'Ochroleuca', very pale cream, but only convincing when seen beside the white. 'Parham', very large deep purplish-blue flowers.

C. pulcherrima Attractive clump-former, to 40 cm (16 in), leaves pinnately divided, toothed, white-hairy beneath, flowers solitary, pure pink, surrounded by yellowish-silver bracts.

C. simplicaulis ✸ ✿ Excellent low carpeter, doubtfully distinguishable from *C. bella* although in my garden they look slightly different (indescribably!) in leaf.

C. triumfettii Usually represented by *C. t.* subsp. *stricta*, similar to *C. montana*, 30 cm (1 ft), leaves narrower and hairier, flowers bluish-pink. A plant offered as *C. stricta* may be the same subspecies but is smaller in all its parts. Subsp. *cana* 'Rosea' similar but flowers pink.

C. uniflora Clump-forming, to 30 cm (1 ft), leaves grey-green, hairy, lanceolate, flowers purplish-pink with large rays, from brownish-silver bracts.

Ceratostigma (*Plumbaginaceae*)

Semi-woody perennials, of varying hardiness, among the few with genuinely 'gentian blue' flowers in late summer and autumn. Although woody they often die down completely in winter except in warm gardens, and grow best in full sun in well-drained soil. *C. plumbaginoides* is rhizomatous; the others form low shrubs, all with simple, alternate, usually bristly leaves, and short terminal or axillary spikes of tubular flowers with five spreading lobes. They are readily propagated from cuttings during summer, or *C. plumbaginoides* may be divided in spring.

C. abyssinica To 50 cm (20 in), leaves narrow, pointed, on reddish stems, flowers 2.5 cm (1 in), deep blue with pointed lobes. Uncommon and the most tender, probably only surviving a few degrees of frost. N. Africa.

C. griffithii Branching red-bristled stems, leaves hairy with purple edges, flowers bright blue, terminal in short heads. A little hardier. Himalayas.

C. plumbaginoides 🏆 To 50 cm (20 in), spreading freely, leaves bright green with hairy margins, often colouring red in autumn, flowers in 2 cm (0.8 in) spikes, hardy to -10 °C (14 °F). It makes an excellent late-flowering border edging. W. China

C. willmottianum 🏆 Semi-shrub, leaves hairy, strongly red-tinged in autumn, flowers pale blue with reddish tubes in spikes. Can be above our size limit, intermediate in hardiness between the two previous species. W. China.

Chaerophyllum (*Umbelliferae*)

C. hirsutum The only species grown, closely resembles a small Cow Parsley, its form, 'Roseum' ✱ being much more desirable, a very elegant 60 cm (2 ft) umbellifer, with the attractive finely cut leaves of Cow Parsley and beautiful sprays of soft pink flowers. Europe.

24 *Chaerophyllum hirsutum* 'Roseum'

Chamaemelum (*Compositae*) (Chamomile)

C. nobilis (syn. *Anthemis nobilis*) The highly aromatic type plant is sometimes used as ground cover, or as a chamomile 'lawn', usually in its non-flowering form 'Treneague', but it has no merit in the border. The form 'Flore Pleno' (See front cover) on the other hand is an attractive low carpeting plant with very finely divided deep green leaves, covered in summer with a succession of creamy-white pompons.

Cheiranthus See *Erysimum*

Chelidonium (*Papaveraceae*)

C. majus The Greater Celandine is the only species, and in its typical form is a weed with an overwhelming propensity for seeding around the garden. Two cultivars are better behaved, and worth growing at the edge of a border or woodland, in sun or shade, but even the double-flowered varieties sow themselves freely and need care to prevent them from overwhelming smaller plants. Europe, W. Asia.

'Flore Pleno' Similar to the type, to 80 cm (30 in), leaves deeply lobed or pinnate, branching stems, loose umbels of small deep yellow double flowers in summer.

Var. *laciniatum* Smaller, leaves very attractive, more deeply cut, grey-green, loose heads of fascinating small flowers with finely divided petals, single or double.

Chelone (*Scophulariaceae*)

Small genus of hardy clump-forming perennials, native to moist soils, with opposite toothed leaves, and stiff, upright leafy stems, and short, dense spikes of unusually-shaped flowers in late summer, the upper lip forming an arched hood with 2-cleft margin, the lower 3-cleft, the interior bearded. They are easy to grow as long as the soil is moist. They can be raised from seed, sown in autumn and kept cool. N. Am.

C. glabra To 60 cm (2 ft) or more, leaves narrow, lanceolate, with very short petioles, flowers in clusters, white or occasionally very pale pink, white-bearded.

C. lyonii Usually taller, leaves broader, oval, on long petioles, flowers pinkish-purple with yellow beard, uncommon.

C. obliqua To 60 cm (2 ft), leaves broadly lanceolate, short-petioled, flowers deep rose, white-bearded, in short spikes on very leafy stems. The most commonly grown species.

Chiastophyllum (*Crassulaceae*)

C. oppositifolium The only species, it is perhaps small for consideration here, but can be a striking wall plant. It flourishes in shade, with good large, rounded, succulent leaves, and long arching sprays of tiny yellow flowers in late spring and early summer, shown to their best advantage when it is planted horizontally, in the company of ramondas and haberleas which enjoy the same conditions. Caucasus.

'Jim's Pride'(syn. '**Frosted Jade**') is a variegated sport which has recently appeared.

Chrysanthemum (*Compositae*)

The various perennials once to be found in this genus have now been placed in *Argyranthemum, Dendranthemum, Leucanthemum, Pyrethropsis, Rhodanthemum*, and other genera.

Chrysogonum (*Compositae*)

C. virginianum The sole representative of the genus, a low-growing, spreading carpeter, branching stems bearing coarse, hairy, ovate leaves, and loose heads of deep yellow flowers to 3 cm (1.2 in) wide, with narrow triangular rays from a yellow disc. It is easily grown even in shade, flowering off and on from late spring to autumn.

Chrysosplenium (*Saxifragaceae*)

The 'golden saxifrages' have recently become more popular with the introduction of the superior Chinese *C. davidianum*. They are undramatic, low carpeting plants with the colouring of euphorbias, and can be used as ground cover in moist shade. They can spread widely in moist humus-rich soils. They have very hairy, rounded or kidney-shaped pale green leaves on stems which root at the nodes, and heads of tiny yellow flowers surrounded by a conspicuous ring of yellow-green bracts in spring. They are easily propagated by division in spring.

C. alternifolia This and the very similar *C. oppositifolium* are native bog plants, similar to *C. davidiana* but more spreading, making a looser carpet with smaller leaves and less conspicuous flowers.

C. davidianum A beautiful mat of yellowish-green, enhanced by flower heads of similar colouring. A pleasing contrast to other more colourful early-flowering woodlanders, like primulas, cardamines and the woodland anemones, or complimenting the yellow *A. ranunculoides* and *A.* x *lipsiensis*.

25 *Chrysosplenium davidianum*

Cichorium (*Compositae*)

C. intybus (Chicory) is quite an attractive garden plant but too large to consider here.

C. spinosum 20–30 cm (8–12 in) Mound, stiff branching spiny stems with a few small leaves, a sprinkling of 5–6-rayed, clear blue flowers in summer. An intriguing spiny chicory which can be grown outside in mild gardens in full sun and well-drained soil, where temperatures do not drop much below -4 °C (25 °F). It can be raised from seed.

Cirsium (*Compositae*)

The Plume Thistles are handsome plants but the majority are either too large to consider here, or are too dangerously free-seeding for use in gardens without meticulous dead-heading.

C. acaule A rosette of typically attractive, finely cut, spiny leaves, one or several stemless heads to 4 cm (1.6 in) in diameter of pinkish-purple flowers. Sometimes confused with *Carlina acaulis*, it may be worth trying in the garden, in very well-drained poor soil, if its seeding is watched. Europe–C. Asia.

C. spinosissimum Rather tall with very attractive, extremely spiny, whitish leaves, and heads of yellow flowers. It rarely looks as good in the garden as in the wild, and seems to need good soil. Alps, Apennines.

Clintonia (*Liliaceae Convallariaceae*)

A genus of charming woodland plants for humus-rich soils in full or partial shade. They are rhizomatous perennials, with large, rounded glossy leaves, and umbels of funnel-shaped flowers, in early summer, followed by conspicuous fruits. They may be raised from seed sown fresh and kept cool until germination. They take at least 4–5 years to reach flowering size.

C. andrewsiana ✱ To 30 cm (1 ft), leaves glossy, 20 cm (8 in), light green, umbels of flowers deep pinkish-red, long-lasting and followed by large deepest blue fruits, which remain on the plant for several weeks. The largest and most striking. W. USA.

C. borealis To 20 cm (8 in), leaves smaller, flowers greenish-yellow, nodding, in smaller and looser heads, followed by very small blue fruits. E., N. Am.

C. udensis (syn. *C. alpina*) Similar in height to *C. andrewsiana*, small loose umbels of flowers, erect, greenish-white, occasionally purple-tinged, bell-shaped, small blue fruits. Himalayas.

C. umbellulata (syn. *C. umbellata*) ✱ Smaller than *C. andrewsiana* but forms good clumps more quickly; dense umbels of pure white flowers, followed by much smaller black fruits. E., N. Am.

C. uniflora is similar to *C. udensis*, 1–2 more open flowers to a stem. Like *C. udensis*, less free-flowering than other species. W., N. Am.

Codonopsis (*Campanulaceae*)

Genus of about 30 species of Asiatic climbing or clump-forming perennials, very variable in leaf, with fascinating, but unpleasantly smelling, pendent flowers, tubular- to star-shaped, often attractively veined, with intriguing markings within their bells. Ideally they should be at a high level, where the inside of the flowers can be seen, but in most gardens they have to be lifted up and peered into to appreciate their main beauty. They have rhizomatous or tuberous roots, and a few can be very invasive, especially some of the twining species. They grow well in sunny borders that do not dry out, or in semi-shade, in humus-rich but well-drained soil. They are easily raised from seed sown in autumn and kept cool through the winter. I have excluded the twining and climbing species, although they include some of the most beautiful.

C. bulleyana Upright to 40 cm (16 in), leaves heart-shaped, hairy, flowers pale blue, dark-veined, 2–3 cm (0.8–1.2 in) long, cylindrical for half their length, then flaring widely but with incurved tips.

C. cardiophylla Very close to *C. clematidea* but leaves cordate with white margins.

C. clematidea Semi upright to 50 cm (20 in), branching stems which soon sprawl, leaves unpleasant-smelling, ovate, pointed, flowers tubby bells with recurving tips, lightly veined outside, beautifully veined and marked with orange and black within.

C. dicentrifolia Close to *C. ovata* but with glabrous leaves.

C. meleagris Upright to 40 cm (16 in), leaves in basal clusters, ovate, almost hairless, nodding bells, only slightly recurving at their tips, heavily purple-veined on the outside, and purple-suffused inside.

C. mollis Upright, taller, stems branching, leaves hairy, ovate, flowers terminal, solitary, tubular towards the base, flaring widely towards the tips, blue with purple at the base, and darker veining within.

C. ovata Erect to 30 cm (1 ft) with finely hairy oval leaves, and solitary pale blue, funnel-shaped flowers, with purple veining inside. One of the best, with a tidier habit than *C. clematidea.*

C. subsimplex Uncommon, upright to 50 cm (20 in), with few, alternate, glabrous, ovate leaves, and several 2 cm (0.8 in) long, pale blue flowers.

Commelina (*Commelinaceae*)

A genus of mainly tuberous-rooted herbaceous perennials, with long, narrow, pale green leaves and small heads of 3-petalled flowers, in some species a clear deep sky-blue, which emerge from a large keel-shaped bract. They will occasionally survive mild winters outside in Britain, especially if well mulched, but they are usually lifted like dahlias and kept frost-free for the winter. They are excellent for well-drained soil in the border in milder areas in sun or light shade, but may seed excessively. They are easily raised from seed sown in early spring and kept warm.

C. coelestis (syn. *C. tuberosa* Coelestis Group) To 50 cm (20 in) or less, from a running root, leaves narrow, lanceolate, sometimes undulant, large terminal bracts from which emerge a succession of clear blue flowers. The best known, and the most striking. C. S. Am.

C. dianthifolia Similar but leaves shorter and narrower, flowers smaller and less impressive, except in colour. This should possibly be considered a subspecies of the very similar *C. tuberosa.* S.W. USA, Mexico.

Convallaria (*Liliaceae Convallariaceae*)

C. majalis 🏆 The Lily of the Valley is the only species and is too well-known to need description here, with its broad leaves and beautifully scented flowers. It has a number of varieties and cultivars worthy of mention including some with exceptionally beautiful leaf variegation. The common type can be very invasive and care is needed in the choice of site to ensure it has plenty of space. The varieties are usually less robust and more appreciative of good conditions of rich moist soil with plenty of leaf-mould, in some shade. Var. *rosea* differs only in having rose-pink flowers, and usually spreads less freely. 'Albostriata', leaves striped longitudinally with white, 'Fortin's Giant', later than the type and larger in leaf and flower, good scent, 'Hardwick Hall', larger, broad leaves narrowly margined with yellow, 'Prolificans', double, might appeal to some, 'Variegata', Similar to 'Albostriata', but stripes are pale yellow, 'Vic Palowski's Gold', ✿ leaves more erect, generously striped with yellow.

Convolvulus (*Convolvulaceae*)

A large genus of annual and perennial shrubs, herbs and climbers, including some serious weeds, and some beautiful plants which can prove invasive when well established. There are several small species which require an alpine house or careful cultivation on the rock garden or scree, and I am excluding these, together with the more vigorous climbers. The remainder include some excellent plants for sunny situations in well-drained soils, which vary greatly in habit but all have comparatively large flowers of typical funnel shape in shades of pink, blue, or white. They may be increased by cuttings in early summer, or those with running roots by root cuttings.

C. althaeoides A low scrambler rather than a climber, to 1 m (3 ft) or more, clambering through shrubs, leaves deeply divided, silvery-grey, flowers exquisite, large pale pink, over a long period in summer. Although sometimes slow to establish, it has a running root and will be invasive, so that it is best planted where its root-spread is limited and it can be appreciated safely. Subsp. *tenuissimus* (syn. *elegantissimus*) even more beautiful, the silvery leaves more deeply incised, and flowers possibly darker. S. Europe.

26 *Convolvulus althaeoides*

C. cantabricus Upright-growing to about 20 cm (8 in), leaves downy lanceolate, flowers 2 cm (0.8 in) wide, pink, solitary or in clusters. Uncommon. S. Europe.
C. cneorum 🏆 Shrubby, to 40 cm (16 in), evergreen, leaves lanceolate, beautiful gleaming silver, flowers large white throughout summer. A superb plant in warm gardens, but only reliably hardy to about -7 °C (20 °F). Med.
C. sabatius (syn. *C. mauritanicus*) 🏆 Mound-forming to 30 cm (1 ft) with trailing stems, leaves ovate, light green, slightly hairy, flowers widely funnel-shaped, usually pale- to mid-blue, in long succession. First-class, but variable in hardiness. 'Dark Form' ✱ much deeper blue. Italy, N. Africa.

27 *Convolvulus sabatius*

Coreopsis (*Compositae*)

Annuals and perennials, mainly N. American, the latter clump-forming with upright stems, lobed or pinnate leaves, and plentiful, large, long-lasting daisy flowers in summer, usually in shades of yellow. They are easy, very colourful plants for a sunny border in good soil, and their flowers are useful for cutting. I have included most of the species available although they are at the upper limit of our size range. They benefit from frequent division and replanting, and are easily increased in this way.
C. auriculata 60 cm (2 ft) or more in good soils, leaves 2-lobed rounded, stems simple or branching, 5 cm (2 in) wide, deep yellow daisies, which last well when picked. 'Schnittgold' (syn. 'Cutting Gold'), large, golden-yellow, 'Superba', more compact, flowers larger with a central maroon blotch.
C. grandiflora Erect to 60 cm (2 ft), leaves linear-lanceolate, simple or 4–5 lobed, hairy, flowers to 6 cm (2.3 in) wide, yellow with deeper centre. Probably the best species for cutting, with several cultivars. 'Astolat', to 40 cm (16 in), flowers large with a dark red central ring, 'Badengold', tall, deep yellow flowers. 'Early Sunrise', only 45 cm (1.5 ft), flowers semi-double, deep yellow. 'Mayfield Giant', similar to 'Badengold', flowers paler yellow. 'Ruby Throat' (syn. 'Rotkehlchen'), flowers with deep reddish-purple throat, sometimes placed within the next species. 'Sunray', to 75 cm (2.5 ft), flowers fully double, deep yellow.
C. lanceolata Differs from *C. grandiflora* in simple lanceolate leaves; flowers yellow with discs of similar colour. 'Goldfink', probably a cultivar of this species, only 25 cm (10 in), flowers golden-yellow, 'Lichstad', flowers bright yellow with a reddish-brown centre, 'Sterntaler', flowers have a brown central ring. 'Sunburst', double.
C. palmata To 70 cm (28 in), leaves palmately divided, hairy-margined, flowers uniformly bright yellow. Uncommon.
C. rosea Compact to 50 cm (20 in), leaves linear, flowers 2 cm (0.8 in) wide, deep reddish-pink with yellow centres, in loose heads. An attractive species, but I find it short-lived; it probably needs good moist soil and frequent division. 'Nana', very dwarf compact.
C. verticillata To 90 cm (3 ft), often less, leaves finely divided, pinnate, flowers few, 5 cm (2 in) diameter, bright yellow, in loose heads. One of the best for the border. 'Grandiflora' (syn. 'Golden Showers') 🏆 flower heads and individual blooms larger, on 60 cm (2 ft) stems. 'Moonbeam', flowers pale lemon-yellow, a delightful cultivar needing good soil to thrive. 'Zagreb', small compact, to 30 cm (1 ft), flowers dark golden-yellow.

Corethrogyne (*Compositae*)

Three species of late-flowering, herbaceous perennials from California. Their hardiness is borderline, with a good chance of surviving to -7 °C (20 °F) planted in a sunny spot in very well-drained soil. Cuttings should be taken in late summer and overwintered under glass as a precaution. Only one species is currently grown in Britain.
C. californica A broad mound of branching stems to 30 cm (1 ft), leaves silvery-grey, tomentose, toothed, flowers 2.5 cm (1 in) wide, soft greyish-pink with yellow centres, in long succession. Not often seen, but well worth growing.

Coriaria (*Coriariaceae*)

A genus of fascinating subshrubs, often herbaceous in cold climates; with a beautiful arching habit and, in most, very attractive fruits, the petals becoming fleshy and brightly coloured around the seeds and staying for a long time on the plant before the birds eventually acquire a taste for them. In good soil they may become rather big to consider here, but I find their long, arching shoots with opposite ovate leaves, spread widely without attaining much more than 60 cm (2 ft) in height in my garden. They are easily raised from seed sown in autumn after removing the fleshy coats, and kept cold.
C. japonica More upright and stiff than *C. terminalis*, stems branching, fruits pinkish-red at first, becoming black as they mature. Japan.
C. kingiana Low runner, branching shoots with long, opposite leaves bearing terminal clusters of abundant small, glossy black fruits. A delightful plant, which may spread far

unless killed by a hard winter; needs careful placing in frost-free gardens. NZ.
C. microphylla Similar to *C. kingiana*, but much bigger with crowded small leaves and brown fruits. NZ, S. Am.
C. nepalensis Similar to *C. japonica* with reddish branching stems and black fruits. Himalayas.
C. terminalis ✱ Usually represented by var. *xanthocarpa* One of the most spectacular of all fruiting plants; long arching stems with conspicuously veined opposite leaves, and long terminal sprays of succulent deep orange fruits. It runs underground but less freely than others described above. Himalayas, China.

Cornus

C. canadensis The only non-woody species commonly grown, spreading rhizomatous, to 20 cm (8 in), leaves ovate, whorled, flowers tiny in rounded heads, surrounded by four large white, petal-like bracts, often flushed pink, followed in some gardens by 6 mm wide red fruits. An excellent low carpeter for moist acid soil in shade, but it can become invasive. N. Am., E. Asia.

Corydalis (*Papaveraceae*)

A large and important genus to the gardener. It includes a great range of plants of differing habit, from plants with definite tubers, some easy to grow, others very difficult, to fibrous rooted or tap-rooted clump-forming perennials. The majority are small plants for the rock garden or alpine house, and I have excluded these, which are mainly tuberous species. The plants described are easily grown non-tuberous species, sufficiently vigorous and freely increasing to make colourful groups in a border, in sun or partial shade in well-drained, humus-rich soil. They all have attractive finely divided, often glaucous leaves, and racemes of typical fumitory flowers, with a tube and two lips, the uppermost with a backward-projecting spur.

They can be raised from seed; several species self-sow with almost excessive freedom. Seed must be sown as soon as ripe, when the elongated capsules are beginning to change from green to cream. It is very easy to leave seed collection too long and to find the seed has been shed. The seed pans should be kept cool and will not usually germinate until the following spring.
C. cheilanthifolia Herbaceous, beautiful leaves finely divided, pinnate, usually bronze-tinged throughout the summer, deepening in autumn. Flowers deep yellow in large upright or spreading spikes, all through late spring and summer. A most attractive plant, equally happy in sun and shade, very free in its seeding, especially in gravel paths. The seedlings are easy to pull up from unsuitable places. China.
C. elata Similar to *C. flexuosa*, taller and more upright, with deeper blue flowers, generally flowering later, retaining its leaves throughout the summer. An exquisite recent introduction with the same requirements. China.

28 *Corydalis elata*

C. flexuosa ✱ One of the most successful introductions of recent years, very easy to grow and propagate in autumn, from the curious small stolons which it produces. It produces a succession of clusters of sky-blue flowers for weeks in spring and early summer; best in rich moist soil in partial shade, but with sufficient moisture it will tolerate full sun, especially in cool, moist climates. In drier gardens it tends to lose its leaves quickly after flowering until early autumn, but it may retain them through the summer if sufficiently moist. Several clones have been named under the original collectors' number: 'China Blue', leaves light green with a slight bronze flush at first, wonderful sky-blue flowers, 'Purple Leaf', reddish stems, persistent purple tinge to the leaves, flowers are a little darker, 'Blue Panda', ✱ an earlier introduction to the USA, only recently becoming generally available, differs in several respects. In my experience it is less tall with more spreading stems. The flowers are a similar sky-blue, but they appear a little later and continue for longer; the leaves are retained better, and the typical small, scaly stolons are less freely produced so that propagation may not be quite so easy. China.

29 *Corydalis flexuosa*

C. linstowiana Clump-forming, ferny dark green leaves on reddish stems and petioles, flowers pale blue, usually marked with white. A very attractive new introduction, proving easy but short-lived in semi-shade, and self-seeding. China.
C. lutea Finely cut green leaves, spikes of bright yellow flowers over a long period; an easy species with the seeding habits of *C. cheilanthifolia*. It flourishes in partial or full shade, but its habits must be remembered when siting it with other small plants. Europe.
C. nobilis Upright to 30 cm (1 ft), leaves bipinnate, green, flowers bright yellow with definite dark brown markings on the lip, in comparatively large clusters. Uncommon, I find it slow to increase, but I have seen it covering a remarkably large area in Copenhagen Botanic Garden. C. Asia
C. ochroleuca Resembles *C. lutea*, but white-flowered with a little yellow on the lip. It seeds around tremendously, its large clumps of fleshy, finely cut leaves being easy to remove if necessary. It has the pleasing gift of seeding into invisible cracks of stone walls, the ideal situation for it. Italy, Balkans
C. saxicola (syn. *C. thalictrifolia*) Leaves yellowish-green, pinnate, with a few rounded lobes, flowers deep yellow in loose clusters, all through the late spring and summer. Not widely grown, but a beautiful plant; not fully hardy but easily raised from seed. Himalayas. China
C. smithiana Very like *C. linstowiana* but with pinkish flowers. A recent short-lived introduction that appears easy and free-seeding.
C. wilsonii Similar to *C. saxicola*, leaves more beautiful, glaucous blue, similar long-lasting loose clusters of deep yellow flowers. Unfortunately it seems to resent winter wet and will only flourish outside in drier areas, although extremely easy to raise and grow under glass. China.

Cosmos (*Compositae*)

C. atrosanguinea ✱ The only perennial species widely grown, a tender plant with dahlia-like tubers which can be lifted and stored in cold areas, or left in the ground in gardens where no more than a degree or two of frost is experienced. Deep planting and mulching in autumn will help to protect the roots. The dahlia-like pinnate leaves do not appear until early summer, and are soon followed by the large solitary, single flowers on branching stems of a unique shade of deep chocolate-purple, and with a remarkably strong scent of chocolate. It continues to flower until the frosts of autumn.

Crambe (*Cruciferae*)

A few annuals and perennials, only two of the latter commonly grown, *C. cordifolia*, a magnificently statuesque plant, far too big to consider here, and our native sea kale, *C. maritima*.
C. maritima To 60 cm (2 ft), leaves large, glaucous, undulant, kale-like, from pinkish young stems, flowers tiny, pure white, in huge rounded heads. It can take up considerable space when producing its striking *Gypsophila*-like flower heads, but to many gardeners the leaves are too redolent of the kitchen garden.

30 *Crambe maritima*

Crassula (*Crassulaceae*)
A genus of tender succulents, with one hardier species for the garden.
Crassula sarcocaulis Rounded mound of semi-woody branching stems to 30 cm (1 ft), leaves small, sessile, pointed, flowers small, pale pink or occasionally white, in large flat-heads. A useful late-flowering plant for a warm, sunny place in well-drained soil.

31 *Crassula sarcocaulis*

Crepis (*Compositae*)

Only two species are grown regularly. They can be propagated by division or by seed sown in autumn.
C. aurea Spreading rhizomes, upright unbranched stems to 30 cm (1 ft), clusters of leaves, toothed or pinnate, dandelion-like, flowers 3–4 cm (1.2–1.6 in), deep orange daisies from reddish buds, mid- to late summer. Easy, worth growing for the colour of its flowers which combine well with the deep rosy-purple of the origanums or paler yellow daisies. S. Europe.
C. incana ✱ A mound of arching, branching stems, leaves

grey, oblanceolate, lobed, flowers abundant, clear soft pink, 2–3 cm (0.8–1.2 in) wide, in late summer. A most desirable species needing very well-drained soil and a warm situation. Greece.

Cuphea (*Lythraceae*)

A genus of annuals and some useful tender perennials which will survive a degree or two of frost in the garden, so that they can be used as border perennials in near frost-free gardens. They are excellent long-flowering plants for containers, which can be kept outside throughout the summer. The red and yellow species combine well with *Bidens*, or with the bronze shades of *Arctotis*. The flowers are tubular with very small spreading lobes. They are extremely easy to root from cuttings taken in late summer and kept under glass until frosts are over.

C. cyanea Sub-shrubby, leaves ovate on branching stems, clusters of cylindrical, 2.5 cm (1 in) long, orange-red flowers, with green tips, all through the summer and early autumn. Mexico.

C. hyssopifolia 🏆 More compact, stems densely covered with dark green, linear leaves, clusters of flowers pale lilac with darker veining, over a similarly long period. Mexico, Guatemala.

C. ignea The 'cigar flower', the most commonly grown species. Like *C. cyanea*, with plenty of axillary flowers, red with black tips; short-lived and should be propagated regularly. Mexico, Jamaica. 'Variegata' has leaves splashed with pale cream.

C. caeciliae ✱ (See plate 2)Ovate leaves on reddish stems, masses of long, tubular, deep reddish-orange flowers. A first-class container plant, always in bloom, very easily propagated.

Cynara (*Compositae*)

The cardoon and globe artichoke are much too big for consideration here but there is one smaller species.

Cynara histrix ✱ 50–80 cm (20–30 in) Leaves very spiny, silvery-grey, pinnate with narrow, toothed segments, flowers several to a stem, large bluish-purple, amid soft purplish-pink bracts. Perhaps the most beautiful of all 'thistles', but not easy to grow, needing a rich but very well-drained soil in a sheltered position. Morocco.

32 *Cynara histrix*

Cynoglossum (*Boraginaceae*)

Annuals and biennials, and a few perennials, with rather coarse leaves but beautiful pure blue forget-me-not flowers in early summer. The perennials described here are easy to grow in any soil, but may become too lax in rich soils. They will tolerate light shade. They may be raised from seed, sown in autumn and kept cool.

C. grande Rounded hairy leaves, upright branching stems, flowers deep blue in loose heads. W.N. Am.

C. nervosum Leaves narrower, white-hairy, flowers small bright blue in very large heads. The most popular species. Himalayas.

D

Deinanthe (*Hydrangeaceae*)

A genus of two species of woodland plant from China and Japan, growing from short, slowly-spreading rhizomes, with rounded, crinkly, toothed leaves, on stems to 50 cm (20 in) but usually less, and clusters of nodding flowers above the leaves in early summer. They are worth growing for their attractive leaves as well as for their intriguing flowers, but are not always easy to please, needing permanently moist, humus-rich, acid soil, in full or partial shade. Peat bed conditions, with small rhododendrons and other ericaceous shrubs suit them well. They can be raised from seed sown as soon as ripe, or by division of established clumps.

D. bifida To 50 cm (20 in), leaves elliptic to ovate, deeply bifid, flowers 2 cm (0.8 in) wide, nodding, saucer-shaped, cream-coloured, with yellow stamens. Japan.

D. coerulea More compact, leaves pointed, flowers a pleasing shade of soft lavender-blue, with blue stamens. The finest species. China.

Delosperma (*Aizoaceae*)

A genus of mainly mat-forming perennials with succulent leaves and many-petalled, brightly-coloured flowers, like those of *Mesembryanthemum* or *Lampranthus*. Many are only suitable for the greenhouse or frost-free gardens, but a few are unexpectedly hardy in the garden, in spite of their distinctly 'tender succulent' appearance. Although they are low-growing they make a dense carpet which is very well-flowered over a long period, usually in late summer. They need full sun and extremely well-drained soil; low fertility may be an advantage. They may be raised from seed, or are easily grown from cuttings or offsets during summer, a wise precaution in case of losses from winter wet or cold. S. Africa.

D. aberdeenense A low, dense, prostrate shrub, flowers small purplish-red.

D. cooperi Low mat of branching stems, leaves small, succulent, cylindrical, flowers abundant, bright magenta, 3–4 cm (1.2–1.6 in) wide, mid- to late summer. Vividly colourful in the garden, hardy to -7 °C (20 °F), probably lower.

33 *Delosperma cooperi*

D. nubigenum Similar to *D. cooperi* but flowers orange-red.
D. sutherlandii Herbaceous, clump-forming from a fleshy rootstock, flowers on short stems larger, solitary, rosy-purple.

Delphinium (*Ranunculaceae*)

A genus of great importance to the gardener, but it is the hybrids which have made it so popular and have had such an impact on the average grower. These are mainly too big to consider here but there remain a number of interesting less widely known species effective in the border, especially when planted in reasonably large groups. They generally have typical 5–7-lobed leaves, and upright spikes of larkspur-like, spurred flowers with spreading outer segments, and small inner segments forming a central bee.

New introductions and reintroductions, particularly from China and N. America have greatly increased the number of species available to gardeners, but many of them are relatively untried. In general the American species do well in very well-drained soil in full sun, but those from the Himalayas and China prefer moist humus-rich soil, and enjoy partial shade in drier gardens. Most of the species can be raised from seed and are easy enough to grow, so that effective groups can be produced. Many of the smaller species have flowers of similar genuine blue shades to the hybrids, colours which are not easy to find in other plants in mid-summer. They combine effectively with the various pink shades of the diascias, and dianthus, or with the yellows of the low-growing hypericums, and asteriscus.

D. andersonii To 50 cm (20 in), few 5-lobed basal leaves, 3 cm (1.2 in) wide, flowers deep blue with a little white in the centre in upright spikes of up to 12. Uncommon, occasionally offered in seed lists, it is typical of many smaller species. W. USA.

D. brunonianum ✱ Variable 20-50 cm (8–20 in), taller in rich soils, dense clump of rounded, shallowly lobed, hairy, toothed leaves, flowers large, dark violet-blue, with even darker centres, hooded by the upper sepal and markedly hairy. One of the finest Himalayan species, it seems short-lived in very rich soil, and needs good drainage, in sun or partial shade.

34 *Delphinium brunonianum*, an unusually robust clump

D. cardinale To 1 m (3 ft) in height, but usually much less, leaves rather sparse, 5-lobed, tending to die away by the time the spikes of red flowers with yellow centres on long petioles appear. A very short-lived perennial, but a good parent to increase the colour range, needing very well-drained soil in a warm, sunny place, and frequent propagation from seed. California.

D. cashmerianum A small Himalayan species to 25 cm (10 in), not always correctly named. The true plant has lobed leaves, other species masquerading as it have deeply divided leaves. The sparse flowers resemble those of *D. brunonianum*, with a shallower hood. It does well in humus-rich soil, and can be effective in a group.

D. delavayi To 80 cm (30 in), leaves divided, toothed, flowers hairy in dense spikes, purple-bluish-violet.

A late-flowering species rarely tried in gardens. China.
D. glareosum Leaves large, deeply divided, flowers deep blue, hairy, in loose heads of ten or more. One of several tuberous-rooted species from N. America, not often seen in gardens as they die down immediately after flowering, and then need fairly dry conditions. They frequently die down after young seedlings are potted, and they must not be discarded as dead.
D. grandiflorum (syn. *D. Chinense*) Leaves broad, 5-lobed with finely divided lobes, flowers to 60 cm (2 ft), variable in colour from a good blue to purple, uncommonly white, in loose heads. A short-lived perennial sometimes considered an annual and grown as such. It makes an attractive group in the front of a border, and will survive longer in well-drained soil in full sun. E. Asia. 'Blue Butterfly', is a strain available from seed, showing some colour variation.
D. likiangense To 40 cm (16 in), leaves deeply divided, flowers few, sky-blue, in loose heads. Uncommon beautiful Chinese species.
D. menziesii To 30 cm (1 ft), leaves finely divided, palmate, flowers few, hairy, long-spurred, deep blue. Tuberous-rooted like *D. glareosum*, with the same requirements. W., N. Am.
D. nudicaule To 60 cm (2 ft) often less, leaves deeply lobed, spikes of flowers orange-red with long spurs and orange or yellow centres. A striking plant, like a smaller version of *D. cardinale*, equally short-lived, should be propagated frequently from seed to maintain a group. It needs excellent drainage. California. Var. *luteum* (syn. *D. luteum*) similar but flowers creamy-yellow.
D. nuttallianum Another tuberous species from W., N. America, with the same requirements as *D. glareosum*. Leaves finely dissected, flowers deep blue with whitish centres.
D. oxysepalum To 40 cm (16 in), leaves 5-lobed, hairy, flowers purplish-blue in upright loose spikes. Uncommon Carpathian species.
D. parishii Leaves hairy, 3-lobed, divided, with narrow segments, flowers 2 cm (0.8 in) long, pale lavender, in spikes of 5–15, early summer. Rare. California.
D. pylzowii Small Chinese species to 30 cm (1 ft), leaves palmate divided into linear segments, flowers 1–3, large, deep violet, hairy, with darker centres. It is one of the easier to grow.
D. semibarbatum (*D. zalil*) Best known as *D. zalil*, to 60 cm (2 ft), leaves finely cut, flowers clear pale yellow in long, upright spikes in summer. A beautiful species with a reputation for difficulty; it seems to be successful in my garden in very well-drained soil in a warm, sheltered position in front of a south wall. It usually sets seed and should be propagated regularly. C., E. Asia.
D. speciosum To 60 cm (2 ft), leaves finely divided, hairy, flowers dark blue in loose spikes. Caucasus, Himalayas.
D. tatsiense ✱ To 30–40 cm (12–16 in), leaves finely dissected, flowers pure deep blue in loose branching heads over a long period in summer. The colour may be paler, especially if the white 'Album' is grown, its seedlings being very pale blue more often than white, unless it is kept isolated. An excellent easy small species with a reputation for being short-lived. In well-drained soil it seems perennial, and can easily be built up into a fine group, self-sowing around the original plants.
D. tricorne Tuberous-rooted, to 60 cm (2 ft) in height, flowers few. dark blue with white centres. N. Am.
D. trollifolium A taller species, sometimes to 1 m (3 ft), leaves finely dissected, flowers deep purple with long hooked spurs in loose spikes of up to 30. W. USA.
D. yunnanense To 70 cm (28 in), leaves lobed, toothed, flowers deep blue in loose spikes. China.

Dendranthemum (*Compositae*)

As a result of the recent revision of the genus Chrysanthemum, a few late-flowering spreading perennials have been removed into this genus. They are all rhizomatous or stoloniferous, making spreading clumps, with typical pinnately-cleft chrysanthemum-like leaves, and upright stems bearing solitary, large, single daisy flowers. They make a good show in the autumn border, with a long flowering season, and they are easily grown in any reasonable soil in sun or light shade, but they tend to exhaust the soil after a year or two, and should be divided and replanted frequently. They are easily increased by division or by cuttings of new growths.
D. weyrichii ✱ To 25 cm (10 in), leaves 5-lobed, the lobes pinnately divided, on branched or simple stems, flowers 4–5 cm (1.6–2 in) wide, clear pink with yellow centres. Excellent for its very late season.
D. yezoense 🏆 Similar to the last, to 40 cm (16 in), flowers solitary with white rays. 'Roseum' good pink.
D. zawadalskii Taller with more divided leaves, flowers large white or pale pink-rayed, an uncommon species. Var. *latilobum* (syn. *D. erubescens*) much taller, to 1 m (3 ft) or more.

Dentaria See *Cardamine*

Dianella (*Liliaceae*/*Phormiaceae*)

An underestimated genus in the garden, where at least some of the species are hardier than is usually suggested; well worth growing for their dark green, sword-like leaves, variegated in some varieties, and their spectacular sprays of deep blue berries in summer. They have short rhizomes from which the broad grass-like leaves arise and sheath the flowering stems. The small flowers, usually blue but occasionally white, with prominent stamens, on long arching pedicels, are held in broad loose heads.

They grow well in humus-rich, well-drained soil in a sheltered sunny bed, or in light shade. In my garden *D. coerulea* and its variegated form have flourished for many years under a south-facing wall, and have survived to -10 °C (14 °F). They can be propagated by seed sown in heat in spring.
D. coerulea Dense clump to 60–70 cm (24–28 in), leaves rough, dark green, keeled, to 60 cm (2 ft) long, wiry branching stems, flowers small, dark blue with yellow anthers in early summer, followed by large bright blue berries, which remain on the plants for weeks. 'Variegata' leaves with a narrow cream

edging, a discreet and attractive variegation, which may revert over the course of several years. S. Australia.
D. intermedia A taller species to 1 m (3 ft), longer leaves, white flowers, similar fruits. New Zealand, Fiji.
D. tasmanica Larger than *D. caerulea*, otherwise similar except anthers brown.

Dianthus (*Caryophyllaceae*)

A genus that presents problems in a book of this sort, containing more than enough material for a book of its own; in fact several have been written on the hybrid Pinks alone. I have excluded all the 'Carnations' as they are not perennial without special care and need constant propagation. Apart from some of these, none can be excluded on the basis of excessive size, and the 'Pinks' are among the most colourful of edging plants for the margins of sunny borders, with a long flowering season and usually a delightful scent. The genus contains many small species which are slow-growing and are better in the more specialized conditions of the rock garden or alpine house. I have excluded most of these. However, there remain other species which are large enough or colourful enough to make some impact in the border, even though their height may be only an inch or two.

The Plant Finder includes over 700 taxa, and the majority of these are hybrids, which have been developed over the years as plants for the border. Where to draw the line with these is the problem, and I have made no attempt with this genus, unlike most of the others, to be comprehensive, preferring to offer a somewhat personal choice, with particular reference to those which persist in the garden for at least a year or two before beginning their usual deterioration, signalling the need for them to be repropagated. To maintain a large collection of cultivars it is necessary to propagate them constantly, in order to replace those that have become straggly or have failed to survive the winter. The best of them, from the gardeners point of view, will make a mound of increasing size, with an abundance of flowers for two or three years with little attention.

To give the species and the hybrid Pinks the best chance of reasonable longevity they should be in light well-drained soil, preferably alkaline, in full sun. Shade tends to make them excessively straggly, and heavy soils cause winter losses. Propagation is easy by cuttings in late summer, or earlier if there is enough space to house the young plants. The cuttings can be 'pipings', the tip of an unflowered shoot pulled gently out of its stem above a node, but these are not always easy to produce and do not seem to have any advantage over a shoot cut cleanly below a node. They are European except where stated.
D. amurensis A loose mat of green leaves, stems to 30 cm (1 ft), flowers 1–3, quite large, reddish-purple, frilly-edged. It tends to become straggly and should be cut back after flowering and propagated frequently. Manchuria.
D. arenarius A mat of narrow, green, grass-like leaves, branching stems to 20 cm (8 in), plentiful solitary white, scented flowers with deeply laciniate petals. Although low-growing this can hold its own in front of a border.
D. barbatus Although 'Sweet William' is usually rightly considered a biennial, I am including the species on the strength of its recently popular 'Nigrescens Group' 🏆, of which a fair proportion of plants will survive at least into a third year. For their first season the leaves are typically dark green, in their flowering year becoming suffused with deepest purple, which combines strikingly with the deep crimson of the flowers. They seem to breed true from seed.
D. carthusianorum Variable, loose mat of narrow linear green leaves, stems to 40 cm (16 in) or more, flowers variable, deep reddish-purple to paler shades of pink or white, in dense flat-heads. An attractive and easy plant, but often fails to produce quite enough flower heads for the height of the stems.
D. deltoides 🏆 Broad mats only an inch or two high, small, deep green lanceolate leaves, completely carpeted with deep pink flowers with a darker central eye for several weeks in summer. An ideal border edging, especially where it can flop across the edge of paving to break up its hard lines. Europe, Asia. 'Albus', pure white, 'Bright Eyes', white with a contrasting broad deep reddish-pink eye, 'Brilliant', bright magenta, 'Flashing Light', dark purple-tinged leaves, deep red flowers.
D. gratianopolitanus The Cheddar Pink, to 20 cm (8 in), a mat of flat glaucous leaves, large scented flowers, clear pink, the petals with toothed margins. Vigorous enough for the border in well-drained soil.
D. knappii Loose mats of green leaves, flowers greenish-yellow in loose heads. Short-lived, and difficult to grow into a good plant, but the colour is interesting; it can be raised from seed.
D. monspessulanus Loose mat of green linear leaves, thin 20–30 cm (8–12 in) stems, flowers 2–5, white or occasionally pale pink, fragrant, with attractively fringed petals. Subsp. *sternbergii* more compact, leaves glaucous.
D. petraeus Loose cushion of green or slightly glaucous grassy leaves, stems 20 cm (8 in), flowers abundant, solitary, short-stemmed, white or pale pink, with deeply fringed petals. Balkans. *D. p.* subsp. *noeanus* More compact with stiff, glaucous, pointed leaves, and similar white flowers.
D. plumarius The parent of many of our Pinks, the species is not widely grown. Loose mound of glaucous blue-green leaves, 30 cm (1 ft) stems, flowers to 3 cm (1.2 in) wide, from white to clear pink, solitary, bearded, strongly scented.
D. seguieri Loose cushion of glaucous leaves, 40 cm (16 in) stems, flowers 1-5, reddish-pink. A rare late-flowering species of woodland.
D. squarrosus Low spreading clumps of dark green, narrow grassy leaves, 15 cm (6 in) stems, flowers solitary, very fragrant, deeply fringed. Russia.
D. superbus Robust loose mat of green, lanceolate leaves, 30 cm (1 ft), branching stems, solitary flowers in shades of pink, or white, petals deeply dissected. It can be somewhat tall and straggly, but the individual highly scented flowers are

attractive; it has been much used in hybridization.

D. sylvestris Loose green mats, spreading, branching stems, flowers pale to purple-pink with toothed petals. Not one of the best but occasionally grown.

Hybrids: There are a vast number of hybrid Pinks, old and new, the majority easy to grow, but some needing frequent propagation to keep them going. The following table gives some of the most reliable, which I have seen and grown, or which have done well in borders in trials without too much attention. Anyone needing fuller information should consult one of the specialist books on the subject. Except where stated they make typical mounds of attractive blue-grey leaves, and flower in summer, usually over a long period.

35 *Dianthus* 'Inchmery'

Name	**Flower**	**Notes**
'Alice'	Semi-double, fringed, white with large reddish maroon centre	Modern hybrid. Long season
'Allspice'	Single, fringed with white margin, deep reddish-purple with two white spots	Old-fashioned, but not difficult
'Annabelle'	Double, fringed, pale rose-pink, darker flecking in the centre.	Modern
'Bat's Double Red'	Semi-double, fringed, even purplish-red difficult	Old-fashioned, but not difficult
'Becka Falls'	Double, slightly fringed, scarlet	Modern, vigorous
'Becky Robinson' 🏆	Double, very pale pink, with a deep reddish-crimson central zone and slightly paler lacing	A modern 'laced pink' Vigorous
'Betty Norton'	Single, fringed, deep pink with maroon eye	1920's, Vigorous, with long late season
'Blue Hills'	Single, deep crimson	Very compact, but easy
'Bovey Belle'	Double, margin serrate, bright pinkish-purple	Good border plant. Tendency to calyx splitting.
'Brympton Red'	Single, large, pinkish-purple, with deeper centre and lacing	Modern, Excellent border plant
'Chastity'	Semi-double, with incurving petals,white with pale	Dwarf, but vigorous enough for the border.
'Constance Finnis'	Single, frilled. white with deep pinkish-red band and lace, creating two large white eyes on each petal	Good border plant
'Dad's Favourite'	Semi-double, white with deep maroon band and narrow lacing	Old fashioned, short flowering at mid-summer
'Devon Glow' 🏆	Double, slightly fringed, purplish pink, paling towards the margins	Modern, long flowering season
'Diane'	Double, toothed, deep salmon-pink, paler at the centre	Modern, long season, easy but tends to be straggly
'Doris' 🏆	Double. lightly fringed, soft pale pink with deeper central band	The most popular, modern, flowers throughout the summer into autumn
'Enid Anderson'	Full semi-double, frilled, deep reddish crimson with dark maroon central band.	Lax growth with 30 cm (1 ft) stems
'Excelsior'	Double, deeply fringed, pale pinkish-mauve with a green eye	Sport of 'Mrs Sinkins', with good scent
'Fusilier'	Single, deep pinkish-red with crimson central band.	Compact. One of the best dwarfs
'Gingham Gown'	Single, fringed, pink with redder central band and lacing like 'Constance Finnis'	Compact, one of the best dwarf laced pinks

Name	Flower	Notes
'Gran's Favourite' 🏆	Double, fringed, white with dark reddish-purple centre, and narrow, much paler lacing	Good for the border, but stems rather long and floppy
'Hidcote' ✸	Double to semi-double, cerise	Reliable semi-dwarf for the border edge
'Highland Fraser'	Single, fringed, purplish-pink, with darker central band and lacing	1930's. Robust and easy, to 15 cm (6 in) high
'Highland Queen'	Similar to the previous, but larger flowers	More vigorous and taller
'Houndspool Cheryl' (syn. 'Cheryl')	Double, lightly fringed, purplish-red throughout	Modern, good border plant to 30 cm (1 ft)
'Houndspool Ruby' 🏆	Double, fringed, pink fading towards the margin, with reddish centre	Modern, 30 cm (1 ft), a good border plant
'Inchmery' ✸ (see plate 35)	Double, fringed, clear pale pink	Long season, late, one of the most beautiful and easiest
'Inshriach Dazzler' 🏆	Single, fringed, brilliant magenta with a violet eye	Modern, spectacular dwarf
'Joy'	Double, deeply fringed, deep pink with paler centre	Good for the border
'La Bourboule' 🏆	Single, fringed, soft pale pink, with white anthers	Low and compact, one of the best
'La Bourboule Albus'	Similar to the above but pure white	
'Laced Joy'	Full semi-double, pale rose-pink with deep maroon centre and some narrow lacing, which often fades	Modern, reliable border plant
'Laced Monarch'	Double, minimally fringed, pink with deep reddish-maroon centre, and paler lacing	Modern, good for the border
'Little Jock'	Semi-double, fringed, purplish-pink with deep crimson centre	Reliable compact dwarf, to 10 cm (4 in) in flower
'London Delight'	Double, finely fringed, pale pink with deepest maroon centre, and deep pink lacing	Good border plant to 30 cm (1 ft)
'Monica Wyatt' 🏆	Frilly double, fringed, deep pink with purplish-red centre	Modern, long-flowering, to 25 cm (10 in)
'Mrs Sinkins'	Very frilly double, deeply fringed, white with greenish centre	Old favourite, still vigorous, with good scent
'Musgrave's Pink' ✸ (see plate 36)	Single, fringed, white with conspicuous green centre	Old hybrid but one of the best in the border, needing little attention
'Nyewood's Cream'	Single, small, creamy-white	A very small plant of unusual colour but a good perennial
'Oakington'	Double, fringed, uniform purplish-pink	Reliable, very floriferous dwarf mat, to 15 cm (6 in)
'Old Mother Hubbard' 🏆	Semi-double, toothed, mid-pink spotted and striped with darker pink	Modern, vigorous, to 35 cm (14 in)
'Old Velvet'	Full semi-double, minimally fringed, rich maroon in the centre fading to purplish-red towards the margin, with white edge	Old fashioned, but not difficult
'Pike's Pink' 🏆	Full semi-double, fringed, very pale pink, with darker central band	One of the most reliable dwarf growers, to 10 cm (4 in)
'Rose de Mai'	Double, fringed, mauve-pink with small darker centre	Early-flowering with long season
'Sam Barlow'	Double usually with split calyx, fringed, white with deepest maroon centre, a spectacular contrast	Old-fashioned, but a reasonable border plant
'Valda Wyatt' 🏆	Double, rose-pink with reddish- pink centre	Modern reliable border plant to 30 cm (1 ft)
'Waithman's Beauty'	Single, frilled with white margin, deep purplish-pink with small white blotches, and white throat	Excellent, reliable, semi-dwarf to 15 cm (6 in)

Name	Flower	Notes
'Waithman's Jubilee'	Deeper in colour than the last with pink blotches and throat	
'Whatfield Gem'	Double, frilled, crimson with pale pink margin	Very dwarf and compact, but easy
'Whatfield Magenta'	Single, frilled, magenta, with pinkish-white throat	Dwarf with very glaucous blue leaves
'Whatfield Ruby'	Single, frilled, deep rose-pink with darker narrow central band, and white anthers	Similar in habit to 'Whatfield Magenta'

36 *Dianthus* 'Musgrave's Pink' & *Viola cornuta*

Diascia (*Scrophulariaceae*)

During the last five years this has become one of the most popular genera of small perennials. Although the low-growing *D. cordata* and its hybrid 'Ruby Field' were grown widely by rock-gardeners previously, it was only after the introduction of the taller and more robust *D. rigescens* that they became widely grown. Enthusiasm for them has increased with the production of hybrids, notably raised by Hector Harrison, with 'new' colours: bluish shades derived from *D. lilacina*, and salmon and apricot shades which seem to have arisen from the use of *D. stachoides* and *D.* 'Ruby Field', although these shades are not obvious in any species.

There are now over sixty hybrids and species in cultivation, with more appearing every month. They are all attractive easy plants, but many are very similar, which makes the choice difficult. Among the most distinct and hardy for the gardener who wants to grow a small selection are *D. rigescens*, *D. vigilis*, and *D. integerrima* among the species, *D.* 'Salmon Supreme' and *D.* 'Blackthorn Apricot' among the salmon shades, *D.* 'Lilac Mist' and *D.* 'Lilac Belle' among the blue-tinged hybrids, and *D.* 'Kate' of an almost unique deeper reddish colour. These have all flourished in the open garden for two or more years with winter temperatures down to -6.5 °C (20 °F), but the newer hybrids are as yet relatively untried in colder gardens.

The species are all native to the Drakensberg mountains and surrounding areas of S. Africa, usually at high altitudes, where rainfall is often high, even in summer. Most of them form a loose mat of branching stems bearing small toothed leaves and abundant upright spikes of flowers which open over a very long period. The individual flowers have a 3-lobed lower lip, the central lobe often very large, and a 2-lobed upper lip with a central translucent yellow 'window', which is often a conspicuous feature. The flowers have two conspicuous spurs usually curving backwards and downwards.

They are extremely easy to grow in ordinary garden soil in sun or light shade, but they resent drought; they benefit from cutting back after flowering. They are ideal for the edge of mixed borders, most of them growing less than 30 cm (1 ft) high but spreading quite widely. *D. rigescens* is taller and can be used further back. Most of their colours associate very well with the lavender-blue shades of the smaller and medium-growing campanulas, and with silver foliage, for example of the less rampant artemisias. The new salmon shades are perhaps less easy to place comfortably in the garden, but they look good with perennials of similar colour like *Agastache* 'Firebird', and with the blue campanulas. A good association in my garden is 'Salmon Supreme' intertwined with *Viola cornuta*.

All the diascias root very easily from cuttings at any time during the growing season, so that it easy to keep a few spare plants through the winter under glass in case the temperature drops unexpectedly low, or the latest hybrid proves to be unexpectedly tender.

D. anastrepta Mat of branching stems to 30 cm (1 ft) long, rooting down, leaves broadly ovate, toothed, flowers deep

purplish-pink with spurs which point outwards rather than downwards. It survives mild winters (to -5 °C) in the garden. Widely grown recently and used in hybridization.
D. 'Appleby Apricot' Similar to 'Salmon Supreme', but flowers a little smaller and broader, spurs curved back and down. It has grown well so far but is relatively untried.
D. barberae Low mat of tangled stems, flowers large, deep rose-pink, spurs pointing outwards and downwards. One of the earliest species to be introduced, although possibly confused with *D. cordata*, similar to its much hardier hybrid *D.* 'Ruby Field', but with larger flowers. It is unfortunately more tender than most.
D. 'Blackthorn Apricot' Flowers very large, salmon, with a broad lip and long curved spurs. One of the best of the new hybrids and proving reasonably hardy.

37 *Diascia* 'Blackthorn Apricot'

D. 'Coral Belle' ✱ Low mat, flowers deep coral. An exciting colour in a new and untried plant.
D. cordata Very similar to *D. barberae* and frequently confused with it, flowers paler, spurs longer, and sepals glabrous, hairy in *D. barberae.* From the gardener's viewpoint the main difference is that *D. cordata* is more hardy. Their hybrid 'Ruby Field' is the best garden plant of the three.
D. fetcanensis (syn *D. felthamii*) More upright bushy habit than *D. cordata* or *D. vigilis*, leaves oval, toothed, flowers deep rose-pink. Another robust species for the garden.
D. 'Hopley's Apricot' Leaves narrow and pointed, flowers salmon, larger than those of 'Salmon Supreme' with slightly shorter and more backward-pointing spurs. Fairly hardy.
D. integerrima More sparse-growing, and runs underground, upright stems to 50 cm (20 in), leaves very narrow, pointed, flowers small, deep pink with a slight bluish tinge, very sharply curved spurs. This has proved very hardy for several years, and even if the top growth is cut by a hard winter it can be relied on to recover from the base,
D. 'Jacqueline's Joy' Compact mat, 15-25 cm (6–10 in) leafy stems, flowers deep pink with a slight blue tinge, a broader lip and short curved spurs pointing back and downwards. It has survived two winters outside in my garden.

D. 'Joyce's Choice' Another good salmon, similar to 'Blackthorn Apricot' except in its slightly smaller flowers.
D. 'Kate' (*D. barberae* x Hopley's Apricot) A striking hybrid with similar foliage to *D. vigilis*, more upright to 40 cm (16 in), flowers large glowing deep reddish-pink with conspicuous yellow 'window' on the upper lip. Quite hardy.
D. 'Lilac Belle' Low carpet, flower spikes to 10–20 cm (4–8 in), masses of very small deep lavender-pink flowers, spurs very small and pointed, slightly darker than 'Lilac Mist', over a very long period. Effective because of the abundance of its flowers rather than their size. It seems quite hardy.
D. lilacina An invaluable parent of the various lilac-tinged hybrids, but hardly worth growing as a garden plant, as the flowers are very small indeed.
D. 'Lilac Mist' ✱ Large spreading flat mat of toothed leaves, abundant long, dense flower spikes to 20–30 cm (8–12 in), flowers pale lavender-pink with darker centres, spurs of medium length, recurve sharply downwards. One of the best of all hybrids, hardy to -8 °C (17 °F) at least. It seems to have inherited the vigour of *D. rigescens* but remains very prostrate until flowering.

38 *Diascia* 'Lilac Mist'

D. 'Louise' The largest -flowered of the salmon shades, compact plant. New and untried.
D. megathura Similar to *D. anastrepta* but spurs tend to turn down at the tips. Not such a good 'doer' in the garden.
D. 'No. 5' Similar to *D. vigilis* in habit, stronger and longer upright stems, clear salmon-pink flowers with a very broad lip slightly paler than the petals.
D. patens Very distinct with long wiry branching stems, very

long leaves even narrower than those of *D. integerrima*, sparse small deep reddish-purple flowers late in the summer. In the garden it runs slowly underground and its long stems clamber attractively into surrounding plants. It seems to be a little more tender than many of the species but certainly survives to -5 °C (23 °F).

***D.* 'Pink Spot'** This appears to be a clone of *D. vigilis* with rather smaller flowers than the best of these.

D. purpurea A very curious species, which I have seen in the Drakensberg, but is scarcely in cultivation. The short-spurred flowers are held in such a manner that they appear upside-down, and are of a deep reddish-purple.

D. rigescens 🏆 The strongest growing of all the species, thick, square, hollow stems to 45 cm (1.5 ft) or more, long triangular coarsely toothed leaves, tall dense spikes of clear deep pink flowers. The best upright vigorous species.

***D.* 'Ruby Fields'** (*D cordata* x *D. barberae*) 🏆 A loose mat of small pale green leaves, flower spikes deep pink with a faint bluish tinge, throughout the early summer. Hardy to -15 °C (5 °F). Probably the first of the many deliberate crosses, and a popular low carpeting plant for the rock garden or front of the border.

***D.* 'Salmon Supreme'** Deeper salmon flowers fading somewhat with age, smaller than 'No. 5' or 'Blackthorn Apricot', and smaller leaves. Very hardy.

D. stachyoides Similar in habit to *D. vigilis* but with conspicuous leafy bracts, flowers deep rose-pink with short spurs directed downwards and outwards. Not a widely grown species, it is less vigorous than many, but a useful parent.

D. tugelensis Like *D. vigilis* in habit, less tall, with deeper pink flowers with backward facing spurs, which are unusual in having swollen tips.

***D.* 'Twinkle'** A vigorous hybrid with wide, deep purplish-pink flowers, with narrow pointed spurs pointing backwards. Somewhat similar to 'Joyces Choice' but more upright, flowers broader.

D. vigilis 🏆 (See plate 16) Possibly the finest species, masses of flowers in loose spikes, of a delicate clear pale pink without a vestige of blue. Very hardy, and usually grows to about 30 cm (1 ft) high, but it has the pleasing habit of scrambling upwards into surrounding plants. There is some variation in flower size and the waviness of the edge of the lip, between various clones introduced from the Drakensberg. The plant offered as 'Jack Elliott' is a good large-flowered clone of *D. vigilis* from seed collected in the Drakensberg.

***D.* 'Wendy'** Similar to 'Jacqueline's Joy', up to 45 cm (1.5 ft) high, the large flowers paler in colour, with a rather narrower and longer lip, and similar short backward-facing spurs.

Dicentra (*Papaveraceae*)

One of the most beautiful of all the genera of small, very hardy perennials, with fine deeply divided, fern-like leaves and generally one-sided racemes of dainty pendent, heart-shaped flowers in spring or early to mid-summer. Some of the species are rhizomatous and these can spread widely in good conditions. Be warned that they can rapidly take over a carefully prepared peat bed. Other species and many of the cultivars are clump-forming and therefore more suitable for association with other small plants in borders. *D. canadensis* and *D. cucullaria* are more delicate plants for the peat bed or alpine house.

The more vigorous hybrids and rhizomatous species do well beneath rhododendrons and camellias and other shade-loving shrubs, growing best in deep humus-rich moist soil or moist woodland. In poor dry soils the clump-forming hybrids in particular are likely to deteriorate quickly, and should then be replanted in fresh soil with plenty of compost or leaf-mould incorporated.

The species and some of their selected forms are likely to hybridize and self-sow, and the mixed seedlings can become a nuisance unless they are removed at an early stage. All can be propagated by division in early spring, and the species can be raised from seed, which should be sown as soon as ripe.

***Dicentra* 'Adrian Bloom'** *D. formosa* x *D. eximia* Clumps of attractive dark green leaves, to 35 cm (14 in), flowers deep reddish-pink, over a long period in early summer. A superb plant that thrives towards the front of a mixed border, preferably in some shade.

***D.* 'Bacchanal'** ✱ Rhizomatous colonizer, leaves unusually pale green, flowers very dark purplish-red. A striking plant which is not widely grown.

***D.* 'Bountiful'** Similar to *D.* 'Adrian Bloom', leaves bluish glaucous, flowers slightly smaller and paler.

D. chrysantha Taller than most of those described, flowers abundant small yellow, leaves glaucous. Very uncommon in cultivation in Britain and said to need more sun. S. California.

D. eximia Like *D. formosa*, but less widely spreading, similar ferny foliage with narrower leaflets, flowers narrower, pink, outer petals less reflexed. A widely grown species. USA.

***D. eximia* 'Snowdrift'** (*D .e.* 'Alba') ✱ (See plate 40) Paler leaves and pure white flowers. An exceptionally beautiful plant that needs good soil to persist.

D. formosa The commonest species in the garden, frequently confused with *D. eximia*. Capable of taking over a specially prepared shade bed, but invaluable for colonizing areas under shrubs. The differences from *D. eximia* are described above. *D. f. alba* is a beautiful white variety. W., N. America. Subsp. *oregona* less common and less rampant, broader very glaucous leaflets and cream-coloured flowers with pink tips to the inner petals. *D. formosa* 'Stuart Boothman' 🏆 smaller growing gentle runner. Flowers similar but darker, leaves much more finely divided, glaucous, one of the most attractive foliage plants. It is normally sterile but should be kept away from other forms of *D. formosa* which will rapidly swamp it in seedlings.

D. 'Langtrees' ♕ Broad glaucous leaflets, loose heads of creamy-white flowers with pink tips. It runs gently underground without getting out of hand.

39 *Dicentra* 'Langtrees'

D. 'Luxuriant' Very robust clump-former, leaves green, flowers deep reddish-pink over a long period.

40 *Dicentra* 'Luxuriant' & *D. eximia* 'Snowdrift'

D. macrantha Leaves pinnate, deeply toothed, on golden stems and petioles, flowers nodding, very large, pale cream with a faint brownish tinge. An exciting species which, in good moist conditions can run far and wide, but is often difficult to establish, producing only a few scattered shoots. China.
D. 'Pearl Drops' Doubtfully distinct from 'Langtrees'.
D. spectabilis ♕ Clump-forming, arching stems to 60 cm (2 ft), leaves deeply lobed, green, flowers large, nodding, deep rose with white tip, early summer. Possibly the most beautiful species of a fine genus, needing good moist, humus-rich soil to show its full beauty. China, Korea. Var. *alba* ♕ an exquisite pure white form, which sometimes seems easier to grow well.
D. 'Spring Morning' Clump-forming, leaves glaucous, flowers abundant pale pink. Probably a selection of *D. eximia.*

Dicranostigma (*Papaveraceae*)

Three annual or short-lived perennial poppies, similar to Glaucium, easily raised from seed, that will usually keep up an appearance of being perennial by self-seeding near to the parent plants. They will grow well in sun or light shade.
D. franchetianum Annual, similar to *D. lactucoides* but taller and looser-growing, beautiful in shade. China.
D. lactucoides Clump-forming, usually biennial rosettes of pinnate toothed leaves to 15 cm (6 in) long, loose sprays of pure yellow flowers to 5 cm (2 in) diameter, on branching stems. Himalayas.
D. leptopodum resembles a more compact *D. franchetianum.* China.

Dictamnus (*Rutaceae*)

A genus of one outstanding perennial, which grows well in rich soil in sun or shade. It can be raised from seed, but takes several years to reach maturity. Once established it will improve for years without further attention. It has the unusual property of producing a volatile oil from the leaves, which can, under the right circumstances, be ignited without damage to the plant, hence the popular name Burning Bush.
D. albus (syn. *D. fraxinella*) ♕ Clump-forming from a woody base, leaves pinnate, aromatic, leaflets toothed, spikes of elegant flowers, white, 5-petalled, with prominent upcurved stamens, on stiff upright stems. *D. a.* 'Purpureus' ♕ Flowers pale pink, heavily veined with deep purplish-pink. S.W. Europe, Asia.

41 *Dictamnus albus*

Dierama (*Iridaceae*)

The common names of 'Wand flower' or 'Angel's fishing rods', are an indication of the beauty and elegance of these perennials from S. Africa, which are hardier in gardens than might be expected. The most commonly grown, *D. pendulum* and *D. pulcherrimum*, form large clumps of long, tough grassy leaves, from which arise long, wiry arching stems, sometimes branched, bearing towards their tips long, tubular, pendant flowers, in shades from white through soft pink to deep purple, on the most slender pedicels. These and their cultivars, however, are too large to consider here. There are a few smaller but equally elegant species or hybrids in cultivation which make most attractive plants where space is limited.

They grow in damp conditions in nature, but experience suggests that they grow as well, and are more perennial, in very well-drained soil in full sun. They happily self-sow in such sites. They are easily grown from seed, but the seedlings should be planted in permanent positions as soon as possible as they take some time to recover from disturbance.

D. dracomontanum (syn. *D. pumilum, D. pendulum* var. *pumilum*) One of the hardier species, usually within our height range; variable in colour. Dwarf forms are sometimes offered as 'Dwarf lilac', 'Dwarf Pink', and 'Dwarf Pale Pink'.

D. pendulum One or two named cultivars probably derive from this species, hybridized with *D. dracomomtanum* (*D. pumilum*). 'Puck', to 60 cm (2 ft), flowers deep rose on rather upright stems, 'Titania', very similar with pale pink flowers.

D. pulcherrimum 'Dwarf forms' are sometimes offered, of uncertain parentage.

Digitalis (*Scrophulariaceae*)

About twenty perennials and biennials, European unless stated, of which our native foxglove and its various seed strains are too large to consider here. They are attractive and easy plants for any shady place, with the exception of *D. dubia* and *D. obscura* which need more sun. They have rosettes of long, usually lanceolate leaves, and similar alternate stem leaves beneath a usually one-sided raceme of tubular- to long-bell-shaped flowers, in summer. They are very easy to raise from seed and frequently seed around, sometimes to excess, which makes them more suitable for the wilder parts of the garden, where this habit can be an asset. They tend to be short-lived if not biennial, so it is important to keep raising them from seed. Some species are notoriously immoral and have to be well-separated if the seedlings are to be true.

C. davisiana Leaves narrow, toothed, flowers pale greenish-yellow with deeper orange veining, of typical foxglove shape, in loose spikes. It usually comes true from seed and is reasonably perennial.

D. dubia A delightful miniature of our native, leaves much whiter and more hairy, flowers clear pink, with darker spotting in 20–30 cm (8–12 in) spikes. It resents much winter wet and needs well-drained soil in the sun. It is difficult to keep pure stocks unless some plants are kept under glass.

D. ferruginea Very leafy stems, long dense spikes of narrow tubular, deep brown flowers, bearded and veined within, sometimes paler orange-brown, with a whitish lip. An unusual looking plant that can attain 1 m (3 ft) or more in its variety 'Gigantea' in good soil. S. Europe. W. Asia.

42 *Digitalis ferruginea & Polygonatum hybridium 'Striatum'*

D. grandiflora (syn. *D. ambigua*) 🏆 Short dense racemes of fat, pale yellow flowers, lightly veined with brown inside. An attractive large-flowered foxglove that needs to be maintained from seed, and usually comes true. 'Temple Bells' a larger-flowered cultivar.

D. laevigata Looser spikes of yellow flowers with a slight brownish tinge, and brown flecking within. A better perennial.

D. lamarckii (*D. orientalis*) Loose spikes of broad, pale, off-white flowers with a long, pure white lower lip and brownish streaking and spotting inside. An uncommon species that is sensitive to winter wet, and needs well-drained soil. Turkey.

D. lanata 🏆 Dense spikes of flowers, small narrow creamy-yellow to fawn, with a prominent whitish lower lip. Fairly perennial and usually seeds around. E. Europe, W. Asia.

D. lutea Leafy spikes of very narrow, pale yellow, downward-facing flowers. A perennial, freely seeding species, which can take over a wide area in sun or shade. W., S. Europe, N. Africa.

D.* x *mertonensis *D. grandiflora* x *D. purpurea* 🏆 An interesting true-breeding hybrid, flowers of similar size to *D. purpurea*, an unusual shade of crushed strawberry with a hint of brown, in shorter spikes. It is not long-lived.

D. obscura ✱ Rosettes of glossy lanceolate leaves, to 40 cm (16 in), loose heads of flowers which can be the nearest to red of the genus, varying between reddish-brown and coppery-orange. A fine, recently popular, perennial species, unusual originating on sunny mountain slopes in Spain, and probably better in sun, at least in cool gardens. It seems to grow best in moist but well-drained soil; if seed set is insufficient, it is easy to propagate from cuttings of new growths in summer.

43 *Digitalis obscura*

D. parviflora Similar to *D. ferruginea*, plants smaller, spikes shorter, flowers small, reddish-brown, darker-veined.
D. purpurea ssp. ***heywoodii*** A beautiful plant needing special precautions to keep the stock true as it seems to cross with any *D. purpurea* within miles. It resembles a very white-woolly version of the latter with smaller spikes of cream to soft creamy-pink flowers.
D. thapsi Similar to *D. purpurea*, to 60 cm (2 ft), stems almost leafless; loose spikes of purple flowers, with darker spots.
D. viridiflora Similar to *D. lutea*, flowers yellowish-green on less leafy stems.

Diphylleia (*Berberidaceae*)

Three species of rhizomatous perennials, of which only one is regularly cultivated. It is a plant for moist shade, with large leaves and heads of small flowers on upright stems in early summer, followed by attractive deep blue fruits on red stalks. Its large leaves look good with other big woodlanders like meconopsis and rodgersias. It can be propagated by seed sown as soon as ripe, or by division in early spring.
D. cymosa Short, thick rhizomes, leaves very large, 2-lobed, to 30 cm (1 ft) wide, with deeply notched segments, flowers in tight heads, small white, 6-petalled, followed by deep greyish-blue berries in autumn.

Diplarrhena (*Iridaceae*)

Two Australasian species, allied to Iris. They have short rhizomes, tufts of long grassy leaves, and erect stems bearing beautiful flowers with 3 large, spreading outer segments and small upright inner segments, in summer. They grow best in well-drained but humus-rich soil in sun or light shade, and are hardy to about 10 °C (50 °F), at least for short periods. They can be raised from seed, or divided.
D. latifolia The taller of the two, to 60 cm (2 ft), flowers larger, white with yellow and violet on the small standards. Tasmania.
D. moraea ✱ 20–30 cm (8–12 in) high, with dense tufts of narrow leaves, slender stems bearing a succession of beautiful, large white flowers, sometimes faintly tinged with mauve, the middle se.g.ment much broader than the outer, with yellow markings on the inner segments, and violet streaks in the throat. The most commonly grown. Tasmania, S. Australia.

Disporopsis (*Liliaceae/Convallariaceae*)

D. pernyi Rhizomatous evergreen woodlander, leaves pointed, elliptic, stems mottled with purple, spikes of long pendent greenish-white bells flaring widely at the greener tips, on long pedicels. A very attractive introduction, with the same restrained beauty as the closely allied polygonatums and disporums. It grows well in acid humus-rich soil in shade. China.

Disporum (*Liliaceae/Convallariaceae*)

Several charming rhizomatous woodland species closely allied to the Solomon's Seals, enjoying similar conditions of moist humus-rich soil in light or full shade. The leaves are simple with conspicuous veins, the pendent flowers bell-shaped or cylindrical, with pointed tips to the petals, in spring or early summer. They are beautiful plants to grow among shrubs and larger perennials like meconopsis and lilies, and although less spectacular than these they have a quiet appealing charm, especially to gardeners who like greenish flowers. Some are capable of running considerably and should not be placed among daintier plants. They are easily raised from seed, or rooted pieces can be separated in spring. I have included all the species likely to be available, although a few are rather tall in the best conditions, as they are in the wild.
D. flavens (syn. *D. sessile* subsp. *flavens*) Clumps of stiffly

upright stems to 70 cm (28 in), flowers 4 cm (1.6 in) long, pale cream, almost cylindrical, in small clusters in the axils of the broad, pale green, pointed leaves, in early summer. Korea.
D. hookeri A running plant, to 30 cm (1 ft), leaves elliptic, 8 cm (3 in) long, flowers to 3 cm (1.2 in), creamy-white, nodding, with petals flaring from the middle, often hidden beneath the leaves. N.W., N. Am. *D. h.* var. *oregonum* widely grown, and very similar, except the leaves are hairy beneath. N.W., N. Am.
D. lanuginosum Taller than *D. hookeri*, leaves narrower pointed, flowers more conspicuous, yellowish-green with petals flaring from the base. E., N. Am.
D. maculatum Similar to *D. lanuginosum* but flowers widely flaring, spotted with purple. Uncommon and one of the most beautiful. E., N. Am.
D. sessile Pointed oval leaves, stems to 40-60 cm (1.3–2 ft), flowers nodding, 3 cm (1.2 in) long, greenish-white, the green intensifying at the pointed tips. One of the commonest and easiest species, which can run quite widely in moist rich soil. Japan. *D. s.* 'Variegatum' ☼ an outstanding foliage plant, the leaves bordered and striped with pure white.
D. smilacinum Running species, to 40 cm (16 in), leaves oval, flowers 2 cm (0.8 in) long, cup-shaped, white, followed by black berries. Korea.
D. smithii Resembles *D. hookeri*, spreads more slowly, stems branching, reddish, flowers cylindrical greenish-cream, 2.5 cm (1 in) long, with short spreading tips. W. USA.
D. trachycarpum Usually taller than *D. smithii*, pure white funnel-shaped flowers with prominent exserted stamens.

Dodecatheon (*Primulaceae*)

Small perennials, mainly of interest to the rock gardener, with some having special requirements like a summer drying off period. They have basal rosettes of simple ovate to lanceolate leaves, and upright leafless stems bearing umbels of striking flowers in late spring, with acutely recurved petals like those of Cyclamen, and a prominent central cone of exserted stamens. A few species are sufficiently robust and easy to include here for planting in mixed borders with ericaceous shrubs, woodland bulbs, primulas etc. They
need rich soil with plenty of humus, in sun where there is enough moisture, or in semi-shade in drier gardens. They can be raised from seed sown in autumn and kept cool.
The following are some of the easiest species for the garden, which received the 🏆 from the Royal Horticultural Society after Trial at Wisley. USA.
D. hendersonii 🏆 Strong-growing to about 30 cm (1 ft), leaves fleshy, slightly toothed, flowers 2 cm (0.8 in) long, nodding, in large umbels, usually deep purplish-pink, with a white ring above the deep purple and yellow cone.
D. meadia 🏆 Similar, generally stronger-growing and taller, flowers similarly variable in colour, with a dark base to the cone and paler yellow stamens, in much larger umbels. 'Album', 🏆 White, a magnificent vigorous and free-flowering plant.
D. pulchelllum 🏆 Very variable, sometimes confused with *D. meadia*, flowers generally fewer, paler pink with more white at the base, stamens very pale yellow. 'Red Wings', Easily grown with vivid deep magenta flowers with orange 'noses'.

Doronicum (*Compositae*)

Invaluable genus of early-flowering rhizomatous herbaceous perennials with large yellow daisy flowers. A few of them are invasive but excellent in the wilder parts of the garden; the remainder will grow well in any reasonably moist border, in sun or partial shade, providing fine splashes of yellow as the daffodils are fading. They contrast well with tulips, for example the dark 'Queen of the Night', or with the early-flowering euphorbias and later hellebores. They can be propagated by division in autumn or early spring. Several of the cultivars are of uncertain origin and I have included them alphabetically.
D. austraicum To 70 cm (28 in), leaves slightly hairy, cordate, with undulant margins, flowers yellow, to 5 cm (2 in) wide, in loose heads on slender stems. A spreading species suitable for the wild garden. C., S. Europe.
D. carpetanum Large clump, leaves hairy, cordate, with long petioles, flowers several, large, narrow-rayed, bright yellow. Uncommon in gardens, but a good plant.
D. columnae (syn. *D. cordatum*) ✱ To 50 cm (20 in), leaves cordate or oval, flowers solitary, bright yellow to 5 cm (2 in) across, on upright stems, in early spring. One of the best early perennials.
***D.* 'Finesse'** Possibly a cultivar of *D. orientale*, to 50 cm (20 in), flowers long-stemmed, solitary, mid-yellow with narrow rays.
***D.* 'Harpur Crewe'** (syn *D.* x *excelsum*) Probably a hybrid or cultivar of *D. plantagineum*, to 60 cm (2 ft), leaves hairy, flowers several, exceptionally large.
***D.* 'Miss Mason'** 🏆 Dense clumps of cordate leaves, a long succession of large narrow-rayed flowers. A fine old favourite for the early border.
D. orientale Similar to *D. columnae*, generally more spreading, larger, leaves more shallowly toothed.
D. pardalianches ✱ Clump-forming, spreading, to 70 cm (28 in) high, with 2–6 flowers to 5 cm (2 in) wide, on slender stems. Invaluable for its longer season than other species.

44 *Doronicum pardalianches*

D. plantagineum Rarely grown except as 'Harpur Crewe', which has larger flowers.
***D.* 'Spring Beauty'** (syn. 'Fruhlingspracht') Low clump-former, flowers large, very double, lacking the Elegance of the singles.

Dracocephalum (*Labiatae*)

This genus contains some of the more attractive hardy labiates for the garden; the range is likely to increase as a result of recent expeditions to China. Although a few are small and more often grown on the rock garden, they are generally suitable for the front of a well-drained border in sun or light shade. They are very similar to nepetas and salvias, with toothed or divided leaves, and leafy terminal spikes of 2-lipped tubular flowers in whorls in summer, varying in colour and including some good blues. They can be raised from seed sown in autumn, or from cuttings of young growth in summer, or by division in early spring.
D. argunense Leaves narrowly lanceolate, entire, short leafy spikes of quite large deep blue flowers. Supposedly one of the larger species to 60 cm (2 ft), but smaller in my garden. N.E. Asia.
D. austraicum Clump-forming, erect stems to 30 cm (1 ft), leaves narrow, entire, pinnate, dense spikes of 3 cm (1.2 in) long bluish-violet flowers. S. Europe–Ukraine.
D. botryoides Low-growing, stems semi-prostrate leaves rounded, hairy, pinnate, upright spikes of 1.5 cm (0.6 in) long, pale pinkish-lavender flowers. Caucasus.
D. bullatum To 25 cm (10 in), leaves oval, reddish-backed on reddish stems, broad dense spikes of dark blue flowers. An attractive species. China.
D. calophyllum 30 cm (1 ft) Leaves pinnate, segments 5–7, narrow, on branching stems, large spikes of deep purplish-blue flowers. China. Var. *smithiana* leaves more finely cut into 7–10 segments, flowers hairy. It is sometimes confused with *D. forrestii*. China.
D. forrestii ✱ Similar to the last but more leafy, leaves with 3–7 segments, darkest blue downy flowers for months, later in summer. Very easy and perennial. China.
D. grandiflorum Clump-forming, stems upright 20–30 cm (8–12 in), basal leaves narrowly cordate, toothed, on long petioles, flowers 4–5 cm (1.6–2 in) long, deep blue in short dense heads. E. Russia. Possibly confused in gardens with the very similar *D. rupestre* from China, generally taller, with broadly cordate basal leaves.
D. hemsleyanum Taller clump-former, to 45 cm (1.5 ft), leaves entire, sessile, oblong, on hairy stems, loose spikes of 3 cm (1.2 in) long purplish-blue flowers. China.
D. isabellae Upright-growing, stems white-hairy, leaves pinnate, flowers 4 cm (1.6 in) long violet in tight whorls. China.
D. renatii Low-growing, stems hairy, leaves oblong, loose upright spikes of 3 cm (1.2 in) long flowers, cream with reddish tubes. N. Africa.
D. rupestre *See* ***D. grandiflora***
D. ruyschianum To 50 cm (20 in), leaves narrowly lanceolate to linear, entire, dense whorls of pale lavender flowers on upright stems. The most widely grown as a border plan. E. Europe–Russia.
D. wendelboi An uncommon species from the Hindu Kush, once described in the wild in glowing terms by Paul Furse as a 'cobalt beauty', and now possibly in cultivation.

E

Echinacea (*Compositae*)

The Cone Flowers are excellent border plants but generally much too tall to consider here when well-grown. The widely grown *E. purpurea* and its cultivars attain over 1 m (3 ft), but *E. p.* 'White Lustre' is usually around 60–70 cm (24–28 in) high in my garden. It is an attractive plant making a spreading clump of simple or lightly toothed ovate-lanceolate leaves, stiff upright stems, and solitary or few 10 cm (4 in) wide, creamy-white flowers, with a prominent central orange-brown cone making a striking contrast, which seems to appeal to most gardeners.

45 *Echinacea purpurea* 'White Lustre'

Echinops (*Compositae*)

The Globe Thistles are easy border perennials, several of which are likely to be too tall to consider. They are extremely easy to grow, and will colonize poor soils, especially if it is reasonably well-drained and in a sunny position. The following are usually under 70 cm (28 in) tall.
E. emiliae A very rare species, occasionally available from collected seed, with deeply divided leaves, and very large jade-green flowers. Sadly it seems very difficult to establish, but would be worth any effort. Turkey.
E. humilis Late-flowering, to 30 cm (1 ft), leaves pinnately divided, white-hairy, flowers steel-blue. Rarely grown. E. Russia.
E. ritro 🏆 Compact growing to 60 cm (2 ft), but usually confused in gardens with the tall *E. bannaticus*. Slowly spreading clump of divided white-hairy, thistle-like leaves,

attractive in themselves, branching stems terminating in circular good blue globes. C., E. Europe, Asia. The stronger coloured cultivars 'Blue Globe' and 'Taplow Blue' are considerably taller and properly belong to *E. bannaticus*.
E. r. ssp. ***ruthenicus*** (syn. *E. ruthenicus*) Similar in size, leaves more deeply divided, dark green with white backs, less branched stems and flowers of a good colour. S.E. Europe, Asia.

Eomecon (*Papaveraceae*)

E. chionantha The sole species, a rhizomatous perennial forming a carpet of long-stemmed, kidney-shaped leaves with wavy toothed edges, flowers white 4-petalled, to 3 cm (1.2 in) wide, in loose heads of a few, on reddish-brown stems, in late spring. It thrives in moist humus-rich soil in shade and can be invasive. It is best planted away from other small plants, among larger shrubs. China.

Epilobium (*Onagraceae*)

Although *E. angustifolium*, the rosebay willow herb, is such a menace in gardens, there are several much smaller species that are well worth growing for their plentiful flowers in summer. Even some of these may be moderately invasive, either by seeding or by running, so that careful watch should be kept on any unknown species. Generally they do best in sunny beds which are not too dry, and they will tolerate light shade. The smallest species are usually grown on the rock garden but are equally at home in the front of a border. They are easily raised from seed, or by division of the spreading species.

I have not included the zauschnerias, which have recently been threatened with inclusion in *Epilobium*, as there seems to be a good chance that the botanists will leave them where they are, and where gardeners are accustomed to find them.
E. chloraefolium Possibly only in cultivation in the form of var. *kai-kourense* is one of the best small species, to 20–30 cm (8–12 in); leaves glossy, oval, red-flushed, pointed, flowers with a long reddish-brown, tubular ovary and 4 spreading, clear pink petals, usually notched at the tips, in loose spikes. It is not invasive and does well in moist shade. NZ.
E. crassum Slow-growing mat-former, stems leafy, leaves spathulate to oval, reddish beneath, flowers solitary, pink-veined white, axillary. NZ.
E. dodonaei Tall spreading species, stems branching upright, usually to 70 cm (28 in), leaves linear, hairy, flowers large, deep rose, in terminal spikes. It may seed freely and is best dead-headed. Europe, W. Asia.
E. fleischeri Similar to *E. dodonaei* but semi-prostrate to 30 cm (1 ft). It is less invasive, flowers good sized. European Alps.
E. glabellum Similar in habit to *E. fleischeri*, variable, 20–30 cm (8–12 in), leaves glossy, oval to triangular pointed, flowers creamy-white, rarely pink in loose heads. NZ.
E. obcordatum Low mat-forming, leaves ovate, toothed, loose clusters of a few comparatively large purplish-pink flowers. Possibly best on the rock garden, late-flowering W. USA.

Epimedium (*Berberidaceae*)

This is an excellent underrated genus, long considered a source of useful, very hardy, ground-covering plants, with attractive foliage especially when it develops autumnal tints. It has recently become equally appreciated for the beauty of the dainty flowers of many of its species, especially the smaller ones, which do not need to be mollycoddled on the rock garden, but can look after themselves in a shady border of good humus-rich soil. The more vigorous will grow reasonably well, even in dry shade among larger shrubs.

All the species have rather leathery leaves which are usually all basal, ternately or pinnately divided, leaves and leaflets long-stalked and sharply toothed. In many species they develop strong autumn colour. Except in the truly evergreen species it is advisable to remove the half-dead remains of the leaves in winter, as they detract from the beauty of the flowers. The flowers, in loose panicles, dancing on slender pedicels, are individually exquisite, like small nodding columbines, with widely spreading sepals, and a central cup formed of the petal limbs, usually with long curved spurs.

They can be raised from seed sown in autumn and kept cool in winter. It may take eighteen months to germinate. They may also be increased by division in spring.
E acuminatum To 50 cm (20 in), leaves long, evergreen, 3-lobed, leaflets lanceolate, spiny-edged, usually flushed with red when young; flowers in loose clusters, large, shallow, sepals palest violet, spreading, petals deep violet-purple, spurs curved. A fine recent introduction. China.
E. alpinum To 30 cm (1 ft), deciduous, leaves long, 4–8 oval, spiny-edged leaflets, flushed pink in spring, flowers small, sepals short, orange-red, petals bright yellow in long loose sprays. S. Europe.
E. x ***cantabrigiense*** (*E. alpinum* x *E. pubigerum*) Usually taller, to 50 cm (20 in), leaves smaller, cordate, sparsely spiny, flowers in a looser inflorescence, small orange-red with insignificant petals.
E. davidii ✱ To 50 cm (20 in), semi-evergreen, leaflets ovate, spiny-edged, tinged slightly with red, flowers in large sprays, bright yellow with long spurs and a deep cup, on reddish stems. An outstanding vigorous species. China.

46 *Epimedium davidii*

E. diphyllum Smaller, evergreen clump, leaves 2-lobed, the leaflets cordate and sparsely spiny, flowers few, small, pure white in loose heads, petals spurless and equalling the sepals in length. Japan.
E. dolichostemon To 35 cm (14 in), evergreen, leaflets 3 sagittate, pointed, spiny, sprays of dainty flowers, very shallow, nodding, sepals white faintly tinged with purple, petals very short deep purple, stamens dark in a prominent boss. A rare and beautiful Chinese species.
E. elongatum Similar to the last, flowers pale yellow with long spreading spurs and undeveloped petal limbs. It is proving easy in the garden.
E. grandiflorum 🏆 Clump-forming, deciduous, from 10-40 cm (4–16 in) high, varying in flower colour, with several named cultivars. Leaves with up to 10 spiny toothed leaflets, usually reddish-tinged or margined in spring, flowers comparatively large with a deep cup, sepals spreading, exceeded in length by the curved spurs, in dense heads, pink to deep purple, white or yellow. Even the smaller forms grow well and increase in a moist shady border with plenty of leaf-mould. Perhaps the most beautiful species. Japan.
Subsp. ***koreanum*** (syn. *E. koreanum*), very different in habit, a more vigorous, spreading plant with much larger leaflets and large pale yellow flowers. 'Album', large pure white, possibly the same as 'White Queen', 'Crimson Beauty', large crimson, a splendid cultivar, 'Enchantress', very large pale pink, superb, 'Lilafee', ✱ one of the smallest, leaves purple-tinged when young, flowers deep violet-purple with paler spurs, 'Nanum', 🏆 very compact, leaves purple-edged, flowers purple, or more often large creamy-white with long spreading white spurs, 'Rose Queen', 🏆 taller, bronzed young growth, flowers in looser sprays, rose-pink with long white or faintly pink-tinged spurs, 'Violaceum', beautiful broad shallow flowers, sepals spreading, pinkish-violet, petals palest pink, spurs long off-white, 'White Queen', 🏆 leaves pale green-edged with purple, flowers large with a deep cup, pure white, sepals and spurs downward-curving.
E. leptorrhizum ✱ To 15 cm (6 in), leaves long, narrow, flushed in spring with purple, margins spiny toothed, flowers exceptionally large, sepals spreading, broad, pale pinkish-purple, petals darker. An exquisite recent introduction from China.

47 *Epimedium leptorrhizum*

E.* x *perralchicum (*E. perraldianum* x *E. pinnatum*) 🏆 Strong-growing evergreen, to 40 cm (16 in), leaflets 3–5, broad, bronze when young, margins long-spined, flowers large deep yellow, with broad sepals and small petals with short reddish spurs. 'Wisley' and 'Frohnleiten', vigorous selections with bright yellow flowers.
E. perralderianum Similar to its hybrid, leaf margins more spiny toothed, flowers smaller. N. Africa.
E. pinnatum Similar to the last, but leaves pinnate or with 5 leaflets, margins not toothed, or sparsely toothed. Subsp. *pinnatum* has more, smaller, toothed leaflets. Iran.
E. p. subsp. ***colchicum*** 🏆 3–5 leaflets, margins entire. N.E. Turkey–Caucasus.
E. pubigerum Evergreen clump-former to 50 cm (20 in), leaflets to 9, rounded, glossy, with small spines, flowers very small, sepals cream or occasionally pale pink, petals yellow, in rather sparse loose panicles. S.E. Europe, W. Asia.
E.* x *rubrum (*E. grandiflorum* x *E. alpinum*) Spreading carpet, leaves deeply purple-tinged in spring and autumn, flowers small but intensely coloured, the sepals scarlet, and the small petals deep yellow. One of the most popular deciduous species.
E. sagittatum Evergreen, leaves trifoliate, leaflets ovate to lanceolate with spiny margins, flowers tiny white or cream. Rarely grown. China.
E. setosum Clump-forming, deciduous, to 40 cm (16 in), leaflets long-pointed, brown-hairy beneath, flowers pure white, short-spurred, in loose sprays. Japan.
E.* x *versicolor (*E. grandiflorum* x *E. pinnatum* subsp. *colchicum*) Vigorous deciduous clump-former, to 30 cm (1 ft), with several named clones. 'Cupreum', leaves with 9 reddish-purple leaflets, green along the veins, flowers aquilegia-like with reddish-pink sepals and short yellow petals in dense clusters, 'Neosulphureum', leaves brown-tinged, fewer leaflets, flowers pale primrose of similar shape, on leafless stems, 'Sulphureum', 🏆 similar but stems leafy with 3–9 leaflets, 'Versicolor' similar to 'Cupreum' but flowers paler.
E.* x *warleyense (*E. alpinum* x *E. pinnatum* subsp. *colchicum*) Spreading evergreen, to 50 cm (20 in), leaflets 5–9 sparsely spiny, flowers large, sepals reddish-orange rounded, petals small yellow, anthers greenish, in generous sprays. Very easy.
E.* x *youngianum (*E. diphyllum* x *E. grasndiflorum*) Variable deciduous clump-former, to 30 cm (1 ft), leaflets 5–9, narrowly ovate, pointed, with spineless margins, often purple-tinged when young, flowers large, purplish-pink or white, in loose sprays. 'Niveum', 🏆 pure white, a widely grown clone with rounded leaflets, 'Roseum', 6–7 leaflets, flowers rose-purple with paler sepals, 'Typicum', leaves pointed, flowers insignificant, greenish-white. Uncommon.

Epipactis (*Orchidaceae*)

Although I have excluded most hardy orchids, notably the cypripediums, because their specialized requirements are more easily satisfied by the alpine grower, and the very easy dactylorhizas because of their tuberous roots and their inclusion in bulb books, it seems reasonable to include this genus as being easy rhizomatous orchids, at least in the case of *E. gigantea.* Both this species and the less commonly offered *E. palustris* do well in the open garden in moist humus-rich soil in partial shade, preferably with leaf-mould as the source of humus. They can be increased by division in spring, making sure that at least one growing point is included in each separated piece.

E. gigantea ✱ Spreading plant, leaves large, oval to lanceolate, markedly ribbed, folded round the upright stems at their bases, flowers large, outward facing, 3–4 cm (1.2–1.6 in) wide, in spikes. Flowers yellowish-green overall and on the outer narrow spreading sepals, with heavy reddish staining on the petals and in stripes down the paler lip. Remarkably easy, capable of covering a considerable area, and even invading the adjoining gravel path in my garden. N. Am.

E. palustris ✱ A more beautiful species because the leaves are narrower and smaller and conceal the flowers less. Flowers paler than *E. gigantea,* with green veining, both lip and petals white. It spreads much less quickly than *E. gigantea,* but is not difficult in the same conditions.

Erigeron (*Compositae*)

A large genus of annual and perennial herbs, often herbaceous, with aster-like daisy flowers, but differing from those of Aster in having more than one row of ray florets. They vary greatly in size, from small and in some cases tricky alpine species, which I have excluded here, to large spreading perennials, few of which exceed 80 cm (30 in) in height. The latter include many excellent cultivars for the border, with a long flowering season mainly in the middle of the summer, and before all the late-flowering asters. The colour range is much the same as that of asters from white, through pale to deep pink, to lavender and deep purple shades.

Most erigerons are easy to grow in a sunny border, especially in rich soils. It is advisable to cut them back after flowering, as they will then often produce a second crop of bloom later in the summer. Frequent division also helps to keep them in good health. They can also be grown from cuttings of young shoots, or the species can be raised from seed, and will often self-sow.

E. alpinus Clump-forming, to 20 cm (8 in), leaves narrow, spathulate to elliptic, downy, flowers single, occasionally 2–3, 3 cm (1.2 in) in diameter, purplish lavender, on short upright stems in summer. Useful at the edge of a border. S., C. Europe.

E. atticus Very similar to *E. alpinus,* more robust, to 50 cm (20 in), leaves very hairy. Europe.

E. aurantiacus Spreading mat-former, leaves hairy spathulate, flowers solitary, bright orange, to 5 cm (2 in) wide. A striking plant with flowers of an unusual colour but it frequently seems to be short-lived. Turkey.

E. borealis Similar to *E. alpinus,* to 30 cm (1 ft), leaves smooth, flowers smaller, purple. N.W. Europe.

E. glaucus Evergreen mounds, leaves very glaucous, spathulate or oval, flowers over a long season in summer, somewhat wishy-washy pale lavender with brownish centres. It is easily grown with good foliage, but it is worth looking out for a cultivar of improved colour. W. USA. 'Albus', white, 'Elstead Pink', good deep purplish-pink, 'Roseus', pure rose-pink.

E. karvinskianus (syn *E. mucronatus*) 🏆 Best known under its synonym, a tangle of slender stems, leaves small narrow, flowers in a never-ending succession, 2–3 cm (0.8–1.2 in) wide, opening white or pale pink and deepening to purple, so that the colours always appear in mixed medley. Its seeding is over-prolific and its appearance somewhat weedy for the border, but it is a splendid plant for the cracks of paving or for old walls, in which it will often find a foothold. Mexico-Panama.

E. multiradiatus Clump-forming to 30 cm (1 ft), leaves lanceolate, toothed, flowers solitary, narrow-rayed, to 5 cm (2 in) in diameter. Himalaya.

E. philadelphicus ✱ Upright leafy stems 40–70 cm (16–28 in), leaves lanceolate to oval, toothed, flowers clear soft pink in generous clusters, around mid-summer. An underrated plant, which seeds around freely, it may be short-lived, but there are always plenty of seedlings to ensure continuity. N. USA, Canada.

48 *Erigeron philadelphicus* with the annual *Omphalodes linifolia*

E. speciosus Clump-forming to 70 cm (28 in), similar in habit to the last but more perennial, flowers purplish-blue, occasionally white, in heads of 1–several. It is rarely grown but is the main parent of the popular hybrids and cultivars. **Cultivars:** All make dense clumps of upright or spreading stems, 45–70 cm (18–28 in), leaves pointed, spathulate to oblanceolate, flowers in large clusters continue to appear over a long period around mid-summer: 'Adria', large, violet-blue, 'Amity', soft lilac-pink, 'Charity', pale lilac, 'Darkest of All', 🏆 deep violet, 'Dignity', deep lilac-pink, 'Dimity' pink and orange, 'Felicity', few-rayed, bright pink, 'Forsters Liebling', 🏆 semi-double, deep reddish-pink, 'Lilofee', semi-double, deep lilac, 'Marchenland', semi-double, large, soft pink, 'Pink Jewel', pale lilac-pink, 'Prosperity', lilac, 'Quakeress', white, flushed pale pinkish-lavender, 'Rosa Triumph', semi-double, pink, 'Rotes Meer', deep red, 'Schneewitchen', pure white, 'Schwarzes Meer', dark violet, 'Sincerity', lilac, 'Sommerneuschnee', white to very pale pink, 'Strahlenmeer', pale violet, 'Violetta' full double, deep violet, 'Wuppertal', semi-double, pale violet.

Eriophyllum (*Compositae*)

E. lanatum The only species commonly grown in Britain, although usually seen on the rock garden it will do equally well at the front of a very well-drained border in full sun. Variable, usually a spreading mound, leaves small white-felted, smothered for weeks in deep yellow 2–4 cm (0.8–1.6 in) wide daisy flowers, in early summer, hardy to at least -6 °C (21 °F) but resents winter wet in heavy soils W., N. Am. Var. *monoense* recently offered in seed lists, more compact, lower-growing, flowers slightly larger with more overlapping petals, possibly even less tolerant of wet conditions.

Erodium (*Geraniaceae*)

Closely resembling Geranium, the erodiums differ in having 5 stamens instead of 10, and usually 'look different' in a way that is easier to see than to describe. The most beautiful are small mat or cushion-forming plants that thrive on the rock garden, but a few larger plants, described here, look fine in front of a border, with interesting finely divided leaves and umbels of attractive flowers, sometimes dioecious, over a long season in late spring or early to mid-summer. The species can be propagated by seed, and both species and hybrids by rooting individual rosettes as cuttings in summer.

E. absinthoides Cushion-forming, to 20 cm (8 in), stems spreading, leaves grey-green ferny, flowers 2 cm (0.8 in) wide, in umbels of 2–8, white to pale violet-purple. It is not widely grown and is one of the more tender species. Greece, Turkey

E. alpinum Similar in size to the last, leaves green, finely divided, umbels of flowers reddish-purple with deeper veining. C. Italy.

E. carvifolium Spreading clump to 30 cm (1 ft), leaves green very finely divided, carrot-like, flowers 4–10, deep reddish-purple, with brownish veining on the lower part of the upper petals, over a long period. One of the best species for the border, and tolerant of partial shade. Spain.

E. castellanum Clump-forming to 20 cm (8 in), leaves green, pinnate, toothed, flowers quite large, deep rose, with a darker veined area towards the base of the upper petals. It seems to be hardy and has a long flowering period. Spain.

E. chrysanthum ☼ Large cushion, to 30 cm (1 ft), leaves beautiful silvery-grey-green, flowers pale primrose, unveined, in few umbels. The plants are dioecious, and the male flowers, as described, are usually very sparse. The female flowers have reddish veining and are more freely produced. Fortunately the foliage is so attractive that it is worth growing for this alone. Vigorous enough for the edge of a border. Greece.

E. daucoides The true species, with very hairy leaves and white flowers, is probably not in cultivation; the plant offered in catalogues closely resembles *E. manescavii* with deep rose flowers.

E. guiccardii Like *E. chrysanthum* with fine silvery leaves, flowers pale to dark rose-purple. A rarely grown species. Balkans.

E.* x *hybridum (*E. daucoides* x *E. manescavii*) Similar to *E. manescavii*, leaves more finely divided, flowers paler and smaller.

E.* x *lindavicum (*E. chrysanthum* x *E. absinthoides* var. *amanum*) Like *E. chrysanthum*, but not quite so silvery, flowers off-white, brown-veined, on taller stems. 'Charter House', superior, with more silvery leaves and pale yellow flowers, with purple stigmas.

E. manescavii Leaves pinnate, coarsely-toothed, flowers deep magenta with darker veining in umbels of up to 20. Robust easily-grown species for the border. Pyrenees.

***E.* 'Merstham Pink'** A mound to 25 cm (10 in), leaves green, finely divided, ferny, flowers rose-pink in sprays over several months. It needs well-drained soil.

E. pelargoniiflorum To 30 cm (1 ft) or more, leaves hairy, grey-green, on branching semi-woody stems, flowers white with pinkish veining and dark blotches on the upper petals, in large loose heads. An interesting species which in some gardens with light sandy soil is over-exuberant in its seeding. It is said to be a little tender, but always seems to leave some seedlings even if winter temperatures drop below -10 °C (14 °F). Turkey.

49 *Erodium pelargoniiflorum*

E. trifolium Upright perennial, leaves ovate, 3-lobed, hairy, toothed, flowers white with purple veining and a darker blotch on the upper petals, in large umbels. Short-lived, but easily raised from seed. Atlas.

Eryngium (*Umbelliferae*)

A genus of annuals, biennials, and perennials, the latter among the most appealing plants for the border for their striking leaves and their long-lasting flowers. Some species are very large, statuesque indeed, and I have confined my descriptions to those likely to stay under 75 cm (2.5 ft) in height. Generally the leaves and flowers, in shades of green, grey and blue, are spiny and thistle-like on branching stems, the flowers opening successively from the top over a very long period, and remaining in good condition even if dried. The 'flowers' consist of a dense central cone of tiny true flowers, surrounded by an involucre of conspicuous deeply divided spiny bracts.

They do best in well-drained soils in a sunny border, and tolerate lime and soils of low fertility well. Whereas they usually stand up well without staking, in rich soils they may become too lanky and fall over. They are easily raised from seed but the cultivars or any special selections must be propagated by root cuttings.

E. alpinum 🏆 50-60 cm (20–24 in) Upright, rosettes of spiny toothed, ovate-cordate leaves, more finely divided stem leaves, flowers large, the cone steely greyish-blue to deep blue, surrounded by finely cut feathery bracts of similar colour. European Alps. A spectacular perennial, especially in its cultivars of improved colour. Several are available: 'Amethyst', leaves finely divided, flowers deep violet-blue, 'Blue Star', flowers deep blue, 'Holden Blue', strong-growing, flowers deep blue, 'Opal', flower heads of a pale silvery-grey-blue, 'Superbum', strong-growing, leaves blue-tinged, flower heads deep blue.

E. amethystinum Branching stems occasionally exceeding 70 cm (28 in), leaves finely divided, leathery, tinged with blue, pinnate below, palmately divided above, flowers 2 cm (0.8 in) wide, true deep blue, surrounded by narrowly lanceolate, silvery-grey-green, spiny bracts. Italy, Balkans.

E. billardieri Branching stems to 70 cm (28 in), basal leaves rounded, bluish-green, more finely divided and spiny on the stems, flowers greyish-blue, rounded heads, with darker blue narrow pointed bracts. Uncommon plant. E. Asia.

E. bourgatii Usually under 40 cm (16 in) high, leaves finely divided, conspicuously white-veined, flower heads large, silvery-blue, surrounded by a ring of long, narrow bracts of similar colour. Pyrenees. A good long-lived very hardy species in well-drained soils varying in colour. 'Oxford Blue', 🏆 a fine cultivar with rich blue flowers and bracts.

E. caeruleum Uncommon, very similar to *E. planum*, but leaves smaller and basal leaves not persistent. Russia.

50 *Eryngium bourgatii*

E. campestre Leaves very spiny, finely cut, bluish, flowers small in large branching panicles, more steely grey-green than blue. Not often cultivated, but quite attractive. Europe–S.W. Asia.

E. creticum Leaves spiny, 3-lobed, cordate, flowers in rounded heads of bluish-purple, amid paler blue spiny bracts. Not widely grown, possibly because it is short-lived. Balkans, Aegean Is.

E. ebracteatum Usually to 7 cm (2.8 in), sometimes taller, rosettes of long, narrow, undivided blue-grey leaves, flower heads dense cylindrical, brownish-purple, with no bracts or very short bracts, on branching stems. An uncommon and unusual species. S. Am.

E. humile Rosettes of leathery glossy leaves, with white finely-spiny margins, flowers 1–3 on short branching stems, pale to deep blue, surrounded by silvery bracts with toothed margins. An exciting small species becoming available from recent seed collections in the Andes.

E. maritimum ☼ Our native Sea Holly, usually under 40 cm (16 in) high, a rounded clump of broad, pale bluish-grey, leathery, somewhat crinkled, 3–5-lobed spiny leaves with paler veins; the flower heads green to greenish-blue, surrounded by very sharp narrow silvery-blue bracts. Europe. It seems to be underestimated as a foliage plant, and is not difficult in very well-drained or sandy soil in full sun.

E. x oliverianum 🏆 Rosettes of dark green undivided cordate leaves, well-branched steel-blue stems, deep blue flower heads and narrow spiny bracts. A hybrid of doubtful origin, but one of the most striking border plants, sometimes exceeding our size limit a little.

E. planum Similar to *E. oliverianum*, branches widely-spreading, flowers smaller, light blue, with narrow silvery-green bracts. Several cultivars with bluer flowers and bracts: 'Blauer Zwerg', ('Blue Dwarf') excellent compact form with very deep blue flowers, 'Roseum', flowers tinged purplish-pink, 'Argentea', flowers silvery-grey, 'Calypso', the leaves edged with creamy-white. It is a spectacular variegation, but unfortunately seems to revert quickly.

E. proteiflorum ✱ Rosettes of long stiff leaves with very sharp curved spines, upright stems, usually with one very large and a few smaller flowers, each consisting of a deep blue cone surrounded by a ring of long lanceolate bracts of a remarkable shade of pale whitish-green, the whole up to 20 cm (8 in) wide. Known incorrectly for many years as 'Delaroux', this has the most spectacular flowers of any species, but is a little tender, only proving satisfactory after a mild winter with temperatures keeping above -6 °C (21 °F). A magnificent plant that can attain 1 m (3 ft), but is usually much less. Mexico.

51 *Eryngium proteiflorum*

E. spinalba To 30 cm (1 ft), leaves finely divided, pale grey-green, flowers in branching heads, whiteish, surrounded by very pale narrow spiny bracts. Not very striking and not often grown.

E.* x *tripartitum 🏆 Hybrid of uncertain origin, close to *E. planum*, with similar widely branching heads of many small flowers, of a superior deep violet-blue colour. It is one of the best plants for the border.

E. variifolium ✪ Usually to 40 cm (16 in), striking rosettes of dark green leaves with very conspicuous broad white veins, dense branching heads of small greyish-blue flowers, very long, narrow, very sharp, silvery bracts. An excellent reliable smaller species.

E.* x *zabellii (*E. alpinum* x *E. bourgatii*) To 45 cm (1.5 ft), differing from *E. alpinum* in its 3-lobed leaves and branching heads of several beautiful long-lasting steel-blue flowers with fewer bracts. One of the best hybrids. 'Jewel', taller with deep blue flowers and larger more finely dissected bracts. 'Violetta', large deepest blue flowers.

Erysimum (*Cruciferae*)

A popular genus of annuals, biennials and perennials, including a wide range of seed strains of wallflowers for bedding. Many of the species were previously included in *Cheiranthus*, and may still be found in some catalogues under that name. The species vary greatly in habit and in hardiness, some being small plants better grown on the rock garden or alpine house, others good plants for the border. There is a large range of hybrids and cultivars that are excellent garden plants, from low spreading carpets to medium sized 'shrubs', with a very long flowering season, mainly in late spring and early summer. They make colourful groups for the front of the sunny border, in a wide range of shades of yellow, orange, purple or lavender, or multicoloured.

Most are hardy in average winters, to -6 °C (21 °F) or lower, especially in well-drained soils, but they tend to be short-lived, or they become woody and straggly after two or three years, even when cut back hard after flowering. They are extremely easy to propagate from cuttings during the growing season, so that any old groups of plants are easy to replace when they deteriorate. Several of the species self-sow very freely, or can be raised from seed.

In the descriptions below I have excluded the annuals and strict biennials, and the smallest 'alpine' species.

E. arenicola Sound perennial, to 30 cm (1 ft), basal rosettes of 4 cm (1.6 in) long lanceolate leaves, flowers 2 cm (0.8 in) wide lemon-yellow in dense upright spikes. W. USA.

E. asperum Variable short-lived species, usually with short spikes of typical bright yellow, but can be deep orange-red in the wild. It can seed around excessively. W., C. USA.

E. capitatum Very similar to the last, but definitely short-lived, usually bright yellow, but said to be mauve occasionally. W., N. Am.

E. concinnum Flowers consistently of a delightful shade of pale lemon yellow in short dense spikes. This seems to me superior to the two previous species, although unfortunately it is also short-lived, but true from seed. W. USA.

E. hieraciifolium Taller, with hairy leaves, hairy branching stems, and flat-heads of yellow flowers in summer. C., N. Europe.

E. linifolium Dense bush to 70 cm (28 in), increasingly woody with age, leaves greyish-green, narrow lanceolate, abundant spikes of deep pinkish-purple flowers over several weeks in summer. One of the best species for the garden, especially in its variegated form. *E. l.* 'Variegatum' ☼ Strikingly creamy-white variegated, more cream than green, with paler mauve flowers. It is a beautiful foliage plant, which survives average winters in my garden.
E. mutabile The true plant is an uncommon Cretan endemic, with prostrate stems to 12 cm (4.7 in) long, flowers small yellow, changing to purple with age. The plant offered in catalogues is more likely to be similar or identical to *E. semperflorens*, resembling *E. linifolium* in its bushy habit, with flowers purplish, often combined with cream or yellow.
E. pulchellum Tuft-forming, rosettes of toothed spathulate leaves, stems to 40 cm (16 in) of bright deep yellow flowers. E. Europe–Asia Minor.
E. scoparium Bushy, narrow untoothed leaves, long loose spikes of pale mauve flowers in mid-summer. It is surprisingly hardy in light soil, but tends to get straggly quickly unless cut back hard. Madeira.
E. semperflorens Similar to *E. scoparium*, flowers usually a mixture of cream and purple, produced throughout the year. Another useful more hardy shrubby species needing the same treatment. Morocco.
E. suffrutescens Uncommon sub-shrubby mound-forming species, leaves narrowly lanceolate, flowers lemon-yellow. California.

Cultivars: Many of these are of uncertain parentage, and I have not grouped them according to their parentage.

Name	Flowers	Notes
'Bloody Warrior'	Deep blood-red, double	Wallflower type, medium height. Needs frequent propagation
'Bowles Mauve'	Mauve, in long spikes, very long season	Large, bushy, with blue-green leaves, very reliable
'Brendon'	Deep yellow, in short spikes from reddish buds	Low, mat-forming, with untoothed leaves
'Butterscotch'	Deep reddish-orange	Low
'Chelsea Jacket'	Blend of purple, brown, and pink	Bushy
'Constant Cheer'	Blend of yellow and purple, long season	Bushy
'Gold Flame'	Deep orange, in short spikes	Low mat-forming
'Harpur Crewe' (See plate 127)	Double, bright yellow, in loose spikes	Medium height wallflower
'Jacob's Jacket'	Similar to 'Constant Cheer'	Bushy
'Jubilee Gold' (See plate 52)	Similar to 'Bredon'	As 'Bredon' but with toothed leaves
'Julian Orchard' ✱	Similar to 'Bowles Mauve', but deeper in colour	Much more compact than 'Bowles Mauve'. Excellent
'Lady Roborough'	Pale yellow fading to cream, from	Low-growing
'Mayflower'	purplish buds	
'Moonlight'	Pale primrose	Low-growing
'Mrs L.K. Elmhirst'	Paler than 'Bowles Mauve'	Leaves greener than 'Bowles Mauve'
'Orange Flame'	Bright orange	Low-growing mat
'Primrose'	Primrose-yellow	Low carpeter
'Rufus'	Deep brownish orange	Old wallflower requiring regular propagation
'Sprite'	Pale yellow	Very low-growing
'Wenlock Beauty' (See plate 52)	Blend of yellow and purple	Bushy

Eumorphia (*Compositae*)

A small genus of uncommonly grown perennials, usually recommended for the greenhouse.
E. sericea Excellent silver foliage plant, a low mound to 30–40 cm (12–16 in) of branching stems, leaves small linear, silvery-grey, a sprinkling of small white daisy flowers in summer. The only species generally available, it is hardier than is usually suggested, surviving temperatures of -6 °C (21 °F) in very well-drained soil at the front of a sunny border. S. Africa.

52 *Erysimum* 'Jubilee Gold' & E. 'Wenlock Beauty'

Eupatorium

Useful tall perennials with broad heads of tiny flowers in mid- to late summer.

E. coelestinum The only species under 80 cm (30 in) likely to be found in lists; a bog or marginal plant, to about 60 cm (2 ft), stems upright, leaves ovate, toothed, 10 cm (4 in) long, dense broad heads of small flowers, bluish-violet fading to purple, in late summer. E., N. Am.

Euphorbia (*Euphorbiaceae*)

During recent years this has become one of the most popular of all genera for the garden. It includes annuals, biennials, and perennials, many of them succulent or cactus-like and only suitable for the greenhouse, but with a fine range of hardy perennials. The majority of the latter have very long-lasting flowers in shades of yellow or greenish-yellow, borne on plants in a remarkably diverse range of sizes and very attractive leaf forms, from tiny low carpeters to rounded cushions and statuesque plants for the back of the border, the different species flowering from late winter to autumn. The almost unique colour of the euphorbias combines particularly well with the deep purples or magentas of such plants as the taller origanums, or many geranium species and cultivars such as *G. psilostemon* or 'Anne Folkard'. The 'flowers' are unusual in consisting of a cup (a cyathium) containing a single female flower reduced to the pistil only, and several male flowers each reduced to a single stamen, the whole usually surrounded by a conspicuous involucre of colourful bracts.

Most species thrive in any reasonable soil in sun or light shade, but a few do better in more dense shade, and others in particularly well-drained soil in very sunny sites. All the euphorbias form a white milky sap, which can be dangerous when pruning or taking cuttings as it is an extreme irritant to the eyes, and can also cause skin sensitivity in a few people prone to allergies. The species can be propagated from seed, preferably sown as soon as ripe and kept cool through the winter, but some hybridization may occur between species in the garden. Cuttings will ensure that distinct forms are maintained, and although taking them is a messy procedure because of the sap, they seem to root quite easily if they are inserted into the cutting medium immediately, without any particular efforts to stop them 'bleeding'.

Several species and cultivars are clearly too tall to include in this book, and I have reluctantly omitted *E. altissima*, *E. characias* and *E. c.* subsp. *wulfenii* in most of their forms, along with *E. longifolia*, *E. mellifera*, *E. palustris* and *E. schillingii*. I have included one or two borderline species like *E. ceratocarpa* and *E. griffithii* and its cultivars, which vary greatly according to soil conditions.

E. acanthothamnos A dense rounded shrub to about 30 cm (1 ft), leaves 1 cm (0.4 in) long, oval, pale green, with woody spines protruding on the older growth, and a sprinkling of small flowers of the typical bright greenish-yellow. It should perhaps be excluded, as it is usually grown in a cold greenhouse, but in gardens where temperatures do not fall below 25 °C (-4 °F) it is suitable for a sunny border. Greece, Turkey.

E. amygdaloides Spreading colonies of upright reddish stems, leaves narrow oblanceolate, flowers in loose spires of yellowish-green, early to mid-summer and sometimes later. An excellent woodland plant, but shade is not essential if the soil is reasonably moist. Europe, S.W. Asia. *E. a.* 'Purpurea' (syn. 'Rubra') a most attractive variety with leaves and flowers deeply tinged with reddish-purple throughout the season, even in self-sown seedlings. 'Variegata', leaves margined cream. *E. a.* var. *robbiae* 🏆 Leaves darker green, broader, flowers more yellow in larger heads, more robust, often invasive except in the wild garden. It is useful to colonize dry shade.

E. anacampseros Resembles *E. myrsinites* in its prostrate habit, leaves similar on pinkish stems, branching heads of small deep, golden-yellow flowers, amid bright green fleshy bracts. A recent acquisition from Turkey, it has survived two winters outside in well-drained soil.

E. capitulata One of the smallest, a low carpet under 10 cm (4 in), densely leafy stems, leaves grey-green, obovate, flowers small yellow with purple glands and no bracts, in flat clusters. Balkans.

E. ceratocarpa ☼ Spreading clump, upright branching stems, reddish in their lower parts, leaves narrow lanceolate, pale green with conspicuous pale veins, flowers greenish-yellow, becoming green, in loose heads throughout summer. A beautiful but uncommon species, on our upper size limit. S. Italy.
E. characias 🏆 This popular species and its subspecies *wulfenii* and numerous cultivars, are generally over 1 m (3 ft) in height, but there are two cultivars that may remain below 75 cm (2.5 ft). 'Humpty Dumpty', compact bushy habit, good large heads of yellowish-green flowers with a red eye, just above the leaves. 'Portuguese Velvet', ✱ ☼ a fine recent arrival in gardens, leaves noticeably downy and blue-green, flower heads long but dense, pale green with purple glands in the centre of each flower.
E. coralloides Easily grown, clump-forming, to 60 cm (2 ft) or a little more, leaves narrow lanceolate, pink-tinged when young, terminal umbels of small yellow flowers amid green bracts. It frequently self-seeds, but not usually to excess. S. Italy.
E. cyparissias An attractive invasive weed, only suitable for wild areas, very drought tolerant. To 30 cm (1 ft), leaves small needle-like, bluish, terminal clusters of yellow flowers sometimes tinged with orange as they age. Europe. There are a few named cultivars which may prove less invasive, but they should still be sited with care: 'Bush Boy', more compact with branching feathery stems, 'Fens Ruby', a new small cultivar with bright reddish-purple new growth, quite invasive, 'Orange Man', persistently orange flowers on short stems, a good colour form if it can be kept within bounds, 'Tall Boy', taller and may attain 50 cm (20 in), and will probably spread as widely.
E. dulcis To 30 cm (1 ft), clumps of upright branched stems, leaves small green, oblanceolate, with reddish autumn tints, heads of greenish-yellow flowers. It is a pretty plant which seeds around excessively and can become a pest. Europe. 'Chameleon' ✱ ☼ Excellent deep purple foliage, and a purple tinge to the deeper yellow flowers. It is outstanding for any gardener who likes purple foliage on a very dainty plant. It colours best in full sun but never becomes really green even in shade. It self-sows less freely than the type and the seedlings seem to come true to colour.
E. griffithii A running perennial to 1 m (3 ft) in height in good soils but usually less, stiffly upright stems with abundant narrow lanceolate leaves with pinkish midribs, terminating in broad heads of orange flowers. One of the best of all euphorbias especially in the form of its superior cultivars. E. Himalaya. 'Dixter' 🏆 red stems and vivid orange-red flowers, the whole plant is suffused with purple, 'Firecharm' better known in the USA and resembling 'Dixter' closely, 'Fireglow' less spectacular than 'Dixter', with flowers of similar colour but with green leaves, 'Wickstead' less well-known and said to have well-coloured young growth and bright orange flowers.
E. hyberna To 45 cm (1.5 ft), leaves broadly lanceolate green with prominent veins, stems with flat-heads of yellowish-green flowers. Some forms acquire rosy autumn tints. It runs gently. W. Europe.

53 *Euphorbia dulcis* 'Chameleon' in front of *E. virgata*

E. jacquemontii Stems 30 cm (1 ft), broad green lanceolate leaves, small heads of green flowers A running plant which can get out of hand, producing scattered shoots over a wide area. W. Himalayas.
E. kotschyanus Bushy species allied to and possibly muddled with *E. macrostegia,* described below, both recently collected from Turkey. I have only seen unflowered specimens of this species, and the leaves seem much narrower.
E. macrostegia ✱ Broad bushy to 70 cm (28 in), leaves unusual, dark green, very glossy, ovate, pointed, very large loose heads of nodding cups, green in the early stages but quickly become deeply tinted with pink, especially in full sun, remaining in good condition for weeks in mid- to late summer. Turkey.
E. × martinii ✱ (*E. amygdaloides* × *E. characias*) Like a compact form of *E. characias*, a rounded bush, with large rather loose heads of green flowers with a conspicuous red centre. It is one of the best euphorbias, especially for smaller gardens.
E. myrsinites 🏆 Low mound of prostrate stems, to 30 cm (1 ft) long, leaves many, obovate pale blue-green, fleshy. In spring the tips of the stems turn up and produce broad flat-heads of typical greenish-yellow flowers. It is one of the finest species for the edge of a border in full sun. S. Europe.
E. nicaensis Upright or spreading plant to 40 cm (16 in), leaves broad, bluish grey-green, lanceolate, on stems which may be pink-flushed, flowers soft greenish-yellow in rounded heads. It is completely different from *E. seguiereana* subsp. *niciciana* (syn. *E. niciciana*). Europe.
E. oblongata Clump-former to 50 cm (20 in), flowers in

very large heads of greenish-yellow over an exceptionally long season in summer. It is very easy to grow and often self-seeds. It is sometimes confused with *E. polychroma*.

E. pilosa (syn. *E. villosa*) Clump-forming, leaves bright pale green, lanceolate, with conspicuous pale veins, on branching stems, flowers small yellowish-green, in abundant flat-heads. W. Himalayas.

E. pithyusa Clump-forming, to 40 cm (16 in), leaves abundant, very small, pale blue-green, domed heads of green flowers with yellow centres. S.E. Europe, N. Africa.

E. polychroma (syn *E. epithymoides*) 🏆 Dome-forming, leaves obovate, sometimes purple-tinged, entirely covered with heads of bright greenish-yellow flowers in late spring for many weeks. It is one of the finest species for a foreground position. S.E., C. Europe. Several excellent cultivars have been named: 'Emerald Jade', smaller with green flowers, colouring well in autumn, 'Major', large bright yellow flowers on a robust plant, 'Midas', another strong-growing cultivar with longer leaves and extra-large bright yellow bracts, 'Purpurea', popular cultivar, leaves purple-tinged, most noticeable in spring, flowers deeper yellow, 'Sonnengold', large bright yellow, 'Variegata', leaves variegated, less easy to grow.

E. pseudovirgata (syn *E. uralensis*) A spreader, to 60 cm (2 ft), leaves narrow lanceolate, flowers small yellowish-green in wide umbels, for a long time around mid-summer. An attractive dainty-looking species, but it may spread excessively in good conditions.

E. rigida ✱ ☼ (syn. *E. biglandulosa*) Semi-prostrate, resembling a large form of *E. myrsinites* with stems leaves and flower heads at least twice as large, stems often tinged pink, leaves pale grey-blue, flowers opening bright greenish-yellow, changing with age to orange and finally to red after several weeks. It is a striking foliage plant at all times, but after a hot summer the flowers develop very early in the year and persist into summer. It has an undeserved reputation for tenderness, certainly surviving to -10 °C (14 °F).

54 *Euphorbia rigida*

E. segueriana subsp. ***niciciana*** ✱ Densely clump-forming, to 30–40 cm (12–16 in), leaves short, linear blue-green, terminal broad umbels of greenish-yellow flowers during a long season in summer. It is one of the finest of the small-leaved species, easy in well-drained soil. Europe–Caucasus.

55 *Euphorbia seguieriana ssp. niciciana* with *Bupleurum spinosum* and *Geranium pratense* a 'Victor Ryder' seedling

E. spinosa Dense rounded mound of branching stems bearing very small light green lanceolate leaves and soft green spines, smothered in summer in tiny deep yellow flowers. It is an attractive foliage plant at all times, resembling *Bupleurum spinosum* but less obviously spiny, and has survived to -10 °C (14 °F) in my garden. C. Med.

E. virgata (syn. *E. waldsteinii*) (See plate 53) A running plant with narrow leaves on thin stems, flowers bright green, yellow-centred. Europe.

E. wallichii A late-flowering upright species, close to *E. schillingii* and *E. longifolia*, but usually to 70 cm (28 in) only; leaves lanceolate with a conspicuous pale central vein, flowers large, bright greenish-yellow, in late summer and autumn. Himalayas.

Euryops (*Compositae*)

A genus of mainly tender shrubs of moderate size from S. Africa, two of which are frequently planted, *E. acraeus* as a hardy plant for the rock garden, and *E. pectinatus* grown as a useful, easily propagated 'filler' in cold gardens, or as a permanent and large feature in frost-free areas. Both are fine foliage plants with large yellow daisy flowers as an added attraction. They need well-drained soil in a sunny sheltered position. They are easily propagated from cuttings in summer or early autumn.

E. acraeus 🏆 Small rounded bush, to 30 cm (1 ft), semi-woody stems, clusters of small linear leaves in a unique shade of pale silvery-blue, combining perfectly with the bright yellow daisy-flowers in early summer. In well-drained soil it survives to -10 °C (14 °F) or thereabouts.

E. pectinatus 🏆 Upright shrubby species, leaves grey-green with deeply incised margins, loose heads of bright yellow daisies on long petioles, in late summer. It only survives mild winters, say to -4 °C (25 °F), but may recover from the base. It is easily propagated by autumn cuttings, overwintered under glass, and these will make large enough plants to make a good showing in gaps in the border or in ornamental containers during the summer.

E. virgineus Upright to 60 cm (2 ft), pale green leafy stems, small yellow daisy flowers in abundant loose heads for weeks in autumn. Probably a little hardier than the last. A very showy plant although the flowers are small.

F

Fascicularia (*Bromeliaceae*)

A fascinating genus of moderately hardy bromeliads, of which two are in general cultivation. They make large rosettes of stiff, leathery, dark-green leaves, with spiny margins. The inner parts surrounding the flowers turn deep crimson during the flowering period, making a striking contrast to the wide centre of many small pale blue flowers. In the mild gardens of Cornwall and the Scillies they grow exuberantly and self-sow, but even in colder conditions they are worth growing, in a warm sheltered position, preferably planted on their sides in sunny retaining walls. They have survived to -6 °C (21 °F) for several years in my garden in Kent. They may be propagated from seed, usually only set in warm gardens. Chile.

F. bicolor Probably the hardier species, leaves to 50 cm (20 in) with brown-scaly backs, outer bracts longer than the flowers.

F. pitcairniifolia Leaves to 1 m (3 ft) long, whitish beneath, bracts shorter than the flowers.

Felicia (*Compositae*)

A genus of annuals and frost-tender perennials from S. Africa, the latter characterized by their extremely prolific, usually bright blue, daisy-flowers, produced over a very long season. In mild gardens with temperatures not falling below-3 °C (27 °F) they are excellent perennials for a sunny border, flowering for most of the summer. They are easily propagated from cuttings, which can be overwintered under glass in colder areas, and rapidly make good plants for containers, put outside in early summer, or for filling gaps in the border.

F. amelloides (syn. *Agathea coelestis*) Rounded bushy, semi-woody, usually to 30 cm (1 ft), leaves sessile ovate, masses of solitary clear blue flowers to 3 cm (1.2 in) diameter, from early summer to autumn. There are several cultivars: 'Read's Blue', larger flowers with yellow centres, 'Read's White', similar with white yellow-centred flowers, 'Santa Anita', 🏆 much larger leaves and larger blue flowers, 'Santa Anita Variegated', 🏆 an excellent foliage plant with cream-variegated leaves and large flowers, 'Variegata', similar in leaf size and flower to the type, leaves cream-edged.

F. amoena More compact than *A. amellus*, leaves narrower, bright pale blue flowers all through the summer. There is a variegated cultivar, *F. a.* 'Variegata'.

F. petiolatus (syn. *Aster petiolatus*) Low shrublet, leaves small, lanceolate, toothed, downy, solitary clear pink daisies on long stalks intermittently during summer. It is one of the hardiest and will survive very mild winters outside.

F. rosulatus (syn. *Aster pappei, A natalensis*) Slowly spreading, rosettes of broad elliptic, very hairy leaves, upright stems with a few narrow leaves, solitary large pale blue flowers to 3 cm (1.2 in) wide. It is a very hardy species which will survive to -6 °C (21 °F).

F. uliginosa Low mat-forming with prostrate stems and small linear leaves, flowers pale lavender, not usually in any abundance.

Fibigia (*Cruciferae*)

A few perennials, of which two are cultivated, mainly for their attractive silver-grey foliage and ornamental fruits, rather than their typical small yellow crucifer flowers. They are easily grown in well-drained soil in full sun, and seem to be long-lived. They are easily raised from seed.

F. clypeata Clump-forming, stems branching, upright, leaves grey-hairy, oval-lanceolate, untoothed, flowers small in dense clusters in early summer, becoming long spikes of very attractive large grey, flattened oval fruits, remaining in good condition for several weeks. Europe-Iran.

F. erythrocarpa Similar to *F. clypeata* but with narrower toothed leaves. Rarely seen in gardens.

Fragaria (*Rosaceae*)

The strawberries are not usually grown as ornamental plants for the border, with the exception of the recently introduced 'Pink Panda', and occasionally the variegated cultivars which can be used as ground-cover in light shade. They can be propagated by rooting runners.

F.* x *ananassa The cultivated strawberry has a cultivar 'Variegata' with leaves blotched and streaked with cream.

'Pink Panda' A new cultivar like a Strawberry except in its flowers, large bright rose-pink with a yellow centre, appearing intermittently through the summer. It grows well in partial shade but its long runners cover a lot of ground very loosely; the flowers are too scattered to have much impact.

F. vesca The wild strawberry has a similar cultivar, 'Variegata', with smaller and more spreading runners.

Francoa (*Saxifragaceae*)

A genus of very beautiful perennials with heuchera-like leaves and slender spikes of long-lasting white to pink flowers in summer. There is some doubt whether the species on offer are in fact varieties of one species. They have an unnecessarily bad reputation for tenderness, or for failing to survive wet winters. A group in my garden has come unscathed through the last five winters, although these have been wetter than usual, and temperatures have been less than -6 °C (21 °F) on several occasions.

F. ramosa Similar to *F. sonchifolia*, looser spikes to 60 cm (2 ft), flowers white or very pale pink spotted with deeper pink.

F. sonchifolia ✱ Spreading clumps, to 50 cm (20 in), leaves dark green hairy, pinnately divided with the lobes broader towards the apex, flowers deep pink in dense terminal spikes, very long lasting, on slender flowering stems. The commonest species in cultivation, possibly muddled with the last, with intermediates often seen.

G

Gaillardia (*Compositae*)

A genus of many annuals and a few perennials, of which only *G.* x *grandiflora* is grown regularly, with several cultivars. They are among the brightest of all border plants, from 40–70 cm (16–28 in) high, producing very large daisy flowers in mid-summer, in shades of bright yellow or red, often bicoloured, above clumps of lobed or pinnate hairy leaves, with toothed margins. The flowers are long-lasting on the plant and when cut, but the plants themselves need staking in the garden. They are very floriferous but often short-lived, especially in heavy rich soils. The cultivars are propagated from root cuttings.

G. aristata One parent of the Croftway hybrids, the species is occasionally grown, leaves softly hairy, greyish-green, pinnate, flowers 10 cm (4 in) wide, deep yellow with a reddish centre.

G* x *grandiflora A range of hybrids between *G. aristata* and the annual *G. pulchella*: 'Aurea Plena', double deep yellow; 'Bremen', scarlet with yellow tips; 'Burgunder', deep purplish-red; 'Croftway', uniform deep yellow; 'Dazzler', orange red with deep red centre; 'Firebrand', coppery-red; 'Goldkobold (Golden Goblin)' deep yellow with darker centre, low; 'Ipswich Beauty', orange with brown centre; 'Kobold (Goblin)' red with yellow tips, low; 'Mandarin', reddish-orange with gold tips; 'Wirral Flame', deep red with paler tips.

Galax (*Diapensiaceae*)

G. urceolata (syn. *G. aphylla*) The only species, a creeping woodlander from N.E. USA, large evergreen glossy round leaves, usually developing good reddish tints in autumn, cordate at the base, with sparsely toothed margins, slender spikes, to 30 cm (1 ft), of tiny white flowers opening from greenish buds in summer. It is an excellent foliage plant with intriguing flowers, for humus-rich acid soil among rhododendrons or other acid-loving shrubs, or at the edge of a shady border.

Galium (*Rubiaceae*) (Woodruff, Bedstraw)

A genus of invasive herbs, not generally suitable for the flower garden, but the species described is a good wild garden plant in shade.

G. odoratum (Sweet Woodruf) Leaves scented and used in pot-pourri, invasive carpeter, with whorls of small pale green leaves, and myriads of tiny white flowers in summer. It associates well in the shady wild garden with vigorous ferns, lamiums, solomon's seals, dicentras, etc.

Gaura (*Onagraceae*)

Only one species is widely grown, *G. lindheimeri*, and this may be too tall in good conditions, but it is frequently around 70 cm (28 in) high or a little less.

G. lindheimeri 🏆 Loosely clump-forming, leaves simple, lanceolate, stems upright, flowers white or pale pink, with four spreading petals above a cluster of long stamens, from red calyces, in slender graceful spires. It is a beautiful, graceful plant for sun or light shade in good soil. There is some variability in flower colour with some cultivars definitely pinker than others. 'Corries Gold', very attractive cream-edged leaves, 'Jo Adela', similarly variegated, 'Whirling Butterflies', to 70 cm (28 in) only, with pure white flowers and red calyces.

Gazania (*Compositae*)

Low-growing annuals and more-or-less frost-tender perennials with many cultivars. They are generally grown as 'bedding plants' in Britain, propagated in autumn from cuttings, overwintered under glass, and planted out in late spring in containers or at the margins of sunny borders In nearly frost-free sunny gardens, in well-drained soil, they make excellent very colourful perennial edging plants. Their leaves may be green or a very good silver; their outstandingly large daisy flowers in a wide range of colours, from white through cream to orange and reddish-purple, often with a darker band or centre.

The following is a selection of the many species and cultivars available. One suspects that some of the names are muddled.

Name	Leaves	Flowers
'Bicton Orange'	Green	Orange
'Cookei' 🏆	Grey	Bronze
'Cream Beauty'	Grey-green	Cream
'Cream & Purple'	Silver	Cream and purple blend
'Flash'	Silver	Orange with blackish ring
G. krebsiana	Grey	Smaller, pale yellow with darker band and dark centre
'Magenta'	Green	Reddish-purple with green band
'Orange Beauty'	Grey-green	Deep orange
'Red Velvet'	Green	Deep red
G. rigens	Green with white reverse	Orange with black basal spot
G. r. 'Aureovariegata'	Green and gold variegated	Gold
G. r. uniflora	Greyish-white	All yellow
'*G. r.* 'Variegata' 🏆	Cream & yellow variegated	Orange with black basal spot
'Silver Beauty'	Silver	Pale yellow
'Slate' ✱	Silver	Blend of Purple and cream
'Yellow Buttons'	Green with white reverse	Small double yellow

Gentiana (*Gentianaceae*)

A large and variable genus, including many superb perennials which can offer unique shades of pure blue, from tiny and sometimes difficult treasures for the rock garden and alpine house, to statuesque plants for the back of the border. Which to include here is a problem, as the most striking are generally considered to be alpines, and yet many are sufficiently vigorous to use as a brilliant edging to borders in sun or partial shade. In addition to the larger-growing plants, I have therefore included a selection of the most reliable easy smaller species, including both *G. acaulis* and some of its allies for spring flowering, and *G. sino-ornata* and some of the many similar species for autumn flowering. Most of the former will grow in neutral or slightly alkaline soils, whereas most of the latter must have acid soil. The species can be grown from seed which is best kept as cold as possible during the winter. The cultivars can be divided or their young growths taken as cuttings in spring.

G. acaulis (syn. *G. kochiana*) 🏆 Spreading mat-forming to 5 cm (2 in), leaves small lanceolate or elliptic, flowers erect tubular to 6 cm (2.3 in) long, with spreading lobes, deep blue in colour with greenish spots within. This is the classic spring-flowering gentian of the Alps, incomparable when it flowers freely, but sometimes not free. It is easy to grow, planted in rich but well-drained soil in sun; flowering seems to be improved by very firm planting in soil enriched by rotted manure. 'Alba', pure white. 'Coelestina', Cambridge blue. There are several other named cultivars, varying in leaf shape, and colour, shape and markings of the flowers, but a recent Trial by the RHS suggests that their names are hopelessly muddled. See them flowering in a nursery or a friend's garden and pick the most floriferous. Europe.

G. andrewsii Clump-forming to 50 cm (20 in), leaves pointed lanceolate, terminal clusters of up to 5 purplish-blue trumpet flowers. E., N. Am.

G. angustifolia Acaulis group, leaves narrow, lobes narrow with ascending tips.

G. asclepiadea 🏆 Willow gentian, a spectacular large clump-forming plant, leaves abundant, lanceolate, on upright or arching stems, to 60 cm (2 ft) or considerably more, flowers numerous, brilliant blue, 4 cm (1.6 in) long, in the axils of the upper leaves, in late summer over a long period. In ideal conditions of well-drained, very rich moist acid soil in partial shade it seeds around freely, and can become very large, but in drier gardens it keeps within the range suggested. C. Europe–Caucasus. 'Alba', white and blue fine white which contrasts very effectively with the blue and seems to come true from seed. 'Knightshayes', usually a little shorter, flowers blue with a conspicuous white throat, 'Nymans', more arching habit and heavily spotted flowers, 'Phyllis', flowers paler blue, 'Rosea', bluish-pink.

56 *Gentiana asclepiadea* white and blue

G. clusii *G. acaulis* group. Leaves hard-tipped, flowers with pointed lobes not spreading. S.E. Europe.
G. cruciata Tufted, leaves broad ovate on semi-prostrate stems, flowers in clusters of several, 2 cm (0.8 in) long, with greenish-blue tubes and brighter blue spreading lobes, in late summer. It is rather leafy for the flower size, but easy in most soils. Europe–Siberia.
G. dinarica *G. acaulis* group. Flowers with no green spots, and narrow pointed lobes. S., S.E. Europe.
G. pneumonanthe Marsh Gentian Small clumps of upright or arching stems to 30 cm (1 ft), clusters of purplish-blue flowers with green lines on the outside in the upper leaf axils, in late summer. It is not very easy, requiring moist soil. Europe.
G. punctata Rather coarse, to 50 cm (20 in), leaves broad, terminal clusters of bell-shaped yellowish flowers with purple spots in late summer. Alps.
G. purpurea Similar to *G. punctata*, flowers pale reddish-purple, with darker reddish spots. C. Europe–Norway.
G. scabra Small clumps, leaves lanceolate, stems upright branching, flowers solitary, narrow blue or purplish, in late summer and autumn. E. Asia.
G. septemfida 🏆 Mat-forming, stems 15–20 cm (6–8 in) long, prostrate or semi-erect, leaves lanceolate to ovate, deep blue trumpets to 4 cm (1.6 in) long, in terminal clusters and in the upper leaf axils in summer. It is one of the easiest to grow, and will tolerate some lime. *G. s.* var. *lagodechiana* 🏆 More prostrate, fewer flowers to each cluster.
G. sino-ornata 🏆 Mat-forming, clusters of semi-prostrate shoots, densely furnished with small narrow leaves, from a persistent, easily divided rootstock; flowers solitary, deep blue in great abundance for several weeks in autumn. It is the most widely grown of a number of similar species and hybrids, all of which need rich moist, acid soil, in partial shade in dry areas, or in full sun in cooler gardens. They are very easily propagated by division in spring before the shoots elongate, and produce a spectacular effect in good conditions. *G. s. alba*, white flowers tinged with green. A selection of other similar species, cultivars, and hybrids, which are easy and can be used in the same way, are described briefly below. 'Angel's Wings', variable, large blue, white, or striped, 'Bernardii', very dark blue, 'Blue Bonnets', sky-blue, white throat, 'Brin Form', deep blue, 'Drake's Strain', short broad, sky-blue, 'Edinburgh' 🏆 mid-blue, 'Edith Sarah', deep blue, striped white, 'Inverleith' 🏆 rich deep blue, 'Kidbrooke Seedling', large, deep blue, 'Kingfisher', large, deep blue, x *macaulayi* 🏆 deep blue, 'Mary Lisle', white tinged blue, 'Royal Highlander', bright blue, several flowers to a stem, x *stevenagensis* 🏆 deep purplish-blue, 'Strathmore', sky-blue, striped silver outside, 'Susan Jane', greenish-blue with white throat, 'Wells Variety', pale blue.
G. trichotoma Clump-forming, leaves narrow lanceolate, upright branching stems to 60 cm (2 ft), small clusters of bright deep blue flowers in the upper leaf axils in summer. It is a promising reintroduction from China.
G. triflora Clumps of lanceolate leaves, branching stems, spikes of narrowly bell-shaped, deep blue flowers streaked on the outside with white. Japan.

Geranium (*Geraniaceae*)

One of the most important of all genera of small and medium-sized perennials for the open garden, with a huge range of species and hybrids for ground-cover and woodland and shady borders, and a few for sheltered sunny positions and the rock garden or alpine house. They vary greatly in habit from small cushions or low mats to 1 m (3 ft) high clumps, usually with a rosette or tuft of palmately divided leaves with further toothed or lobed divisions, and tight umbels or spreading panicles of 5-petalled flowers, upward-facing or nodding, varying in colour from white to deepest magenta, often with conspicuous veining. The flowering period is mainly from late spring until late summer.

In general the hardy geraniums are easy to grow in any reasonable soils, favouring those with plenty of humus; the majority thrive in partial or even deep shade. Many species are ideal for ground-cover, running freely and rooting down as they go, but care is needed with these to keep them away from more precious and smaller plants. They grow well between larger shrubs such as rhododendrons, and the smaller species make an ideal edging to a mixed border. A few species are slightly tender and need a sheltered, sunny position in well-drained soil to survive the winter, but these often keep going by self-sowing, even when the parent plants die.

The species can usually be raised from seed, preferably sown when fresh, and kept cool in winter. The hybrids and selected cultivars should be propagated by division, or from cuttings. These are best taken from young growths as soon as they become long enough in spring, as they can become much more difficult to root later.

In the list that follows I have excluded annuals, biennials, and the species definitely needing rock garden or alpine house treatment.
G. albanum Scrambling evergreen, leaves rounded, divided to half way, 8–9 lobes coarsely toothed, long prostrate stem,

loose heads of flowers 2 cm (0.8 in) wide, bright pink minimally notched, paler in the centre and conspicuously veined with purple. Not spectacular, but an easy plant for the border or ground-cover, and will clamber into shrubs. Caucasus, Iran.

G. albiflorum Like *G. sylvaticum*, to 40 cm (16 in), stems branching, purple, leaves deeply divided, rounded, lobes deeply toothed, flowers small white or pale purple, petals notched and violet-veined. An uncommon species. C., N. Asia.

***G.* 'Ann Folkard'** (*G. procurrens* x *G. psilostemon*) ✸ Spreading scrambling plant with prostrate stems, leaves yellowish-green, flowers large, deep magenta with a black eye, all through the summer. A superb hybrid which never roots down like *G. procurrens*, but clambers through nearby shrubs or other perennials, in sun or light shade, looking particularly fine with euphorbias or the yellow-leaved hostas.

57 *Geranium Ann Folkard & Hosta Frances Williams*

G. aristatum To 60 cm (2 ft), leaves coarsely lobed, hairy, grey-green, toothed, loose heads of flowers similar to those of *G. phaeum*, larger, with reflexed pale mauve petals, deeper at the base and heavily veined with deep mauve. An excellent easy plant with a long flowering period. S.E. Europe.

G. asphodelioides Variable, large clump-forming. *G. a.* subsp. *ashodelioides* leaves rounded, sharply divided to at least 2–3, flowers small white or pale pink, long narrow petals with darker veining, in broad loose heads. S. Europe. Subsp. *crenophilum* differs in having broader-petalled deep pink flowers. Subsp. *sintenisii* leaves with narrower lobes, red-tipped hairs on the leaves and sepals, flowers many, usually pale pink, smaller than those of the type. These are excellent plants for a sunny border. Two cultivars: 'Prince Regent', flowers purplish-pink, darkly veined, 'Starlight', pure white.

G. canariense Rosettes of large leaves on a 'trunk' above ground, 40 cm (16 in), leaves divided to the base into 3–5, the divisions with many toothed lobes, flowers in dense heads, deep pink paling at the base. It is a splendid species for a sheltered sunny spot, resembling *G. palmatum* but more tender. Canary Is.

G.* x *cantabrigiense (*G. macrorrhizum* x *G. dalmaticum*) Intermediate in habit and leaf form between the parents, flowers like those of *G. dalmaticum*. Two clones are commonly cultivated: 'Cambridge', dense carpet of pale green leaves with profuse purplish-pink flowers. 'Biokovo', looser-growing, white flowers tinged faintly with pink at the base, 'St Ola', fine white unmarked flowers. They make excellent low ground-cover or border edging.

G. cinereum Small cushion-forming, attractive rosettes of greenish-grey deeply cut leaves, sprays of a few soft pink flowers finely veined with deep pink, and with a paler greenish centre. This describes *G. c.* var. *cinereum* Generally looked upon as excellent rock garden plants, *G. cinereum* and its varieties have sufficient vigour to be used at the edge of a sunny border in well-drained soil. They frequently self-sow and hybridize with each other. Pyrenees. 'Album', pure white. *G. c.* var. *subcaulescens* 🏆 Very vigorous, leaves dull green, flowers large, deep magenta veined with dark red, with a black centre. A dramatic plant when its large cushions are completely covered in flowers; it contrasts magnificently with silver or grey foliage, for example of *Artemisia* 'canescens'. E. Europe, Turkey. It seems to be variable and some clones have been named. 'Guiseppii', flowers softer in colour, darker in the centre but lacking the central black area, 'Splendens', 🏆 less harsh in colour, with white margins to the base of the broad petals. 'Ballerina' (Var. *cinereum* x var. *subcaulescens*), similar to the former in habit but usually stronger-growing and more persistent, flowers beautifully marked, pale pink, heavily veined with violet-purple, and with a dark centre of similar colour, 'Lawrence Flatman', the same parentage and very similar, flowers darker, more vigorous.

58 *Geranium cinereum var. subcaulescens* with *Artemisia alba* 'Canescens' & *Silene uniflora*

G. clarkei Spreading rhizomatous species allied to *G. pratense*, to 50 cm (20 in), growth more lax and spreading, leaves similar, deeply divided to the base, with narrow lobes, similar heads of upward-facing flowers, variable in colour, usually white with pale purplish veins, or deep purple. It can spread vigorously in good conditions in partial shade, and should not be allowed to overwhelm smaller plants. Kashmir. Several cultivars have been named. 'Kashmir Blue', strong-growing, pale blue, 'Kashmir Pink', large pale pink, 'Kashmir Purple', purple, 'Kashmir White' (syn. *G. rectum* 'Album') white.
G. collinum Bushy to 40 cm (16 in), leaves sharply toothed, with narrow lobes, loose heads of rather small pale to dark pink flowers with faint darker veining. An easy plant but not one of the most spectacular. S. Europe, Asia.
G. dalmaticum 🏆 Dense carpet, leaves small rounded, glossy, deeply cut into wedge-shaped divisions, flowers pink with a conspicuous boss of red-tipped stamens, and reddish calyces, in compact heads. 'Album', white, usually faintly tinged pink. These are excellent long-lived plants for a sunny position in well-drained soil. S.E. Europe.
***G.* 'Dilys'** ✱ Low carpeting plant, leaves deeply divided with pointed lobes, flowers deep purplish-pink in profusion over a very long season from mid-summer to autumn. It is an exceptionally good new hybrid for sun or partial shade.

59 *Geranium* 'Dilys'

G. endressii 🏆 Spreading rhizomatous, leaves deeply lobed on prostrate or semi-upright stems, masses of good-sized clear pink flowers over a long period. It is one of the most reliable and floriferous species, in sun or light shade but it can take up a lot of space. Pyrenees. 'Wargrave Pink', has paler pink flowers and is less vigorous.
G. erianthum Clump-forming to 50 cm (20 in), leaves deeply divided into overlapping sharply toothed lobes, compact heads of a few pale to deep lilac-purple flowers with light to dark veining and almost black anthers. A variable species not widely grown but not apparently difficult in a woodland situation. 'Calm Sea', beautiful tall cultivar, very pale blue, darker-veined flowers, 'Neptune', darker blue and very robust. E. Asia.
G. eriostemon *See* ***G. platyanthum***
G. fremontii Clump-forming, thick woody rootstock often partially above ground, leaves coarsely lobed, upright stems bearing loose branching heads of flat flowers, deep to pale pink with paler centres and some darker veining. It grows best in sun but often dies off in patches. S.W. USA.
G. gracile Similar to *G. nodosum*, to 40 cm (16 in), leaves deeply divided into 5, the divisions unlobed but toothed, flowers similar, funnel-shaped, deeply-veined pink. It is an easy plant, less invasive than *G. nodosum*. Turkey-Caucasus.
G. himalayense Spreading, rhizomatous to 40 cm (16 in), a dense carpet of deeply divided leaves with broad toothed lobes, loose heads of exceptionally large cup-shaped deep blue flowers. Himalayas. It is one of the finest species for ground cover, with several named cultivars: 'Gravetye' (syn. *E. h. alpinum*) 🏆 More compact, flowers even larger with a deeper purple centre, 'Irish Blue', flowers smaller and paler with a dark centre, 'Plenum' (syn. 'Birch Double') less vigorous, leaves smaller, flowers small double, pinkish-purple.
G. ibericum subsp. ***ibericum*** Clump-forming to 50 cm (20 in), leaves hairy, deeply divided, with many lobes, toothed, dense heads of shallowly cup-shaped, upward-facing flowers, pinkish violet with darker veining. Subsp. *jubatum* differs in having glandular hairs on the pedicels. They are good easily grown in sun or light shade. Caucasus, Turkey.
***G.* 'Johnson's Blue'** 🏆 (*G. himalayense* x *G. pratense*) Creeping clump-forming, similar to *G. himalayense* but taller, branching heads of large deep lavender-blue flowers, paler towards the base, produced over a very long period. It is one of the finest of the larger hybrids, and flourishes in sun or shade.
***G.* 'Joy'** ✱ Spreading dense carpet, to 30 cm (1 ft), leaves small rounded, divided, greyish-green, flowers in great abundance, soft purplish, outward-facing, with violet veining. It is an outstanding new hybrid.
G. kishtvariense Bushy rhizomatous, leaves deeply divided, toothed, heads of several deep rose-purple flowers with dark veining and white markings at the base of the petals, and dark anthers. It is a fairly recent introduction from the Himalaya, which is proving easy in gardens and not invasive. Kashmir.
G. lambertii Lax trailing plant to 40 cm (16 in), leaves 5-lobed, toothed, loose heads of pendent flowers, white or palest pink with maroon veining at the base and conspicuous maroon anthers. It is a beautiful species which will clamber into surrounding plants, in sun or partial shade. Himalaya.
G. libani Summer-dormant, clump-forming, leaves deeply divided into 5 lobes, notched and toothed, flowers violet-blue with notched petals, in late spring. It is a lovely plant for a warm sunny position in well-drained soil.
***G.* 'Little Gem'** Low growing, spreading gradually, leaves small glossy cut to the mid-point and shallowly lobed, small loose heads of comparatively large flowers of an unusual very

bright shade of purplish-pink, with a hint of magenta. A new hybrid that promises to be an excellent low carpeter for the front of the border.

G. macrorhizum Densely carpet-forming to 30 cm (1 ft), leaves sticky, aromatic, compact heads of flowers over a long period, variable in colour, usually deep purplish-pink or white with red calyces and red anthers. It is one of the best low ground-cover plants, very easy in sun or shade. S. Europe. Several excellent cultivars have been named: 'Album', 🏆 one of the best, white contrasting well with the red calyces, 'Bevan's Variety', the darkest with deep magenta flowers, 'Czakor', lower-growing, deep magenta flowers with darker calyces, 'Ingwersen's Variety', 🏆 leaves pale green, glossy, flowers pale pink, 'Lohfelden', more compact and low-growing, very pale pink with darker veining and orange anthers on red filaments, 'Pindus', similar in habit to 'Lohfelden' but broad-petalled reddish-purple flowers, 'Spessart', white, but the name is sometimes applied to a deep magenta cultivar, 'Variegatum', leaves splashed with cream, but rarely seems (to me) very effective, 'Velebit', similar to 'Pindus' but with narrow widely-spaced petals.

G. maculatum Loosely clump-forming to 70 cm (28 in), leaves sparse, deeply divided into narrow, toothed lobes, heads of several soft pink flowers, paler in the centre, in late spring and early summer. It does well in moist soils. *G. m. albiflorum* excellent white flowered form. N.E. USA.

G. maderense 🏆 The largest species, very large rosettes of deeply divided lobed glossy leaves, on a thick reddish stem which becomes elongated into a considerable 'trunk' during the two or more years to flowering, the flowers purplish-pink deepening to violet in the centre, in a very large, dense head. It is a magnificent plant, but only suitable for the greenhouse or mild gardens, as it requires at least two mild winters to achieve flowering size. It usually dies after flowering, setting plenty of seed, but likely to hybridize with *G. palmatum* if that is also grown. Madeira.

60 *Geranium maderense* in a hot corner with *Euphorbia mellifera*

G.* x *magnificum (*G. ibericum* x *G.platypetalum*) 🏆 Very similar to *G. ibericum*, sterile hybrid, flowers deep bluish-purple, veined. It is one of the best and easiest to grow, and will cover a considerable area.

G. malviflorum Clump-forming, leaves divided almost to the base, pinnately lobed towards the apex; compact clusters of bluish-purple flowers, with some white at the base and dark veining, in late spring or early summer. It is a tuberous-rooted species allied to *G. tuberosum* but strong-growing enough for the border in well-drained soil. S. Spain, N. Africa

G.* x *monacense (*G. phaeum* x *G. reflexum*) Intermediate in habit, leaves blotched or unblotched, flowers similar with reflexed petals, reddish-purple, with a distinct white ring at the base and a deep violet-purple band above it. 'Muldoon', a cultivar with heavily purple-blotched leaves, var. *anglicum*, leaves unblotched, flowers with minimal white at the base and a broader dark band.

G. nervosum Very variable in height and leaf shape, leaves sticky, hairy, widely lobed, broad heads of purplish-pink flowers with notched, darkly veined petals. N. USA.

G. nodosum Spreading rhizomatous, to 30 cm (1 ft), leaves deeply divided, glossy, toothed but not lobed, flowers funnel-shaped, pale to deep pink, conspicuous darker veining, in loose heads. It grows very easily even in poor dry conditions, and can spread excessively by seed and by its rhizomes. S. Europe. Cultivars are sometimes offered, differing mainly in depth of colour e.g. 'dark form' and 'pale form', 'Svelte Lilac', dark-veined lilac, paler in the centre, 'Swish Purple', deep purple with white eyes, 'Whiteleaf', a particularly good dark-flowered selection, the petals paler at the margins.

G. oreganum Similar to *G. pratense*, less vigorous, leaves similar, loose heads of large, deep pink, upward-facing flowers with white centres. It seems easy in partial shade. W. USA.

G. orientaltibeticum Low spreading carpeter, leaves deeply divided with narrow lobes, conspicuously marbled with cream, flowers rich pink with white centres. Its propensity for spread belies its small size and it can overwhelm small rock plants. China.

G.* x *oxonianum (*G. endressii* x *G. versicolor*) Variable fertile hybrid, robust, usually taller than its parents, leaves broadly lobed, sometimes blotched with brown, flowers larger in shades of pink and usually veined. Several cultivars are offered in catalogues: 'A.T. Johnson', 🏆 more compact than *G. endressii*, flowers a beautiful clear silvery pink, 'Claridge Druce', one of the most popular, a tall strong-growing cultivar, shallowly funnel-shaped, rose-pink veined flowers with notched petals, 'Hollywood', pale pink with particularly dark veining, 'Prestbury White' ('Prestbury Blush'), white tinged faintly with palest pink, 'Rose Clair', purplish-pink with faint veining but the name is in some doubt, 'Southcombe Double', small double pink flowers with petaloid stamens, 'Thurstonianum', a curiosity, petals very narrow, deep purplish-pink, white at the base, 'Wargrave Pink', 🏆 clear pink 'Winscombe', similar to *G. endressii*, very variable in colour on any one plant, from almost white to deep pink as they age, some veining appearing in older flowers.

G. palmatum 🏆 Similar to *G. maderense* and often offered in its place, it differs in having a much less developed 'trunk' beneath the rosette of leaves, and in having large, very diffuse heads of purplish-pink flowers, over a very long period of summer. It is considerably more hardy, and makes a striking feature in a sheltered sunny border, self seeding freely. On the rare occasions when old plants are killed by frost, with temperatures below -15 °C (6 °F), young self-sown seedlings soon take over. Madeira.

61 *Geranium palmatum*

G. palustre Loose bushy, to 40 cm (16 in), leaves lobed with a few teeth, loose heads of purplish-pink faintly veined flowers. C., S. Europe.
***G.* 'Patricia'** ✱ A new hybrid, large mounds of foliage with abundant branching heads of bright magenta flowers with dark centres. It is a very promising plant with similar colouring to *G. cinereum* var. *subcaulescens* and *G. psilostemon*, but intermediate in size.
G. phaeum (Black Widow) Clump-forming to 70 cm (28 in), leaves with 7–9 shallowly cut toothed lobes, often stained purple, profuse one-sided heads of nodding flat flowers, typically deep blackish-purple (var. *phaeum*) or pink (var. *lividum*), usually with white at the base. It is easily grown in the shade, and may flower again after its mid-summer flush. Several cultivars have been named: 'Album', pure white, as robust as the type, 'Joan Baker', excellent, tall with large reddish-purple flowers, 'Langthorn's Blue', flowers violet-blue, 'Lily Lovell', popular cultivar, leaves pale green, flowers large deep mauve, 'Majus', large-flowered, pink, 'Mourning Widow', particularly dark flowers 'Samobor', ✱ very fine foliage plant with strikingly brown-blotched leaves, 'Variegatum', leaves blotched purple, edged and splashed cream.
G. platyanthum (? syn. *G. eriostemon*) Clump-forming to 50 cm (20 in), leaves hairy, cut to half way and shallowly lobed, large dense pyramidal heads of pale violet outward-facing flowers. It is a good easy species for a shady place. E. Asia.
G. platypetalum Clump-forming to 40 cm (16 in), leaves hairy rough, divided to the middle and toothed, dense heads of deep purplish-blue flowers, often over a long period. Turkey, Caucasus.
G. pogonanathum Mound-forming with a very thick rootstock, partially above ground, stems clambering, loose branching heads of pink flowers with recurving petals. It is an attractive species but not very free to increase. China.
G. pratense (Meadow Cranesbill) Upright plant to 80 cm (30 in) or more, leaves deeply divided, narrow-lobed, large heads of 4 cm (1.6 in) wide outward-facing flowers, in shades of lilac-blue to purple and white. It is one of the best species for the border or for the wild garden, in sun or light shade, with a number of cultivars, of which the following are a selection. Europe–E. Asia. *G. p. f. albiflorum*, pure white, 'Galactic', excellent milky white, strong-growing, 'Mrs Kendall Clark', 🏆 probably the most popular, vigorous, large heads of silvery-lilac flowers with pale veining, 'Plenum Album', double white, 'Plenum Caeruleum', double pale lilac, 'Plenum Violaceum', 🏆 very fine double dark blue-violet, 'Rose Queen', outstanding, palest, pink-veined with purple, and orange anthers, 'Silver Queen', large, white, faintly tinged with palest violet, and black anthers, 'Victor Ryder', good reddish-purple leaves and blue flowers (see plate 55).
G. procurrens Viciously spreading carpeter with long trailing stems rooting deeply at every node, and a scattering of deep purple heavily veined flowers. The flowers are an attractive colour and it is proving a good parent, but in many gardens, including my own, it has become a menace, difficult to remove without weed-killers. Himalayas.
G. psilostemon 🏆 Large bushy to 1 m (3 ft), leaves deeply cut, narrow-lobed, toothed, large branching heads of deep magenta flowers with a black centre and black veining. It is a first-class large plant for the border. Turkey. The cultivar 'Bressingham Flair' is more compact and has less strident paler flowers.
G. pulchrum Shrubby to 1 m (3 ft), leaves silvery hairy, deeply cut, branching heads of pale pink flowers. It is not widely grown and its hardiness is in some doubt. S. Africa.
G. pylzowianum Low-growing, spreading, leaves deeply divided, narrow-lobed, loose heads of purplish-pink flowers, not always freely produced. Vigorous enough for the edge of the border. W. China.
G. reflexum Similar to *G. phaeum*, flowers smaller, petals more reflexed. S. Europe.
G. renardii 🏆 Mound forming to 25 cm (10 in) high with attractive grey-green, shallowly lobed leaves, and numerous dense heads of white flowers heavily veined with pale grey-violet. It is one of the finest species with unique foliage, very long-lived without spreading excessively. Caucasus. *G. R.* 'Whiteknights', equally attractive, differing in its pale blue flowers veined with dark blue, making a looser plant. 'Philippe Vapelle', a hybrid with *G. platypetalum*, very similar in habit and leaf but with deep purplish-blue flowers.

62 *Geranium renardii* 'Phillippe Vapelle'

G. richardsonii Clump-forming to 50 cm (20 in), leaves deeply divided with pointed lobes, loose heads of flowers, variable in colour, usually pure white with a greenish centre, but occasionally pink. The best white forms are very beautiful. W., N. America.
G.* x *riversleaianum ✱ *G. endressii* x *G. traversii*) Low-growing carpeters with deeply divided hairy leaves, and abundant flowers over a long period. They are fine easy plants which have always proved hardy in my garden but might be expected to be tender in temperatures approaching -18 °C (0 °F). Several clones have been named: 'Mavis Simpson', ✱ beautiful broad dense carpet, smothered in clear pale pink flowers, paler in the centre and faintly veined, 'Russel Pritchard', one of the most popular, similar in habit with large deep magenta flowers.
G. rivulare Small clump-forming, leaves finely cut, narrow-lobed, compact heads of white flowers veined with pale violet. Var. 'Album', pure white. Europe.
G. robustum Upright bushy plant to 80 cm (30 in), leaves deeply divided, silvery backed, large pinkish-purple flowers, with white centres. It is an attractive plant only hardy in nearly frost-free gardens. S. Africa.
***G.* 'Salome'** ✱ *G. procurrens* x *G. lambertii* Very like 'Anne Folkard' in habit, long trailing, leaves yellowish-green, scattered palest violet flowers with a very dark violet centre and dark veining. The colour is unusual and the flowers appear over a very long season from mid-summer to autumn on stems which scramble into any surrounding vegetation.
G. sanguineum Low mound-forming, slowly spreading rhizomes, leaves deeply cut with very narrow lobes, and masses of usually solitary flowers, very variable in colour from white to deep magenta. Although often planted on the rock garden they make excellent plants for the front of the border in sun or light shade, preferably in well-drained soil. Many cultivars are available, the following being among the best: *G. s.* 'Album', 🏆 is one of the finest, rather taller and looser than many, pure white, 'Cedric Morris', tall, rose-purple, 'Elsbeth', low-growing with hairy calyces, flowers deep purple, 'Glenluce', compact, large clear pale pink, 'Jubilee Pink', one of the best, neat-growing, large pinkish-magenta, *G. s. lancastriense* is correctly *G. s. striatum*, 'Minutum', a tiny miniature, safest on the rock garden, 'Shepherd's Warning', 🏆 one of the best, compact and very floriferous, flowers a little nearer to magenta than those of 'Jubilee Pink'. *G. s. striatum* 🏆 Dwarf, usually to about 15 cm (6 in), spreading well, flowers clear soft pink. It thrives in well-drained soil. 'Splendens' is a tall strong-growing variety of *G. s. striatum*, with pale pink, darker-veined flowers.
G. sessiliflorum Very small, leaves small rounded, divided, deeply bronzed in *G. s.* subsp. *novae-zelandae* 'Nigricans', flowers tiny whitish. It is perhaps too small for consideration here, but it seeds around so freely that its rosettes of bronze leaves become quite noticeable at the edge of a border, and it is the parent of some new hybrids which will probably prove more suitable, with bronze or olive-green leaves. NZ. My only experience is with 'Sea Spray', a low mat of dark olive-green leaves, with a long succession of white flowers faintly tinged with pink, larger than those of *G. sessiliflorum*.
G. sinense A curiosity resembling *G. phaeum*, very small dark flowers with sharply recurved petals and a very prominent proboscis of stamens. China.
G. soboliferum Rare compact species, leaves finely cut, ferny, deep magenta veined flowers in late summer. It may need very moist conditions. C., E. Asia.
G. sylvaticum Clump-forming to 70 cm (28 in), leaves deeply divided with abundantly toothed lobes, large loose heads of flowers, varying in colour between white and purplish-pink. It is any easy robust plant for sun or shade, with several named cultivars: *G. s. f. albiforum*, white, sepals and stamens pink, *G. s.* 'Album', 🏆 leaves paler, uniformly pure white, 'Amy Doncaster', small, rich violet-blue, one of the deepest coloured of all, 'Angulatum', rare, very large, petals broad rose-pink, 'Birch Lilac', deep lilac, 'Mayflower', 🏆 popular cultivar, blue-violet with white eyes, *G. s. f. roseum*, pink petals, var. *wanneri*, pale pink with deep rose veining.
G. thunbergii Loosely spreading ground-cover, leaves deeply cleft, hairy, with pointed lobes, flowers small white to deep pink in late summer. It is not one of the best.
G. transbaicalicum Similar to *G. pratense*, reddish stems, leaves very finely divided, brown-edged, flowers deeper pinkish-blue. E. Asia.
G. traversii var. ***elegans*** ✱ Low spreading, attractive leaves grey-green, hairy, rounded, loose sprays of soft silvery-pink flowers. This is one of the most beautiful low-growing species, which I find almost hardy in a sheltered, sunny spot in well-drained soil. It frequently produces self-sown seedlings and these usually take over if the parent plant dies, in temperatures below -12 °C (10 °F). The type *G. traversii* has white flowers and is rare in cultivation. Chatham Is.
G. tuberosum Small tuberous-rooted clump-forming, leaves very finely divided, fern-like, small sprays of purplish-pink

veined flowers, in late spring and early summer. It is an attractive little plant which seems to need a warm, sheltered place in full sun in well-drained soil to persist; probably not hardy below -8 °C (17 °F). Med.
G. versicolor (syn. *G. striatum*) Ground-covering plant to 40 cm (16 in), long spreading stems, leaves brownish-blotched, loose sprays of white flowers with a network of deep rose-pink veins. It can cover a lot of ground even in dry situations, and produces its striking flowers over a long season from mid-summer to autumn. Two varieties with white unmarked flowers are occasionally seen, var. *album*, and 'Snow White'. S.E. Europe.
G. viscosissimum Closely allied to *G. nervosum*, variable, upright clump-forming to 60 cm (2 ft), heads of large pale pink flowers with pale veining and a white centre. It is an easy plant, with good flowers in its best forms. W., N. America.
G. wallichianum Variable, trailing, usually to 40 cm (16 in) but often less, long semi-prostrate shoots, many loose sprays of light to dark purplish-pink flowers, with white centres and darker pink veining. It is an excellent plant especially in its cultivars, easy and reliable in shade. Himalaya. 'Buxton's Variety', 🏆 compact, floriferous, flowers lilac-blue with a large round white centre, 'Syabru', ✸ compact with beautiful very dark magenta flowers with dark purple veins.
G. wlassovianum Bushy to 30 cm (1 ft), leaves brown-stained, loose heads of flowers, variable colour, usually dark purplish-pink with darker veining. It grows well in sun or light shade. E. Asia.
G. yesoense Bushy habit, to 40 cm (16 in), leaves very finely divided, narrow-lobed, pale pink or white paired flowers. It does well in damp areas. Japan
G. yunnanense A recent reintroduction from China, similar to *G. pogonanthum*, flowers nodding, pink, bowl-shaped in small heads. It needs plenty of moisture.

Geum (*Rosaceae*)

About 50 perennials, mainly clump-forming, sometimes spreading by rhizomes, with dense clusters of hairy leaves, usually pinnate, and solitary or loose clusters of flat to cup-shaped 5-petalled flowers, in bright shades of yellow, white, orange or red, mainly in early summer. They are among the earliest really colourful plants for the border, of small to medium size, with a long flowering period, but their intense shades of red, orange and yellow need some care in placing, well away from more pastel shades. They thrive in rich but reasonably well-drained soil, but usually need dividing every three years or so to keep them in good condition. They can be propagated by division, or the species are easily raised from seed.
G. × borisii (*G. bulgaricum* × *G. reptans*) The true hybrid is a compact cushion-forming plant with bright yellow pendent flowers, but the name is sometimes used for a form of *G. coccineum*.
G. bulgaricum Uncommon, upright growing, leaves hairy, pinnate, with large terminal leaflets, flowers in loose heads, nodding, yellow to orange. Balkans.
G. chiloense Clump-forming to 60 cm (2 ft), leaves hairy with equal leaflets, heads of scarlet upward-facing flowers from early to mid-summer. Chile. Its excellent cultivars are more widely grown: 'Dolly North', to 50 cm (20 in), large yellow tinged with orange,'Fire Opal', 🏆 tall, semi-double reddish-orange on purple stems, 'Georgenberg', low-growing, abundant flowers, a pleasing shade of golden-yellow, 'Lady Stratheden', 🏆 medium-tall double deep yellow, 'Mrs J. Bradshaw', 🏆 old favourite, semi-double orange-red, needs frequent replanting, 'Princess Juliana', 45 cm (1.5 ft) orange, 'Rijnstroom', coppery-orange, 'Rubin', smaller, semi-double deep red.
G. coccineum Similar to *G. chiloense*, slightly shorter, leaves having larger terminal leaflets, flowers more cup-shaped. Balkans. It is usually seen as one of its cultivars: 'Coppertone', compact to 25 cm (10 in), soft pale orange, 'Fuermeer', taller, orange red, over a long season. 'Prince of Orange', similar orange, 'Red Wings', tall with masses of semi-double scarlet flowers, 'Werner Arends', similar to 'Red wings', deep orange.
G. elatum Small clump-forming, leaves hairy pinnate, flowers usually solitary, large single deep yellow. It is variable and may be larger with several flowers to a head. It is uncommon, but imported seed is sometimes available. Himalaya.
G. 'Lemon Drops' To 35 cm (14 in) with heads of pendent greenish-yellow flowers with orange stamens, and reddish calyces.
G. montanum 🏆 Low-growing, carpeting, 5-10 cm (2–4 in), rosettes of glossy pinnate leaves with a very large terminal leaflet, flowers 1–3 bright yellow. It is an easy plant for the edge of a border, growing best in humus-rich soil in sun. C., C. Europe.
G. parviflorum Clump-forming to 30 cm (1 ft), leaves hairy pinnate, loose heads of small white flowers.
G. pentapetalum (syn. *Sieversia pentapetala*) A low mat of glossy pinnate leaves, 2–3 cm (0.8–1.2 in) wide solitary white flowers on 8 cm (3 in) stems. It is an attractive plant for moist peaty soil. E. Asia, Japan.
G. pyrenaicum Clump-forming to 50 cm (20 in), pinnate leaves with a large cordate terminal leaflet, heads of I-4 bright yellow 3 cm (1.2 in) wide flowers. Pyrenees.
G. rivale (The Water Avens) Slowly spreading rhizomatous plant to 30 cm (1 ft), leaves hairy pinnate with large terminal leaflets, loose heads of nodding flowers on long petioles, with large pinkish-brown calyces and small off-white to pink petals. It has a certain charm and is widely grown but the flowers are small for the quantity of leaf; the more colourful named varieties and cultivars (possibly hybrids) have more impact. Europe, N. Am. *G. r.* 'Album' ☼ Leaves paler, calyces pale green, flowers greenish-white, shows up well in the border, its soft colouring presenting no problems between other plants, 'Leonard's Variety', flowers larger, deep orange-

pink in conspicuous heads on dark stems, held well above the leaves, 'Lionel Cox', similar to the last but bright yellow.
G. triflorum Similar to *G. rivale* more compact, leaves evenly pinnate, finely divided, ferny, conspicuous clusters of deep reddish-purple nodding or upright flowers from pink calyces. Var. *campanulatum,* excellent variety which seems more strongly coloured, with the flowers mainly upturned.

Gillenia (*Rosaceae*)

A genus of two species of beautiful clump-forming perennials, with almost sessile 3-lobed leaves, and branching wiry stems to 1 m (3 ft), but often much less, bearing many dainty white or pale pink flowers with long, narrow petals in mid- to late summer. They thrive in moist humus-rich soil in sun or partial shade, either in the border or in a more informal woodland setting among shrubs, where they will combine well with dactylorhizas, meconopsis, and other later flowering woodlanders after most of the rhododendrons and other shrubs are over. They can be propagated by division or preferably by seed, which is not produced very freely in my experience and needs careful searching out.
G. stipulata Uncommon in cultivation, differing from *G. trifoliata* in its larger leaf stipules and smaller flowers with less conspicuous calyces. S.E. USA.
G. trifoliata 🏆 As described above, the red calyces contrasting well with the very pale flowers. It is an exceptionally beautiful plant with a long flowering season, easily grown, and standing well without support. W., N. Am.

Glaucidium (*Paeoniaceae*)

G. palmatum 🏆 The one species, a clump-forming perennial to 40 cm (16 in), with large, palmately lobed leaves, and pale lavender poppy flowers 6–8 cm (2.3–3 in) in diameter, in late spring or early summer. It is an outstanding plant with good leaves and wonderful large satiny flowers, which needs moist rich soil with abundant humus, in full or partial shade. It is best left undisturbed, and can be raised from seed. Japan. The white var. *leucanthum* ('Album') is rare and perhaps even more beautiful.

63 *Glaucidium palmatum*

Glaucium (*Papaveraceae*) (Horned Poppy)

A genus of annuals, biennials, and short-lived perennials, with attractive blue-grey lobed or deeply dissected leaves, and loose heads of large poppy flowers, followed by very long, narrow seed capsules. Even the perennials are short-lived, but they self-seed freely and usually maintain a colony without much help from the gardener. They need the hottest, sunniest part of the garden in well-drained rather poor soil to be remotely perennial. They are easily raised from the abundant seed.
G. flavum The only perennial widely grown, to 70 cm (28 in), with rosettes of bluish-grey, fleshy basal leaves, stem leaves which clasp the branching stems, and terminal large golden-yellow flowers for a long time in summer. Although this is the typical colour it can be a good deep orange in *G. f. fulvum* (syn. *aurantiacum*). I grow a colony which arose from seed from a solitary orange plant among hundreds of yellow on Lesbos. Recent generations have come true to colour.
G. grandiflorum A delightful smaller more compact species with deep crimson flowers with a black blotch. Although said to be perennial, it was very short-lived in my experience, and sadly failed to set seed.

Grindelia (*Compositae*)

A genus including several clump- or mound-forming perennials, with large, bright yellow daisy flowers, only one of which is widely grown. They need a sunny, sheltered position in well-drained soil; they are more perennial in soils which are not too rich. They can be propagated by seed sown in autumn or by cuttings of new growth in summer.
G. chiloense A sprawling mound of semi-prostrate branching stems to 70 cm (28 in), leaves lanceolate, toothed, flowers 5 cm (2 in) wide, yellow from sticky resinous buds, over a very long season from mid-summer on. It flowers well in full sun, the bright colour combining well with the dark blue of *Lavandula* 'Hidcote', or the deeper blue campanulas, or the reddish-purple of some origanums. Patagonia.
G. robusta An uncommon species, more upright and taller, and probably less hardy. California.
G. squarrosa Similar in habit to *G. chiloensis,* with broader leaves and heads of several smaller yellow flowers. W., C., N. America.

Gunnera (*Gunneraceae*)

A genus of waterside perennials, well-known for their enormous leaves, with a few very low stoloniferous, mat-forming species grown for their attractive leaves and their ornamental fruits. Most of the latter group are too small to consider here, but the species described below make interesting small-scale ground-cover for the front of a moist shady border in humus-rich soil. They are doubtfully hardy below -7 °C (20 °F). They can be propagated by seed or by division.
G. flavida Dense mat of broad, toothed, wavy-edged,

brownish-green leaves, with upright brush-like spikes of yellow fruits. NZ.

G. hamiltonii Similar to the last, leaves bluish-green, oval, rarely producing its red fruits in cultivation. Stewart Is.

G. magellanica The most vigorous, leaves dark green, rounded, robust enough to make attractive ground cover. It rarely fruits. S. America.

G. prorepens Similar to *G. magellanica* but leaves purple-tinged, and plenty of deep red fruits. NZ.

Gypsophila (*Caryophyllaceae*)

A genus of annuals and perennials, varying greatly in size and habit, from tiny alpine cushions, which I have excluded, to low carpeting plants suitable for walls or a border edge, to the well-known large *G. paniculata*, with great clouds of tiny flowers. Although in good conditions the latter is above our height range, many of its cultivar are considerably shorter. All thrive in well-drained soils in full sun. *G. paniculata* is invaluable for filling gaps with its large flower heads, especially planted around Oriental poppies, tulips, or other early bulbs planted in a border, which leave a gap by mid-summer. They can also be used to separate 'difficult' colours. The species may be grown from seed, and these and the cultivars can be propagated from cuttings of young shoots in early summer. The cultivars of *G. paniculata* are usually propagated commercially by grafting onto two-year-old seedlings of the species.

G. cerastioides Low mat-forming, leaves small grey-green, flowers solitary or clustered, white or pale pink, 1 cm (0.4 in) (0.4 in), with darker pink veins. It makes a low mat for the front of a border but is less vigorous than *G. repens*. Himalayas.

G. pacifica An uncommon plant similar to *G. paniculata*, taller with larger pink flowers. E. Asia.

G. paniculata Like the last this is often over 1 m (3 ft) in height, but some of its cultivars are shorter. It makes a mass of branching stems with lanceolate blue-green leaves, and great panicles of small white or pale pink flowers in summer. C., E. Europe, Asia. The following are some of the best cultivars: 'Bristol Fairy' 🏆 double white, usually short-lived unless propagated regularly, 'Compacta' and 'Compacta Plena' dwarf, single and double white flowers respectively. The latter is very reliable and long-lived but shorter than 'Bristol Fairy', 'Flamingo', double pink on a bushy plant, tends to be short-lived, 'Pink Fairy' similar but more perennial, 'Snowflake' tall double white, 'Rosy Veil' 🏆 excellent dwarf to 30 cm (1 ft), pale pink.

Gypsophila repens Low mat-forming, a wide carpet of small bluish-green leaves, smothered in summer in loose heads of white or pink flowers. It can be used at the edge of a border and makes a very fine wall plant to give some colour after the early aubrieta, phlox and alyssum are over. *G. r. alba*, similar single white, 'Dorothy Teacher', 🏆 compact, slower-growing, pale pink, deepening with age, 'Dubia', more compact, reddish stems, very pale pink, *G. r. fratensis*, good compact pink, 'Letchworth Rose' and 'Rosea', pink, with the longer stems of the type, making them ideal for trailing down retaining walls.

H

Hacquetia (*Umbelliferae*)

H. epipactis 🏆 The only species, a small clump-forming perennial with a dense rootstock, flowering in late winter or earliest spring, the very short stems lengthening to 10 cm (4 in) over the long flowering period. The 'flowers' are composed of a dense cluster of tiny bright yellow true flowers surrounded by a ring of large green bracts resembling petals, in good condition for several weeks, by which time the glossy green 5-lobed leaves have appeared. Although it begins to flower at a height of only 10 cm (4 in) or less, it eventually attains about 20 cm (8 in) and, although it is so small, its substantial roots and its habit of self-seeding freely make it more suitable for a mixed border among shrubs than for the rock garden. 'Thor' ☼ a stunning new introduction, leaves strikingly margined creamy-white, floral bracts similarly margined and streaked. They grow best in partial or full shade in moist humus-rich soil, and can be raised from seed sown fresh, although sufficient seedlings can usually be found around the plant. C. Europe.

64 *Hacquetia epipactis* 'Thor'

Haplopappus (*Compositae*)

A large genus of annuals and perennials, only one perennial commonly grown. Generally of low semi-shrubby habit, with rosettes of toothed leaves, and usually solitary, comparatively large daisy flowers in profusion. They need well-drained soil in full sun, and can be propagated by seed or by cuttings.

H. glutinosus (syn. *H. coronopifolius*) Mat-forming to 15 cm (6 in), leaves sticky, narrow lobed or pinnate, flowers solitary, 1-5 cm (0.4–2 in) wide, bright yellow, narrow-rayed on long

peduncles, in summer. Patagonia.
H. macrocephalus Low shrublet to 8 cm (3 in), leaves glossy, toothed, ovate-spathulate, hairy, very deep orange daisies in summer. A recent relatively untried introduction from the Andes, the flower colour can also be pink to purple.

Hedysarum (*Leguminosae/Papilionaceae*)

A genus of perennials and shrubs with attractive hairy pinnate leaves and heads of large colourful clover-like flowers in summer. The shrubby *H. multijugum* is tall, and the only species seen regularly in gardens is *H. coronarium*. They grow best in very well-drained soil in the sunniest possible position.
H. coronarium Mound of long straggling stems, many upright dense heads of bright purplish-red flowers for a few weeks in summer. It is a very colourful plant which I find short-lived or liable to flower itself to death.

Helenium, Helianthus, Heliopsis (*Compositae*)

Ever-popular daisy-flowered perennials, but all are too large to consider here, if they are reasonably well-grown.

Helichrysum (*Compositae*) (Everlasting flower)

A large genus of shrubs, perennials, and annuals, of very variable habit, from tiny alpines to large shrubs, many with exceptional silver foliage as well as good everlasting flowers. Some are of borderline hardiness except in nearly frost-free gardens, but even in cold gardens those with fine foliage are useful to combine with other plants in ornamental containers. I have omitted the many species which resent winter wet and need alpine house or rock garden treatment, including some recently introduced small species from South Africa, which may prove easier and hardier than expected. I have also omitted the definitely shrubby species, most of which are now to be found under *Ozothamnus*. Some species set good seed and can be propagated from it, and the majority are easily increased by cuttings.
H. ambiguum Clump-forming, to 30 cm (1 ft), leaves alternate, spathulate, white-downy, flowers small yellow in 5 cm (2 in) wide heads. An excellent foliage plant that only flourishes outside in near-frost-free gardens in very well-drained soil. Spain, Balearic Is.
H. arenarium Clump-forming, stems upright or procumbent to 40 cm (16 in), densely set with grey-white lanceolate or spathulate leaves, flowers yellow to orange in mid- to late summer. Hardier than the last but needs very well-drained soil in full sun. Subsp. *aucheri*, leaves even whiter, spathulate. Europe–W. Asia.
H. bracteata (syn. *Bracteantha bracteata*) Usually seen as a seed strain of annual 'everlasting flowers', but two cultivars 'Dargan Hill Monarch' and 'Skynet' are perennial in warm gardens, upright growing with white-felted leaves and broad heads of large 'everlasting flowers', deep coppery-orange in the former and pinkish cream in the latter.
H. 'County Park Silver' Low carpeter, a mat of branching stems with small very silver leaves, a fine foliage plant. Although usually grown with winter protection, its vigour and resistance to winter wet make it worth trying as a border edging, except perhaps in very wet areas.
H. heldreichii Silver mound to 30 cm (1 ft), densely leafy silver stems, leaves linear, flowers insignificant, straw-coloured. Easy to grow and propagate, an outstanding and quick-growing silver foliage plant, hardy with overhead protection to keep the worst of the rain off, and hardy outside in drier gardens, especially as a wall plant.
H. italicum (syn. *H. angustifolium*) Shrubby to 60 cm (2 ft), stems upright or semi-prostrate, branching, leaves small, very narrow, grey-green to white, flowers small yellow in dense heads. It seems reasonably hardy in suitable conditions. S. Europe. subsp., *microphyllum* more compact, leaves smaller, very silver, a useful container plant.
H. milfordiae 🏆 Low mat-forming, rosettes dense white-woolly, large white flowers opening from deep crimson bracts. It is a beautiful plant which is proving unexpectedly hardy in very well-drained soil. S. Africa.
H. orientale Dense clump to 30 cm (1 ft), 5 cm (2 in) long grey felted leaves, flat-heads of bright yellow flowers, in early summer. A popular alpine house plant for its fine foliage and bright long-lived flowers, but it is remarkably hardy and tolerant of wet if planted in well-drained soil in a sheltered sunny position or in a wall. Greece.
H. petiolare 🏆 Spreading sub-shrubby, leaves rounded, grey-white, short-petioled, felted, on long trailing stems which clamber into surrounding plants, flowers greyish-white, insignificant. S. Africa. Several cultivars are available, varying in leaf size and colour. They are all first-class plants to grow among others and provide contrasting foliage, either in containers or as temporary fillers in cold gardens, or as permanent features of frost free gardens. They are easily propagated from cuttings in late summer to overwinter under glass. 'Limelight', popular cultivar, leaves yellow tinged, which can look unhealthy (to me), probably most effective in light shade, 'Roundabout' a miniature edition of 'Variegatum', much more compact with leaves half the size but very prone to reversion to the larger form, 'Variegatum' excellent foliage plant, grey leaves generously variegated with cream. It looks particularly good with the yellow flowers of other 'container plants' like *Cuphea cecileae* or *Euryops pectinatus*.

65 *Helichrysum petiolare* with *lobelia* and a *white pelargonium* in a hanging basket

H. plicatum Very similar to *H. orientale*, taller and less silver, flowers deeper yellow. It needs the same conditions. S.E. Europe.
H. rupestre (syn. *H. fontanesii*) Similar to *H. heldreichii* with yellow flowers. It is more generally grown, and possibly more hardy. W., C. Med.
***H.* 'Sulphur Kight'** Recent hybrid, 30–40 cm (12–16 in), leaves grey felted on upright stems, flowers good pale yellow in large heads, remaining in good condition for along time.
H. scorpioides Upright-growing to 40 cm (16 in), leaves grey-green with white-hairy backs, stems densely leafy below, more sparingly above, flowers solitary, yellow, to 2.5 cm (1 in) wide. S.E. Australia.
H. splendidum (syn. *H. trilineatum*) 🏆 Loose shrubby habit to 70 cm (28 in), leaves small, narrow, very silver, flowers bright yellow. It is one of the best 'silvers', and can be used in the same way as *H. petiolatum* in containers or in warm gardens, but it is hardier. S. Africa.
H. stoechas Bushy species to 50 cm (20 in), similar to *H. italicum* and *H. splendidum*, excellent silver-grey leaves, 2 cm (0.8 in) long, heads of globular yellow flowers.
H. thianschanicum Mat-forming, leaves lanceolate silver-grey, flowers long-lasting flat-heads of deep yellow. Another good recent introduction, easy to grow but it resents winter wet without some protection. It should be an excellent plant for the front of a sunny border in drier areas.

Helipterum (*Compositae*)

About 60 annuals and perennials, only two of the latter being seen occasionally in gardens. They are very similar to helichrysums with silvery leaves and heads of yellow or white 'everlasting' flowers in summer. Like many of the helichrysums they need very well-drained soil and protection from winter wet in areas of high rainfall. They may be propagated from seed or by cuttings of the current year's shoots.
H. albicans Variable, a mound of upright or semi-prostrate stems to 30 cm (1 ft), leaves white-felted, spathulate or oblanceolate, flowers solitary, 2.5 cm (1 in) wide, deep yellow. S.E. Australia. Subsp. *incanum*, leaves longer, narrower, and more silver, flowers paler yellow fading to white. Subsp. *alpinum*, more compact, flowers white.
H. anthemoides More bushy, to 30 cm (1 ft), leaves grey-green narrow, flowers white opening from reddish buds. S.E. Aust.

Helleborus (*Ranunculaceae*)

Some 15-20 species of perennials, perhaps the finest of all plants apart from bulbs for late winter and early spring in the garden. A small group of them has stems which are evergreen for two years and carry all their leaves. They then flower and the old stems are replaced from the base. The majority have clumps of leaves and flowering stems arising from ground level. In most species the leaves are divided from the base into three or more segments, which may be further divided, and usually have toothed margins. The flowers may be single to several to a stem, cup-shaped, in a variety of colours, with five colourful sepals, which take the place of the petals of most flowers, the latter reduced to a ring of nectaries, which are usually inconspicuous, and a cluster of many stamens.

The ideal conditions for growing hellebores are an alkaline, rich but reasonably well-drained soil, with abundant humus, in partial shade, but remarkably good plants can be grown in acid soils, and in full sun if the humus content and moisture are adequate. Hellebores look great grouped together, but they are perhaps seen at their best in combination with early bulbs like snowdrops, aconites, various forms of *Anemone blanda*, *A. apennina*, *A. ranunculoides* and *A.* x *lipsiensis*, *A. nemorosa*, erythroniums and trilliums, and the smaller narcissi, early perennials such as pulmonarias and cardamines, and among such shrubs as hamamelis, corylopsis, and camellias and early rhododendrons. Later their interesting foliage combines well in the shade with ferns, hostas, and other leaves of contrasting shape.

Although hellebores can be increased by division, the plants take a long time to recover and unless it is considered essential to propagate a particular cultivar, it is better to raise them from seed whenever possible, sowing the seed as soon as it is ripe and keeping it cool until germination. Several nurseries are now raising very good strains from seed by hand pollination and selection, and these are excellent value, whereas a division from a cultivar will always be slow to establish. A fungus disease causing black spots on the stems and leaves can be an important problem in some gardens, and often necessitates the early removal of diseased leaves, and a regular spray with a systemic fungicide.

In the descriptions that follow I have concentrated on the species, and have only described a few named hybrids and cultivars, as they are difficult to acquire. For a more detailed account the reader should consult the excellent 'Hellebores' by Graham Rice and Elizabeth Strangman, and 'Hellebores' by Brian Mathew, the former containing more information about hybrids.
H. argutifolius (syn. *H. corsicus*) 🏆 Substantial semi-woody stems, sometimes over 1 m (3 ft), large glossy dark green leaves, divided into 3 overlapping leaflets with spiny margins. In their second season the stems produce large heads of up to thirty green cup-shaped flowers, remaining in good condition for several weeks. It is a very widely grown substantial plant with magnificent foliage, frequently self-seeding around the garden, almost to excess in good conditions. Unless seedlings are needed the plants look better if the old stems are cut away after flowering. Corsica and Sardinia.
H. atrorubens The plant usually grown under this name is correctly *H. orientalis* subsp. *abchasicus*. The true species is smaller, leaves with 5 segments, the outer leaflets further divided, to 15 divisions in all, with toothed margins, and loose heads of 4–5 cm (1.6–2 in) wide flowers, which vary between green and purple, usually purple-backed. NW. Yugoslavia.
H. corsicus *See* ***H. argutifolius***
H. cyclophyllus Very similar to *H. odorus*, leaves rounded,

dying down in autumn, divided into seven, outer leaflets further divided, white hairs on the backs, and finely toothed margins. The flowers bright pale green throughout, to 6 cm (2.3 in) wide, mainly facing outwards. It is easy to grow but the early growth may be frosted in cold gardens.

H. dumetorum One of the smallest, usually to 25 cm (10 in), leaves divided into 10-12 narrow, toothed leaflets, flowers small deep-green nodding. It is a delightful little plant for a shady spot.

H.* x *ericsmithii (*syn. H.* x *nigristern*) (*H. niger* x *H.* x *sternii*) An excellent but variable hybrid, with features of both parents. Leaves glossy dark green, divided like those of *H. niger*, margins spiny toothed, pale veins, flowers large, white or pink-flushed, tinged with green especially at the base, deeper pink on the outside. It is a magnificent plant in good conditions, but is prone to attack by black spot unless the old leaves are removed in autumn and it is sprayed regularly.

H. foetidus Robust early-flowering plant, evergreen stems bearing large glossy deep-green leaves divided into narrow, toothed leaflets, large loose heads of 2 cm (0.8 in) wide pale green flowers with a purplish band around the tips of the petals, amid prominent pale green bracts, a striking feature even before the flowers open. It is an extremely easy plant which self-sows freely, in sun or shade, and rarely suffers from disease. Its evergreen leaves can be an important feature of the winter landscape. Europe. A few cultivars are occasionally available: 'Bowle's Form' very robust, leaves more finely divided, larger heads of flowers, 'Green Giant' tall, leaves finely divided, bracts of brighter green, 'Wester Flisk' ✪ widely grown group with reddish stems and petioles, which add to the beauty of the plants.

H. lividus 🏆 Small uncommon plant like *H. corsicus* in habit but to only 35 cm (14 in), 3-lobed leaves, dark green with pale veining, untoothed edges, and purple-tinged backs, flowers, in early spring, cup-shaped, basically green but strongly flushed with purple on the outside and usually within. Generally recommended for the alpine house, it can be grown well outside in well-drained soil in a sheltered position, surviving temperatures to -10 °C (14 °F). It is easily raised from fresh seed, but is very liable to hybridize with *H. corsicus* if it is grown anywhere near, hence the frequency with which seedlings of the hybrid are offered as *H. lividus*. Majorca.

66 *Helleborus lividus*

H. mutifidus Very variable, with four subspecies differing mainly in their natural distribution and in the number of leaf divisions, from twelve to a hundred or more, always dying down in winter. Flowers green, rarely flushed on the outside with purple, usually not more than 4 cm (1.6 in) wide. Subsp. *bocconei* twenty coarsely toothed leaf divisions, flowers green, paler with age. Italy. Subsp. *istriacus* twelve divisions, flowers relatively large, occasionally purple-flushed. N. Italy to N. Slovenia. Subsp. *multifidus*, leaves more finely divided, with as many as forty segments, flowers small very deep green. From mountains further south. The most southerly subsp. *hercegovinensis*, leaves beautifully divided, with a hundred or more leaflets, flowers pale yellowish-green. All grow well in partial shade in well-drained soil, but are fairly slow to build up into good clumps.

H. niger 🏆 The Christmas Rose is the most popular and largest-flowered of all the hellebores, and usually flowers after Christmas. 30 cm (1 ft) high clump of evergreen leaves, segments seven to nine rather widely separated, margins untoothed or sparsely toothed, flowers large, beneath the 7 cm (2.8 in) wide leaves, white with a greenish centre and usually some pinkish staining at least on the outside, more marked with age. Sadly it is not the easiest to grow well, doing best in alkaline soil rich in humus, in partial or full shade. Subsp. *macranthus,* flowers larger, leaves finely toothed. C., S. Europe Several cultivars and cultivar groups have been named at times, usually with extra large flowers and not, one suspects, always maintaining their original qualities. The following are frequently offered: 'Blackthorn Strain', excellent seed strain, developed from crossing two named cultivars, flower stems very tall and tinged with purple, flowers white, pink in the bud, and increasingly pink with age. 'Potters's Wheel' was the finest of all seed strains when first offered, flowers huge white, with green nectaries and green at the base of the petals, rarely as good as it was originally, the name is usually given to a good large-flowered plant. 'White Magic', another good strain, stems extra-tall, leaves unusually small, lighter green, a profusion of flowers, that become pink as they age.

H.* x *nigercors 🏆 (*H. niger x H. corsicus*) Robust hybrid, flowers very profuse, to 4 cm (1.6 in) across, white, or cream tinged with green, usually with a central green stripe down each petal, on tall leafy stems with 3-lobed toothed leaves, further flowers on short leafless stems. It is one of the finest hybrids, but usually needs precautions against black-spot disease.

H. x nigristern *See* ***H. ericsmithii***

H. odorus Very similar to *H. cyclophyllus*, leaves 5-lobed, hairy, the outer divisions further divided, more likely to survive the winter, flowers green most often a pale yellowish shade. It is one of the easiest of the green-flowered species to grow in a shady position. S.E. Europe.

H. orientalis This name is applied to most of the hybrids in general cultivation. The true plant is uncommon, leaves leathery, toothed, evergreen, divided into up to eleven segments. There are three subspecies: subsp. *orientalis* flowers white tinged with green, nectaries green, subsp. *abschacicus* flowers and nectaries purple-tinged, varying in depth of colour, correctly includes *H. atrorubens* hort, a robust plant with very deep purple flowers early in the season, subsp. guttatus flowers white spotted with pink or red. The name 'Guttatus' is sometimes applied to hybrids with spotted petals.

67 *Helleborus orientalis*, a good white cultivar

'Orientalis Hybrids': This is the popular name, more correctly perhaps *H.* x *hybridus*, for most of the vast range of hellebores available to gardeners. Any gardener who grows a modest collection of hellebores will be aware that seedlings are likely to appear without any great effort, and that they are in the main quite pleasing. However, a visit to one of the nurseries breeding hellebores and developing seed strains of uniform excellence will immediately show what can be done and perhaps suggest that most of ones own haphazardly bred plants would be better discarded. The finest named hybrids of all may be available rarely and at a high price, but these have been used as parents in the development of superior strains, often sold on the basis of colour. Excellent deep pink to purples are commonplace and blackish-purple flowers with an attractive 'bloom' seem to be of increasing intensity. There are some excellent vigorous whites, and clear yellows are improving. Some of these plants seem to come almost true from seed, in particular the best of the white strains I find that seedlings of a particularly dark *H. torquatus.* hybrid produces plants of dark reddish-purple, although not quite of the same intensity. 'Guttatus' hybrids seem to retain the spotting in their progeny even with open pollination. Recently some very attractive small double-flowered plants have been appearing, derived from double-flowered *H. orientalis*, and from a double *H. torquatus*, and these will become increasingly popular.

H. purpurascens An uncommon early-flowering species, to 30 cm (1 ft), completely herbaceous, leaves divided into some twenty-five narrow, toothed leaflets, flowers, to 5 cm (2 in) wide, vary but are usually green within and purple outside, or may be more evenly purple throughout. It will tolerate more sun than most species. E. Europe.

H.* x *sternii (*H. argutifolius* x *H. lividus*) A very variable hybrid that combines the features of its parents to differing degrees. It can be almost as large as *H. argutifolius* with some purple flushing on the back of the leaves and stems, conspicuous veining, and a pink tinge to the flowers. At the opposite extreme it can closely resemble *H. lividus* but usually with more toothed leaves and less marked purple backing. 'Boughton Beauty Strain', closer to *H. argutifolius*, 'Blackthorn Strain' to *H. lividus*, the latter exceptionally fine with marbled leaves, dark purple stems, and pink flushed flowers. *H.* x *sternii* is a very easy plant in full sun or part shade, and is likely to self seed with the seedlings becoming closer to *H. argutifolius*.

H. thibetanus A hellebore to dream about, very recently introduced from China and not yet available commercially. The leaves are divided into seven leaflets with sharply toothed margins, and the flowers are deeply cup-shaped, large, opening white and rapidly becoming clear pale pink with darker veining, fading to green. China.

H. torquatus Until recently this was much coveted as the 'blackest' flowered of all but it has now been studied more fully in the wild and found to be very variable. Although the flowers can be green within and deepest purple without, the classic concept of the plant, they can be pure green, resembling *H. mutifidus*, or have any combination of green and purple. They are all attractive small plants with rounded leaves finely divided into linear segments. They are slow-growing but not difficult in partial shade. W. Balkans.

H. vesicarius An unusual species that can only be grown in the open in areas with dry summers, as it requires the same treatment as a bulbous plant with no water after the leaves die down. In early winter it produces a clump of large pale buttercup-like divided leaves followed by clusters of small cup-shaped flowers with a ring of purple towards the tips of the petals like those of *H. foetidus*. The flowers are followed by remarkable green inflated seed pods as much as 7 cm (2.8 in) long which, in nature, eventually break off and blow away as 'tumbleweeds'. Turkey.

H. viridis Slow-growing, leaves deciduous with up to 20 divisions, sometimes tinged purple when young, flowers dark green to 5 cm (2 in) wide. There are two subspecies: subsp. *viridis*, from S. Europe, young leaves downy beneath, leaflets finely toothed, subsp. *occidentalis*, a native of Britain and N. Europe. young leaves smooth, older leaves coarsely toothed. They are slow-growing, but not difficult in partial shade.

Helonias (*Liliaceae/Melanthiaceae*)

H. bullata The only species, closely allied to Heloniopsis, uncommon rhizomatous plant, to 20 cm (8 in), rosettes evergreen, leaves very glossy lanceolate to 40 cm (16 in) long, flowers with six narrow pink petals and prominent pale blue anthers in short dense spikes. It needs moist humus-rich soil in sun or semi shade, at pond margins or among shrubs. E. USA.

Heloniopsis (*Liliaceae/Melanthiaceae*)

Three or four evergreen clump-forming perennials, of which only one, with several varieties, is widely grown. They are very attractive plants, easily grown in rich but well-drained soil in partial shade, that does not become too dry. They can be propagated by division, or by seed, if this is set, sown as soon as ripe.

H. orientalis (syn. *H. japonica*) Rosette-forming, 20 cm (8 in), leaves glossy lanceolate to 20 cm (8 in) long, sometimes flushed purple, often forming growth-buds at their tips, which then root or can be rooted. Flowers in heads of up to ten, nodding with narrow petals to 2 cm (0.8 in) long and long style and anthers protruding, usually pale to deep pink but sometimes white. Japan. Var. *breviscapa* is sometimes offered, with white or very pale pink flowers. Var. *yakushimensis* a very dwarf compact variety only 10 cm (4 in) high, with pale flowers.

Hemerocallis (*Liliaceae/Hemerocallidaceae*)

The Day Lilies are a genus of invaluable perennials for the border, making dense clumps of attractive arching pale green leaves, from which arise loose branching stems bearing a long succession of typical lily-like flowers, that individually only last for a day but appear in such profusion that this is never a noticeable disadvantage. The range of flower colour is now very large, from white through all shades of yellow to deepest bronze, and shades of pink to deep red or purple, with the additon of doubles and ruffled flowers. To many gardeners the most attractive are those with a multitude of small flowers, like 'Golden Chimes' and 'Corky', rather than a few very large flowers. They are easily grown in rich moist soil, and benefit from splitting up and replanting every few years if they become less floriferous.

Hemerocallis are becoming increasingly popular with an ever-larger range of new hybrids appearing from year to year, many of them raised in the USA. The majority are too large to consider here, but I have briefly described below some of the species and cultivars readily available in Britain that are likely to remain under 75 cm (2.5 ft) in height. Smaller cultivars are being developed constantly and my list may give little idea of the number currently available in N. America. Golden Chimes and Corky, both 🏆 plants are a little tall.

Name	Height	Flowers	Notes
'American Revolution'	To 60 cm (2 ft)	Deep blackish-red	
'Bertie Ferris'	To 60 cm (2 ft)	Yellow	
'Blushing Belle'	70 cm (28 in)	Pale blush	Early
'Burning Daylight'	70 cm (28 in)	Orange self	
'Cherry Cheeks'	70 cm (28 in)	Deep pink, pale yellow throat and stripe	Late
'Chicago Apache'	To 60 cm (2 ft)	Ruffled deep scarlet	
'Chicago Petticoats'	60 cm (2 ft)	Pink, slightly frilled	Early
'Chicago Royal Robe'	65 cm	Deep reddish-purple, yellow throat	Early
H. dumortieri	50 cm (20 in)	Deep yellow	Large clump with few flowers
'Eenie Weeny'	30 cm (2 ft)	Deep yellow	Long-flowering
'Fairy Tale Pink'	To 60 cm (2 ft)	Ruffled, shell-pink	
'Frans Hals'	60 cm (2 ft)	Bicolour, orange, and deep orange-red with an orange stripe	Late
'Gentle Shepherd'	To 40 cm (16 in)	Creamy-white	
'Golden Prize'		Large, golden-yellow	
'Hope Diamond'	to 40 cm (16 in)	Ceamy-white with greenish centre, widely open	Early
'Joan Senior'	65 cm (26 in)	Creamy-white, small green throat	Early
'Kindly Light'	To 60 cm (2 ft)	'Spider', with long, narrow petals, citron-yellow	
'Little Grapette'	30 cm (1 ft)	Bluish-purple	
'Lusty Leland'	To 60 cm (2 ft)	Deep red, throat and reverse gold	

Name	Height	Flowers	Notes
H. middendorfii	To 75 cm (2.5 ft)	Orange-yellow, widely open	
H. minor	50-60 cm (20–24 in)	Deep yellow, long-tubed, brownish-backed	Leaves narrow to 40 cm (16 in) long
'Nova'	55 cm (22 in)	Lemon yellow, green throat	
'Pardon me'	60 cm (2 ft)	Bright red, yellow throat	
'Red Precious' 🏆	55 cm (22 in)	Deep orange-red, yellow central stripe	
'Ruffled Apricot'	To 60 cm (2 ft)	Ruffled, apricot	
'Siloam Button Box'	To 60 cm (2 ft)	Small cream, maroon eye	
'Siloam Purple Plum'	45 cm (1.5 ft)	Deep reddish-purple, small green throat	Early
'Stafford'	70 cm (28 in)	Crimson, yellow central stripe, yellow throat	
'Starling'	70 cm (28 in)	Deep brownish-purple, yellow throat	Early
'Stella Doro' 🏆	30 cm (1 ft)	Uniform deep yellow	
'Wally Nance'	60 cm (2 ft)	Deep red, yellow throat	Early
'Yellow Petticoats'	To 60 cm (2 ft)	Double, yellow	

Hepatica (*Ranunculaceae*)

A genus of exquisite small clump-forming perennials with three to five lobed leaves, evergreen or deciduous, usually leathery and often purple-backed, and solitary flowers with 6–10 petals, in shades of blue, pink, or white, in early spring. They seem to thrive more in some gardens than others, and can make wonderful large clumps with a great number of flowers. They enjoy good feeding, and should be planted in moist, humus-rich, but well-drained soil, in partial shade. Although small and suitable for the rock garden, they are excellent in providing early colour at the edge of a shady border or among shrubs. They can be propagated by division, but they resent disturbance, and are better raised from seed which should be sown as soon as ripe and kept cool until germination the following spring.

H. acutiloba To 20 cm (8 in), leaves 3-lobed, the lobes pointed and longer than wide, flowers to 2 cm (0.8 in) wide, usually deep lilac-blue, occasionally white or pink. E., N. America

H. americana Similar but 10–15 cm (4–6 in) high, leaf-lobes rounded and broader than long, often tinged with purple, flowers usually similar, but also white, pink, purple, or double blue. E., N. America.

H.* x *media (*H. nobilis* x *H. transsilvanica*) 🏆 'Ballardii' is the cultivar usually on offer, a magnificent plant with very large rich blue flowers. It is doubtful whether the original plant is still available, but the name covers some good large-flowered plants.

H. nobilis (syn. *H. triloba*) 🏆 Usually 10–15 cm (4–6 in) high, leaves large with three rounded or oval, often purple-flushed lobes, flowers 2.5 cm (1 in) wide, usually 6-petalled, in shades of pale to deep blue, pink to deep reddish, or white. Doubles are sometimes seen, particularly of blue and reddish-pink varieties. Europe. Var. *japonica* lobes more pointed, 6-9 petals, usually white or very pale pink. Var. *maxima* an uncommon plant with larger leaves, not matched by the flowers.

H. transsylvanica (syn. *H. angulosa*) 🏆 Taller and more robust than *H. nobilis*, leaves larger, with somewhat lobed margins, flowers up to 4 cm (1.6 in) wide, with 8-10 petals, lilac-blue to purple, pink or white, occasionally with doubles.

Hesperis (*Cruciferae*)

Some 60 species of biennials and perennials, usually short-lived and sweetly-scented, including our native Sweet Rocket, which is useful in the wild garden and has superior cultivars for the border. All are easily raised from seed, and the cultivars can be grown from cuttings of new growth in spring.

H. matronalis Sweet Rocket To 80 cm (30 in) or more, with branching stems bearing masses of single, very fragrant, typical crucifer flowers in shades of lilac to white. It self seeds very freely and is best in a wilder part of the garden. 'Alba' and 'Alba Plena' are single and double-flowered white cultivars. 'Lilacina Flore Plena' is an uncommon but excellent double lilac that was almost lost as a result of virus infection but has now been 'cleaned up' and its vigour restored. The doubles are less vigorous and usually under 70 cm (28 in), excellent easy plants for the border in sun or light shade.

Heuchera (*Saxifragaceae*)

Evergreen or deciduous perennials making large dense clumps of rounded hairy leaves, often marbled or tinted with grey or brownish purple. The larger species have upright stems to 50–70 cm (28 in), bearing tiny bell-shaped flowers in elegant loose spires, in shades of green, pink, and red. in mid-summer and often later. Their delicate beauty has always appealed, but they have become more popular recently as colourful border plants with real impact, as the colour range and size of flower has been improved, especially by the work of Alan Bloom. More recent work in the USA. has concentrated on their leaves and some superb foliage plants are appearing, in addition to the well-tried 'Palace Purple'. These make very effective ground-cover at the edge of borders or in light woodland among rhododendrons or other shrubs, combining well with other shade-loving perennials like meconopsis or primulas. There are several small species with a dainty charm that makes them worth growing in shady beds among other small plants or in the crevices of shady walls. They are all easily grown in humus-rich moist soil in partial shade, or in sun if the ground remains moist. The species are readily raised from seed, and the cultivars can be increased by division in autumn.

In the following descriptions I have included the hybrids or cultivars with their likely parents, but several of doubtful origin are listed under *H.* x *brizoides.*

H. americana ✿ Variable, usually 40–50 cm (16–20 in), leaves rounded, cordate, hairy, with toothed lobes, often mottled with grey or purple, flowers tiny in loose spikes, greenish from red calyces. I have grown some very pleasing foliage plants from wild-collected seed, and there are now some excellent selections coming into cultivation, especially in the USA: 'Chocolate Veil' leaves very large chocolate-purple with lighter markings, 'Emerald Veil' leaves purple-backed, green with silvery marbling, 'Pewter Moon' (one of the first of these, leaves reddish-purple overlaid with a pewter 'bloom', 'Pewter Veil' leaves pink-tinged, becoming green with silver markings, 'Ruby Veil' leaves remaining deep red with some silvery markings, 'Ruby Ruffles' similar to the last but leaves ruffled, 'Velvet Knight' even darker than 'Chocolate Veil'.

H.* x *brizoides Hybrids of *H. sanguinea* with *H. micrantha* and probably *H. americana,* usually to 60 cm (2 ft), resembling *H. sanguinea,* but with a wide range of colours. 'Apple Blossom' tall, pale pink, 'Bresssingham Hybrids', tall, elegant, from white through pale to deep pink to red, 'Chocolate Ruffles', leaves ruffled with dark brown tips and purple edges, flowers small purple,'Coral Cloud', crimson, 'Firebird', deep red, 'Firefly', orange-pink, 'Green Ivory', robust, abundant flowers green and white, 'Lace Ruffles' similar to 'Chocolate Ruffles', but leaves green and silver, 'Mary Rose' and 'Pretty Polly,' pink flowers, larger in the latter. 'Red Spangles', 🏆 one of the brightest and best, large orange-red, 'Schneewittchen', ✸ excellent large pure white flowers over a long season, 'Scintillation', 🏆 good marbled foliage, flowers white tipped with bright pink, 'White Blush' leaves green and silver, flowers pale pink from reddish buds. Various other hybrids are occasionally offered.

H. chlorantha To 80 cm (30 in), leaves 5–7–lobed, oval, toothed, flowers pale green in loose spikes. N.W. Am.

H. cylindrica Similar to *H. chlorantha* To 60 cm (2 ft), dense spikes of greenish-cream flowers. N.W. Am

H. grossularifolia ✸ To 40 cm (16 in), but in my experience usually much smaller, leaves rounded, toothed, lobed, flowers comparatively large pure white. It is one of the best small species, with sufficient vigour for the edge of a shady border. N.C. USA.

H. hallii Similar to *H. grossularifolia* flowers greenish-white flushed with pink.

H. micans Small-growing, flowers deep reddish-pink in short spikes. S.W. USA.

H. micrantha Variable, to 50 cm (20 in),leaves oval, 5–7–lobed, toothed, to 8 cm (3 in) wide, tall very loose panicles of tiny white flowers. Although the flowers are so small it is a remarkably graceful plant to grow among shrubs. W. USA. There are several more dramatic cultivars: 'Carousel' leaves glossy, heavily patterned with silver, flowers rose, 'Palace Purple, 🏆 the most popular cultivar, leaves deep purple, loose sprays of pinkish flowers. It is an exceptionally fine foliage plant when vegetatively propagated. 'Ruffles', new cultivar obtainable in the USA, leaves ruffled green, flowers pure white. Some cultivars listed under *H.* x *brizoides* are placed here by some authorities.

68 *Heuchera micrantha*

H. parvifolia To 15 cm (6 in), with kidney-shaped leaves and white or cream flowers in small spikes. Uncommon. S. USA.

H. pilosissima Rarely grown, to 60 cm (2 ft), leaves hairy, cordate, shallowly lobed, flowers pale pink in compact heads, on brown-hairy stems. California.

H. pubescens To 60 cm (2 ft), leaves rounded, cordate, sharply toothed, lobed, spikes of green flowers, sometimes flushed with purple. E., C. USA. 'Alba' flowers pure white.

H. pulchella One of the smallest, leaves deeply lobed, toothed, dense spikes of pale pink flowers. S. USA.

H. rubescens Leaves rounded, 3–5-lobed with narrow teeth, flowers pink, usually green-tipped, in one-sided loose heads.

An attractive species of medium height. W., C. USA

H. sanguinea An excellent species, much used in hybridization, to 60 cm (2 ft), leaves rounded hairy, 5–7 lobed, flowers in loose panicles, unusually large bright red. S. USA. Some cultivars have been named: 'Alba' white, 'Frosty' leaves heavily marbled with white, flowers red, 'Snowstorm', leaves margined with white, flowers deep rosy pink.

H. versicolor To 20 cm (8 in), leaves hairy-margined, oval, short spikes of pink flowers becoming red with age. S. USA.

H. villosa Variable, 30-70 cm (28 in), leaves rounded, hairy, cordate with pointed, hairy lobes, petals narrow. S.E. USA.

x ***Heucherella*** (*Saxifragaceae*)

Bigeneric hybrids between *Heuchera* and *Tiarella*, with the same delicate beauty of flower, but lacking the invasive tendency of *Tiarella*. They enjoy the same conditions as heucheras.

H. alba (*H. brizoides* x *Tiarella wherryi*) 'Bridget Bloom' is usually grown, clump-forming, heuchera-like lobed toothed leaves, usually mottled brown at first, often developing autumn colour later. Flower spikes soft pink in early summer 'Rosalie', ✸ a recent even more beautiful cultivar, leaves more reddish-brown, finer spikes of clear pale pink flowers.

H. tiarelloides (*H. brizoides* x *T. cordifolia*) 🏆 A spreading stoloniferous plant, forming a dense carpet of leaves with narrow spires of tiny pink flowers. It makes good ground cover without being too invasive.

Hieracium (*Compositae*)

A very large genus of annuals and perennials, very few of which are garden-worthy. Most of them seed excessively, and those with attractive foliage should be dead-headed. A few, notably the orange-flowered *H. aurantiacum*, are too invasive for any but the wildest garden, and are likely to prove ineradicable. Propagation is only too easy by seed.

H. lanatum Clump-forming, leaves very large, pointed, white-felted, flowers small yellow dandelions in loose sprays through the summer. The leaves are splendid but the flowers detract from them.

H. maculatum Clump-forming with deep green leaves heavily blotched or spotted with blackish-purple. The leaves are quite attractive, but the flowers are not, and it will seed everywhere.

H. villosum Clumps of very white-hairy grey-green leaves, and larger dandelions than those of *H. lanatum*. It is probably worth growing if dead-headed.

Horminum (*Labiatae*)

H. pyrenaicum The only species, evergreen, rosette-forming, leaves basal, rounded, crinkly, toothed, flowers to 2 cm (0.8 in) long in dense one-sided spikes, violet-blue, tubular, mid- to late summer. It can be raised from seed and is quite effective as a border edging.

Hosta (*Liliaceae/ Hostaceae*)

A genus of some 40 species of clump-forming herbaceous perennials with magnificent foliage in a remarkable range of colours and textures, and attractive spikes of lily-like flowers in shades of white and lavender to purple. With the appreciation of the importance of foliage in the garden, its beauty less ephemeral than that of flowers, hostas have become immensely popular, with a constant influx of new cultivars in Britain and particularly in the USA, and hundreds are available to gardeners. This presents problems in a book of this kind, and in the descriptions that follow I have been extremely selective, choosing mainly those that have stood the test of time, and in many cases have received the 🏆 Gardeners wishing to widen their range should consult the specialist books on the subject, and see them displayed at our Shows and in gardens and specialist nurseries. When choosing them at a nursery or a Show, bear in mind that their ultimate size of leaf and height will be much greater in the garden.

In general hostas grow best in deep rich soils with plentiful humus in partial shade. They make a perfect edging of beautiful leaves from spring to late autumn, the perfect foil to taller perennials, especially those that thrive in some shade like lilies, meconopsis, the taller campanulas and astilbes. Once planted they are best left alone for several years, as they will develop larger leaves of better colour when they are well established. The cultivars must be propagated by division in early spring, if necessary. The species can be raised from seed, but unless this is wild-collected there is likely to be a great variation in the seedlings.

'August Moon' Pale green leaves deepening to gold, large, crinkled, and gold at maturity. Flowers tall, pale lavender. mid-season. A vigorous plant that colours best in shade.

69 *Hostas* at the edge of a partially shaded border, with *Ourisia macrocarpa* in the background

'Big Daddy' Leaves large, crinkled, blue. Flowers, pale lavender, early. Plant in shade.
'Blue Angel' 🏆 Leaves very large, unpuckered, blue. Flowers palest lilac. It is one of the best 'blues' for shade, but slow to reach its full potential.
'Blue Moon' Leaves small, rounded, pale blue. Flowers purplish-blue in dense spikes, mid-season. It colours well in shade but is slow to establish.
'Blue Wedgwood' Leaves medium, blue, triangular, heavily crinkled. Flowers lavender mid-season. Very good but slow to mature.
'Buckshaw Blue' Leaves medium, very blue and cupped. Flowers white, faintly tinged grey. Plant in shade.
H. crispula 🏆 Leaves large, cordate, with a wavy edge, and conspicuous broad white margin. Flowers tall, pale mauve, in mid-season. A superb plant in good soils in partial shade.

70 *Hosta crispula*

H. fluctuans 'Variegated' Leaves very large, waved, green with a wide cream margin. Flowers very tall, pale lilac. It is one of the most spectacular, but may take several years to reach full size.
H. fortunei Leaves medium-large, heart-shaped, green. Flowers tall, deep mauve, late season. The plain-leaved form is less popular than its varieties and cultivars with similar flowers in shades of mauve. All do best in shade. *H. f.* 'Albomarginata' 🏆 a fine variety with leaves irregularly margined with white, var. *albopicta* 🏆 excellent, leaves waved, cream with a green margin when young, but changing to green later, var. *aurea* 🏆 leaves medium sized, a beautiful soft yellow early in the season, fading to green later, var. aureomarginata more vigorous, leaves larger, yellow-edged, darker flowers, var. *hyacinthina* 🏆 leaves grey-green, slightly crinkled, with a very narrow white margin, flowers large violet, a good easily-grown variety.
'Francee' 🏆 Leaves heart-shaped, broad, greyish-green with a an irregular pure white margin. Flowers medium-tall, pale lilac. A first-class vigorous plant for the garden.
'Frances Williams' 🏆 (See plate 57) Leaves large rounded, greyish-blue, incurving at the edge, with a broad, irregular yellow margin which diffuses into the green. Flowers white, early. Tends to scorch in the sun, but is superb in partial shade.
'Ginko Craig' Low-growing, leaves narrow with a broad pure white edge. Flowers purple, late. An outstanding and easy hosta for shade.
'Gold Edger' Leaves small, cordate, golden. Flowers pale lilac, mid-season, one of the best smaller golden hostas, needing some sun to colour well.
'Gold Standard' Leaves large, becoming rich golden-yellow, irregularly margined with green. Flowers pale lilac, mid-season. It needs to be grown in partial shade, with sufficient sun to ensure the gold developing.
'Golden Medallion' Leaves medium, cupped and crinkled, pure golden-yellow in some sun. Flowers white, early. An attractive slow-growing plant.
'Golden Prayers' Leaves small, golden. Flowers pale lavender. Like most of the gold-leaved hostas it needs some sun to colour well.
'Golden Sunburst' A golden sport of 'Frances Williams', with leaves that burn in full sun, and are green in full shade.
'Golden Tiara' 🏆 Leaves small, green with gold edge. Flowers rich purple at mid-summer. One of the best compact growers for edging.
H. gracillima Leaves medium-small, lanceolate with undulate margin, glossy green. Flowers pinkish violet.
'Hadspen Blue' Leaves medium, pointed, very glaucous blue. Flowers short, lavender. One of the bluest of all in partial shade.
'Halcyon' 🏆 Leaves medium-large, broad, greyish-blue. Flowers pale violet, mid-season. One of the most reliable 'blues' for shade, and the best of the 'Tardiana Group'. (*H. tardiflora* x *H sieboldiana* 'Elegans').
'Honeybells' 🏆 Leaves large, waved, light green. Flowers late, in large spikes, very pale lilac. Very robust, and will grow in sun if the soil is moist.
'Hydon Sunset' Leaves very small, broad at the base, gold, liable to fade to green later. Flowers deep purple. A good edging plant for partial shade.
'June' Leaves medium, golden-yellow with a bluish-green edge. A recent sport of 'Halcyon', and one of the most striking hostas.
'Krossa Regal' 🏆 Leaves very large, glaucous-blue, slightly waved. Flowers in very tall spikes, pale lavender, mid-season. One of the most reliable large hostas for partial shade.
H. lancifolia 🏆 Leaves medium-large, narrow, glossy green. Flowers dark violet, late in the season. A fine mound-forming edger.
'Lemon Lime' Leaves small, waved, gold. Flowers lilac in short spikes, mid to late season. One of the more vigorous small golden cultivars.
H. longisima Leaves very long and narrow, green, in 20 cm (8 in) high mounds. Flower spikes comparatively tall, pale

violet, late. It does best in damp soils.
'Love Pat' Leaves medium, cupped, glaucous-blue. Flowers white, early. It is a very good new 'blue'.
'Midas Touch' Leaves medium-large, cupped, gold. Flowers late, pale lilac. Slow-growing, but a good gold with some sun.
H. minor Leaves small, waved, dark green. Flowers deep mauve in mid-season. One of the smallest, but quite strong-growing with excellent flowers.
H. montana Leaves large, oval, glossy dark green. Flowers tall, pale violet, mid-season. The flowers colour is variable. *H. m.* 'Aureomarginata' leaves with a broad yellow margin, flowers almost white. It is a spectacular plant, but is often slow to establish.
H. nigrescens Leaves medium-large, cupped slightly, glaucous-blue on very long petioles. Flowers very tall, pale lavender, in mid-season.
'Northern Halo' Sport of *H. sieboldiana* 'Elegans', leaves crinkly, often cupped, blue with a white margin.
'Pastures New' Leaves medium-small, grey-green, cordate. Flowers pale lavender, well above the leaves. A vigorous mound-former with good flowers.
'Pearl Lake' Leaves medium, grey-green. Flowers lavender, on pinkish stems., early to mid-season. A good dense mound.
'Piedmont Gold' Leaves large, wavy-edged, deep yellow. Flowers very pale lavender on short stems. It needs partial shade, and is one of the best large golds.
H. plantaginea Leaves large, oval, glossy pale green. Flowers large, white, on tall spikes. Usually grown as *H. p.* 'Grandiflora' 🏆 with larger flowers. It flowers best with some sun.
H. rohdeifolia* f. *albopicta Leaves medium-small, lanceolate with a yellow edge that fades with age to white. Flowers long-stemmed purple, in mid-summer.
'Royal Standard' 🏆 Leaves large, deeply veined, pale green tending to turn yellowish. Flowers pure white in fine loose spikes. It is a first-class vigorous hosta that will tolerate sun.
'Shade Fanfare' 🏆 Leaves large, oval with a slightly waved margin, greyish-green with an irregular but generally wide creamy-white margin, that may turn yellow in sun. Flowers tall, lilac, mid-season. One of the best large hostas for a shady border.
H. sieboldiana Leaves large, cupped and puckered, glaucous blue. Flowers large, pale lilac, early. It is a magnificent and popular plant, especially as the cultivar *H. s.* 'Elegans' 🏆 with even more heavily textured leaves.
H. sieboldii 🏆 Not to be confused with the last, leaves medium-sized lanceolate, green with a white edging, flowers violet in late summer. A vigorous medium-sized grower.
'Snowden' A hybrid between *H. sieboldiana* and *H. fortunei* 'Aurea'. Leaves large, glaucous pale blue. Flowers large, white, at mid-summer. A wonderful plant in semi-shade with plenty of moisture.
'Sugar and Cream' Sport of 'Honey Bells' with large cream-edged green leaves, and white flowers. Excellent and vigorous in semi-shade.

'Sum and Substance' 🏆 Leaves huge, thick, and glossy, greenish gold. Flowers tall. lavender, late in the season. It is possibly the largest-leaved of all, and a most spectacular plant when well- established, in a site with a fair amount of sun.

71 *Hosta* 'Sum and Substance'

'Summer Fragrance' Leaves medium-large, somewhat waved, green with a cream margin. Flowers scented, pinkish-blue, on tall stems in late summer.
'Tall Boy' ✱ Leaves medium large, green. Flowers very tall. deep purple over a long period from mid-summer. It is one of the finest species for flower.
H. tardiflora Leaves medium, lanceolate, glossy dark green. Flowers deep lilac, very late.
H. tokudama Leaves medium,cupped and puckered, blue. Flowers short-stemmed, greyish-white, mid-season. It grows best in shade. *H. t. f. aureo-nebulosa* leaves yellow with a broad irregular bluish margin, *H. t. f. flavo-circinalis* leaves blue with a broad creamy-yellow margin.
H. undulata* var. *undulata 🏆 Leaves green with a wide creamy-yellow centre. Flowers pale purple in early summer. It is less vigorous than other varieties of *H. undulata*: *H. undulatat* var. *albomarginata* (syn. 'Thomas Hogg') leaves white-edged, very wavy, flowers tall, pale purple, early, var. *erromena* 🏆 leaves green undulate, flowers paler on tall stems. Var. *univittata* 🏆 a very popular variety, leaves with a

wide cream central band, flowers violet.
H. ventricosa 🏆 Leaves large, dark green, with a slightly waved margin. Flowers large deep purple on long stems. It is vigorous, making a fine green mound. Var. *aureomarginata* 🏆 differs in having a pale yellow margin later becoming white. It is one of the best variegated hostas, when established. 'Aureo-maculata' leaves with a central yellow splash which eventually turns green. Much less vigorous.
H. venusta 🏆 Leaves tiny, cordate, dark green. Flowers deep lavender on 15–20 cm (6–8 in) stems. A delightful miniature, small enough for a shady rock garden but vigorous enough for the front of a border.
'Wide Brim' 🏆 Leaves large, bluish-green with a wide creamy-yellow rim, that widens as the season progresses. flowers lavender, mid-season. It keeps its colour well in shade.
'Zounds' Leaves like those of *H. sieboldiana*, but large, puckered and gold. Flowers pale lilac, early. it is one of the best gold-leaved plants for light shade.

Houttuynia (*Saururaceae*)

One invasive herbaceous perennial with a few cultivars.
H. cordata Spreading rhizomatous perennial to 50 cm (20 in), leaves very dark green, pointed, cordate, often red-margined at first and with red-tinged veins, short upright spikes of minute yellow flowers, surrounded by 4–6 pure white petal-like bracts, in mid-summer. It spreads very widely indeed, often without many flowers in any one place. The cultivars are less invasive but their spreading propensity should not be underestimated. Wet conditions make them more invasive. 'Chameleon' leaves strikingly variegated, with a green centre and a broad red margin streaked yellow. It can be invasive even in dry soils, and should never be planted among precious plants, except as a water plant in a pot standing at the edge of a pool, where it can be very effective. 'Flore Pleno' widely grown cultivar, differing only in having a larger number of white bracts forming a cone. 'Variegata' is probably the same as 'Chameleon'.

Hylomecon (*Papaveraceae*)

H. japonicum (syn. *Stylophorum japonicum*) The only species, clump-forming, to 30 cm (1 ft), leaves pale green, 5–7-lobed pinnate, with toothed margins, flowers mainly solitary pure yellow poppies to 4 cm (1.6 in) wide, in early summer. It is a delightful plant for humus-rich soil in partial shade, easily raised from seed sown in autumn.

Hypericum (*Guttiferae*)

A very large genus, the majority of which are shrubs or semi-shrubby perennials, from prostrate mats to large bushes. Although they vary enormously in habit, most have simple opposite leaves, and typical yellow 5-petalled flowers starry or cup-shaped flowers with a prominent boss of yellow stamens. In the descriptions below I have only included a selection of the hardier mat-forming or semi-prostrate species, suitable for the edge of a sunny border. Their low mounds of leaves smothered in summer with masses of yellow flowers combine well with blue flowered perennials like campanulas. Those described grow best in well-drained soil in a sunny position, and are easy to propagate from cuttings at any time during the growing season, or from seed. Many are of border-line hardiness.
H. cerastioides (syn. *H. rhodoppeum*) Mat-forming, to 25 cm (10 in), leaves downy, oval, abundant open flowers, deep golden-yellow, to 4 cm (1.6 in) wide, in summer. It is one of the easier and hardier species.
H. coris Mound-forming, to 20 cm (8 in), leaves very small linear, abundant small starry deep yellow flowers faintly marked with red. It is quite hardy.

72 *Hypericum coris*

H. elongatum (syn. *H. hyssopifolium*) ✱ Short-lived perennial, to 30 cm (1 ft), at first mat-forming with small blue-green leaves, becoming erect in its second season, with dense upright spikes of small yellow starry flowers. It is an unusual species, but sometimes behaves as a biennial, setting plenty of seed, from which it is easily raised.
H. olympicum 🏆 Sub-shrubby, a mound to 20 cm (8 in) high, leaves small oval glaucous blue-green, solitary or loose heads of bright yellow, narrow-petalled flowers with a large boss of stamens. It is one of the most reliable perennials and is very hardy. *H. o.* 'Citrinum' (*H. o. f. uniflorum* 'Citrinum') 🏆 flowers soft lemon yellow, a beautiful colour which combines better with other plants than the harsh yellow of the type. *H. o. f. minus* smaller in all its parts and less vigorous, with a paler yellow form 'Sulphureum', as well as a form with cream-variegated leaves 'Variegata'.
H. orientale (See plate 89) Cushion-forming, leaves small, deep green, toothed, lanceolate, a long succession of deep yellow flowers 2–5 cm (0.8–2 in) wide in summer. It is not as attractive or as widely grown as *H. olympicum*, but is extremely hardy and tends to self-seed.

Iberis (*Cruciferae*)

About 30 species of annuals and low-growing evergreen perennials or subshrubs. A few are small plants for the rock garden or alpine house, but the majority are large enough for the front of a border or a wall, and are among the most popular of easy 'rock plants' to combine with alyssum and aubrietia in sheets of colour in late spring. They are easily propagated by cuttings in summer, or by seed of the species.

I. gibraltarica Semi-shrubby evergreen to 30 cm (1 ft), leaves thick, 2.5 cm (1 in) long, spathulate, sparsely toothed, dense heads of pure white flowers in summer. Less hardy than *I. sempervirens*, with which it may be confused. Morocco and Gibraltar.

I. saxatilis Similar to *I. sempervirens*, but more compact, flowers white often becoming pinkish with age. S. Europe.

I. semperflorens Similar to the last, leaves larger, spathulate, flowering in late autumn and winter. It is scarcely hardy enough for the open garden in average temperatures, but is excellent in nearly frost-free gardens, or in the cool greenhouse. W., S. Italy.

I. sempervirens 🏆 The most widely cultivated, a spreading mat to 20 cm (8 in), leaves thick, deep-green, 2 cm (0.8 in) long, and masses of flowers in 5 cm (2 in) wide heads in late spring and summer. Med. 'Little Gem' (syn. 'Weisser Zwerg') a compact form, smaller in all its parts, possibly a form of *I. saxatilis*. 'Snowflake' 🏆 the finest cultivar, with even more profuse and larger flower heads.

Incarvillea (*Bignoniaceae*)

Around 12 species of annuals and herbaceous perennials, either acaulescent with basal rosettes of pinnate leaves and upright stems bearing several large gloxinia-like flowers, or caulescent with semi-shrubby habit and leafy stems bearing similar but smaller flowers. The spectacular acaulescent group grow best in rich moist soil in partial shade, or in full sun in cooler gardens, the caulescent species need sunnier conditions in very well-drained soil. They may be raised from seed sown in autumn and kept cool, or rather more quickly with bottom heat under glass, or established clumps can be divided. The more shrubby species can also be grown from cuttings during summer.

I. arguta Caulescent semi-woody, branching stems to 60 cm (2 ft), leaves 5–9-lobed pinnate, with 2–3 cm (0.8–1.2 in) long toothed leaflets, flowers tubular in terminal loose heads, clear pink, to 3.5 cm (1.4 in) long, in late summer. It seems hardy, at least to -6 °C (21 °F) in well-drained soil in a sunny border.

I. delavayi Acaulescent, a large species, 40–50 cm high, leaves to 30 cm (1 ft) long, with up to 20 leaflets with toothed margins, the terminal leaflet smaller, flowers up to 10, to 8 cm (3 in) long, rose-pink with a yellow throat, early to mid-summer. It is an easy species in rich moist soils. China. Var. *alba* ✸ a superb white variety with a yellow throat, 'Bees Pink' strong-growing cultivar with paler pink flowers.

I. lutea Acaulescent, to 60 cm (2 ft) tall, with 30 cm (1 ft) long leaves with toothed lanceolate leaflets, more widely spaced than those of *I. mairei* and with the terminal leaflet of similar size to the others, and racemes of up to 20 large yellow flowers. Seed has only recently been introduced and it has a reputation for taking a long time to flower.

I. mairei (syn. *I. brevipes*) Acaulescent, to 30 cm (1 ft), leaves to 20 cm (8 in) long, with 5–9 oval finely toothed leaflets, the terminal one much larger than the remainder, flowers deep purplish-pink, yellow in the throat, to 6 cm (2.3 in) long, with large spreading lobes. Several seed collections have been made recently. China. *H. m. grandiflora* leaves shorter with only 3–5 leaflets, flowers exceptionally large. 'Frank Ludlow' dwarf form with particularly large flowers. 'Nyota Sama' a little taller with paler pink flowers.

73 *Incarvillea mairei*

I. olgae Caulescent, similar to *I. arguta*, but taller with leaves more sparsely toothed, and flowers smaller with shorter tubes. It seems to be more difficult to grow and perhaps more tender.

I. sinensis Caulescent species to 50 cm (20 in) but usually less, leaves finely divided to 12 cm (4.7 in) long, loose racemes of 3 cm (1.2 in) long flowers, deep pink or creamy-white. 'Alba' widely grown and very floriferous creamy-white, unfortunately annual or biennial, subsp. *variabilis* uncommon, pink, said to be perennial. China.

I. zhongdianensis Acaulescent, generally smaller than *I. mairei*, leaves 10–15 cm (4–6 in) long, with entire, and almost equal leaflets, heads of up to 8 large purplish-pink flowers, yellow with purple lines within, to 5 cm (2 in) long. It is a recent reintroduction from China (as *I. compacta*) which is proving amenable in cultivation.

74 *Incarvillea zhongdianensis*

Inula (*Compositae*)

About 90 annuals and perennials, many of the larger ones too tall to be considered here. The perennials are clump-forming, herbaceous, with simple usually toothed leaves, and upright stems bearing solitary or many yellow daisy flowers in summer. The smaller species do best in well-drained soil in full sun, and are suitable for the front of a border as well as the rock garden, the larger in any reasonable loam, as long as it is not too dry.

I. candida 20–30 cm (8–12 in), leaves white-hairy, rounded to lanceolate, clusters of a few small yellow short-rayed flowers. It has the whitest of leaves, and looks very fine as a foliage plant in rock crevices in the wild, or as a wall plant in warm dry gardens. It resents excessive winter wet, and is unlikely to be hardy below -6 °C (21 °F). Greece.

I. ensifolia Clump, to 40 cm (16 in), leaves narrowly lanceolate, hairy, to 8 cm (3 in) long, solitary yellow daisies to 4 cm (1.6 in) wide in summer. An easy front of the border plant, combining well with the blues of campanulas. C. Europe–Caucasus. 'Compacta' small-growing, flowers dark yellow. 'Gold Star' intermediate in height with paler flowers.

I. grandiflora A little larger than *I. ensifolia*, leaves broader, toothed, flowers to 6 cm (2.3 in) wide. Possibly the same as *I. orientalis*, generally taller.

I. hookeri ✱ Spreading, 60–70 cm (24–28 in) upright branching stems, leaves very hairy, lanceolate to oblong, flowers 1–3, narrow-rayed to 6 cm (2.3 in) wide, from very hairy buds. It is a magnificent vigorous perennial near to our size limit, or sometimes taller, with most attractive shaggy buds and greenish-yellow flowers, over a long period in mid- to late summer. Himalaya.

75 *Inula hookeri*

I. orientalis *See* ***I. grandiflora***

I. royleana Similar in habit to *I. hookeri*, to 60 cm (2 ft), leaves longer and broader toothed, flowers very large, deep yellow, solitary, to 10 cm (4 in) wide, with broader rays. It is a robust plant in moist soil, but less spreading than *I. hookeri*.

I. verbascifolia Uncommon in cultivation, like a larger version of *I. candida*, leaves less hairy, linear bracts below the flowers. It needs similar conditions and will only thrive in warm gardens.

Iris (*Iridaceae*)

In this very large and important genus I have been selective, excluding the species that are bulbous or have stout rhizomes. The genus has been split into several subgenera, some with several Sections, and I have mainly followed this classification in deciding which to include. The Subgenus Iris contains plants with well-developed rhizomes and a prominent beard, usually on the falls, and includes the bearded or Pogon irises, so popular in the border, as well as the Hexapogon, Oncocyclus and Regelia sections, and I have excluded all these. I have also excluded the Nepalensis Subgenus, that mainly require special treatment under glass, and the bulbous Subgenera, Xiphium, Hermodactyloides, and Scorpiris (Juno).

The plants described belong to the Subgenus Limniris, containing two Sections, Lophiris, (the Evansias), and Limniris, a very complicated section with 16 Series, and of these I have only omitted those that are too tall or are best grown under glass. Although their leaves and flowers vary considerably, the latter all have the typical iris shape, with three upright standards, and three falls that consist of a generally narrow, semi-upright, basal haft, and a broad fall which often has a beard, crest, or ridge in the centre. Their cultural requirements vary from Series to Series, and I have therefore included the Series after the name of the species as a general guide, detailing any exceptions.

Lophiris Section The 'Evansia' irises, characterized by a frilly crest on the falls. They are mainly woodlanders in nature, and grow best in humus-rich but well-drained soil in partial shade, except in cool gardens where they will tolerate full sun.

Limniris Section, The Series

Californicae An important group of beautiful irises, from the Pacific coast of N. America, mainly on acid soils in the open or in light woodland. They seem surprisingly neglected, considering their beauty and ease of cultivation in neutral or acid well-drained soils in light shade, or in full sun in cooler gardens. They are typically fairly dwarf with one or two flowers ,with spreading falls, to a stem, in early to mid-summer.

Ensatae *See* ***I. lactea.*** *I. ensata* is in the *Laevigatae*

Foetidissimae *See* ***I. foetidissima***

Hexagonae Water irises, requiring permanently moist rich soil, in sun, or in partial shade if the moisture is less certain.

Laevigatae Mainly tall moisture-loving plants, including the 'Kaemferi' irises. They thrive in rich permanently moist soil, with plenty of sun, but some resent excessively wet soils in winter.

Longipetalae Two species similar to the Californiaornicae, but native to calcareous soils that are wet in spring but dry in summer. They do better in drier and sunnier sites than the Cailfornicae, but must be kept moist in spring.

Prismaticae *See* ***I. prismatica***

Ruthenicae *See* ***I. ruthenica***

Sibiricae A large and important group of generally tall deciduous irises, mainly from moist woodland or mountain sites in C., E. Asia. They are easily grown in rich soil that is not too dry in the growing season.

Spuriae A variable group, some from open grasslands, others from alpine areas. They are generally easily grown in rich but well-drained soil in full sun, but a few do better in partial shade. Several are too large to consider here, including *I. crocea*, *I. monnieri*, *I. orientalis*, and *I.spuria* and most of its subspecies.

Tenuifoliae Uncommonly grown species from the steppes of Asia, needing an open sunny position in the garden.

Tripetalae A small group characterized by having markedly reduced standards, hence the appearance of 'three petals'. It includes *I. setosa*, a variable but easily grown species for moist acid soil in sun or very light shade.

Unguiculares A popular group of winter-flowering plants for hot dry conditions.

Vernae *See* ***I. verna***

The Species:

I. bracteata *Californicae* Clump-forming with short rhizomes with wiry roots, leaves broader than most of the group, to 30 cm (1 ft) long, short leafy bracts up the 30 cm (1 ft) stems each subtend two 6 cm (2.3 in) wide flowers, pale yellow in colour with purplish veining and a deeper yellow patch in the centre of the spreading falls.

I. brandzae *See* ***I. sintenisii***

I. bulleyana *Sibiricae* A very recent reintroduction from China, that may be a hybrid of *I. chrysographes* and *I. forrestii*, both of which it resembles, or a species. Variable, generally 40–50 cm (16–20 in), leaves long like those of *I. chrysographes*, flowers 1–2, large, deep violet -blue with very variable white spots and streaks, and yellow at the base. The various forms seen in the wild are all attractive, and one hopes that they will be as easy to grow as *I. chrysographes*, needing moist humus-rich soil in sun or light shade.

I. chrysographes ✱ *Sibiricae* Variable, usually 30–50 cm (12–20 in), leaves narrow, grey-green, flowers usually two, dark reddish to blackish-violet. with drooping falls, usually lined with deep yellow but sometimes unmarked, and spreading standards. It is a wonderful waterside plant in permanently damp sites, especially in its popular near-black form, that looks wonderful among the soft yellows of *Primula sikkimensis* or *P. florindae*. China. Several cultivars, some of which may have *I. forrestii* blood, as they hybridize freely, 'Black Knight' and 'Inshriach' are particularly dark, var. *rubella* and 'Margot Holmes' flowers reddish-purple, the latter with yellow streaks in the throat.

I. chrysophylla *Californicae* Variable in height to 20 cm (8 in), leaves narrow grey-green, flowers rather slender, pale to deep yellow with deeper yellow veining. It is one of the least common of the Pacific Coast irises in cultivation, and may be a little tender.

I. clarkei *Sibiricae* A Himalayan species, similar in habit to I. *chrysographes*, leaves broader, stems often branched, flowers with more spreading standards, dark blue to purple, with a large white patch veined with dark blue on the falls. It is not widely grown, and does not need such wet conditions.

I. confusa *Lophiris* Clump-forming with upright slender bamboo-like stems with a fan of broad leaves at the top of each. Stiff, branching flower stems appear from the fan in spring and bear a succession of rather small flowers, opening flat, white with a yellow crest and blotch, and some purple spotting. It is the largest of the evansias, and strictly too tall to consider here, as it can attain 1 m (3 ft). China.

I. cristata ☼ *Lophiris* One of the smallest. generally 8–10 cm (3–4 in), spreading widely by its branching rhizomes, small fans of leaves, comparatively large flowers, usually lavender-blue but variable in colour in nature, the falls almost flat with a white patch in the centre and three yellow or orange ridges. It is an exquisite iris for the front of a moist shady border with other small plants. It tends to exhaust its soil and needs replanting every two or three years. E., N. Am.

I. douglasiana *Californicae* Large clumps of coarse dark green leaves flushed with reddish-purple at the base, branched stems, flowers 2–3, 8 cm (3 in) wide, varying in colour between pale lilac and deep purplish-blue, rarely white. It is the best known and most robust of the group, but seems to me somewhat coarse compared with the others. There may be better forms!

I. ensata (syn. *I. kaemferi*) *Laevigatae* Leaves variable to 50 cm (20 in) long with a conspicuous central vein, flower stems usually unbranched, with 2–4 very large flowers, purple or reddish, with yellow at the base of the spreading falls, and small standards. One of the most magnificent irises, with huge flowers, usually seen as one of its many cultivars. The species usually grows to 60–90 cm (2–3 ft) and the cultivars are taller, and I have not described them individually. They like very moist rich soil, but do better in borders which are not too boggy in winter.

I. fernaldii *Californicae* Clumps to 40 cm (16 in), leaves narrow, grey-green, to 40 cm (16 in) long, slender stems, flowers 1-2, pale yellow with a darker central line on the falls, with faint purplish veining. It is relatively untried, but an attractive species.

I. foetidissima *Foetidissimae* Almost too well-known to need description, our native Gladwyn iris forms tufts of leathery bright green glossy leaves, branched stems from 50–80 cm (20–30 in), inconspicuous greyish-yellow flowers, tinged to some degree with purple, followed by a cluster of vivid orange-red seeds which persist for a month or two in winter. The evergreen leaves and brilliant seeds are worthwhile features of a very undemanding plant, that seeds itself around almost to excess, even in very dry shade. Two yellow varieties var. *citrina* and var. *lutescens* have flowers of a clear yellow, and varieties are sometimes seen with yellow fruits. 'Variegata' excellent foliage plant with leaves striped with cream.

I. forrestii *Sibiricae* ✱ Clump-forming with very narrow grassy leaves, and unbranched stems with two flowers, clear yellow streaked with purple on the haft and faintly on the rest of the falls, with upright standards. A beautiful species that does not need wet conditions. China in alpine grassland.

76 *Iris forrestii*

I. fulva *Hexagonae* 40–70 cm (16–28 in), leaves moderately wide, flowers 5–6 cm (2–2.3 in) wide with pendent falls and standards in an unusual shade of orange-red or copper. It is the only widely grown species in the series, and is a remarkably striking plant when it does well in moist rich soils, but it does not seem easy.

I x ***fulvala*** (*I. fulva* x *I. brevicaulis*) The hybrid is easier to grow, but the flower colour is more 'ordinary', a rich deep purple.

I. gracilipes *Lophiris* Dwarf clump-forming evansia, 10–15 cm (4–6 in), leaves very narrow, flowers 3–4 cm (1.2–1.6 in) wide similar to those of *I cristata* with a large white blotch, veined with purple, crest mainly white. It is equally beautiful and requires similar conditions to *I. cristata*. Japan, China.

I. graminea spuriae 20–40 cm (8–16 in) Leaves abundant narrow, longer than the flowers stems, flowers 1-2, to 8 cm (3 in) diameter, violet-purple with a greenish-winged haft and a white patch on the falls, veined with violet. Very easy and persistent but tends to hide its flowers among the leaves.

I. hartwegii *Californicae* One of the smaller plants of the series, leaves very narrow, flowers 1-2, with unusually narrow falls and standards, pale yellow or lavender, with darker veining. It seems reasonably easy in partial shade. Three subspecies are grown: subsp. *australis* to 40 cm (16 in), flowers dark violet-blue, subsp. *columbiana* flowers larger pale yellow with darker veining, subsp. *pinetorum* flowers

narrow, pale cream with darker yellow markings, and a frilly edge to the falls.
I. hexagona *Hexagonae* Rare, leaves long, broad, stems branching to 80 cm (30 in), flowers very large, purplish-blue with a yellow patch on the falls.
I. innominata *Californicae* ✱ Deep yellow with Milium effusum aureum Very variable, clump-forming, to 25 cm (10 in), leaves very narrow dark green, often reddish-flushed at the base, to 15 cm (6 in) long, flowers one or two, 6–7 cm in diameter, most commonly yellow with wavy-edged spreading falls and upright standards, but very variable, including pale cream to deep orange, and pale lavender or pink to deep purplish-blue. It is an outstanding iris in all its forms and is easy to grow in humus-rich well-drained soils at the edge of a border in light shade, or in sun if there is plenty of moisture. Named cultivars are sometimes offered reflecting the various colour forms: 'Alba' white with some yellow on the haft, var. *lilacina* pale lavender, 'Rose' pale purplish-pink, 'Spinners' an outstanding deep yellow tinged and veined with brown.

77 *Iris innominata*, a pale variety

I. japonica *Lophiris* Similar to *I. confusa*, but lacking the upright 'canes', Its stolons root freely and produce fine large leaf-fans at ground level, upright stems to 40–75 cm (16–30 in), and flowers, produced in a long succession, larger than those of *I. confusa*, white or in shades of pale to deep purple, with a waved and frilly margin, and deep yellow crest with small violet blotches on each side of it. Individually the flowers are exceptionally fine and the plant does not seem difficult, proving very perennial in my garden in a warm, sunny bed, and apparently equally happy in partial shade. Japan, China.
I. kerneriana ✱ *Spuria* To 30 cm (1 ft), leaves grassy, flowers 2–4, large, lemon-yellow, with reflexing falls with a darker central blotch. I have found this beautiful species quite easy in full sun in rich soil. Turkey.
I. lactea *Ensatae* Clump-forming to 50 cm (20 in), leaves leathery grey-green, flowers 2–4, narrow, from blue to purple with paler very narrow falls. It is easily cultivated in a sunny position. E. Asia.
I. lacustris *Lophiris* Tiny, very similar to *I. cristata* except in its smaller and narrower leaves, and shorter stems, and needing the same treatment. C., N. Am.
I. laevigata *Ensatae* 🏆 Similar to *I. ensata*, but leaves wider, without a prominent midrib, and flowers usually smaller and narrower, purplish-blue or white, with a yellow haft. There are many cultivars of similar size to those of *I. ensata*. They are among the easiest irises to grow in wet conditions including shallow water, and make splendid groups with several cultivars together.
I. lazica *Unguiculares* Differs considerably from *I. unguicularis* in having fans of broad spreading glossy green leaves, and dark lavender flowers with white falls streaked with the same colour. It flowers much later, in early spring, and does not require hot dry conditions to flower well. Turkey.
I. longipetala *Longipetalae* Cups of glaucous leaves to 50–60 cm (20 in–2 ft), flowers to 8, white, veined with lavender on the long drooping falls. It grows well in dry conditions as long as it is moist in spring. W. USA.
I. macrosiphon *Californicae* Variable 15-25 cm (6–10 in) leaves very long, flowers 2 to a stem, varying from white to deep golden-yellow and from pale to deep violet, frequently with darker veining. Unfortunately it also varies in hardiness and some forms will not survive except in very mild gardens.
I. milesii *Lophiris* Distinct from other evansias in having a thick rhizome, large fans of leaves to 60 cm (2 ft), flowers stems 40–70 cm (16–28 in), flowers large pinkish-purple, with spreading falls, with wavy margins and a yellow crest. Easy in a sunny border. Himalayas.
I. missouriensis *Longipetalae* Similar to *I. longipetala*, leaves narrower and longer, flowers fewer on a stem, colour variable between pale and deep lilac, with or without a yellow blotch, falls heavily veined. It is easily grown and seems to do better in full sun and a drier situation than the Californicae.
I. munzii *Californicae* To 70 cm (28 in), leaves wide grey-green, fine flowers, 2–4, in shades of blue to purple, with wavy margins to the falls and standards. Sadly it is very tender, and only suitable for the greenhouse or near frost-free gardens.
I. prismatica *Prismaticae* Creeping with slender rhizomes, leaves narrow grassy to 60 cm (2 ft) long, thin upright stems, flowers 1–3, 5–6 cm (2–2.3 in) wide, from off-white to pale lavender, with greenish, purple-veined haft. I have found it easy and reliable in partial shade in moderately dry conditions.
I. purdyi *Californicae* Resembling *I. bracteata* in its stem leaves, all leaves heavily stained with red at the base, flowers large white or cream, sometimes with a hint of blue, and with pale purple spotting on the falls. It is a beautiful species that deserves to be more widely grown.
I. ruthenica *Ruthenicae* Variable, clump-forming, leaves long, grassy, to 30 cm (1 ft), flowers 1-2, with white falls heavily veined and margined with violet-blue, without a crest or central stripe, and upright standards of the same colour throughout. It is an easy plant, sometimes rather leafy, in any

soil that does not dry out. It varies greatly in size, and a small var. *nana* is sometimes seen, with 5 cm (2 in) leaves and very short flower stems. E. Asia.

I. sanguinea *Sibiricae* Similar to and often confused with *I. sibirica*, usually under 70 cm (28 in) high, leaves longer, glaucous, flowers 1–3, reddish-purple with a yellow haft veined purple, and small standards. S.E. Russia to Japan.

I. setosa *Tripetalae* ✸ Very variable, with some named varieties. It has short thick rhizomes, stems 20-50 cm (8–20 in), leaves 20-50 cm (8–20 in) long, purple-tinged at the base, flowers one to several, usually 6 cm (2.3 in) wide, in shades of blue or bluish-purple, or white in *I. s. alba*, with an exceptionally broad blade to the pendent falls, and very small narrow standards It is a most beautiful species with flowers of an elegant shape, for the front of the border in moist rich soil. E. Asia, N. N. America. Var. *arctica* (var. *nana*) dwarf, flowers purple veined and streaked with white. Var. *major* and subsp. *hondoensis* are robust, flowers purplish-blue on 70 cm (28 in) stems.

I. sibirica Very variable in height but usually over 60 cm (2 ft), with narrow green leaves much shorter than the branching stems, flowers 2–3 from pale blue to deep violet-blue flowers with a white centre to the falls, all veined with darker blue, except the small standards of uniform colour. This is an extremely easy plant for any but the driest conditions, forming increasing clumps for years without attention, especially at the waterside. C. Europe–C. Russia. There are many excellent named cultivars offered commercially, but they are generally too tall for consideration here.

I. sintenisii *Spuria* Densely clump-forming, leaves grassy, flowers slender, usually solitary, dark blue, with dense darker veining on the whitish falls. it is easy, needing less moisture than most irises. E. Europe. Turkey. Subsp. *brandzae* is very uncommon, and on the only occasion on which I have grown it, it seemed more compact with less veined flowers.

I. spuria *Spuria* Excellent large plants for the border with a wide range of subspecies and cultivar, mainly large. C. Europe. Subsp. *maritima* is smaller than the others, to 50 cm (20 in), with quite small flowers, cream with dark purple veining on the haft and dark blue on the blade of the fall.

I. tectorum ✸ *Lophiris* Plump rhizomes and fans of broad leaves, 30 cm (1 ft), flowers 2–4, large and flat, with the standards held horizontally, lilac, heavily veined with deeper purple, and a frilly white crest with a few darkspots. It is an exceptionally beautiful species and not difficult in well-drained soil in sun or very light shade. China. There is also a fine white form 'Alba'.

I. tenax *Californicae* To 30 cm (1 ft), leaves narrow green, red-stained below, flowers slender pale to deep lavender, less commonly cream to yellow. It is one of the easiest species to grow in woodland conditions.

I. tenuifolia *Tenuifoliae* Rare, dense clumps of upright narrow leaves to 30 cm (1 ft) long, flowers short-stemmed, lilac to deeper blue, with heavy dark veining and a central yellow line on the falls. The flowers tend to be somewhat lost among the leaves, and are not freely produced even in full sun. C., E. Asia

I. tenuis *Lophiris* Similar to a taller *I. cristata*, creeping, with 30 cm (1 ft) long, narrow leaves, branching stems, flowers 3 cm (1.2 in) wide, lilac with a flat yellow crest. Unfortunately it is notoriously difficult to flower in the garden. Oregon.

I. tenuissima *Californicae* Rare, narrow grey-green leaves, flowers 1-2, pale yellow with purple veining on the widely spreading falls on slender stems. It is a beautiful species and does not seem to be difficult. W. USA.

I. unguicularis *Unguiculares* 🏆 Spreading dense clusters of rhizomes which tend eventually to deteriorate in the centre, and tough narrow leaves, among which appear the large long-tubed flowers in shades of lavender, with dark veining on the haft and a yellow patch on the falls, in long succession in winter and earliest spring. It is one of the most popular of all irises for its splendid winter flowers, which can be cut in bud and last well in water. It grows well in the hottest available site, preferably under a south wall. The dead leaves should be removed, and some gardeners trim all the leaves before flowering, producing a very shorn appearance for a while, soon improving.

Several cultivars have been named: 'Alba' creamy-white apart from a yellow median line, 'Angustifolia' smaller with white fall margined with blue, 'Mary Barnard' excellent, large deep violet-blue, 'Oxford Dwarf' is probably a form of *I. u.* 'Cretensis' with small leaves and flowers with white falls, veined violet, and lavender at the tips, with an orange median line, 'Walter Butt' very large pale lavender.

78 *Iris unguicularis*

I. unguicularis 'Cretensis' from Crete and the Peloponnese, much more compact with narrow grassy leaves and flowers like 'Oxford Dwarf.' A magnificent plant in nature but unfortunately rarely flowers well, if at all, in the garden. It performs better in a bulb frame.

I. uromovii *Spuria* Probably a form of *I. sintenisii*, with particularly narrow leaves.

I. verna *Vernae* Tiny, clump-forming, 4–6 cm (1.6–2.3 in),

with fans of grey-green or dark green leaves to 12 cm (4.7 in) long, flowers to 5 cm (2 in) diameter, lilac-blue with an orange stripe down the centre of the fall. It is rare in gardens but is apparently not difficult in humus-rich soil. S.E. USA.
I. versicolor *Laevigatae* Spreading with stout rhizomes, to 75 cm (2.5 ft), leaves broad, branching stems carry several large flowers, pale lilac to deep purple, with spreading falls, with a central yellow or white blotch veined with purple. Easy in wet conditions. E. USA.
I. virginica *Laevigatae* Closely allied to *I. versicolor*, stems usually unbranched, flowers a purer shade of blue, with hairs on the signal patch on the falls. Var. *shrevii* differs in having a branched stem. E. USA.
I. wattii *Lophiris* A tender Evansia resembling *I. confusa*, even larger bamboo-like branching flower stems, flowers considerably larger, lavender-blue with a white blotch and ridged crest, and yellow spots, and more pendent falls. It is only hardy in nearly frost-free gardens, and needs similar treatment to *I. confusa*. E. Asia.
I. wilsonii *Sibiricae* Similar to *I. forrestii*, taller, leaves glaucous, flowers larger, with more spreading standards. It is liable to hybridize with other species in the garden. China.

Isopyrum (*Ranunculaceae*)

About 30 herbaceous perennials, of which only the one described is widely grown. They are delightful dainty woodlanders, similar to anemonellas, needing humus-rich soil in partial shade that never dries out. They can be grown from seed sown as soon as ripe and kept cool, or by division in early spring.
I thalictrioides A slowly spreading rhizomatous plant to 15 cm (6 in), leaves glaucous, thalictrum-like, biternate with 3-lobed leaflets, flowers white, 5-sepalled, saucer-shaped, in loose axillary clusters, 1-2 cm wide, spring. Although small it is suitable for the front of a shady border. C. Europe–Himalayas.

Isotoma See **Solenopsis**

J

Jaborosa (*Solanaceae*)

20 species of perennials from the Andes, only one of them widely grown in gardens, but with the possibility of others appearing from recent seed-collecting expeditions. Some may be of borderline hardiness, needing very well-drained soil in a sunny position, and they may be invasive.
J. integrifolia Running rhizomatous, leaves dark green, simple, oval, to 10 cm (4 in) long, flowers large, solitary, white with a long greenish tube and long, narrow reflexing petals, in long succession. It has exceptionally beautiful flowers, strongly perfumed in the evening, let down by its uninteresting leaves. In my garden it has been hardy to at least -12 °C (10 °F), losing its leaves in most winters, and it is decidedly invasive.

79 *Jaborosa integrifolia*

Jasione (*Campanulaceae*)

About 20 species of annuals and small tufted perennials with entire basal leaves and dense scabious-like heads of tiny flowers with conspicuous stamens. They are suitable for the edge of a sunny border in well-drained soil, and can be propagated by seed sown in autumn or by division in spring.
J. crispa (syn. *J.humilis*) 15–20 cm (6–8 in) Leaves narrow with hairy margins, heads of blue flowers in summer. Spain.
J. heldreichii (syn. *J. jankae*) Similar to *J. montana*, generally shorter, more hairy, and with smaller flowers heads to 1 cm (0.4 in) wide. Balkans to Turkey.
J. laevis (syn. *J. perennis*) 20–30 cm (8–12 in) Leaves narrow hairy, larger flower heads to 4 cm (1.6 in) diameter. W. Europe. 'Blue Light' (Blaulicht') is a compact cultivar with bright blue flowers.
J. montana 15–40 cm (6–16 in) Short-lived, sometimes annual, leaves very narrow, crenate, 2–3 cm (0.8–1.2 in) wide flower heads over a long season in summer. Europe.

Jeffersonia (*Berberidaceae*)

Two species of herbaceous perennials from woodland in N. America and N. Asia. They are among the most beautiful of all shade-loving plants in leaf and flower, and although small they are very good perennials, in the right conditions of moist humus-rich soil in shade. They are best propagated from seed, preferably sown as soon as ripe.
J. diphylla Clumps of basal leaves deeply divided into two greyish-green kidney-shaped lobes with scalloped margins, glaucous beneath, to 25 cm (10 in), flowers solitary, white cup-shaped in late spring. N.E. Am.
J. dubia ✱ Leaves deeply purple-tinged, rounded, flowers cup-shaped, with 6-8 clear lavender-blue or rarely white petals, in early to mid spring, usually appearing before the leaves. E. Asia.

Jovellana (*Scrophulariaceae*)

Genus of six tender perennials of which two are sufficiently hardy to grow in gardens with winter temperatures above -7 °C (20 °F). They closely resemble small-flowered calceolarias, with typical pouched flowers, usually white or off-white, spotted with purple or violet. They are easily grown in moist, rich but well-drained soil, in sun or partial shade, and they can be increased by cuttings in summer.

J. sinclairii Low semi-woody plant to 30 cm (1 ft), leaves ovate, toothed, hairy, loose one-sided heads of small nodding white bells, heavily spotted within with purple, in summer. NZ.

J. violacea Taller, especially in frost-free gardens, semi-shrubby, leaves similar to those of *J. sinclairii*, more upright and densely bushy, flowers similar, usually very pale violet with darker spots and some yellow in the throat. It has survived several winters in my garden and is a pretty bush with a scattering of flowers for several months. Chile.

Jurinea (*Compositae*)

Spineless thistle-like biennials or perennials, rarely grown in gardens. The plant described is one that I grew for several years and seemed easy in a sunny site in well-drained soil, with no propensity for excessive spread.

J. spectabilis Clump-forming to 50 cm (20 in), leaves glossy dark green, lanceolate with shallowly-toothed margins, upright stems bearing deep rose thistle-like flowers to 5 cm (2 in) wide in summer.

K

Keckiella (*Scrophulariaceae*)

A small genus closely allied to and previously included in Penstemon. *K. cordifolia* has been grown for some time and other species have been introduced recently from collected seed. The species I have grown are not fully hardy, and all have branching semi-woody stems bearing bright green narrowly-oval to lanceolate toothed leaves, and vivid deep scarlet flowers with narrow tubes and short flaring segments, in the leaf axils, in mid- to late summer. They can be increased from seed sown in autumn, or by cuttings during summer.

K. cordifolia Long spreading woody stems from a central rootstock, reaching over 1 m (3 ft) into surrounding shrubs, or forming a loose mound to 60 cm (2 ft) or more, with a very long succession of 3 cm (1.2 in) long scarlet flowers. It is a fascinating plant that has proved hardy in front of a south wall, but cut to the ground in hard winters.

K. corymbosa Compact bushy growth to 30 cm (1 ft), with leaves and flowers similar, on a smaller scale, to *K. cordifolia*. It is a delightful shrublet but will probably not survive below -5 °C (23 °F) in the garden.

K. lemmonii Limited experience suggests that this is similar to *K. ternata* but is more tender.

K. ternata Similar to *K. cordifolia* but smaller with self-supporting arching shoots to 50 cm (20 in), and orange-red flowers. It has survived several mild winters, to -7 °C (20 °F).

Kirengeshoma (*Saxifragaceae*)

Probably one species, although two names are on offer for slightly differing plants. It is a magnificent clump-forming perennial, often above our size limit but around 60–80 cm (24–30 in) high in less than perfect conditions. It needs rich moist soil in semi-shade, tolerating more sun in wetter sites. It can be increased (reluctantly) by division, or by seed sown in autumn, the seedlings slow to appear and to mature.

K. palmata ✱ Leaves palmately incised, acer-like, stems branching, often red-tinged, flowers creamy-yellow, shaped like dangling shuttlecocks, in loose heads. Japan.

K. koreana Doubtfully distinct, but with less deeply incised leaves and more upright-facing flowers with wider-spreading petals. Korea.

Knautia (*Dipsacaceae*)

Some 60 annuals and perennials, of which only *K. macedonica* is widely grown, apart from our native field scabious *K. arvensis* that is sometimes grown in the wild garden. *K. macedonica* is a first-class easy perennial for any reasonable soil in the sunny border. It can be increased by cuttings of early growths in summer, or by seed sown in autumn.

K. macedonica ✱ (See back cover photo) Clump-forming to 50 cm (20 in), leaves hairy, simple or deeply divided, spreading branching stems, flowers scabious-like, solitary, tightly-double, 5 cm (2 in) across, in a pleasing shade of deep purplish-crimson, with white anthers, in mid-summer for several weeks.

Kniphofia (*Liliaceae*/*Asphodelaceae*)

A genus of spectacular evergreen perennials, that combine fine large rosettes of leaves with striking spikes of flowers to enliven any sunny border in the second half of summer. The spikes vary greatly in the density of the individual flowers which are usually narrowly tubular with short straight or flaring perianth lobes. Many kniphofias are too large to consider here, but the few smaller species and the increasing number of dwarf hybrids described below make a splendid contribution to the central area of a border. The hotter red and orange colours may need some care in placing, but they combine well with later lavender-blue and white campanulas, with *Perovskia atriplicifolia*, and the deep reddish-purple of the origanums. The pale white to cream cultivar are easier even with pink shades.

The main essential in cultivation is a light well-drained soil, in a sunny position. They do not thrive to the same extent in heavy soil in cooler gardens. They can be increased by division in spring, or the species may be raised from seed.

All the species described are native to S. Africa.
K. citrina Closely related to the commonest species *K. uvaria*, but smaller, and having creamy-white to pale yellowish-green flowers.
K. galpinii The garden plant under this name is *K. triangularis* subsp. *triangularis*, the true plant being a little larger, flower spikes red at the tip shading downwards to pale orange, with straight lobes. The two plants have made an important contribution to the dwarfer hybrids.
K. rufa 60–90 cm (2–3 ft) Flowers drooping, widely spaced, most often creamy-yellow, sometimes orange or white in nature.
K. snowdenii To 80 cm (30 in), flowers very widely spaced and drooping, pale orange. It is a very elegant species, with a reputation for tenderness. It has been successful in front of a south wall down to at least -7 °C (20 °F).
K. triangularis The most widely grown dwarf species, to 70 cm (28 in), differing from *K. galpini* in having flowers in a uniform shade of soft orange, possibly paler at the base, with flaring lobes. It is a beautiful plant which persists well in very well-drained drained soils.

The Dwarf Hybrids

These are of mixed parentage, and I have not attempted to elucidate. The height depends on growing conditions, and some may become as high as 1 m (3 ft), but are usually considerably less.

Name	Height	Flowers	Notes
'Ada'	50-60 cm	Deep yellow	
'Apricot'	To 75 cm (2.5 ft)	Yellowish apricot	Slender
'Bees Sunset' 🏆	To 80 cm (30 in)	Pale orange	Narrow leaved
'Bressingham Comet'	50 cm	Orange, red-tipped	
'Brimstone' 🏆	To 60 cm (2 ft)	Green in bud, opening yellow	Late
'Buttercup' 🏆	To 80 cm (30 in)	Light yellow	Early
'Candlelight'	To 50 cm (20 in)	Yellow	Slender, narrow leaved
'Corallina'	To 70 cm (28 in)	Deep brownish-orange	
'Enchantress'	50-60 cm	Pale coral, red-tipped	
'Goldelse'	To 70 cm (28 in)	Deep yellow	Slender, early
'Goldfinch'	To 80 cm (30 in)	Deep yellow	
'Jenny Bloom'	To 90 cm (3 ft)	Creamy-coral	Very slender, may become tall
'Little Elf'	To 70 cm (28 in)	Clear pale orange	Slender, grassy leaves
'Little Maid' 🏆	40–50 cm	Cream	Grassy leaves, slender
'Maid of Orleans'	50-70 cm (28 in)	Creamy-white	
'Modesta'	To 60 cm (2 ft)	Pink buds opening cream	
'Sunningdale Yellow' 🏆	To 70 cm (28 in)	Bright yellow	
'Torchbearer'	To 70 cm (28 in)	Pale primrose	
Yellow Hammer'	To 70 cm (28 in)	Deep yellow	

L

Lamium (*Labiatae*)

A genus of annuals and perennials, the latter including mainly low mat-forming species useful as ground-cover, with a few clump-forming plants for the border, and one or two plants for the scree or alpine house. They are easy plants to grow and some of them are decidedly invasive, *L. galeobdolon* in particular being unsuitable for anything but the wild garden. The many forms and cultivars of *L. maculatum* also need some thought in placing. Although very low-growing they can cover a lot of ground, and do not fit in well among the less robust border plants.

All may be propagated by division or by cuttings, and they frequently self-seed, usually with inferior plants as a result.
L. album The white dead nettle is not suitable for the garden but variegated forms might be considered: 'Friday' leaves with a central patch of gold surrounded by two shades of green, 'Goldflake' golden-striped, 'Pale Peril' young growth tinged with gold, but it later resembles the weedy species. Europe–W. Asia.
L. galeobdolon (syn. *Lamiastrum galeobdolon*) Widely spreading, 20–30 cm (8–12 in), coarse mottled ovate leaves, stems of yellow dead-nettle flowers. Only suitable for difficult shady areas, as it will overrun most other plants. Europe–W. Asia. There are several improved cultivars: 'Florentinum' probably the best for ground-cover, leaves pleasantly mottled with silver, some purple colouring towards the centre, 'Hermann's Pride' lower and slower growing, narrower leaves streaked with silver: 'Silver Carpet' ✿ ('Silberteppich') a far superior, slow-growing plant, with very attractive silver leaves veined with green. It needs and deserves good soil to do well.

80 *Lamium galeobdolon* 'Silver Carpet'

81 *Lamium* 'White Nancy'

L. garganicum Very variable usually clump-forming, to 20–40 cm (8–16 in), leaves hairy, rounded or kidney-shaped with crenate margins, flowers, varying in size, generally purplish-pink or white, in loose clusters in summer. The best forms are excellent with large flowers carried above the foliage, but it can be over-leafy with poor flowers. Subsp. *pictum* (syn. *L. g. striatum*) excellent compact-growing plant, 10–15 cm (4–6 in), smaller leaves, abundant narrow pale pink flowers deeper pink towards the tips of the lips. Europe, N. Africa to W. Asia.

L. maculatum Vigorous mat-forming, leaves triangular or rounded, toothed, usually whitish in the centre, comparatively large short leafy spikes of dead-nettle flowers, in shades of pink to purple, or white, often for several weeks in summer. Europe, N. Africa to W. Asia. The best cultivars, notably 'Beacon Silver' and 'White Nancy', are very attractive, but quite invasive. Many of the plants seen, especially those resulting from self-sowing, are mediocre and best in wild areas, where their self-sowing and spread might be useful. 'Album' pure white, 'Aureum' yellow -tinged leaves and pink flowers, less vigorous than most, 'Beacon Silver' excellent, leaves silver apart from a narrow green margin, flowers purplish-pink, 'Cannon's Gold' similar to 'Aureum' with purple flowers, 'Chequers' a broad central silver stripe and purplish-pink flowers, 'Immaculate' deep green leaves and deep purple flowers, 'Pink Pewter' leaves tinged overall with silver, good deep pink flowers, 'Red Nancy' similar silver leaves to 'Beacon Silver', red flowers, 'Roseum' similar to the type in leaf, pleasing pure pink flowers, 'Sterling Silver' leaves silver throughout, deep purple flowers, 'White Nancy' one of the finest, leaves silver very narrowly margined with green, flowers pure greenish-white.

L. orvala Upright-growing, bushy, to 40 cm (16 in), large ovate nettle-like leaves, whorls of deep purplish-pink flowers streaked with white at the tips of the stems. This is one of the most attractive species and well worth growing, although perhaps a little leafy to achieve top rank. *L. o.* 'Album' is similar with pure white flowers. E. Europe.

Lathyrus (*Leguminosae/Papilionaceae*)

A large genus of annuals and perennials, the latter mainly climbing plants not included here, and a few valuable clump formers, easily grown in sun or light shade, with leaves pinnate or divided into several lobes, and typical pea-flowers in late spring or summer, in a range of sizes and colours. They are readily raised from seed.

L. aureus Loose erect clumps to 50 cm (20 in), leaves glossy, 4–8 leaflets, 8–12 cm (3–4.7 in) spikes of up to 20 nodding or outward-facing flowers, long, narrow, curved, in an unusual shade of deep gold. It thrives in a partially shaded position among meconopsis and other woodland plants. Balkans.

82 *Lathyrus aureus*

L. cyaneus Erect clumps to 35 cm (14 in), leaves of 4–8 narrow leaflets, flowers 4–8, lilac-blue, paler at the base, in loose spikes. Not to be confused with *L. vernus* 'Cyaneus'. Caucasus.
L. davidii Similar to *L. aureus*, taller, leaves pale yellowish-green with broader leaflets, flowers very similar. It is a most attractive but very uncommon species. E. Asia.
L. japonicus (syn. *L. maritimus*) Low mat with prostrate stems to 60 cm (2 ft) long or more, leaves with 4–10 glaucous, rounded leaflets, flowers few, purplish-blue, in short loose spikes. It needs well-drained soil and can cover a lot of ground, best among shrubs or robust perennials. N. Europe.
L. laevigatus (Syn. *Orobus laevigatus*) Variable, generally similar to *L. aureus*, which is included in it by some authorities, flowers yellow. Europe, Asia.
L. laxiflorus Clump-forming, 2 downy leaflets to each leaf, spreading or semi-upright stems to 40 cm (16 in) long, loose heads of rather small bluish-purple flowers. white at the base. S.E. Europe–W. Asia.
L. multiceps Bushy to 40 cm (16 in), leaves with 2 narrow leaflets, flowers in dense spikes of up to 6, pale to deep violet-blue with a white keel. It is a recent introduction from the Andes, but should be hardy.
L. niger (syn. *Orobus niger*) Upright clumps to 60 cm (2 ft), up to 12 lanceolate leaflets, spikes of up to 10 small deep violet flowers, fading to lilac. S. Italy.
L. vernus (syn. *Orobus vernus*) 🏆 Compact clumps to 40 cm (16 in), up to 8 glossy, broadly lanceolate to oval leaflets, loose spikes of small purplish flowers, tending to become bluish with age. Europe. There are a number of selected cultivars in a range of different colours: 'Alboroseus' bicoloured clear pink and white, one of the most beautiful, 'Albus' white, 'Caeruleus' and 'Cyaneus' in shades of purplish-blue, the latter particularly attractive, 'Flaccidus' looser growing with longer stems, purple, 'Roseus' clear deep pink. All are excellent perennials for a partially shaded border, doing best in rich moist soils, flowering in late spring and early summer with trilliums and the early rhododendrons.

Leptinella (syn. *Cotula*) (*Compositae*)

A genus of low-growing carpeting annuals or perennials, mainly from New Zealand, some very invasive unless used in paving cracks or a similar controlled situation. One or two (the best) are tricky alpine plants, notably *L. atrata* and *L. dendyi*, and are excluded. The following are creeping perennials rooting at their nodes, with attractive finely divided pinnate leaves, and small rayless 'button' flowers. If grown in paving or along the edges of paths they will withstand some walking on, and they are probably safest not in the beds themselves. Propagation by division is easy.
L. pectinata Mat-forming, leaves hairy, grey-green, pinnate, white flowers heads. Subsp. *villosa* much more hairy, flowers yellow or orange. Subsp. *willcoxii* less hairy green leaves and reddish yellow flowers. They all tend to be invasive in gardens.
L. potentillina Mat-forming, leaves finely divided, hairy, with toothed leaflets, often reddish-tinged, small yellow flower heads. Wide spreading but perhaps less of a problem than *L. pectinata* and *L. squalida*.
L. pyrethrifolia More robust loose carpet to 50 cm (20 in), leaves dark green, narrow-lobed, creamy heads of flowers. Another invasive species. Var. *linearifolia* has undivided linear leaves, and smaller heads of paler flowers.
L. rotundata Densely mat-forming to 30 cm (1 ft), leaves yellowish-green, hairy, flowers greenish-white. It is less invasive.
L. squalida Variable robust mat-former, with attractive ferny bronze-tinged leaves, and white flowers. It makes a handsome mat but is usually too invasive for anywhere but a path.

Leucanthemum (*Compositae*)

Most species have now been removed into other genera such as *Pyrethropsis* and *Rhodanthemum*, and only the old garden favourites remain, best known as *Chrysanthemum maximum* and its hybrid *C.* x *superbum*. with their large range of cultivars, and *C. vulgare*, the ox-eye daisy. They are all easily grown border plants with deep green simple or pinnate leaves, and single, semi-double or double, white daisy flowers, excellent for cutting, in mid- to late summer. They do best in good rich soil in sun, and should be divided every few years to retain their vigour and floriferousness.
They are generally a little tall when well-grown and staked, and I have only included a limited choice.
L. maximum Clump-forming to 1 m (3 ft), single white daisies, nearly always represented by a form of *L. superbum*. Pyrenees.
L. superbum (*L. maximum* x *L. lacustre*) A very large range of cultivars varying mainly in height and the number of petals (rays), usually white, surrounding a yellow disc. The doubles may be anemone-centred or fully double. 'Aglaia' 🏆 excellent semi-double, 'Bishopstone' popular single that has possibly superceded the older 'Phyllis Smith', 'Cobham Gold' the only cultivar with a yellow tinge, but it is less robust, 'T.E. Killin' 🏆 and 'Wirral Supreme' 🏆 among the best semi-doubles, 'Esther Read' and 'Starburst' good full doubles, 'Little Princess' ('Silberprinzesschen') dwarf.
L. vulgare The Ox-eye Daisy, with its single flowers, is useful for naturalizing in the wild garden. Several cultivars are occasionally available, and these tend to be under 70 cm (28 in) in height. 'May Queen' flowers unusually early.

Liatris (*Compositae*)

A genus mainly of perennials from the N. American prairies. Only one is widely grown, *L. spicata*, but others are occasionally available from seed lists, and will probably become more popular, as they are very attractive and easy clump-forming border plants with narrow leaves and dense spikes of flowers that open from the top, usually rosy-purple or white, in late summer, very attractive to butterflies They can attain 1 m (3 ft) in height but in my experience are usually around 60–70 cm (24–28 in). They resent excessive winter wet and do better in well-drained soil, surviving to at least -10 °C (14 °F). They can be propagated by division or by seed when this is set.

L. ligulistylis Clumps of narrow grassy leaves, inflorescence unusual with a few large, purple, widely-spaced flowers, on 30 cm (1 ft) reddish hairy stems in early summer.

L. pycnostachya Leaves linear, hairy upright stems to 1 m (3 ft), very dense spikes of reddish-purple flowers in late summer. It grows better on dry soils than *L. spicata.*

L. scariosa Similar to *L. pycnostachys*, shorter, looser, more open spikes of purple flowers. 'Alba' and 'Grandiflora' have white flowers, considerably larger in the latter.

L. spicata Clump-forming, stems stiffly upright, hairless, usually to 70 cm (28 in), leaves abundant narrow, flowers rosy-purple in long dense spikes in late summer. It is an excellent plant, especially in moist soils, in sun or partial shade. The white 'Alba' is outstanding in semi-shade with a dark background, 'Kobold' to 40 cm (16 in), flowers violet, 'Floristan Weiss' and 'Floristan Violett' seed strains grown for their long spikes of white and violet flowers respectively.

83 *Liatris spicata* 'Alba'

Libertia (*Iridaceae*)

Several perennials with short rhizomes, a compact cluster of fibrous roots, and fans of grassy leaves in dense clumps, usually with wiry, upright, branching stems, bearing loose heads of small white flowers, with three spreading petals. They are easy and generally hardy plants for a sunny or lightly shaded position in humus-rich soil, with good evergreen clumps of leaves and charming flowers in early summer. They can be increased by division in spring or by seed sown in autumn. The following are the species most generally available.

L. breunioides Uncommon, like a small *L. ixioides*, to 30 cm (1 ft), leaves occasionally bronze-tinged.

L. caerulescens Similar to *L. ixioides*, more tender with pale blue flowers. A blue libertia sounds a great asset, but its tenderness and small wishy-washy blue flowers are disappointing, unless I have been unlucky in growing a poor form. Chile.

L. elegans Uncommon, very small white flowers on 30–40 cm (12–16 in) stems. Chile.

L. formosa Rigid leaves to 40 cm (16 in) long, branching stems to 80 cm (30 in) but usually less, loose spires of many dense umbels of creamy-white flowers over a long period. It is very easy and hardy. Chile.

L. grandiflora Similar to *L. ixioides*, leaves to 50 cm (20 in) long, flowers and seed capsules larger. NZ.

L. ixioides Leathery green leaves with a pale midrib to 30 cm (1 ft) long, and 30-60 cm branching stems bearing wide panicles of many umbels of 2–8 pure white flowers. NZ.

L. paniculata Linear grassy leaves to 50 cm (20 in) long, branching stems of similar length, broad panicles of small white flowers. It is possibly a little more tender. S.E. Australia.

L. peregrinans Spreading rhizomatous species with more scattered leaf fans than *L. ixioides*, considerably shorter, flowers similar, with darker orange anthers. NZ. 'Gold Leaf' ✿ deep golden sword-like leaves, a very attractive foliage plant, although slow-growing in poor soils.

L. pulchella Small clump-forming, 10–15 cm (4–6 in), leaves narrow, grassy, flowers 3–6, pure white, on thin pedicels, in solitary terminal clusters. A delightful miniature. S. Australia, NZ.

Ligularia (*Compositae*)

L. hodgsonii The only small species in a race of fine, large, moisture-loving perennials, 60–80 cm (24–30 in), leaves toothed cordate or oval, large flat-heads of deep yellow to orange daisy flowers to 2–5 cm (0.8–2 in) diameter.

Limonium (*Plumbaginaceae*) (Statice)

Mainly perennials and shrubs, some of doubtful hardiness, variable in habit and leaf formation, with broad panicles made up of small dense spikes of 5-petalled flowers, often emerging from colourful calyces, on branching wiry stems.

The larger hardy species and cultivars are excellent border plants with a long flowering season, and are generally easily grown in full sun, but some need protection in cold gardens. The flower heads of many species dry well, retaining their colours, and are invaluable in dried arrangements. The smallest species are often used on the rock garden but can also hold their own at the edge of a border if the soil is well-drained.

L. bellidifolium Small clump-forming, to 20 cm (8 in), with spreading panicles, containing many non-flowering spikes and some dense spikes of pale violet-blue flowers. Europe.

L. caesium Clumps of upright stems, leaves narrowly linear, glaucous, flowers clear pale pink in terminal long loose spikes. A most beautiful species, but difficult to propagate, hardy to at least -7 °C (20 °F) in the garden. S.E. Spain.

L. cosyrense 30 cm (1 ft), leaves narrowly spathulate, wide heads of solitary 8mm long pink flowers among many non-flowering shoots. S. Italy.

L. gmelinii Rosettes of broad dark green leaves, 60 cm (2 ft), broad panicles of blue flowers. It is uncommon but is good in a sunny border, tolerating dry conditions. E. Europe.

L. gougetianum Small species to 20 cm (8 in) or less, with dense well-flowered blue panicles. N. Africa, Balearic Is.

L. latifolium (syn. *L. platyphyllum*) Large leathery dark green oval leaves, and myriads of blue flowers with whitish calyces, on branching wiry stems. It the most popular species, a striking plant giving the same cloud-like effect as a gypsophila, in the front or middle of a border, with several named cultivars of improved colour, including 'Robert Butler' and the very dark 'Violetta'. C., S.E. Europe.

84 *Limonium platyphyllum* 'Robert Butler'

L. mouretii Clumps of rosettes of broad glossy oblanceolate leaves, with shallow lobes and crinkly margins, flowers small white, in loose sprays, emerging from conspicuous reddish-brown calyces. A most attractive, rarely-grown species, easy in well-drained soil. N. Africa.

L. paradoxum Clump-forming to 30 cm (1 ft), leaves lanceolate, many dense spikes of a few bluish-violet flowers. Wales and Ireland.

L. platyphyllum *See* ***L. latifolium***

L. tataricum (syn. *Goniolimon tataricum*) Clump-forming, leaves obovate, broad panicles of flowers, variable in shades of bluish-purple.

Linaria (*Scrophulariaceae*) (Toadflax)

A widespread genus of annuals and perennials, the latter often short-lived, which thrive on poor well-drained soils, and usually self-sow freely. They vary greatly in habit but all have typical antirrhinum-like 2-lipped spurred flowers with a raised palate on the lower lip, often of a contrasting colour. Most of the species have a delicate beauty, often combined with a thuggish ability to cover the garden in their progeny, which tend to differ from the original plants as they hybridize freely. The worst offenders are probably best in the wild garden. Seed is the easiest method of propagation, but division or cuttings of new shoots may be a possibility.

I have excluded the annuals and some of the smallest species like *L. alpina* as more suitable for the rock garden.

L. aeruginea Small clump-former to 25 cm (10 in), leaves tiny, glaucous, linear, masses of 2 cm (0.8 in) long flowers in dense racemes, usually yellow with purple markings, or purple, with a paler spur. *L. a.* var. *nevadensis* has yellow or yellow and white flowers, and seeds sufficiently to ensure that it is always with us. S. Spain, Portugal.

L. dalmatica (syn. *L. genistifolia* subsp. *dalmatica*) ✱ Upright growing to 60 cm (2 ft), leaves very glaucous, lanceolate or ovate, with spires of 4 cm (1.6 in) long pure yellow flowers over a long period around mid-summer. It is unique in being a sound perennial that does not seed excessively, and substantial enough to have impact in the border. It is surprisingly little known. C. and S. Europe.

L. genistifolia Similar to *L. dalmatica* but usually shorter, with narrower leaves and smaller flowers. C. and S. Europe–Turkey.

L. purpurea Clump-forming to 50 cm (20 in), leaves linear, glaucous, flowers in terminal spikes, lavender-blue. An attractive plant with which it is difficult not to have a love-hate relationship. In my own garden it is treated as a weed as it seeds prodigiously from the top of various walls, but everyone admires it. C., S. Europe. The cultivars may be less menacing: 'Canon Went' pink, with only a tinge of purple, 'Springside White' pure white.

L. triornithophora ✱ Short-lived perennial to 50 cm (20 in) or more, leaves glaucous, lanceolate, flowers long-spurred, pale pink or deep bluish-purple, in several whorls, usually of three. These look remarkably like long-tailed birds perched together. It is a beautiful plant, well worth maintaining from seed, especially if you have a good colour form.

Lindelofia (*Boraginaceae*)

A few uncommonly-grown Himalayan hardy clump-forming perennials, with long, narrow hairy leaves, and upright leafy stems with fine deep blue flowers in the leaf axils and at their tips. They do best in rich moist soil that is well-drained as they resent excessive winter wet. They may be propagated by seed or by division.

L anchusoides Clumps of 20 cm (8 in) long silver-hairy leaves, upright branched stems to 90 cm (3 ft), flowers 1 cm (0.4 in)-wide, bright blue, funnel-shaped, in terminal heads.

L. longiflora Similar and more widely grown, flowers larger, deep purplish, with spreading lobes.

Linum (*Linaceae*) (Flax)

A large genus of annuals, shrubs and perennials, with several first class plants for the border, variable in leaf, with blue, yellow, or white flowers, usually shallowly saucer-shaped, in early to mid-summer. There are several small species best on the rock garden. The larger species vary in hardiness and are sometimes short-lived, but they are easy in full sun in well-drained soil, and make an excellent display for several weeks, although the individual open 5-petalled flowers may be fleeting. They can be propagated from seed or from cuttings.

L. arboreum 🏆 Dense bush, leaves glaucous, spathulate, 2 cm (0.8 in) long, flat-heads of 2 cm (0.8 in) wide deep yellow flowers. It may not survive hard winters, but cuttings can be overwintered under glass. E. Med.

L. austraicum Similar to *L. perenne*, leaves and flowers smaller. C., S. Europe.

L. campanulatum Erect, woody-based, to 30 cm (1 ft), leaves spathulate or obovate, heads of 3–5 large yellow flowers, similar to *L. flavum*. Med. from Spain to Italy.

L. capitatum Rosette-forming, upright 20–30 cm (8–12 in) stems, heads of 5-10 yellow flowers to 3 cm (1.2 in) wide. Balkans.

L. flavum Clump-forming, 40–50 cm (16–20 in) stems, leaves spathulate or obovate, large heads of up to 20 or more deep yellow flowers. 'Compactum' similar, much more compact. S., E. Europe–Russia.

L. leonii Similar to *L. narbonnense*, shorter and more bushy, tiny glaucous leaves, and loose heads of much paler blue flowers. It is a recent arrival in gardens and seems to be reasonably hardy. S. Europe.

L. monogynum Upright-growing, 40–50 cm (16–20 in), leaves glaucous, loose heads of white or occasionally very pale blue flowers. NZ.

L. narbonnense Clump-forming, stems upright or spreading, branching, leaves glaucous, lanceolate, flowers sky-blue with small white eyes in loose sprays. It is very effective for several weeks in groups in the front of a border. 'Heavenly Blue' 🏆 flowers of an even better blue. S.W. Europe.

L. perenne Similar to *L. narbonnense*, taller, more upright, with slightly paler flowers. C., E. Europe. *L. p. album* identical in habit, flowers pure white, producing a long-lasting white effect, especially good among the early campanulas.

L. tenuifolium Short-lived upright perennial, leaves needle-like glaucous, heads of pale to deep pink veined flowers. It seeds freely.

Liriope (*Liliaceae*/ *Convallariaceae*)

A small genus of evergreen rhizomatous perennials, sometimes confused with *Ophiopogon*, from E. Asia, making clumps or spreading colonies of thick grassy leaves, with dense upright spikes of small muscari-like or starry flowers in late summer or autumn, followed by conspicuous fruits. They thrive in reasonably rich moist acid or neutral soil in full or partial shade, and provide welcome late colour in the front of borders or among shrubs, associated with *Gentiana asclepediaea*, especially in its white form, lilies and other woodland plants. They may be propagated by division or from seed.

L. exiliflora Spreading dense mats, arching 30 cm (1 ft) long leaves, open spikes of starry violet flowers. It is usually grown in the form of 'Ariaka-janshige' with beautiful white-striped leaves.

L. gigantea Similar to the last, leaves longer, flowers and fruits larger.

L. graminifolia Possibly a form of *L. spicata*, similar with larger leaves and more widely-spaced flower on the spikes.

L. muscari 🏆 Large dense clumps of leaves, to 50 cm (20 in), long dense spikes of violet-blue flowers over a long period in autumn, followed by glossy black 'berries'. It is an invaluable plant for autumn flowers in shade, and has several cultivars: 'Gold-banded' compact, with a broad gold band down the margin of each leaf, 'John Burch' leaves with a central yellowish band, flowers large, 'Majestic' tall, leaves narrow, flowers dark, 'Monroe White' excellent, flowers pure greenish-white, 'Royal Purple' flowers darker purple in profusion, 'Silvery Midget' dwarf to only 20 cm (8 in), leaves white-variegated, 'Variegata' leaves yellow-margined, taller than 'Gold-banded'.

L. spicata Spreading colonizer, 25–40 cm (10–16 in), leaves arching, short spikes of pale violet flowers. 'Alba' white, 'Silver Dragon' compact with white-striped leaves.

Lithodora (*Boraginaceae*)

A few shrubby perennials, some of them typical upright bushy plants which I have excluded as 'real shrubs', and some low woody-stemmed mat-formers, previously well-loved as lithospermums, which I describe below. They are among the truest gentian-blue-flowered of all plants, and are easy to grow in humus-rich, acid to neutral soil, in sun or very light shade, eventually forming remarkable pools of colour for several weeks at mid-summer.

They can be propagated from cuttings, preferably in the middle of summer, when they root easily, or at other times in mist.

L. diffusa The popular species previously known as *Lithospermum prostratum* makes a low spreading mat with small hairy leaves on branching woody stems and masses of pure blue tubular flowers with spreading lobes. 'Alba' rather small white, less effective, 'Cambridge Blue' paler blue than the commoner cultivars, the old favourites 'Grace Ward' 🏆

and 'Heavenly Blue' 🏆 (see plate 105) deep gentian blue flowers, a little deeper and larger in the former, 'Picos' a recent introduction, much more compact, with flowers of good colour.
L. oleifolia 🏆 Probably best on the rock garden, but will settle down and run underground at the edge of a very well-drained bed, leaves grey-green, hairy, larger than those of *l. diffusum*, flowers that can be a good clear blue, but often open pinkish.

Lithophragma (*Saxifragaceae*)

A small genus of which only one species is generally grown, an attractive little plant, easy in moist humus-rich soil in full or partial shade, and in some gardens invasive. It is increased by division in spring or by seed.
L. parviflorum Clump-forming species, to 25 cm (10 in), with small tubers on its roots, rosettes of deeply 3-lobed hairy leaves, rounded in outline, and loose spikes of soft pink flowers 1.5 cm (0.6 in) across, with deeply frilled petals.

Lithospermum (*Boraginaceae*)

The most garden-worthy have been removed into Lithodora, and only the species described is grown regularly.
L. purpureo-coeruleum A rhizomatous colonizer, upright stems to 60 cm (2 ft), leaves 5–7 cm (2–2.8 in) long, glossy, lanceolate, flowers 2 cm (0.8 in) long, purple, in loose heads, becoming bright blue with age. It is an attractive but invasive plant for the wild garden or similar situation, tolerating poor dry conditions.

Lobelia (*Campnulaceae*)

A large genus of annuals and perennials. Many of the perennials are small plants best suited to the rock garden, and others are too tall to describe here, including the moisture-loving *L. cardinalis*, *L. fulgens*, and their hybrids. Those described are easy border perennials, sometimes of doubtful hardiness, best in moist rich soils. Most are clump-forming with simple toothed leaves in rosettes and on upright stems, and spikes of tubular 2-lipped flowers , the lower lip being larger than the upper and 3-lobed. They are among the most colourful plants for a moist sunny bed, flowering generally in the latter half of summer. They can be propagated by division, by seed, or by cuttings of the new growths in summer.
L. laxiflora ✱ (See plate 160) Spreading rhizomatous, to 60 cm (2 ft), stems upright, very leafy, leaves narrowly lanceolate, flowers scarlet with contrasting orange-yellow throats. In a hot summer it is a very striking plant, but fails to flower freely in wet seasons, and then seems over-leafy. It has a reputation for tenderness, but in temperatures above -10 °C (14 °F) its invasiveness is likely to be more of a problem, and it should be planted where its spread can be restricted. S. USA, Mexico.
L. sessilifolia 50 cm (20 in) clumps of slender stems, leaves narrowly lanceolate, toothed, flowers violet in the leaf axils at mid-summer. E. Asia.
L. siphilitica Clump-forming, to 60 cm (2 ft), leaves broadly lanceolate or oval, large dense spikes of blue flowers in late summer. The colour is variable and in the best forms is an exceptional true blue, splendid for the late border. 'Nana' a reliable compact form to 30 cm (1 ft), 'Alba' a good white. E., N. Am.

Lomatium (*Umbelliferae*)

Not widely known in cultivation, it is a genus of some 60 perennial species from N. America, with beautiful finely dissected leaves, and large umbels of small yellow or white flowers. In my experience they do not seed excessively and are among the most desirable umbellifers for a sunny border. They may be grown from seed but germination is erratic, best sown as fresh as possible and kept cold through the winter.
L. columbianum Under this name I have a species with dramatic finely dissected leaves to 30 cm (1 ft) and broad deep yellow umbels.
L. dissectum ✱ Leaves finely divided, appearing with the umbels of tiny deep yellow flowers in early spring, flowers and leaves then lengthening gradually to about 30 cm (1 ft), and remaining good for several months. It is a delightful plant, likely to tempt growers to try other species.

85 *Lomatium dissectum and chionodoxas*

Lotus (*Leguminosae*)

About 100 annuals and perennials, including wayside weeds like *L. corniculatus* the Bird's-foot Trefoil, which can be used in the wild gardens, and a few excellent species tender in most British gardens but fine plants in nearly frost-free gardens. Generally they make low mats of 3-lobed or pinnate leaves, with plenty of typical pea flowers, characterized by their beaked keels. They can be propagated from seed or by cuttings of new shoots in early summer.
L. berthelotii 🏆 Tender low mat-former with branching stems up to 80 cm (30 in) or more long, with small silver

linear leaflets, and masses of deep reddish-orange flowers in long succession in late spring and early summer. It is a most striking plant, especially in a tall container or in a wall where its stems can hang down. It is not frost-hardy but is magnificent in frost-free gardens. Canary Is.
L. maculatus 🏆 Very similar to the last but with deep yellow flowers tipped with orange-red. Tenerife.
L. maritimus (syn. *Tetragonolobus maritimus*) Low mat-forming, rooting at its nodes, leaflets large, grey-green, hairy, flowers large clear yellow. It is reasonably hardy, probably to at least -7 °C (20 °F) and deserves to be more popular, although it could become invasive in warm gardens. Europe–W. Asia.
L. sessilifolius (syn. *L. mascaensis*) Similar to *L. berthelotii* with intensely silver stems and leaves and clear bright yellow flowers. Tenerife.

Lupinus (*Leguminosae*)

A large genus of annuals, perennials and shrubs, mainly from N. America, with a scattering from Europe, N. Africa, and S. America. They are mainly known to gardeners as the ever-popular hybrids and cultivars derived from *L. polyphyllus*, first as the tall 'Russell Lupins' that have now lost their vigour and are largely unobtainable, and more modern hybrids that include some strains small enough to consider here. Any plant enthusiast who visits the USA in summer will appreciate that there are many exciting species that are untried or little tried in our gardens. I describe a few below as they are now being introduced as collected seed. They vary enormously in size and habit, but all have the typical leaves and flowers.I have omitted a number of small temperamental species needing rock garden or alpine house treatment, and several large species.

They are readily increased by seed and some species can be increased by cuttings in summer.
L. albifrons ✱ Compact shrub, to 70 cm (28 in) in my garden, leaves small silvery, on branching woody stems, short spikes of blue and white flowers. An attractive mound of silvery-grey-green throughout the year, and a sound perennial in well-drained soil.
L. alopecuroides Uncommon, to 50 cm (20 in), looser growing than the last with white woolly stems and leaves, and white bracts between whorls of blue flowers. It seems less easy than *L. albifrons.*
L. argenteus Uncommon, short-lived, to 50 cm (20 in) high, leaves larger, grey-green, hairy beneath, spikes of lavender-blue flowers. It is not as effective in leaf as the name suggests.
L. chamissonis ✱ Densely shrubby to 70 cm (28 in), small hairy leaves less silver than *L. albifrons* but still attractive at all seasons, and compact spikes of blue flowers around mid-summer. It is one of the most perennial species.
L. humifusus Semi-prostrate, stems very hairy, loose spikes of a few large blue flowers. It is an Andean species, not fully tried, but it survives mild winters in the garden.
L. littoralis Running prostrate species, usually under 30 cm (1 ft), loose in habit, leaves hairy, flowers pale to deep blue. It has less beautiful foliage than many species, but is easy to grow.
L. sericeus (syn. *L. ornatus*) Clump-forming, to 50 cm (20 in), leaves very silvery hairy, 7 cm (2.8 in) long spikes of blue flowers in mid- to late summer. A beautiful plant in nature, it is not easy in the garden as it resents winter wet.
L. tarijanensis Prostrate perennial, stems and leaves very white hairy with narrow leaflets, flowers blue. A promising plant that is relatively untried outside.
L. variicolor (syn. *L. versicolor*) (See plate 154) A large-growing semi-prostrate species with long branching stems and green leaves, and flowers in a range of colours, purple, blue, yellow, white, or pink. It seems easy and fairly hardy but becomes tall.

Hybrids: The original Russell hybrids and many of those raised subsequently are too large to be considered. There are a few seed strains, developed for their compact size and full range of colours, including bicolours, from pure white through soft cream to yellow shades, pinks reds and oranges, and pale blue to deep blue, purple or violet. These are likely to be found as Garden Gnome, Minarette, and Dwarf Gallery in catalogues.

Lychnis (*Caryophyllaceae*)

Some 30 annuals and perennials, the latter usually short-lived but freely seeding, sometimes to excess. Some species have attractive white-woolly or reddish-purple leaves, and the flowers colour varies from white to scarlet through shades of pink or magenta. They are easily grown, but persist better in well-drained soil. They may be raised from seed or in some species by division.
L. alpina Small tufted, to 15 cm (6 in), rosettes of narrow spathulate leaves, dense clusters of purplish-pink, occasionally white, 1 cm (0.4 in) wide flowers, in summer. Although small it can be used as an edging to a bed, and it does not seed excessively. Widespread.
L. x ***arkwrightii*** (*L.* x *haageana* x *L. chalcedonica*) Leaves dark purple, 40 cm (16 in) stems, flattish heads of brilliant scarlet flowers. 'Vesuvius' is a particularly well-coloured selection. They are striking plants of a colour that needs careful placing, exciting with the strongest yellows, or with white.
L. chalcedonica 🏆 Clump-forming, to 60 cm (2 ft), leaves ovate, somewhat sticky, flat-heads of many small vivid scarlet flowers. W. Russia. An easy and popular perennial with several cultivars: 'Alba' white usually with a tinge of pink, 'Carnea' soft flesh-pink, 'Flore Pleno' double red, 'Grandiflora' extra large red, 'Rosea' pale pink, with a double 'Rosea Plena'.
L. coronaria Short-lived, or biennial, clump-forming to 70 cm (28 in), leaves grey hairy, loose heads of a few magenta

flowers. It maintains itself in the garden by seeding freely, and it can become a menace in this way unless judiciously deadheaded. Europe. The white 'Alba Group' 🏆 are perhaps more attractive, but seed freely. Intermediates have been named, 'Angels Blush' pale pink, 'Atrosanguinea Group' much darker pink flowers, 'Oculata Group' white with a pink centre.

L. flos-cuculi Ragged Robin only suitable for the wild garden, but there is an attractive compact form 'Nana' only to 20 cm (8 in) with rose-pink flowers. Europe–W. Asia.

L. flos-jovis Rosettes of hairy grey-green leaves, stems to 30 cm (1 ft), loose heads of deep purplish-pink flowers. It is short-lived but seeds freely. Europe. Alps.

L.* x *haageana Similar to *L* x *arkwrightii*, but usually less tall.

L. micqueliana Clump-forming, 50 cm (20 in), leaves sparsely hairy, green, heads of a few large vermilion flowers. Japan.

L. viscaria Rosettes of deep green lanceolate leaves without hairs, to 70 cm (28 in), large heads of many deep purplish-red flowers. Europe–W. Asia. Var. *nana* half the size of the type, Var. *atropurpurea* much darker, 'Alba' single white, Albiflora double white, 'Plena' and 'Splendens Plena' 🏆 double, the latter with larger deeper magenta flowers.

L.* x *walkeri (*L. coronaria* x *L. flos-jovis*) 'Abbotswood Rose' 🏆 Rosettes of grey hairy oval leaves, 30–40 cm (12–16 in), compact heads of rose-pink flowers.

L. wilfordii Clump-forming to 50 cm (20 in), leaves sparsely hairy oval, flowers few, large, deep red with finely laciniate petals. Korea, Japan.

L. yunnanensis Slender to 20 cm (8 in), leaves narrow, lanceolate, flowers solitary or 2–3, white with bifid petals. China.

Lysichiton (*Araceae*)

Two moisture-loving species, with fine large leaves and great upstanding aroid flowers in summer, the better-known yellow-flowered, *L. americanum* 🏆 becoming too big to describe here. They need very damp soil, preferably at the margin of a pond, where their roots can reach the water, and are perhaps the finest of all plants for such a situation, well worth the wait of several years for them to become fully established. They can be propagated by division, or by seed.

L. camtschatcense 🏆 Clump-forming, leaves large glossy to 40 cm (16 in) long, magnificent white arum-like flowers in spring.

Lysimachia (*Primulaceae*)

About 150 annuals, shrubs and perennials, usually rhizomatous and often invasive, with simple leaves and generally with dense spikes of yellow or white 5-petalled flowers. in summer. They range from low mats to upright plants over 1 m (3 ft) high, and many are near our height limit. They are very easy to grow, thriving best in moist conditions, with due regard to their invasive tendency in good conditions. They can be propagated by division in autumn or spring, or the species by seed. I have exclude the fine *L. ephemerum* as being too tall. and *L. punctata* and *L. vulgaris* as tall and excessively invasive.

L. barystachys Upright clump-former to 60 cm (2 ft), leaves hairy, lanceolate, alternate, dense racemes of nodding white flowers. E. Asia.

L. ciliata Invasive colonizer, usually too tall in reasonable soil. I have included it for its recently-introduced cultivar 'Firecracker' ✿, leaves deep purple, rounded, upright spikes to 80 cm (30 in) of 2 cm (0.8 in) wide nodding or outward-facing flowers. It has excellent foliage combining well with the colour of the flowers, but promises be as invasive as the type. N. Am.

L. clethroides 🏆 Spreading colonizer, near to or exceeding our size limit, abundant lanceolate leaves and small white flowers in intriguing dense spikes that arch over in the middle. Not excessively invasive in dryish soils, an excellent perennial for the middle of the border, combining well with phlox, delphiniums etc. China, Japan.

86 *Lysimachia clethroides*

L. fortunei Clump-forming, upright reddish stems to 50 cm (20 in), narrow lanceolate leaves, and loose spikes of white or pink-tinged flowers. China, Japan.

L. henryi Clump-forming, stems prostrate, oval leaves, and dense terminal upright clusters of deep yellow flowers. China.

L. japonica Low spreading mat, oval leaves to 2.5 cm (1 in) long, yellow flowers solitary, axillary, in early summer. 'Minutissima' tiny form, probably too small for the border.

L. lichiangensis Erect branching stems to 50 cm (20 in), leaves narrow lanceolate, spikes of pale pink widely bell-shaped flowers, with darker veining. It is a new and little tried plant that sounds attractive.

L. nummularia (Creeping Jenny) Low mat-forming evergreen, decidedly invasive, but quite attractive with small

rounded glossy leaves and solitary cup-shaped flowers. 'Aurea' 🏆 leaves golden-yellow, less invasive, but still needs careful placing away from small treasures.
L. thyrsiflora Rhizomatous, with 50 cm (20 in) hairy stems, leaves lanceolate, long dense racemes of funnel-shaped flowers. It is a bog-loving plant and will grow in shallow water.

Lythrum (*Lythraceae*)

Two species are widely grown, *L. salicaria*, the Purple Loosestrife, and *L. virgatum*, but they are generally too tall for consideration, apart from one or two uncommon cultivars. They grow best in moist rich soil and provide some excellent late summer colour. *L. salicaria* 'Happy' and 'Purple Dwarf' only 60 cm (2 ft) high with leafy shoots carrying dense spikes of reddish-purple, and deep purple flowers respectively.

M

Maianthemum (*Liliaceae/ Convallariaceae*)

Genus of three creeping rhizomatous plants, with simple conspicuously-veined leaves, and dense terminal spikes of small white flowers in early summer. They need moist humus-rich soil, in which they may be invasive. In fact they are unsuitable for ideal peat-bed conditions, as they will infiltrate all the other plants in it. They may be propagated by division in spring.
M. bifolium A rapid spreader, leaves heart-shaped, hairy beneath, flower stems 10–20 cm (4–8 in). An attractive little plant that needs careful placing, preferably among robust shrubs. W. Europe–Japan. Var. *yakusimense*, is a beautiful miniature.
M. canadense An uncommon species differing in its oval leaves. N. America.
M. kamtschaticum (syn *M. dilatatum*) Different in having larger hairless leaves on longer stems, and taller spikes of larger flowers. It is less widely grown. W., N. America.

Malva (*Malvaceae*)

M. moschata The only species small enough to consider, clump-forming, leaves dark green, dense spikes to 60 cm (2 ft) or more of pale pink mallow flowers. *M. m. alba* 🏆 (see back cover plate) superb pure white form which self-seeds very freely.

Mandragora (*Solanaceae*)

Six species, of which only two are grown regularly at present. They make large flat rosettes of dark green leaves, wrinkled, and hairy along the veins, with a cluster of flowers among the leaves, in autumn. These are pale to deep violet, widely-open bells, to 4 cm (1.6 in) long, with broad triangular lobes, followed by large yellow to orange fruits. They are the mandrakes of old, once considered to have magical powers, as the swollen roots often take on human shapes. They are interesting plants for a sunny position in well-drained soil, but not great beauties. Introduction of Chinese species would awaken more enthusiasm for them. They may be raised from seed.
M. autumnalis As described above, but leaves glabrous. Med.
M. officinarum (syn *M. acaulis*) The Mandrake. This is as described but the flowers are usually greenish-white with narrower lobes. N. Italy, Yugo.

Margyricarpus (*Rosaceae*)

M. pinnatus (Syn *M. setosus*) One species, a low spreading sub-shrub to 50 cm (20 in), leaves dark green, finely divided, pinnate, stems branching, inconspicuous small greenish flowers, followed by striking large white fruits in late summer. An excellent fruiting plant for a sunny border or a wall. Andes.

Marrubium (*Labiatae*)

Some thirty species of woody-based evergreen perennials, with very hairy or felted leaves and insignificant dead-nettle-like flowers. Those described are the most attractive, grown for their fine white-woolly foliage. They need full sun and very well-drained soil as they resent excessive winter wet. They are best cut back hard after flowering like the similar ballotas, to retain a reasonably compact habit. They may be propagated by cuttings.
M. cylleneum ☼ A dome to 40 cm (16 in), leaves woolly, rounded, grey-green, short spikes of insignificant cream flowers hidden amid woolly bracts. 'Velvetissimum' ✿ more striking, with slightly yellowish pale green felted leaves. They are excellent foliage plants if kept tidy by cutting back hard after flowering or after winter damage.
M. incanum Intensely white-woolly, otherwise similar to the last and possibly more sensitive to winter wet.

Matthiola (*Cruciferae*)

Mainly annual and biennial plants, including the ever-popular border stocks, with their supreme scent, derived from *M. incana*. The few perennial species are semi-shrubby with grey hairy leaves, and spikes of stock-like flowers in summer, and they are not widely grown. They grow best in very well-drained soil, preferably alkaline, and can be raised from seed or from cuttings of young growth.
M. fruticulosa Variable, to 60 cm (2 ft), leaves linear-lanceolate, grey, flowers pinkish-purple, 4-petalled, scented over a long period in early to mid-summer. *M. f. valesiaca* a delightful miniature to 20 cm (8 in), short upright spikes of similar flowers. It tends to run

underground in light soils, without being too invasive. 'The white perennial stock' may be a cultivar or hybrid of *M. fruticulosa*. It is a first-rate plant for a sunny border in well-drained soil, a mound of grey leaves to 80 cm (30 in) or more with an abundance of typical white flowers throughout most of the summer. It seems to be a sound perennial for several years and can be increased by seed or cuttings.

M. scapifera More clump-forming to 25 cm (10 in), leaves narrow woolly, loose spikes of rosy-purple flowers in early summer. It is relatively untried but might be suitable for the front of a border, with excellent drainage.

Meconopsis (*Papaveraceae*)

A glorious race of large-flowered poppies, mainly from the Himalayas and requiring a moist atmosphere and moist humus-rich soil in partial shade to grow satisfactorily. They thrive in northern areas of Britain, and are difficult in normal dry summers in the South. Most of them are too large to consider here, and several of the smaller species are definitely monocarpic and will be excluded. Those described are perennial, but may be short-lived, especially in dry areas. Droughts are frequently fatal except for *M. cambrica*, a plant which is difficult to kill and can be a menace in the well-ordered garden, although an attractive addition to the wild garden. All the species can be raised from seed. The few cultivars should be propagated by division.

M. cambrica with *Cardamine bulbosa* Tap-rooted, rosettes of long-stemmed pale green pinnate leaves, branching spikes to 50 cm (20 in) of clear yellow 4 cm (1.6 in) wide flowers in early to mid-summer. A most attractive poppy that self-sows freely even in dry shade and should be dead-headed or planted in a wild area. Var. *aurantiaca* has orange flowers, and there are double forms of both the yellow and the orange, and single and double red forms, 'Frances Perry' and 'Muriel Brown'.

87 *Meconopsis cambrica* & *Cardamine bulbosa*

M. delavayi Rare, tricky, small perennial to 20 cm (8 in), flowers deep purplish-blue, nodding, with a large boss of yellow stamens. Recent seed collections may make it more common, at least in damp areas.

M. punicea A remarkable species, rosettes of very hairy leaves, 30–40 cm (12–16 in) stems, huge deep scarlet pendent flowers in summer. It is difficult to grow, probably needing very moist conditions in summer, much drier in winter.

M. quintuplinervia 🏆 Spreading clumps, leaves yellow-hairy, oval, stems to 30 cm (1 ft) solitary, pale lavender, nodding bell-shaped flowers in early summer. It is the easiest and commonest of the smaller perennial species, as long as it never becomes dry.

M. simplicifolia Generally biennial or a short-lived perennial to 50 cm (20 in), with lanceolate hairy leaves on long petioles, and 6 cm (2.3 in) wide flowers, varying in colour from a good bright blue to purple.

Meehania (*Labiatae*)

Two species are cultivated, both stoloniferous, herbaceous or semi-evergreen perennials, from woodland habitats, with low spreading stems bearing opposite, oval, hairy, toothed leaves and terminal heads of quite large deep violet-blue 2-lipped flowers with some white markings in the leaf axils, in early summer. They are among the more striking labiates and deserve to be more widely grown. They thrive best in moist humus-rich soil in partial shade, and can be propagated by cuttings.

M. fargesii As described, but only moderately stoloniferous, flowers larger, carried above the leaves, pale to deep violet, with the lower lip and throat white spotted and streaked with violet and red. W. China.

M. urticifolia More stoloniferous, flowers darker violet with less white on the lip, tending to be more hidden among the leaves. E. Asia.

Melittis (*Labiatae*)

M. melissophyllum The sole species, deciduous clump-forming perennial to 50 cm (20 in), leaves oval, downy, toothed, flowers in whorls of several, large, 2-lipped, good clear pink to purple or white with a pink blotch on the lower lip, summer. Although leafy the flowers are large enough to stand out well, and it makes a good plant for the front of the border or woodland, in reasonably moist soil. It can be propagated by division, or by cuttings of the young shoots. W.C. Europe–Ukraine.

Mentha (*Labiatae*)

Generally invasive herbs used for their culinary properties. There are attractive variegated and gold-leafed forms, but they are too invasive for the border.

Mertensia (*Boraginaceae*)

A genus of exceptionally beautiful blue-flowered perennials, mainly from N. America and E. Asia, the larger American species and some of the Asiatic species being easier to grow than the small alpines, which will not be considered here as they need careful cultivation in the alpine house or rock garden. They vary greatly in foliage and habit but have blue bell-shaped flowers, in spikes or clusters, in late spring and early summer. The following species should succeed, growing best in humus-rich well-drained soil, in sun or light shade. They may be propagated from seed, preferably freshly sown as soon as ripe.

M. ciliata To 60 cm (2 ft) loosely-growing, leaves lanceolate grey-green on branching stems, loose sprays of small nodding clear blue bells in summer. It thrives in woodland conditions. Rocky Mts.

M. echioides 15–20 cm (6–8 in) Clump-forming, leaves lanceolate, hairy, grey-green, dense heads of narrowly bell-shaped blue flowers on upright stems. It is one of the best small species.

M. primuloides Similar in habit to *M. echioides*, with usually one-sided racemes of a few long, narrow deep blue bells.

M. pterocarpa (syn. *M. rivularis japonica*) ✱ Clump-forming, leaves very glaucous rounded, flowers large blue in loose sprays on branching stems. An excellent plant for the front of the border in humus-rich soil in partial shade.

M. pulmonarioides (syn. *M. virginica*) 🏆 The tallest and most robust, to 60 cm (2 ft), leaves ovate, flowers narrow, blue, with spreading lobes, nodding in large heads. It is a splendid perennial for moist shade, best known by its synonym, but it dies down rapidly after flowering, and may suffer from having other plants planted on top of it.

Micromeria (*Labiatae*)

A few garden-worthy woody perennials resembling thymes, with small aromatic leaves and short spikes of small 2-lipped flowers. They are mainly small plants for the rock garden or border edge in well-drained soil in full sun. They can be propagated by seed or by cuttings.

M. thymifolia The only species regularly grown, a low evergreen bush to 40 cm (16 in), leaves tiny, smothered in summer with myriads of tiny white or palest lavender flowers. It resents excessive winter wet.

Mimulus (*Scrophulariaceae*)

One hundred and fifty species of annuals, perennials and shrubs, variable in habit but usually with simple opposite leaves, and tubular flowers with five spreading lobes, in a variety of colours, most often yellow or orange, but also white, pink, red or heavily spotted. They are mainly of small to medium size and include some of the most brightly-coloured plants for moist borders or pond edges, easily grown in suitable soils but often a little tender or short-lived, and a few excellent perennials of more restrained colouring which will tolerate drier conditions in the border. There are also several semi-shrubby species allied to *M. aurantiacus* (syn. *Diplacus glutinosus*) which will tolerate drier soils but are less hardy than most of those described.

They can be propagated by division or cuttings, or the species can be raised from seed.

***M.* 'Andean Nymph'** 🏆 Probably a true unnamed species, a low spreading mound to 20 cm (8 in), leaves ovate, toothed, flowers abundant in summer, pale pink, deeper on the upper lip and with a yellow tinge on the lower, spotted especially in the throat with reddish-purple. It is a good perennial that enjoys moist rather than wet soils. Andes.

M. aurantiacus (syn. *M. glutinosus, Diplacus glutinosus*) 🏆 Shrubby or semi-shrubby, leaves narrow, very sticky, typically shaped flowers with widely spreading lobes in shades of deep orange in long succession. A valued greenhouse shrub with a very long flowering season throughout the summer, in warm gardens a good perennial which eventually can exceed our size limit. It will tolerate several degrees of frost especially in front of a sunny wall, and can easily be propagated from cuttings to overwinter under glass. It grows best in rich soil and will tolerate moderately dry conditions. Var. *puniceus* flowers deep reddish-orange to crimson. W. USA.

M. bifidus ✱ Very similar to *M. aurantiacus* but flowers pale creamy-yellow. It should be hardier, being native to the Sierra Nevada at fairly high altitude, but in my experience needs a sheltered spot.

M.* x *burnetii (*M. cupreus* x *M. luteus*) Similar to *M. luteus*, dwarfer, flowers orange with a dark-spotted yellow throat.

M. cardinalis Clump-forming, 50–80 cm (20–30 in), or more in good moist soils, leaves ovate to elliptic, on upright branching stems, axillary narrow-tubed flowers with broad spreading scarlet lobes, with a few yellow spots in the throat. It is one of the most striking but short-lived species, easily grown in sun or partial shade and easily raised from seed. The colour may vary, and pink varieties are occasionally available. W. USA.

M. guttatus The Common Large Monkey Flower Spreading stoloniferous species to 60 cm (2 ft), upright or semi-prostrate, flowers axillary to 4 cm (1.6 in) long, bright yellow with red spots in the throat, on very leafy stems, in summer. In the wet conditions that it enjoys it can be decidedly invasive, by seed and by it stolons and rooting stems. It frequently becomes naturalized besides stream and ponds, so beware! N. Am.

M.* x *hybridus (***M. luteus*** x ***M. guttatus***) A range of excellent hybrids, some more complicated in origin. They are ideal marginal plants that are unlikely to get out of hand, but in my experience are usually short-lived and should be propagated regularly. They are 20–30 cm (8–12 in) in height unless stated. The following are among those most readily available.

Hybrids:
'Bees Scarlet' deep scarlet, 'Calypso Hybrids' unusually large flowers in shades of red, purple, and deep yellow, 'Highland' hybrids 'Orange', 'Pink', 'Red' ♉ and 'Yellow' excellent low-growing plants with a long flowering season, 'Hose in Hose' double brownish-orange as the name describes, 'Inshriach Crimson' a low carpeter, crimson, 'Malibu' and 'Mandarin' strong-growing with orange flowers, the latter particularly floriferous, 'Whitecroft Scarlet' and 'Wisley Red' similar low-growing plants with deep red flowers.
M. lewisii ♉ Clump-forming usually to about 70 cm (28 in), leaves finely toothed oblong-elliptic, loose heads of deep rose-pink flowers, tinged with orange and spotted with purple in the throat. An excellent plant of a soft colour, thriving in reasonably moist rich soil in partial shade or in full sun with abundant moisture. N.W. Am.

88 *Mimulus lewisii*

M. longiflorus Very similar to *M. aurantiacus*, flowers palest cream or pale salmon. California.
M. luteus Very similar to *M. guttatus*, flowers yellow with large red blotches on the lobes and in the throat. It is almost as invasive, and will quickly colonize damp areas.
M. moschatus Similar in habit to *M. guttatus*, with sticky foliage and considerably smaller flowers. It was once musk-scented but now this is rarely noticeable. N. Am.
***M.* 'Popacatapetl'** Probably a hybrid or cultivar of *M. longiflorus*, flowers pure white. A fine recent introduction, which is proving unexpectedly hardy.
M. primuloides Mat-forming, under 10 cm (4 in), flowers comparatively large, bright yellow, solitary in summer. A good perennial that needs dividing when it begins to deteriorate, to maintain its vigour. W. USA.
M. ringens Upright growing, tall stems to 80 cm (30 in), leaves lanceolate, toothed, flowers narrow, bluish-lilac in summer. A sound perennial of unusual colour, but one could wish that the colour was as striking as that of the other species. N. Am.
M. tilingii Clump-forming, stoloniferous, leaves elliptic on semi-prostrate stems, large yellow flowers with red ridges in the throat. It is one of the hardiest moisture-loving species. N.W. Am.

Mitella (*Saxifragaceae*)

A few mat or clump-forming evergreen rhizomatous perennials, resembling the smaller heucheras. They have a quiet charm with attractive leaves and upright spikes of small white or greenish flowers. They thrive in moist shady borders and can eventually take over a lot of space with their natural spread combined with very free seeding. They are therefore better among shrubs than among small perennials. They can be propagated by division or by seed.
M. breweri The only widely grown species, leaves glossy dark green, kidney-shaped, to 5 cm (2 in) wide, upright spikes to 20 cm (8 in) of many tiny yellowish-green flowers. W., N. Am.
M. caulescens Similar to *M. breweri* leaves larger, flowers in slightly taller spikes. W., N. Am.
M. diphylla Uncommon species, leaves pale green, shallowly lobed, spikes to 40 cm (16 in), sparse, very small, white flowers. E., N. Am.

Moltkia (*Boraginaceae*)

Six species of dwarf shrubs and one clump-forming perennial, all except *M. aurea* (probably not in cultivation) with attractive deep blue to purple flowers.
M. doerfleri (syn. *Lithospermum doerfleri*) Spreading rhizomatous perennial, leaves narrow, hairy, lanceolate on upright stems, dense nodding clusters of deep bluish-purple flowers, in summer. It is rarely grown and can be a little invasive, but it is an attractive plant for the border.
M.* x *intermedia (*M. petraea* x *M. suffruticosa*) ♉ Semi-shrubby to 30 cm (1 ft), leaves linear to lanceolate, large loose sprays of narrow pure blue flowers. Excellent for edging a sunny border.

89 *Moltkia x intermedia & Hypericum orientale*

Monarda (*Labiatae*)

A few annuals and perennials from N. America, from which a large number of hybrids have been raised. They form dense mats of basal leaves and upright leafy stems terminating in a dense head of narrow 2-lipped flowers, the upper lip upright and the lower usually long and curved downwards, generally surrounded by bracts which are often ornamental. This is a popular genus of colourful late summer-flowering perennials, in shades of pink to purple or red, or white, for the sunny border in rich soil. Some of their colours seem to me somewhat 'muddy' but the clear pinks, reds and whites are delightful at a time when such colours are becoming scarce. Mildew can be a problem in some gardens, but mildew-resistant cultivars are being developed. They are usually near our height limit and may be taller in good conditions. They can be propagated by division.

I describe the species in general cultivation, and have briefly described the hybrids, mainly between *M. didyma* and *M. fistulosus*, in a table.

M. bradburyana (syn. *M. russeliana*) Uncommon species, to 60 cm (2 ft), leaves glaucous, untoothed, broad heads of small pale pink flowers spotted with purple.

M. didyma Bergamot 70–100 cm (28–40 in) Square stems, leaves hairy, toothed, ovate, 5 cm (2 in) wide heads of crimson flowers with red calyces surrounded by reddish bracts. The species does best in moist soil, and is worth growing, together with several cultivars described below with the hybrids.

M. fistulosa Similar but stems more branched, hairy calyces, flowers bluish-purple with paler pink bracts. It tolerates drier conditions.

M. menthifolia Similar to the last, usually less tall, stems unbranched, recurving pinkish bracts, and purple flowers.

M. punctata To 60 cm (2 ft), flowers pale yellowish, dotted with brown, surrounded by very large reflexing white bracts. The appearance is very unusual but sadly it seems to be short-lived in the garden.

Cultivars and Hybrids

Name	Height	Colour	Notes
'Adam'	Tall	Light red	
'Aquarius'	Medium	Pale purplish-pink	Mildew resistant
'Beauty of Cobham' 🏆	Tall	Bluish-pink	Purplish leaves
'Blue Stocking' (syn 'Blaustrumf')	Tall	Dark violet	
'Cambridge Scarlet' 🏆	Tall	Deep scarlet	
'Capricorn'	Medium	Purple	Mildew resistant
'Cherokee'	Tall	Rose pink	Some mildew resistance
'Comanche'	Tall	Dark purple	Some mildew resistance
'Croftway Pink' 🏆	Tall	Clear rose-pink	
'Dark Ponticum'	Medium	Purple	
didyma 'Alba'	Medium	White	
'Elsie's Lavender'	Medium	Pale lilac	Mildew resistant
'Kardinal'	Tall	Reddish purple	
'Libra'	Medium	Reddish-pink	Mildew resistant
'Loddon Crown'	Medium	Maroon	
'Mahogany'	Medium	Deep red	
'Mohawk'	Tall	Deep mauve	Some mildew resistance
'Morgenrote'	Tall	Salmon	Early
'Ou Charm'	Medium	Very pale pink	
'Pale Ponticum'	Tall	Pale lavender	
'Pawnee'	Tall	Lilac	Some mildew resistance
'Pisces'	Medium	Deep pink	Mildew resistant
'Prairie Night	Tall	Violet	Late
'Sagittarius'	Medium	Pale lilac	Mildew resistant
'Scorpio'	Tall	Purple	Very mildew resistant
'Sioux'	Tall	White tinged palest pink	Some mildew resistance
'Schneewichen'	Low	Creamy white	
'Vintage Wine'	Medium	Reddish purple	

Monardella (*Labiatae*)

A small genus of annuals and perennials, of which two are regularly grown. They are woody-based, making low mounds of simple, aromatic, opposite leaves, with dense clusters of

2-lipped flowers surrounded by conspicuous bracts. They are attractive plants but only suitable for warm gardens in well-drained soil in full sun.

M. macrantha Bushy growth to 25 cm (10 in), leaves ovate, 4 cm (1.6 in) wide heads of vivid scarlet flowers surrounded by a whorl of purplish bracts.

M. odoratissimum Similar in habit, leaves lanceolate, smaller heads of pale purple flowers amid purplish bracts. This seems somewhat hardier than the last, but will probably not survive below 20 °F (7 °C).

Morina (*Morinaceae*)

Genus of a few species of fascinating perennials of real character, with long, dark green, spiny leaves, and upright stems, to 80 cm (30 in), bearing whorls of tubular flowers with five spreading lobes, two above and three below, white, pink, or creamy-yellow, in summer. They grow best in humus-rich soil with good drainage, and seem to resent excessive winter wet, although they are hardy to 12 °F (-10 °C) or lower. They may be raised from seed, pricking out the seedlings early, especially of the less common species, as they resent disturbance.

M. coulteriana Clump-forming, leaves to 15 cm (6 in) long, margined with slender spines, dense spikes of pale creamy-yellow whorled flowers with 2 cm (0.8 in) long curved tube and 8mm lobes. Unfortunately, though very desirable, it has proved difficult to germinate and establish from collected seed.

M. longifolia ✱ Leaves slightly longer and darker, very spiny, stiff upright stems bearing up to eight or more whorls of flowers, opening white and rapidly becoming deep rose-pink. It is an exceptionally beautiful perennial. Himalayas.

90 *Morina longifolia & Arisaema candidissima*

M. persica This is very similar to *M. longifolia*, with more spiny leaves and more slender flower spikes. It seems to be less easy to grow. E. Europe–C. Asia.

Myosotidium (*Boraginaceae*)

M. hortensia The only species, a challenging plant grown for its magnificent rounded, deeply-veined, glossy leaves to 30 cm (1 ft) long, and large sprays of forget-me-not blue flowers in early summer. A native of the Chatham Islands it is generally thought to need mulching with seaweed, but recently it has been found rather easier than its reputation suggests, grown normally in rich soil in partial shade. The flowers are not always a very good blue! It is a wonderful sight at Inverewe garden, but is probably not hardy below 20 °F (-7 °C). It can be raised from seed sown fresh.

Myosotis (*Boraginaceae*)

The Forget-me-nots are a genus of some fifty annual, biennials, and perennials, the short-lived species being popular garden plants for bedding. There are a few interesting small perennials including several white and yellow-flowered species from New Zealand, but these are realistically only suitable for the rock garden or alpine house. The only sound perennial worth using is *M. scorpioides*, which can be propagated from seed or division.

M. scorpioides (Marsh Forget-me-not) An invasive rhizomatous perennial with typical leaves and loose sprays of bright blue, yellow-centred flowers in summer. It is a good marginal plant or may be grown in shallow water, but it should be avoided where space is limited. Europe.

N

Nemesia (*Scrophulariaceae*)

A genus of popular annuals, and a small number of perennials, probably correctly varieties of *N. coerulea*, which are only hardy in mild winters but are very easy to raise from cuttings. Their very long flowering season makes them ideal plants for the front of a sunny border or a container.

N. caerulea (syn. *N. fruticans*, *N. foetens*) Clump-forming to 30 cm (1 ft), upright or semi-prostrate stems, abundant small narrow leaves to 1-5 cm long, loose spikes of attractive 2-lipped flowers, the upper lip 4-lobed, the lower usually 2-lobed, with a short spur. The flowers are produced in a long succession throughout most of the summer, especially if the old flowers stems are cut off. S. Africa. Three varieties seem to be currently available: *N. coerulea* itself usually a pale rather wishy-washy lavender, 'Innocence' white with a yellow throat, 'Joan Wilder' (syn. 'lilac-blue') a considerable improvement, flowers deep bluish-lavender, 'Woodcote' (syn.

N. umbonata 'Woodcote') ✱ an uncommon variety with much deeper violet-purple flowers.

Nepeta (*Labiatae*)

A large genus of mainly herbaceous perennials of upright or spreading habit, usually within our height limits but occasionally a little taller when well-suited. Their leaves are often aromatic, opposite, usually toothed, green or more often grey-green, the flowers tubular or funnel-shaped with a long tube and two lips, the upper 2-lobed, the lower 3-lobed with a larger central lobe. The flowers, in summer, are arranged in whorls which may be wide apart up the stem or in tight heads, in varying shades of blue or white, or yellow in *N. govaniana*.

They are useful easy garden plants for well-drained borders in full sun. Many are repeat flowering if they are cut back after the first flush is over. The species may be raised from seed, and most are easily grown from cuttings. They tend to suffer in very wet winters and it is as well to overwinter spare rooted cuttings under glass. Some of the less common species are recent introductions from China, and may well become more popular.

N. camphorata Clump-forming to 60 cm (2 ft), leaves scented, cordate, whorls of white flowers, purple-spotted on the lower lip. S. Greece.

N. cataria The common European catmint, a spreading plant to 80 cm (30 in), leaves grey downy, upright spikes of small white flowers dotted violet. Europe–C. Asia. It is widely naturalized but is not one of the best. 'Citriodora' is lemon-scented.

N. clarkei Clump-forming to 80 cm (30 in), leaves ovate-lanceolate on upright stems, close whorls of good deep lilac flowers with white on the lower lip, from dark calyces. It is a very promising hardy species. Himalayas.

N* x *faassenii (*N. racemosa* x *N. nepetella*) The most popular catmint for border edging, spreading clumps of branching stems, to 30 cm (1 ft) or more, grey toothed leaves, sprays of small pale violet flowers over a very long period, especially if it is cut back after flowering. It thrives in hot well-drained situations. Cats really love it and are likely to lie on it! Several cultivars probably belong here: 'Porzellan' leaves narrower, soft blue, 'Six Hills Giant' magnificent, stronger-growing and hardier, flowers larger darker, 'Snowflake' low-growing spreader, pure white, 'Souvenir d'Andre Chaudron' sometimes considered a cultivar of *N. sibirica*, widely-spreading, leaves grey, flowers large deep blue.

N. govaniana ✱ An elegant clump-former for partial shade, leaves pale, toothed, large loose panicles of pale yellow flowers on long pedicels. It will tolerate considerable shade and is ideal to lighten a dark corner. Himalaya.

N. grandiflora Upright to 70 cm (28 in), whorls of rather small dark purple flowers among leafy bracts. E. Europe–Caucasus.

N. longipes ✱ Excellent, tall growing, upright stems bearing grey-green toothed leaves, long spikes of lilac-blue flowers in closely-spaced whorls.

91 *Nepeta longipes*

N. melissifolia Tall, tending to run underground, leaves ovate, grey, spikes of blue flowers spotted on the lower lip with red. Greece.

N. nepetella Very variable, usually a spreading mound to 30 cm (1 ft), leaves greyish, short spikes of white flowers with a faint rose tinge. In ssp. *amethystina* the flowers are a good deep blue.

N. nervosa One of the best, 40–50 cm (16–20 in), leaves lanceolate, green, veined, upright dense spikes of pure blue flowers with white on the lip. Himalayas.

N. nuda Tall, leaves ovate, grey, branching heads of pale lavender flowers. Subsp. *alba* white. S. Europe.

N. phyllochlamys Low carpeting plant to 15 cm (6 in),

leaves white felted, short spikes of off-white flowers. It needs very well-drained soil, and is likely to be short-lived. Turkey.
***N.* 'Pool Bank'** A tall plant of uncertain origin, branching heads of deep blue flowers from purple calyces. A vigorous garden plant.
N. prattii To 80 cm (30 in), leaves narrowly ovate, dense whorls of bluish-violet flowers. China.
N. racemosa (syn. *N. mussinii*) Similar to *M.* x *faaseni*, to 30 cm (1 ft), masses of deep violet flowers over a long period in early to mid-summer. 'Superba' stronger-growing and very floriferous, good dark flowers. Caucasus. Cultivars listed under *N.* x *faasennii* may be found under this name.
N. sibirica Vigorous clump-former, leafy stems to 80 cm (30 in) or more, loose terminal heads of deep violet-blue flowers among the leaves. E. Asia.
N. sintenisii Rare and unusual species to 60 cm (2 ft), leaves whitish, hairy, dense terminal heads of white flowers.
N. stewartiana Like *N. sibirica*, flowers longer-tubed, purple, the lower lip heavily spotted with darker violet. Uncommon. China.
N. subsessilis To 40 cm (16 in), leaves glossy, toothed, ovate, flowers deep lavender in large round heads. China.
N. tuberosa Rhizomatous, leaves cordate-ovate, spikes of deep purple flowers on upright spikes to 70 cm (28 in). S.W. Europe.

Nierembergia (*Solanaceae*)

Several annuals and colourful perennials from S. America, most of the latter short-lived and tender in average gardens, but with one good mat-forming white-flowered perennial *N. repens*. The more tender species, notably *N. coerulea*, have a long flowering season and grow strongly from overwintered cuttings, making excellent plants for patio containers, or for the front of a sunny border. *N. repens* is easily propagated by division. Nomenclature of some species is in doubt and the synonyms below are used as frequently as the correct names.
N. coerulea (syn. *N. hippomanica*) 🏆 Semi-woody to 40 cm (16 in), leaves small, spathulate, pointed, flowers in long succession, cup-shaped, lilac-blue to pale violet, to 2 cm (0.8 in) wide.
N. repens (*N. rivularis*) Low running carpeter, herbaceous, leaves light green, spathulate, large white deep cups with yellow eyes, to 3 cm (1.2 in) wide. Although often said to need moist soil, I find it runs and flowers most effectively in light sandy or gravelly soil. 'Violet Queen' occasionally offered, with violet flowers. One wonders whether it is a hybrid as the colour is not found in wild populations.
N. scoparia (syn. *N. frutescens*) Similar to *N. coerulea*, of shrubby habit to 50 cm (20 in), leaves narrow, flowers pale to deep violet.

O

Oenanthe (*Umbelliferae*)

Several species of spreading clump-formers with divided leaves and typical umbels of cow parsley-like white flowers in summer. They require moist soil and only one species is grown regularly. It can be propagated by division, frequently layering itself.
O. javanica Spreading, to 30 cm (1 ft), leaves finely divided, grey-green, umbels of white flowers. It is usually seen in the very attractive variety 'Flamingo' in which the whole plant has a pink tinge and the leaves are variegated with a white margin. It needs a moist soil.

Oenothera (*Onagraceae*)

About 100 species of annuals, biennials and perennials, many of them excellent garden plants. They are immensely variable, from densely rosetted cushions to tall upright growing clumps, with a range of low to medium carpets and mounds between, usually with strikingly large flowers in shades of yellow, white or pink. The clump-forming species and their cultivars are fine border plants to provide strong yellows in mid-summer, and the lower-growing plants will make substantial edging plants. They combine well with the purplish-red of *Lythrum* 'Firecandle' or less dramatically with the taller blue or white campanulas. A few merit the common name of evening primroses, but a large proportion keep their flowers open throughout the day. They vary in cultural requirements from difficult species for alpine house or scree to plants suitable for the average border. They can be raised from seed, or from cuttings in early summer.

I have excluded the more tricky alpines and the biennials, although the latter can become a spectacular and sometimes all too permanent feature by their self-sowing. A visit to the western USA cannot fail to impress with the number of fine oenotheras growing in semi-desert conditions and not in cultivation or rarely seen. These relatively untested species are well worth trying, first in very well-drained soil in a sunny position, before venturing them in ordinary garden soil.
O. acaulis Densely rosetted, stemless or short-stemmed, leaves 10–20 cm (4–8 in) long pinnate, clusters of very large pure white flowers, opening in the late afternoon and fading to pink by morning. A beautiful plant but rarely long-lived, even with the very good drainage and sunny position that it needs, in a bed or on a wall. Chile.
O. caespitosa Similar to *O. acaulis* but leaves narrow, lanceolate, shallowly toothed. If it survives several winters it builds up into a dense woody mound. N.W. Am.
O. californica Relatively untried, low carpeter to 15 cm (6 in), leaves lanceolate grey-green, flowers large white maturing to deep pink. May be a runner!
O. flava Similar in habit to *O. acaulis*, stemless, flowers small

yellow to 3 cm (1.2 in) wide. S. USA. to Mexico.
O. fremontii Clump-forming to 20 cm (8 in), leaves silvery lanceolate, 3–4 cm (1.2–1.6 in) wide yellow flowers. S. USA.
O. fruticosa Clump-forming, upright, leafy, often reddish stems to 80 cm (30 in), leaves lanceolate, entire, to 7 cm (2.8 in) long, flowers deep yellow in generous heads in the upper leaf axils. Probably the best species for the border, with several excellent subspecies and cultivars. E. USA. 'Fireworks' 🏆 the most popular, tall, red stemmed, leaves purple-tinged, ssp. *glauca* (syn. *O. tetragona*, *O. youngii*) 🏆 leaves broader, toothed, more compact. 'Erica Robin' young leaves yellow becoming tinged pink, comparatively small flowers, 'Fruhlings Gold' yellow-margined leaves and large deep yellow flowers, 'Lady Brookborough' a reliably perennial more compact cultivar, var. *riparia* (*O. riparia*, *O. tetragona* var. *riparia*) ✸ very different in habit, making a mound of semi-prostrate stems to 30 cm (1 ft), flowers medium-sized yellow in long succession, a fine plant for the front of a border, 'Yellow River' to 40 cm (16 in) like a larger *O. f.* var. *riparia* with bright red stems.
O. glabra hort. A dubious name usually applied to a compact growing *O. fruticosa* with a purple tinge to the leaves.
O. kunthiana Uncommon, clump-forming to 40 cm (16 in), leaves pinnate, clusters of small white flowers. S. USA.
O. macrocarpa (syn. *O. missouriensis*) 🏆 Mound-forming to 30 cm (1 ft), long reddish semi-prostrate stems, leaves narrow, lanceolate, with pale midribs, a long succession of very large deep yellow flowers. It is one of the most beautiful species, capable of occupying a considerable space. S. USA.
O. pallida Mound of spreading branches, leaves lanceolate, 5 cm (2 in) wide white flowers fading to pink. Another uncommonly grown semi-desert species. S. USA.
O. perennis (syn. *O. pumila*) Clump-forming to 25 cm (10 in), leaves lanceolate or spathulate, short spikes of 2 cm (0.8 in) wide deep yellow flowers on leafy stems. E., N. Am.
O. rosea Upright clump-forming to 30 cm (1 ft), flowers very small, deep pink. A disappointing plant, especially when compared with the next, but it is not invasive. S. USA, S. Am.
O. speciosa Rapidly spreading rhizomatous, leaves narrow, green, on upright stems to 40 cm (16 in), terminal sprays of 4 cm (1.6 in) wide white flowers, opening in the daytime and fading to pink. The plant usually seen in gardens is probably 'Rosea' (syn. *O. berlandieri*). Having fallen in love with this in a garden in Nevada I eventually obtained it from collected seed and it accords with the description above except that the flowers are a fine soft pink in colour. It is the most beautiful of all species but it is decidedly invasive in well-drained soils, and may be regretted! S. US–Mexico.

92 *Oenothera speciosa*

O. tetragona *See* ***O. fruticosa*** under which various cultivars and varieties often attributed to *O. tetragona* in catalogues may be found.

Omphalodes (*Boraginaceae*)

A genus of about 20 species of annuals and perennials, of which only four are widely grown. I am excluding the annual *O. linifolia*, and the tricky alpine species *O. luciliae*. The remaining two perennials are creeping rhizomatous species with simple leaves and sprays of deep blue or white flowers with a short tube and five sprea ding petals. They are among the best spring-flowering plants for moist shady conditions, associating beautifully with trilliums and the later-flowering cardamines and wood anemones. They can be raised from seed, or by division in spring.
O. cappadocica 🏆 Dense spreading clump, 25 cm (10 in), leaves glossy ovate-cordate to 10 cm (4 in) long, loose sprays of many small bright blue flowers with white eyes, carried prominently above the leaves. Turkey–W. Rusia. 'Alba' pure white, 'Anthea Bloom' lighter blue leaves greyish, 'Cherry Ingram' ✸ a vigorous cultivar, with considerably larger deep blue flowers, a definite improvement on the type, 'Starry Eyes' distinctive flowers, deep blue at the centre and white towards the edge of each petal.

93 *Omphalodes cappadocica* 'Cherry Ingram' at Washfield Nursery

O. verna Similar to *O. cappadocica*, usually with larger leaves, fewer-flowered, and earlier in spring. It is less striking, but is easier to grow in less than ideal soils, and its earlier flowering is useful. 'Alba' a reliable white form. S. Europe.

Ononis (*Leguminosae*)

Some 75 species of annuals and perennials, sometimes shrubby, and often spiny, with pinnate or trifoliate leaves. Comparatively large pink or yellow pea-flowers are held in the upper leaf axils in summer, often for several weeks. Those described do best in alkaline well-drained soils in hot positions, and some are invasive if grown in borders. A few species need to be grown in the cold greenhouse. They can be raised from seed or from cuttings of young growth.

O. cristata (syn. *O.cenisia*) Mat-forming, leaves with 3 narrow leaflets on hairy stems, sprays of deep pink flowers with white keels over a long period. Although usually grown in the alpine house it is worthy of trial in the open in warm well-drained gardens. S. Europe.

O. natrix Shrubby, leaves pale green, trifoliate, large pure yellow flowers in loose sprays. An attractive non-invasive species that deserves to be more widely grown. Europe.

O. repens Invasive mat-forming species to 30 cm (1 ft), leaves simple or trifoliate, a long succession of pink flowers in loose heads. It is probably safest in the wild garden. Europe.

O. rotundifolia Upright species resembling *O. natrix*, dense clusters of slightly smaller rose-pink flowers for many weeks. S. Europe.

O. spinosa Lower shrubby habit than the last, single flowers in the leaf axils. Europe–Asia.

Onosma (*Boraginaceae*)

About 150 evergreen very hairy perennials, with simple leaves on spreading stems from a central rootstock, and dense pendant clusters of narrowly tubular flowers, often bi-coloured, in summer. They grow best in very well-drained soils in a sunny position and are excellent wall plants, where their nodding flowers can be appreciated and where excessive moisture, which they resent in winter, can run off. Several of the smaller species are best under cold glass except in areas of low rainfall, but the more robust, described below, can be used in the front of a sunny border in suitable soil, except in very wet and cold gardens. They can be propagated by seed sown in autumn or by cuttings of new growth in summer.

O. alboroseum Spreading perennial, a mound of semi-prostrate hairy stems to 25 cm (10 in), leaves lanceolate to oblong, terminal clusters of white flowers with pink tips deepening in colour with age. One of the hardiest in the garden, given good drainage. Turkey.

O. echioides Similar to *O. alboroseum* but flowers pure pale yellow. An uncommon species in gardens, but not difficult. S. Europe.

O. frutescens Similar to *O. alboroseum*, flowers smaller, pale yellow tinged to a greater or lesser extent with purple. Greece.

O. nanum ✱ Smaller clump-forming, to 20 cm (8 in), leaves small narrow and clusters of clear pale yellow flowers. It is one of the most attractive, but it seems to be short-lived. It is easily raised from seed, and frequently self-sows in light soils. Turkey.

94 *Onosma nanum*

O. stellulatum Similar to other yellow-flowered species, but flowers rather small. Yugoslavia.

O. tauricum 🏆 One of the most vigorous, similar to *O. alboroseum*, but flowers yellow sometimes paling to white. S.E. Europe–Turkey.

Ophiopogon (*Convallariaceae*/ *Liliaceae*)

A few species of evergreen perennials, sometimes rhizomatous, with clumps of grassy foliage and upright spikes of small spherical or bell-shaped flowers, followed by fleshy fruits. They are mainly small plants of moist woodland easily grown in similar conditions in the garden, at the edge of a shady bed or among shrubs, a few capable of extensive ground-cover. Several are excellent foliage plants. They can be propagated by division in spring or raised from seed sown fresh.

O. bodinieri A recent arrival in gardens, clumps to 20 cm (8 in) high, long arching dark green leaves, upright spikes of nodding white flowers, faintly tinged pink. China.

O. chingii Another recent introduction, smaller clumps of very narrow leaves, spikes of white flowers, followed by blue fruits. China.
O. intermedius Clump-forming, leaves to 30 cm (1 ft) long, short spikes of many white or pale lilac flowers, in early summer, followed by violet fruits. A vigorous leafy ground-covering plant. 'Argenteomarginatus' leaves margined in white. China.
O. jaburan Large clump-forming, leaves to 60 cm (2 ft) long, shorter spikes of white flowers in late summer. Unfortunately it is only hardy in near frost-free gardens. Several leaf forms may be available, 'Vittatus' the only one commonly grown has creamy margins to the leaves.
O. japonicus Spreading rhizomatous, clumps of dark green arching leaves, short racemes of white to purple bell-shaped flowers in late summer, followed by blue fruits. It makes good ground cover, but can very invasive in moist humus-rich soils. Several cultivars are available: 'Albus' white, 'Compactus' and 'Minor' much more compact.
O. planiscapus Vigorous clump-forming, leaves arching or upright to 30 cm (1 ft) long, dense spikes of white flowers tinged with purple in late summer, followed by small deep blue fruits. Most commonly grown as the cultivar *O. p.* 'Nigrescens' 🏆 with the blackest leaves of any plant, easily grown in sun or shade, but colours best in the sun. It does not seem to me easy to place in the garden, but makes a good background to dwarf narcissi such as *N. asturiensis*, or can be combined with the golden leaves of appropriate hostas, or grasses such as *Hakonochloa macra* 'Aureola'.
O. wallichianus Like a slightly smaller *O. jaburan*, unusually large white or pale purple flowers. It is of doubtful hardiness, but worth trying in mild gardens.

Origanum (*Labiatae*)

About thirty species of perennials, often semi-woody, and sometimes rhizomatous. Most have hairy, conspicuously-veined, entire, greyish leaves, often sessile, and narrow tubular flowers hidden among strikingly coloured hop-like bracts, pale green, pink or deep reddish-purple, which remain attractive for many weeks, usually deepening in colour with age. They are wonderful garden plants, the smaller species best on the rock garden or front of the border in well-drained soil in full sun, the larger species excellent in the foreground of the border, where their deep purple bracts combine particularly well with yellow-flowered perennials.

The species can be raised from seed or the perennials increased by cuttings of young shoots or by division of the rhizomatous species. I have only included the easier alpine species which can hold their own at the edge of a border, as several species need some protection from winter wet. I have excluded the pot herbs, apart from some of the more colourful leaf forms of Marjoram. The parentage of many of the cultivars is uncertain and I have described them alphabetically rather than under one of their probable parents.

O. acutidens Mound to 30 cm (1 ft), leaves ovate glaucous, loose heads of insignificant flowers amid a cluster of fine light green bracts. Similar to *O. rotundifolium* but taller and looser in growth, and generally less effective. Turkey.
O. 'Barbara Tingey' ✱ A beautiful cultivar, closely resembling 'Kent Beauty', slightly smaller bracts which colour later in the season.
O. 'Buckland' Similar to 'Kent Beauty' in its flowers, leaves smaller more hairy, on more upright stems. It is one of the finest of the small cultivars.
O. calcaratum (syn *O. tournefortii*) Small clump-former, leaves very hairy, greyish-green, narrow clusters of green bracts that rapidly become pink and deepen. Sufficiently easy to grow at the edge of a well-drained bed.
O. 'Erntedank' Clump-forming to 50 cm (20 in), leaves bluish-tinged green, upright panicles of small pink flowers amid conspicuous deep reddish-purple bracts. It is one of the finest of the larger cultivars for the border.
O. 'Herrenhausen' 🏆 (See plate 132) Similar to 'Erntedank' with a purple tinge to the young leaves, somewhat paler flowers and bracts. It hybridizes freely with *O. laevigatum* 'Hopley's' producing variable intermediates.
O. x hybridum (*O. dictamnus* x *O. stypileum*) Small creeping species, to 30 cm (1 ft), leaves slightly hairy, grey-green, upright clusters of pinkish bracts, deepening with age.
O. 'Kent Beauty' ✱ Perhaps the best of the low mound-forming species, hairy grey-green rounded leaves, completely hidden in mid- to late summer by pendent clusters of hop-like bracts to 5 cm (2 in) long, pale green at first but quickly deepening to deep rose-pink, and remaining attractive for weeks. A plant for well-drained soil in full sun.

95 *Origanum* 'Kent Beauty'

O. laevigatum ♕ Clump-forming, running slowly underground, leaves blue-green on stiff upright stems to 70 cm (28 in), flowers small tubular, deep purple, in diffuse branching panicles, with small purple bracts, that are less conspicuous than in other species. The abundance of small flowers in late summer make it one of the most beautiful easy border perennials. Turkey. 'Hopley's' is usually described as a variety of *O. laevigatum*, but differs considerably and may be a hybrid with *O. vulgare*. The upright stems are little-branched, with widely spaced whorls of purplish-pink flowers. Another excellent easy plant.

O. libanoticum Similar to *O. rotundifolium*, mound-forming with small flowers hidden among large bracts, that remain green, with only the faintest tinge of pink. It seems easy to grow but is less satisfying than *O. rotundifolium* or the cultivars with deep pink bracts. Lebanon.

O. microphyllum A low dense sub-shrub, to 30 cm (1 ft), leaves tiny grey, abundant small clusters of little pink flowers amid purple bracts. In spite of a reputation for tenderness I find it survives our average winters in the open and is well worth growing. Med.

***O.* 'Norton Gold'** Like *O. laevigatum*, with yellow leaves and pink flowers. Possibly a hybrid of it.

***O.* 'Nymphenburg'** A hybrid of *O. laevigatum* similar to 'Erntedank' deep pink flowers and large very deep purple bracts.

96 *Origanum* 'Nymphenburg'

***O.* 'Rosenkuppel'** ✱ Similar to the last, a little more compact, even darker flowers and bracts, a superb border plant.

O. rotundifolium ♕ A low mound of bluish-green rounded leaves, hidden from mid- to late summer in large clusters of beautiful pale green bracts. The unusual shade of green make it one of the best small species, a parent of most of the cultivars of similar habit.

O. vulgare (Marjoram) Very variable, usually similar to *O. laevigatum* in habit, with clusters of pale lilac flowers protruding from small dark purple bracts. Apart from its use as a pot herb it is generally grown in gardens in one of its more ornamental foliage forms: Var. *album* white, Ssp. *hirtum* shorter, leaves and stems very hairy, compact heads of white flowers, 'Aureum' leaves yellow, becoming greener in late summer, 'Aureum Crispum' similar with wavy-edged leaves, 'Thumble's Variety' large pale yellow leaves and white flowers.

Osteospermum (*Compositae*)

Some 70 annuals and perennials, sometimes sub-shrubby, mostly from S. Africa, varying in habit from low mats to upright clumps, with very large daisy flowers in shades of white, pink to purple, or yellow, produced over a very long period. Some species are hardy to -10 °C (14 °F), others need to be kept almost frost-free, and the ever-increasing number of hybrids and cultivars are very variable in this respect. Their very long flowering season and ease of propagation from cuttings make them among the most valuable of plants for ornamental containers or as spectacular foreground plants in the border.

Cuttings can be rooted at any time and it is wise to overwinter some plants of any variety under frost-free glass. Seedlings will also flower within a year but these will vary considerably if several different cultivars are grown – hence the profusion of new names! I have described below the commonly grown species and a selection of hybrids of which I have experience, but the enthusiast will find many more in catalogues. Hardiness, and more particularly length of flowering season, should be the guiding factors in choosing plants for the garden.

O. barberiae *See* ***O. jucundum***, to which plants in cultivation should probably be referred.

O. ecklonis Subshrub to 50 cm (20 in) or more, leaves lanceolate, entire or toothed, on branching stems, a long succession of 5–7 cm wide flowers, with deep bluish central discs and white rays backed with bluish-purple. The type plant is more tender than var. *prostratum* ♕ a flat mat only 15–20 cm (6–8 in) high in flower, leaves toothed lanceolate, hardy to -10 °C (14 °F). Its hardiness makes it ideal for the garden, although it may not be quite as floriferous as some of the cultivars.

O. jucundum (*O. barberiae*) ♕ Similar in habit and hardiness to *O. ecklonis* var. *prostrata*, leaves usually entire, flowers deep purplish-pink with dark purple discs. Var. *compactum* ✱ lower-growing, flower stems shorter, flowers slightly smaller, even deeper in colour. It seems to be one of the hardiest.

97 *Osteospermum jucundum var. compactum*

Cultivars: The following are some of the best, but there could be even better awaiting trial: 'Blue Streak' upright, flowers like those of *O. ecklonis* with a bright blue reverse, not very hardy, 'Bodegas Pink' variegated foliage similar to 'Silver Sparkler' but with the reddish-purple flowers of *O. jucundum*, less robust and more tender, 'Buttermilk' 🏆 very attractive upright plant with large soft yellow flowers with dark centres, flowering period shorter than that of many cultivars. Other yellows are appearing which may have a longer season. 'Cannington hybrids' mainly upright, available in a variety of shades of pink or white, usually with contrasting backing to the rays, 'Hampton Court Purple' prostrate with deep purple flowers, 'Lady Leitrim' one of the most hardy, a broad carpet of semi-prostrate stems, flowers white becoming pink with age, 'Langtrees' moderately low-growing with pink flowers, fairly hardy, 'Pink Whirls' 🏆 upright, unusual flowers in which the petals are constricted in the middle and have inrolled margins, giving a unique appearance that has made them popular with many gardeners. In my experience they are not always reliably 'whirled', tending to revert to straight margins, and are tender, 'Silver Sparkler' 🏆 ☼ upright, clearly variegated leaves with cream margins, typical white, blue-backed flowers, superb in a container with a very long flowering period, but will not survive average winters outside, 'Tresco Purple' large-growing, flowers very substantial, deepest purple. Although very good in flower it is tender and has a short flowering period, 'Weetwood' excellent very hardy cultivar, resembling *O. ecklonis* var. *prostrata* but more compact, with white rays with a green reverse, 'Whirligig' 🏆 differs from 'Pink Whirls' only in having white flowers.

98 *Osteospermum* 'Silver Sparkler'

Othonna (*Compositae*)

A genus of mainly tender perennials and shrubs from S. Africa, of which only one has proved suitable for the rock garden or border.

O. cheirifolia (syn. *Othonnopsis*)
Evergreen woody-based perennial, low spreading stems, leaves 5–8 cm (2–3 in) long, fleshy, glaucous, spathulate, grey-green, 3 cm (1.2 in) wide yellow daisies over a long period in summer. It is an interesting and attractive plant which survives moderate winters in well-drained soil in full sun. It can be propagated by cuttings.

Ourisia (*Scrophulariaceae*)

A fascinating genus of mainly evergreen perennials from S. America and Australasia, cushion or mat-forming, variable in leaf, with tubular flowers in early to mid-summer, with 5 spreading lobes, mainly white in the Australasian species and pink or red in the S. American. The smaller species are best in the alpine house or rock garden, the larger in moist humus-rich soil in semi-shade, and all thrive in moist areas and are difficult in dry gardens. In good conditions the larger species with their whorled flowers contrast well with meconopsis and moisture-loving primulas. They seem to exhaust the soil quickly and should be replanted every two or three years into fresh well-fed soil.

They can be raised from seed, which is very fine and should be sown on the surface of an ericaceous compost, or from cuttings. The following list includes the easier species suitable for the open garden.

O. caespitosa Prostrate mat, rooting at the nodes, leaves small glossy spathulate, slender upright stems carrying paired 2 cm (0.8 in) wide white flowers in summer. Although very low-growing this is vigorous enough for the edge of a shady bed. Var. *gracilis* smaller leaves and smaller solitary flowers. NZ.

O. coccinea Spreading carpet, leaves oval toothed, upright stems to 25 cm (10 in) loose heads of 3 cm (1.2 in) long scarlet flowers with prominent cream-coloured stamens. In good conditions this is a very striking plant which can spread vigorously. In my own dry garden it needs plenty of water to get it to grow and flower well. Chile.

***O.* 'Loch Ewe'** (*O. coccinea* x *O. macrophylla*) Excellent hybrid resembling *O. coccinea* but flowers clear soft pink, in whorls when it grows well.

O. macrocarpa ✱ (See plate 69) Spreading clumps of rosettes, leaves conspicuously veined, glossy, oval, to 10 cm (4 in) or more long, upright stems to 50 cm (20 in), several whorls of up to ten 3 cm (1.2 in) long white flowers on long pedicels. In poor conditions or in exhausted soil the number of whorls is reduced, often to one. It is a fine plant and seems quite easy even in drier gardens. NZ.

O. macrophylla Very similar to *O. macrocarpa*, larger more hairy leaves, and smaller flowers. They may be confused in gardens.

***O.* 'Snowflake'** *O. macrocarpa* x *O. caespitosa* 🏆 Low carpet to

10 cm (4 in) in flower, leaves small glossy, comparatively large single or paired white flowers. It is easier and more robust than *O. caespitosa.*

Oxalis (*Oxalidaceae*)

A large genus of small annuals and perennials, often bulbous, notorious for containing some of the worst garden weeds, but containing also some supremely beautiful, well-behaved perennials. They mainly have attractive trifoliate leaves, and funnel-shaped to open 5-petalled flowers. Apart from the menaces they vary in their requirements from moist woodland to open conditions in well-drained soil. Their small size makes most of the sun-loving species more suitable for the rock garden, but several of them are easy enough to grow in the front of a mixed border. They can be raised from seed or by splitting of the bulbs.

Several 'new' species have recently been introduced from Andean seed and are relatively untried as to hardiness and invasive tendencies, and it would not be wise to try them in the garden until they have been carefully tested within the confines of a pot. Most of those described below are reasonably hardy and can safely be planted in the garden.

O. acetosella (Wood-sorrel) Creeping perennial with small white flowers veined with purple, only suitable for the shady wild garden. N. hemisphere.

O. adenophylla 🏆 Tuberous-rooted, densely clump-forming, leaves very glaucous, up to 12 leaflets, 2.5 cm (1 in) long white flowers in spring, with purplish veining, often with a pink or purple flush to the petals. One of the most beautiful, easily increased by division to produce a decent sized colony for a sunny site, with good foliage at all times and unusually large flowers. The colour varies, 'Rosea' being a good deep pink. S. Am.

O. deppei *See* ***O. tetraphylla***

O. depressa (syn. *O. inops*) Slowly spreading, surprisingly hardy, rhizomatous, leaves green, trifoliate, comparatively large clear pink flowers in summer. It has never proved invasive with me but some growers have had problems with it. S. Africa

O. enneaphylla 🏆 Similar to *O. adenophylla*, leaves smaller, glaucous, flowers usually slightly smaller, white or pink with deeper veining, but very variable in colour with several named varieties. It is perhaps the finest and most reliable species for the rock garden, or in front of other small perennials, in well-drained soil. S. Am., Falkland Is. 'Alba' large pure white, 'Minutifolia' very dwarf form, only suitable for the rock garden or trough, 'Rosea' and 'Rubra' deep pink and darker reddish-pink.

O. hirta Upright growing to 20 cm (8 in), sessile hairy green leaves, heads of deep reddish-pink flowers in autumn. It is much more tender than other species mentioned, but would be an excellent plant for frost-free gardens with dry summers. S. Africa.

O. 'Ione Hecker' 🏆 (*O. laciniata* x *O. enneaphylla*) Resembling the latter, but with pale violet-blue flowers heavily veined with darker violet, almost as 'blue' as the very tricky *O. laciniata*. It is a beautiful easily grown hybrid readily increased by division.

O. magellanica Dainty low rhizomatous carpeter, small bronze-tinged leaves, small white flowers in late spring and summer. It can be invasive in moist soil but takes a long time to get out of hand planted beneath shrubs in shade. Australasia.

O. obtusa Low slowly spreading mat, leaves hairy grey-green, a sprinkling of large soft pink flowers in late spring. I find it takes a log time to cover much ground and does not produce as many of its fine flowers as one could wish.

O. oregana Similar to *O. acetosella*, larger in all its parts, flowers white or pale pink, veined, in summer. It may become somewhat invasive in good moist conditions. N.W. USA.

O. purpurea Spreading clusters of bulbs, very attractive hairy grey-green leaves, large yellow or purple flowers in autumn or winter. Usually grown as 'Ken Aslet', with bright yellow flowers, it is said to need frost-free conditions, but has survived several mild winters in my garden. The flowers are produced sparingly but the leaves make it worth while. In hot frost-free gardens it could be superb!

O. squamata 10–15 cm (4–6 in) Mound of pale green leaves with a huge number of deep rose flowers. Still at the trial stage, this recently introduced Andean seems easy to grow and shows no sign of spreading excessively at the root, but might self seed if more than one is grown. It is hardy to at least -5 °C (23 °F).

O. tetraphylla (syn. *O. deppei*) A large-leaved species to 30 cm (1 ft) in flower, with broad notched leaflets with a conspicuous purple band towards the base, flowers in loose heads, deep reddish-pink. It is a popular house plant mainly grown for its foliage, but hardy enough to use in the open in mild gardens. 'Iron Cross' is particularly striking with the leaflets having a large deep purple blotch occupying the base.

O. versicolor A spectacular small species with clusters of small leaflets at the end of 10–15 cm (4–6 in) stems, abundant white flowers with each petal edged with crimson, so that the closed or half-open flowers display a remarkable candy-striped effect. It is very easy and increases freely, but unfortunately can only be grown outside in near frost-free gardens.

P

Pachysandra (*Buxaceae*)

Four species of rhizomatous evergreen perennials, making a dense carpet 20–40 cm (8–16 in) high, with handsome leaves and upright spikes of small unisexual white flowers in late spring, the male flowers numerous at the top of the spike and the female fewer at the base of the spike. They are mainly used as ground cover in light to deep shade, and can be invasive in good soils. They are easily propagated by detaching

rooted pieces in spring or by stem cuttings later.
P. axillaris To 40 cm (16 in), leaves ovate, toothed, white flower spikes in the upper leaf axils. It spreads less quickly than *P. terminalis*. China.
P. procumbens To 30 cm (1 ft), leaves grey-green, toothed, sometimes with brownish mottling, spikes of white flowers with pink anthers, from stems below the leaves. S.E. USA.
P. terminalis The commonest and most vigorous, leaves leathery, greyish-green, sparsely toothed, shorter spikes of white flowers. This is the species to choose for substantial evergreen groundcover. Japan. 'Green Carpet' lower growing, smaller finely toothed leaves 'Variegata' leaves margined with creamy-white, less rampant than the type.

Paederota (*Scrophulariaceae*)

P. bonarota The only species in cultivation, a mound to 20 cm (8 in), leaves glossy, oval, toothed, arching spikes of many small tubular blue flowers with prominent stamens, resembling those of Veronica, in which it has been included in the past. It is an easy cushion plant for walls or for the edge of a well-drained, sunny border.

Paeonia (*Ranunculaceae*)

Some thirty species of herbaceous perennials and evergreen shrubs, and an enormous number of hybrids between them. They are among the most beautiful of all herbaceous plants with their excellent leaves, often tinged with purple, and their huge single or double flowers in early summer. They are easy to grow and will persist for years undisturbed in a sunny or lightly shaded border, if the initial soil preparation has been carried out properly, incorporating plenty of well rotted manure or compost, and feeding regularly by further mulching with manure or by top-dressing with bone-meal or a general fertilizer in spring. If their flowering deteriorates they are probably starved and should be lifted, divided, and replanted in rich soil. They can be increased by division but take some time to recover from the disturbance. The species may also be raised from seed, which should be sown fresh and the seed pots kept cold through the winter until germination.

Most of the species come within my size limit and I have included the two or three which exceed it for the sake of completeness, and because size depends very much on the soil preparation. I have exclude all the shrubby species except the small *P. potaninii*. The hybrids present me with a major problem as many are larger than the species, they are almost all beautiful, and their are far too many of them in cultivation to describe. I have a particular love of the species, and I have not found it too difficult to exclude all the hybrids except those that have received the 🏆. I would strongly advise any gardener wanting to grow a selection of these to see them in flower at a specialist nursery, or on show at Chelsea or elsewhere.
P. anomala To 50 cm (20 in), leaves finely divided, glossy deep green, very large, almost flat, red flowers with a boss of deep yellow stamens, in early summer. Russia.
P. broteroi To 40 cm (16 in), lower leaves biternate with the leaflets further divided, upper leaflets entire, flowers large, bright red, with yellow stamens in early summer. Spain and Portugal.
P. cambessedesii 🏆 Usually to 30 cm (1 ft), leaves ternate, pinnately divided, the leaflets glossy greyish-green above, markedly purple beneath, the flowers in late spring somewhat variable in colour, generally deep rose-pink, saucer-shaped, with a large boss of yellow stamens. A magnificent small species with a reputation for tenderness, usually seen in the cold greenhouse, it has survived the last ten winters in well-drained soil in a sunny spot in the open, with temperatures to -10 °C (14 °F) occasionally. Balearic Is.

99 *Paeonia cambessedesii*

P. daurica To 50 cm (20 in), leaves biternate, leaflets rounded, large pinkish-red bowl-shaped flowers in early summer. S.E. Europe–Caucasus.
P. 'Defender' 🏆 A fine American hybrid, probably of *P. peregrina*, large bowl-shaped flowers of a remarkable shade of bright coppery red.
P. emodi ✱ Robust species to 80 cm (30 in) or more, masses of light green leaves deeply divided into narrow segments, very large pure white flowers with yellow stamens in late spring. It is one of the most beautiful of all the species and seems to be reasonably easy to grow in the border, especially

in light shade. W. Himalayas.

P. lactiflora The parent of most of the herbaceous hybrids in gardens. 'Whitleyi Major' 🏆 is probably closest to the type, one of the finest of all the white flowered 'species', leaflets divided into about 10 narrow segments, with red stems and often a reddish flush, outstandingly large, white, deeply bowl-shaped flowers in summer. The following hybrids have also been awarded the 🏆. They are all likely to grow taller than most of the species described: 'Bowl of Beauty' 🏆 one of the most popular of the 'Imperial' paeonies with the stamens replaced by small 'petals', so that the flowers have a broad frilly centre, a shape that seems to me more attractive than most of the true doubles, 'Duchesse de Nemours' 🏆 very full pure white double, with the added quality of a good scent, 'Felix Crousse' 🏆 deep reddish-pink, 'Festiva Maxima' 🏆 similar flowers to 'Duchesse de Nemours' 🏆 but with a deep crimson blotch at the base of most of the petals, 'Laura Dessert', 🏆 large flowers with white fringed petals and a very large creamy-yellow petaloid centre, 'Monsieur Jules Elie' 🏆 fully double rose-pink, 'Sarah Bernhardt' 🏆 an old hybrid, exceptionally large fully double pale pink flowers, late in the season.

P. mascula Variable, usually to 60 cm (2 ft), about 9 broad oval leaflets, flowers variable in colour, white to deep purplish-pink or red. An easy garden plant but the flowers tend to be even more fleeting than usual. Widely distributed. Europe–W. Asia. Subsp. *arietina* 12-15 leaflets narrower and hairy beneath. E. Europe–Turkey. Subsp. *russii* broader leaflets, shorter, purple-tinged stems. Corsica, Sardinia, S. Italy, Greece.

P. mlokosewitschii 🏆 To 60 cm (2 ft) or a little more. reddish-tinged stems, leaves biternate, glaucous, slightly greyish-green, leaflets broad obovate, soft yellow deeply bowl-shaped flowers, with deeper yellow anthers, well above the leaves in late spring. It is the most glorious species, and not difficult, but the flowers, as with so many species, are fleeting.

P. mollis Red-flowered single, probably of garden origin, to 45 cm (1.5 ft), leaves pale green with many leaflets, hairy beneath, almost globular deep purplish-pink flowers in summer.

P. obovata 🏆 To 50 cm (20 in), purple-tinged stems and grey-green leaflets, hairy on the reverse, large solitary deep purplish-pink flowers in late spring, var. *alba* 🏆 white with a red centre partly hidden by the yellow stamens. It is one of the finest whites and a reliable species in the border, thriving in partial shade. E, Asia.

P. officinalis Widespread species in S. Europe, and a very old favourite in gardens, with several subspecies and cultivars, all very easy to establish. Subsp. *officinalis* usually to 60 cm (2 ft), leaves biternate, each leaflet deeply divided into several narrow pointed lobes, large single red flowers usually with a hint of pink in the hue. S. Europe. 'Alba Plena' popular double white, usually with a faint pinkish tinge on first opening, 'Anemoniflora Rosea' 🏆 deep pink with a centre filled with yellow petaloid stamens margined with red, an exceptionally fine reliable cultivar, Subsp. *banatica* and subsp. *humilis* differ in their leaf segmentation, the former with only the central leaflet further lobed, the latter having all the leaflets divided to one third of their length, 'Rosea Plena' 🏆 very large flowered fully double, somewhat darker than 'Rosea Plena Superba', 'Rubra Plena' 🏆 similar but deep crimson.

P. peregrina To 50 cm (20 in), leaves divided into 9 leaflets with shallow pointed lobes, flowers dark red, deeply cupped. An easy early-flowering species, most often grown as its cultivar 'Otto Froebel' ('Sunshine') 🏆, one of the most striking singles, with brilliant light scarlet flowers. S. Europe.

P. potaninii Generally classed a shrubby species, I include it on account of its low spreading habit, under 60 cm (2 ft), running underground, leaves attractive, deeply divided pale green, flowers small (to 6 cm (2.3 in) wide) red or creamy-white, over quite a long period in earliest summer. For some reason, the white form has proved much easier to grow in my garden. China.

P. x *smouthii* (*P. lactiflora* x *P. tenuifolia*) Resembling *P. tenuifolia* but taller, with leaves slightly less finely divided, and red flowers slightly larger with less overlapping petals.

P. tenuifolia ✱ ☼ To 50 cm (20 in), leaves pale green, finely divided into linear segments so that they look truly ferny, flowers comparatively large bright red or soft pink with yellow stamens. A unique species, always eliciting attention with its beautiful filigree leaves. Seed is sometimes available and may come true, especially if you collect your own. Frequently it becomes obvious in the young plants that the leaves are not sufficiently finely divided. S.E. Europe–Caucasus.

100 *Paeonia tenuifolia* 'Rosea'

P. veitchii To 50 cm (20 in), creeping, many long, narrow pointed leaflets, 1–3 deep purplish-pink, rarely white, nodding flowers to a stem. Best in partial shade. Var. *woodwardii* shorter stems, usually to only 30 cm (1 ft), leaves hairier. China.

P. wittmanniana A robust species to 1 m (3 ft) or more, large oval glossy leaflets, fine cream-coloured flowers with crimson stigmas surrounded by yellow anthers, in late spring. Caucasus–Elburz.

Papaver (*Papaveraceae*)

A genus even more popular and widespread in gardens than the paeonies, with somewhat similar flowers in the larger species. Although their simple elegant flowers vary little in shape, the species vary enormously in size and habit, from small annuals and perennials often used on the rock garden, through annuals, biennials, and perennials of intermediate size, to the well-loved large perennial Oriental Poppies, available in a wide range of cultivars. They mainly flower in early summer.

They are generally easily grown in sunny borders, but the smaller species do best in very well-drained soils, and should be catered for in a rock garden or in the foreground of a border if suitable drainage can be provided. Unfortunately the larger perennials are very floppy and need supporting at an early stage. They also die down untidily, but as soon as the leaves begin to brown all the top growth can pulled off and a neighbouring clematis like *C. heracleifolia* or *C. durandii* or a lathyrus trained over the gap. The species can be raised from seed very easily, in fact the annuals and biennials are better sown in situ, or alternatively pricked out early with minimum root disturbance which they seem to resent. This is the best treatment for the perennial species. The hybrids, particularly the Oriental Poppies, can be increased by division or by root cuttings.

I describe below the genuinely perennial species, some of which are short-lived, and I have omitted the largest cultivars of *P. orientale*.

P. alboroseum A small species to 10 cm (4 in), resembling the Iceland Poppies, leaves hairy, pinnately-lobed, flowers solitary white or palest pink, usually with a yellow blotch at the base of each petal. It is a pretty poppy that can be used in the same way as *P. alpinum*. N.E. Russia–Alaska.

P. alpinum Variable to 20 cm (8 in), leaves hairy, finely divided, grey-green or green, solitary flowers 2.5–4 cm across in shades of white, yellow, and orange-red. The name is in some doubt and several other similar species could be included in it, including the European *P. burseri*, *P. kerneri*, *P. rhaeticum*, and *P. sendtneri*, and perhaps the Japanese *P. miyabeanum*. These are all small short-lived species, usually self-seed freely, and often hybridize, making retention of the species difficult. In very well-drained soil they are easily grown and can be used as a border edging as well as on the rock garden.

P. atlanticum To 30 cm (1 ft), similar to and often confused with *P. ruprifagum*, differing in pinnately-lobed, toothed leaves, stems silky-hairy, larger 5 cm (2 in) wide orange flowers. It seeds very freely and should be dead-headed if this is to be controlled. The double form flore-pleno has beautiful semi-double flowers and seeds less freely, but produces a proportion of single flowers. These are most attractive poppies that flower off and on for most of the summer. N. Africa.

P. bracteatum *See* ***P. orientale***

P. burseri ✱ Allied to *P. alpinum*, leaves sparsely hairy, flowers pure white single, with a boss of yellow stamens. It is the whitest and perhaps the most beautiful of the group.

***P.* 'Fireball'** A cultivar of uncertain origin, at one time offered as *P. orientale* 'Nanum Flore Pleno', and now thought to be a form of *P. lateritium*. It runs freely underground, producing tufts of very bristly divided leaves like those of *P. orientale* on a very small scale, and abundant upright hairy stems, to 30 cm (1 ft), flowers fully double reddish-orange, fading quickly to dingy white at their edges. Very easy and very perennial and looks marvellous for about a week, then rapidly becomes a mess until the old growth can be torn out like an oriental poppy. It is much admired!

101 *Papaver* 'Fireball'

P. heldreichii *See* ***P. spicatum***

P. kerneri A good yellow-flowered *P. alpinum*. S.E. Alps.

P. kluanense Very similar to *P. radicatum*, to 15 cm (6 in), flowers greenish-yellow single. W. Canada.

P. lateritium Similar to *P. atlanticum* leaves coarsely toothed, hairy, lanceolate, hairy stems, flowers similar to *P. atlanticum* but sometimes brick red, with a shorter flowering season in early summer. Turkey.

P. miyabeanum ✱ Similar to *P. alpinum*, flowers pale yellow with a tinge of green. It is my favourite plant in this group, but short-lived and not always self-sowing as one would like. It is well worth collecting seed. Japan.

102 *Papaver orientale* 'Black and White'

P. nudicaule (Iceland Poppy) Probably not the true Iceland Poppy, but one of its parents, the true perennial species can attain 50 cm (20 in), with tufts of pinnate hairy leaves and solitary cup-shaped, yellow, 4–6 cm (1.6–2.3 in) wide flowers. C.–E. Russia. Strains of mixed Iceland Poppies may be sold under this name, and although they are strictly perennial they are very short-lived and better treated as biennials or annuals.
P. orientale Almost too well-known to need description, stoloniferous (usually), large clusters of very bristly pinnately lobed leaves to 30 cm (1 ft) long, bristly stems to 90 cm (3 ft), leafy towards the base, very large single red or orange-red cup-shaped flowers with a small black blotch or no blotch at the base of the petal. The Oriental Poppies of gardens also include *P. bracteatum* (*P. o.* var. *bracteatum*) 🏆 taller with each flower subtended by 4–5 sepal-like bracts, and a larger black blotch at the base of each petal. These poppies and their cultivars have the most sumptious flowers in a considerable range of colours. They are not particularly easy to place in the colour scheme of a border, but the reds look magnificent in front of the huge greenish-yellow flowers of *Euphorbia characias* ssp. *wulfenii* 'Lambrook Gold'. Most of the cultivars are too tall to consider here, but the following are some of the smaller-growing.

Variety	Height	Colour
'Allegro'	60–70 cm (28 in)	Scarlet with black blotch
'Black and White' 🏆	70–80 cm (28–32 in)	White with a black blotch and a dark centre
'Curlilocks'	65–75 cm (26–30 in)	Orange-red with large black blotch and fringed petals
'Dwarf Allegro'	40–50 cm (16–20 in)	As 'Allegro'
'Helen Elisabeth'	To 70 cm (28 in)	Deep pink
'Ladybird'	50–60 cm (20–24 in)	Vermilion with black blotch
'Marcus Perry'	60–70 cm (24–28 in)	Orange-scarlet
'Midnight'	To 75 cm (2.5 ft)	Pinkish-orange, very large
'Oriana'	60–70 cm (24–28 in)	Orange with black centre, petals ruffled
'Patty's Plum'	50–70 cm (28 in)	Soft mauve, a very unusual shade
'Picotee'	60–70 cm (28 in)	White with an orange frilled edge
'Prinzessin Victoria Loise'	65–75 cm (26–30 in)	Pinkish-salmon with black blotch
'Turkenlouis' 🏆	60–80 cm (28–32 in)	Soft pink, pale centre

P. paucifoliatum A rare species, of which seed has recently been reintroduced, like a smaller edition of *P. orientale*, to 50 cm (20 in), flowers smaller bright red with a similar dark blotch. It seems to clump up more slowly but is proving a good perennial. Caucasus.
P. pilosum Very similar to *P. spicatum*, more variation in colour from orange to scarlet more rounded seed capsules. Turkey.
P. radicatum Very similar to *P. nudicaule*, rare in gardens, best known as part of the Iceland Poppy group. N. hemisphere. Pyrenees–S. Alps.
P. rupifragum Very similar to, and confused with *P. atlanticum*, leaves less hairy and smaller, flowers with more red in the colour. It has a long flowering season throughout the summer, and is a very free seeder. Dead-heading is advisable! S. Spain.
P. sendtneri A delightful white-flowered *P. alpinum*. C., E. Alps.
P. spicatum (syn. *P. heldreichii*) Clumps of pale green white-hairy toothed leaves, 40–50 cm (16–20 in) upright spikes of almost stemless, large, soft orange flowers opening over a long period on each spike. It is a very attractive foliage plant and the flowers are beautiful, especially when grouped together for impact. It is one of the most perennial, as I still have plants from the seed collection over twenty years ago. Turkey.

Paradisia (*Liliaceae*/*Asphodelaceae*)

Two species of clump-forming perennials, leaves narrow, grass-like, upright spikes of pure white, funnel-shaped, lily-like flowers, with prominent upturning white style and filaments, and yellow anthers. They are very attractive, their flowers of a brilliant pristine whiteness, ideal for the middle of a border. They are easily raised from seed.
P. liliastrum St Bruno's Lily. The smaller plant, to 50cm

(20 in) if well-grown. It seems to need good drainage but is not very drought tolerant. S. Europe. The variety 'Major' ✸ is more robust.

P. lusitanica Larger clumps of broader leaves, much taller flower spikes, often well above our height limit, flowers more open with reflexing petals. It is very easy and seeds about in sun or shade, and once a colony is big enough the flowers should be dead-headed, or the seeds distributed to the many gardeners who do not grow it!

Parahebe (*Scrophulariaceae*)

Mainly low shrubs closely allied to Hebe. I have excluded all but one, a more typical perennial.

P. perfoliata 🏆 Clump-forming to 30 cm (1 ft), leaves rounded bluish-green, clasping the stem, loose sprays curving at their tips of pale blue flowers, an outstanding perennial for any sunny border.

Paris (syn. *Daiswa*) (*Liliaceae/ Trilliaceae*)

A small genus of fascinating herbaceous woodland plants, starting into growth late in the spring from slowly spreading rhizomes, with stiff upright stems bearing a symmetrical whorl of leaves towards the top, just beneath the solitary green flowers with usually 4 narrow sepals and narrower petals in summer. They have a quiet appealing charm and the longest lasting flowers of any perennials, and are reasonably easy to grow in moist humus-rich soil in shade. They can be raised from seed but are slow-growing in the seedling stage, taking 5–8 years to reach flowering size.

P. incompleta Rare species, to 30 cm (1 ft), a whorl of 6–12 leaves, to 10 cm (4 in) long, flowers on a short stalk above the leaves, four pale green sepals and no petals. Turkey–Caucasus.

P. japonica (syn. *Kinugasa japonica*) Resembling a pure white *P. polyphylla*, but probably unavailable, certainly difficult, and on the top of many a 'wants list'! Japan.

P. polyphylla (syn. *Daiswa polyphylla*) ✸ Upright stems to 60 cm (2 ft), or more in good conditions, a whorl of 5–9 purplish-stalked leaves, large flowers with 4–5, green, 8 cm (3 in) long, lanceolate sepals, and linear petals of almost the same length. The ovary is violet, becoming brown after several months, and opening to expose the vivid red fleshy seeds, while the flowers are still in pristine condition, three or four months after they appear. Himalayas–China. *P. p.* var. *tibetica* (syn. *P. tibetica*) To 20 cm (8 in) or less, leaves 7–10 lanceolate, stalkless, 5 sepals half the length of the leaves, shorter thread -like petals, and green or yellow ovary. W. China. *P. p.* var. *yunnanensis* (syn. *P. yunnanensis*) lower growing to 20–30 cm (8–12 in), with yellow sepals and petals and a green ovary.

103 *Paris polyphylla*

104 *Paris polyphylla* fruit

P. quadrifolia Our native species, the only one commonly grown, similar to *P. incompleta* as described, except in the presence of four linear green petals, rarely taller than 20 cm (8 in). Europe, Asia.

Parochetus (*Leguuminosae*)

A genus of two species of low mat-forming perennials with leaves almost indistinguishable from clover, and pea flowers of the clear brilliant blue seen in only a few plants, over a long period. They are easily grown but not fully hardy. *P. africana* is a good hanging basket plant for winter flowering. They can be propagated by division or by cuttings.

P. africana The commoner species, which until recently was usually named *P. communis*. A vigorous trailer, shoots rooting at the nodes, typical clover leaves with a dark U-shaped mark on each leaflet, flowers all through the winter in mild gardens. The similarity to clover should be borne in mind as it is easily mistaken when out of flower. E. Africa.

P. commmunis The true plant is similar but tuberous-rooted and deciduous, and spreads less freely. Himalayas, China.

Patrinia (*Valerianaceae*)

A small genus of clump-forming perennials, with lobed leaves and loose sprays of many small, usually yellow flowers, generally late in the season. They grow best in humus-rich soil in partial shade, and deserve to be more widely grown to lighten up a shady corner in late summer or autumn. They can be propagated by division or by seed sown as soon as ripe, and kept cool.

P. gibbosa Clump-forming to 30 cm (1 ft), leaves oval, pointed, 15 cm (6 in) long, pinnately lobed, rounded heads of small bright yellow flowers. Japan.
P. palmata *See* ***P. p. triloba***
P. scabiosaefolia To 60 cm (2 ft) or more in good soil, leaves pinnate, toothed, colouring in autumn, upright stems bearing large heads of small bright yellow flowers in late summer and autumn. Surprisingly uncommon in gardens. E. Asia.
P. triloba The most widely grown species, to 20 cm (8 in), leaves 5-lobed toothed, reddish in autumn, comparatively large loose heads of yellow flowers in late summer. An excellent plant for late colour at the edge of a shady border. Var. *palmata* ✸ is the most frequently offered plant, and differs in very minor particulars.
P. villosa To 15 cm (6 in), uncommon, leaves simple ovate, flat-heads of creamy-white flowers. Korea, Japan.

Pelargonium (*Geraniaceae*)

A large genus of tender perennials, but with two hardy species, of which *P. endlicherianum* is usually grown on the rock garden or in the alpine house. They are clump-forming from thickened woody rhizomes which build up into a woody mound, with rounded leaves and upright stems, bearing umbels of intriguing magenta flowers with two large broad upper and three insignificant lower petals, in summer. They may be raised from seed, or portions of woody rhizome with leaves can be cut off and rooted in a propagator.
P. endlicherianum A fascinating species with dark green rounded or kidney-shaped leaves, and stems to 20 cm (8 in) or a little more. It seems to be hardy to -10 °C (14 °F) or probably less. Turkey, Syria.
P. quercetorum A dense mound of woody rhizomes, large palmately lobed leaves, dense umbels of similar but larger flowers on 40-60 cm (1.3–2 ft) stems. A rarely grown but striking species which seems quite easy in ordinary well-drained soil in full sun. It deserves to be more widely grown. Turkey–N. Iran.

Penstemon (*Scrophulariaceae*)

A large North American genus of mainly evergreen perennials, from tiny alpine mat-formers through compact shrubs to large upright clump-forming plants for the border. All have tubular flowers with five spreading lobes forming an upper and lower lip. Many species are difficult or short-lived in the garden, especially the small alpines from high altitudes, and many are tender to a greater or lesser degree.

A very large number of colourful cultivars for the front or middle of the border have been raised, and the naming of these has become confused. A recent Trial of this group by the Royal Horticultural Society has done much to sort out the confusion, and the best of them have been given the Award of Garden Merit. They are all very colourful plants for the front or middle of any border, but are of marginal hardiness. I have described these briefly in the table below, together with a few others which I have found particularly good in the garden.

In considering the species I have concentrated on those that have proved reasonably reliable as plants for the front or middle of the border, given good drainage, and I have omitted the small difficult species that are more likely to be successful in the alpine house or rock garden.

The species can be raised from seed, but they may hybridize if several are grown together. All may be propagated from cuttings, best taken in early summer in the species, but easy at most times in the case of the border cultivars. The latter should be propagated regularly in late summer so that plants can be overwintered under glass, for replanting after the frosts of spring are over.
P. alpinus Clump 15–60 cm (6–24 in) high, congested heads of 2–3 cm (0.8–1.2 in) long blue flowers, usually tinged purple. Some excellent blue forms.
P. angustifolius Clump 10–40 cm (4–16 in), leaves narrowly lanceolate, dense heads of flowers 1.5–2 cm (0.6–0.8 in), pinkish to blue. Early but usually short-lived.
P. attenuatus Clump to 60 cm (2 ft), leaves oval to lanceolate, entire, flowers whorled like *P. procerus*, yellow or rich purple. Easy, and good in its best forms.
P. azureus Sub-shrubby, 20–60 cm (8–24 in), leaves silvery, lanceolate, heads of 2–3 cm (0.8–1.2 in) purplish-blue flowers. One of the more perennial 'blue' species for the border but not the brightest.
P. barbatus Clump 30–70 cm (28 in) with stiffly upright stems, leaves glossy, lanceolate, loose spikes of narrow, tubular, scarlet flowers at mid-summer, rarely pink, white or yellow. A good, striking, perennial species in mild gardens, easier than some others of similar colour.
P. barrettiae Sub-shrubby, 30 cm (1 ft), leaves bluish-green, toothed, oval, masses of pale lavender to purple flowers. Use in the front of a border in well-drained soil, or on the rock garden.
P. campanulatus (*P. kunthii*) ✸ Clump to 50 cm (20 in), leaves narrowly lanceolate to ovate, toothed, long spikes of very narrow, generally reddish-purple flowers. It is said only to be winter-hardy in mild gardens but has proved one of the best perennial species in my garden, if temperatures remain above -7 °C (20 °F). Flower colour varies from wild collected seed, including a pleasing deep pink.
P. cardwellii Dense shrub to 30 cm (1 ft), flowers large, violet-purple. Usually grown on the rock garden but in well-drained soil one of the easier shrubby species.
P. confertus Clump to 40 cm (16 in), small cream-coloured whorled flowers. Closely allied to *P. procerus*, a reliable and reasonably hardy perennial.
P. davidsonii Like *P. barrettiae* in habit, to 20 cm (8 in), leaves small, glossy green, flowers lilac to purple in clusters. Var. *menziesii* 🏆 more compact, with pinkish-lavender flowers paler in the throat. Among the most perennial shrubby species.
P. digitalis 50–100 cm (20–40 in) Upright species, leaves

lanceolate frequently tinged purple, flowers white in tall spikes often flushed faint purple. One of the most hardy and reliable perennials for the border, and I find it happy in partial shade. Easily raised from seed, and plants with good leaf colour should be selected. 'Husker Red' A particularly good purple-leaved selection.

P. eatonii Like *P. barbatus*, flowers in long slender one-sided spikes of vivid scarlet. A striking species for a sheltered site in well-drained soil, but less easy to keep than *P. barbatus*.

P. eriantherus Clump to 30 cm (1 ft), stems and oblanceolate leaves hairy, flowers in clusters, large, with spreading lobes, pale to very deep lavender, yellow in the throat. Usually grown on the rock garden, but I have had it for several years in a well-drained border.

P. fruticosus Upright shrub, 15–40 cm (6–16 in), leaves oval to broadly lanceolate, leathery, flowers bluish-lavender in clusters well above the leaves. Var. *scouleri* 🏆 narrower toothed leaves, flowers lavender or white, among the most satisfactory and hardy species. I find *P. f. scouleri albus* 🏆 a first class front-of-the-border plant which always smothers itself in white flowers for two or three weeks in summer. It contrasts well with Lithodora 'Heavenly Blue'.

105 *Penstemon fruticosus* var. *scouleri albus* & *Lithodora diffusa* 'Heavenly Blue'

P. glaber Clump to 50 cm (20 in), leaves glossy lanceolate, flowers deep blue to purple. Moderately easy in well-drained soil.

P. gracilis Upright to 60 cm (2 ft), leaves narrow lanceolate in rosettes, pale flowers in loose heads, off-white to pink. Allied to *P. digitalis*, uncommon in gardens.

P. hartwegii 🏆 Upright to1 m (3 ft), leaves narrow glossy, very large red flowers, white in the throat, in striking spikes, with a good white variety. One of the most spectacular of the taller penstemons and a major contributor to the border hybrids. Usually short-lived except in sheltered gardens.

P. heterophyllus Semi-shrubby to 40 cm (16 in), leaves blue-green lanceolate, flowers blue, often tinged with purple from yellowish buds, in upright spikes over a long season in summer. A long-lived perennial, but the flower colour varies in the purity of its blue. 'Blue Gem' compact with good blue flowers, 'Blue Springs' intermediate in height with clear pale blue flowers, 'Heavenly Blue' more reliably blue in colour, subsp. *purdyi* ✱ to only 20 cm (8 in), flowers brilliant azure in large spikes. I find this reliable in well-drained soil, and one of the bluest of all, but its seedlings are often more like the type, with purplish flowers.

P. hirsutus Very variable, clump-forming, 8 cm (3 in) (var. *pygmaeus*) to 50 cm (20 in), leaves ovate or broadly lanceolate, often tinged purple, flowers large, pale to deep violet, white in the throat, in dense spikes. Very easy and reliable species for the border, its best forms a most attractive colour. Var. *pygmaeus* Flowers more white than violet, popular for the rock garden but possible at the edge of a border. It is very small and the flower colour seems to me wishy-washy. Good intermediates with purple leaves and deep violet flowers to 20 cm (8 in) can be found.

106 *Penstemon hirsutus*

P. isophyllus 🏆 Like *P. hartwegii*, less bushy with broader leaves and long, narrow red flowers, cream towards the base, possibly longer-lived.

P. jamesii Stiffly upright to 40 cm (16 in), often less, leaves narrow, blue-green, unusually broad pale lavender bells with golden hairs in the throat, in dense one-sided spikes. It is reasonably perennial.

P. kunthii *See* ***P. campanulatus***

P. laetus Subshrubby to 70 cm (28 in), spikes of attractive large purple flowers. Uncommon except as its subspecies *roezlii* with narrower lanceolate leaves and blue flowers, often confused in trade sources with *P. roezlii* of gardens, a compact shrubby plant allied to *P. newberryi*.

P. lyallii Upright clump to 60 cm (2 ft) or more, leaves long, narrow, flowers pale violet in loose heads. My plants have proved similar to *P. digitalis* but darker and equally easy to grow. More compact growing plants under this name are possibly impostors.

P. newberryi 🏆 Shrubby, similar to *P. fruticosus*, but more prostrate with rooting stems, and flowers mid to deep

rose-pink in clusters in early summer. A fine easy plant in well-drained soil.
P. ovatus Clump 30-90 cm (1–3 ft) high, leaves cordate, flowers variable from clear blue to purplish. It is a reliably perennial species, and an excellent blue in its best forms.
P. pinifolius 🏆 Low shrub, leaves tiny light green needles, flowers narrow, vivid orange-red, in loose spikes. 'Mersea Yellow' identical apart from deep yellow flowers. Among the most popular of all penstemons, and although excellent rock garden plants they can equally well be used at the border edge.
P. procerus Mats 8-40 cm (3–16 in) high, leaves small, very narrow, glossy, flowers small tubular in one to several whorls on upright stems, usually deep blue-tinged purple, occasionally creamy-yellow or white. Easily grown with good drainage, but the flowers have less impact than those of many other species. Subsp. *tolmei* 20 cm (8 in) high or less, broader leaves, more widely grown, especially in rock gardens.
P. richardsonii Low mound, stems prostrate or semi-upright, leaves narrow, toothed, flowers 2.5 cm (1 in) long, deep purplish-pink to lavender in loose sprays in late summer. Useful and unusual species in its late flowering and low spreading habit, making it a good wall plant. It is easy and hardy in my garden.
P. rostriflorus Like *P. barbatus*, to 70 cm (28 in), but stems more spreading, flowers nodding, long, narrow, orange-scarlet, in long spikes. It tends to be short-lived except in dry warm gardens.
P. rupicola 🏆 Sub-shrubby mat like *P. barrettiae* but leaves glaucous, toothed, flowers comparatively large, colour pink to reddish-purple. It is one of the best and most reliable of the shrubby species.
P. serrulatus Clump 60 cm (2 ft) or often less, leaves glossy, toothed, flowers deep purple or blue in spikes. Reasonably long-lived in the border.
P. smallii Clump with very leafy upright stems, leaves pale green often tinged red, toothed, flowers rose-pink in terminal clusters. An attractive and reasonably easy plant.
P. strictus Stiffly upright to 60 cm (2 ft), leaves spathulate to lanceolate, flowers large deep blue in spikes. One of the more reliable border penstemons.
P. utahensis Clump, 30–50 cm (12–20 in), flowers in spikes, vivid carmine. Uncommon, but it seems to be one of the hardier red-flowered species.
P. venustus Clump to 40 cm (16 in), leaves large, grey-green, large purple flowers in one-sided spikes. An easy plant for a well-drained border. N.W. USA.
P. virens ✱ Mat to 15–20 cm (6–8 in), leaves dark green, glossy, oval to lanceolate, flowers vivid deep blue in dense heads. Excellent blue colour and glossy foliage make this one of the finest of all the blue-flowered species.
P. watsonii Resembling *P. procerus*, flowers smaller, purplish-blue, in less dense whorls.
P. whippleanus Rosette-forming mat to 20–40 cm (8–16 in), leaves glossy, oval, flowers nodding in whorls, a unique shade of greyish-violet. This is one of the soundest perennial species in my garden.
P. wislizenii (syn. *P. barbatus* subsp. *coccineus*) Similar to *P. barbatus*, more branching habit, flowers more vivid red.

Border Cultivars

The table below describes the flowers of some of these. They all make upright clusters of stiff stems with oval to lanceolate leaves, and I have only mentioned the leaves when they are unusual.

Name	Flowers	Notes
'Alice Hindley' 🏆	Pale mauve, white throat	
'Andenken an Friedrich Hahn' (syn. 'Garnet') 🏆	Deep carmine, few white throat markings	Very reliable and hardy
'Apple Blossom' 🏆	Narrow pale pink, white throat, white streaking outside	Multiple stems and narrow leaves
'Beech Park' 🏆	Like 'Osprey' but flowers smaller with a wider pink area	
'Catherine de la Mare' 🏆	Bluish-purple	Low sprawling habit
'Cherry Ripe' 🏆	Narrow red flowers on long pedicels	
'Chester Scarlet' 🏆	Very large bright red flowers, deeper red in the throat	
'Connie's Pink' 🏆	Deep reddish-pink, narrow flowers	
'Evelyn' 🏆	Narrow, pale pink with narrow leaves	One of the best and hardiest
'Hewell Pink Bedder'	Reddish-pink	Glaucous leaves
'Hidcote Pink' 🏆	Mid-pink streaked outside with white, dark streaks in the throat	Glaucous leaves

Name	Flowers	Notes
'King George'	Large scarlet, white throat streaked red	
'Margery Fish' 🏆	Deep blue to purplish-blue	Low sprawling habit
'Maurice Gibbs' 🏆	Large broad purplish-red, white throat	
'Osprey' 🏆	Large white, pink margin to the lobes	
'Papal Purple'	Soft deep lavender, white throat	Fairly short
'Pennington Gem' 🏆	Soft pink, white throat streaked red	Moderately hardy
'Port Wine' 🏆	Deep reddish-purple, dark mouth	
'Raven' 🏆	Deep reddish-purple, dark-veined white throat	
'Rich Ruby'	Deep reddish-purple	
'Rubicundus' 🏆	Very large broad red flowers, white-mouthed	Tender
'Schoenholzeri' ('Firebird') 🏆	Pinkish red, compact spike	Very hardy
'Sour Grapes'	Mixed shades of purple and blue	Flowers in 'bunches'
'Stapleford Gem' 🏆	Mixed shades of purple and blue, paler than Sour Grapes	Very hardy
'White Bedder' 🏆 (see plate 107)	Creamy white with black anthers	Moderately hardy

107 *Penstemon* 'White Bedder'

Persicaria (*Polygonaceae*) (syn. *Polygonum*)

Most of the plants so well-known as Polygonum species have now been transferred by botanists into Persicaria, but are more likely to be found in catalogues under their previous name. A genus of some 100 species of annuals, perennials, and shrubs, many of them tall, very invasive, and unsuitable for gardens. I describe below the smaller most ornamental perennials. They may be upright or spreading, with simple alternate leaves and dense spikes or loose heads of small bell-shaped to tubular flowers with petaloid sepals, generally pink or white. They are not perhaps the most exciting of perennials and they need choosing with care to avoid the menaces, but they are easily grown in sun or partial shade, some even tolerating dry shade, and several make good ground cover. A few need very moist conditions. They may be raised from seed or by division or cuttings.

All the following are synonymous with the equivalent Polygonum species

P. affinis Vigorous low ground-cover to 40 cm (16 in) high, leaves lanceolate, flowers rose-pink in dense spikes, mid-summer to autumn. Himalayas. 'Darjeeling Red' 🏆 deep crimson. 'Donald Lowndes' 🏆 pink with good autumn leaf colour. 'Dimity' (syn. 'Superba') white faintly tinged pink, deepening to reddish with age. These are among the most colourful species with a reasonable balance of flower to foliage.

P. amplexicaulis Vigorous clump to 80 cm (30 in), leaves broadly lanceolate clasping the stems, flowers like *P. affinis*, but red, generally smaller. Himalayas. Var. *pendula* Spikes nodding. 'Alba' white, 'Atrosanguinea' deep crimson. 'Arun Gem' more prostrate, flowers in curved spikes, deep pink with brownish tips. 'Firetail' 🏆 compact, good crimson. 'Inverleith' low-growing, short dark crimson spikes. 'Rosea' strong-growing with pale pink flowers. All are easily grown, especially in moist soil, but one might wish for more 'flower power', accompanying the leafiness.

P. bistorta Invasive carpeter, leaves oval, flowers pale pink in dense spikes. 'Carneum' flowers deeper in colour in shorter wider spikes. 'Superba' 🏆 tall, flowers rich pink. These are definitely plants to be avoided in small gardens but may be useful where extensive ground cover is needed.

P. campanulata Stoloniferous clump-former to 90 cm (3 ft), leaves ovate, white-backed, flowers bell-shaped white or pale pink, in loose spikes on upright branching stems. 'Alba' and 'Southcombe White' white, the former more spreading. 'Rosenrot' deep pink. They need moist conditions in partial shade to thrive well.

P. capitata Low carpeter, leaves broad with purplish V-shaped zone, flowers in dense round heads just above the leaves, over a long season. A very attractive ground cover that can be invasive, but curbed by frost below about -7 °C (20 °F). Himalayas.

P. macrophylla Clump to 30 cm (1 ft), leaves ovate, flowers large, pink to red, in broad spikes or heads. A well-behaved plant rarely seen in gardens. Himalayas–China.

P. milletii Like *P. bistorta*, more compact and less invasive, flowers crimson. Himalayas, China.

P. tenuicaulis ✱ Low mat-former to 10 cm (4 in), leaves oval, dark green, purple flushed beneath, flowers white, in dense spikes just above the leaves in early spring. In complete contrast to all the other species this is a perfectly behaved and very attractive little carpeter for moist shade in humus-rich soil.

P. vaccinifolia Spreading mat to 15 cm (6 in), prostrate stems reddish, slender, branching, flowers bistort-like, pink, in narrow dense spikes in late summer and autumn. A good late flowering carpeter, best in moist soils, where it can be invasive.

P. virginiana Rarely grown but the cultivar 'Painters Palette' is popular with leaves variegated in gold and pink.

Petrocoptis (*Caryophyllaceae*)

Seven Pyrenean perennials of which only two are grown regularly. Although mainly seen on the rock garden they are easily grown and suitable for the front of the border or for growing in a wall. They are clump-forming with a semi-woody base and typical campion-like flowers in summer. They are easy to raise from seed but frequently prove short-lived.

P. glaucifolia (syn. *Lychnis lagascae*) Branching to 20 cm (8 in), leaves glaucous, lanceolate, and flowers 3 cm (1.2 in) wide, carmine or white, in loose heads. N. Spain.

P. pyrenaica Similar, leaves in basal rosettes, flowers pale pink or white.

Petromarula (*Campanulaceae*)

One species endemic to Crete, often a conspicuous feature of rocky cliffs or even of old buildings, where it grows out of tiny cracks, but very rarely grown in gardens. It is well worth trying and has grown well in my garden planted in and above a low wall, flowering profusely in early to mid-summer once established. It can be raised from seed.

P. pinnata Rosettes of dark green pinnate leaves 10–30 cm (4–12 in) long, erect or semi-erect 30–50 cm (12–20 in) stems, large sprays of myriads of 1 cm (0.4 in) wide, pale violet-blue flowers, with strongly recurving narrow petals and a prominent style. It may be short-lived.

108 *Petromarula pinnata*

Petrorhagia (*Caryophyllaceae*)

20 species of annuals and perennials, of which only one is grown regularly. It can be raised from seed or by cuttings, the latter essential for the cultivar.

P. saxifraga (syn. *Tunica saxifraga*) 🏆 Mound-forming, leaves small linear, on slender branching stems, flowers pale pink or white, shallowly cup-shaped, in abundant loose sprays in late summer. 'Rosette' Similar, but deep pink double flowers. A charming plant with the airy effect of a gypsophila, for the front of a well-drained sunny border, or wall.

Phlomis (*Labiatae*)

About 100 species of perennials and shrubs, mainly from the Mediterranean but extending through Asia to China. They are clump-forming, or erect shrubs, with attractive leaves and large whorls of 2-lipped flowers, the upper hooded, usually in shades of yellow or pink to purple, on upright stems. They are invaluable plants for the sunny border, with beautiful leaves at all times and good flowers, thriving especially in well-drained soils, but the majority are too tall to consider here. In addition to those described below some smaller species have recently been introduced from China, but are relatively untried in gardens. They can be raised from seed or from cuttings.

P. cashmeriana Clump to 60 cm (2 ft), leaves lanceolate, grey-green, white-woolly reverse, flowers in several whorls, comparatively large, deep pink, marked darker purple on the lower lip. A most attractive species, but in my experience far from easy to keep going. Himalayas.

P. italica Small very upright shrub under 80 cm (30 in), leaves whitish-green, very downy, broadly lanceolate, flowers pale pink in upright spires of 4–6 whorls in late summer. An easy plant for the border but straggly with age and may then need replacing. Hardy to around -10 °C (14 °F). Balearic Is., (not Italy).

109 *Phlomis italica & Lavatera* 'Burgundy Wine'

P. lanata ✱ ☼ Compact more spreading shrub to 60 cm (2 ft), leaves rounded, downy, yellowish-green, flowers deep yellow, solitary or whorled, in summer. Less hardy than most of the shrubby species but survives to at least -7 °C (20 °F). Crete.

Phlox (*Polemoniaceae*)

A genus of about 70 annuals and perennials, from North America, varying greatly in cultural requirements and habit, from tight alpine cushions, through spreading mats. to small and large upright clump-formers. Although varying greatly in their foliage and inflorescence, their individual flowers are generally similar, narrowly tubular at the base with five widely spreading lobes (petals) which may be notched at their tips, and often have a contrasting colour in the throat.

From the gardeners point of view they fall mainly into three groups. The smallest are tight cushions or low mats, some needing care in the alpine house or rock garden, but others robust enough to make a carpet of colour at the edge of a border in well-drained soil, particularly the large number of cultivars of *P. douglasii* and *P. subulata.* The second group are beautiful woodlanders needing moist humus-rich soil in partial shade, carpeting or clump-forming plants that are ideally placed between shrubs or other taller shade-lovers like lilies, meconopsis, polygonatums, disporums etc, and flower profusely in late spring and early summer. The third group contains the tall border phlox cultivars, which I will exclude, and a few others of intermediate size, that all thrive on very rich soils with adequate moisture. As a guide to their requirements I have marked them (Gp 1), (Gp 2) or (Gp 3).

Although the species can be raised from seed when available most phlox are easily grown from cuttings, or in the case of the larger cultivars from root cuttings, the latter method diminishing the dangers of eelworm attack, to which they are prone.

P. adsurgens 🏆 (Gp 2) Low mat of semi-prostrate stems rooting at the nodes, leaves ovate, flowers clear soft pink with pale eye and a dark streak down the centre of each petal, in loose clusters on short upright flowering shoots to 20 cm (8 in). It is one of the most beautiful of this group but not always easy to please. 'Red Buttes' Darker flowers of excellent shape with more overlapping petals. 'Wagon Wheels' Strangely popular, with very narrow petals.

P. × arendsii (***P. divaricata × P. paniculata***) (Gp 3) Plants about 40 cm (16 in), flowers in good large clusters in early summer before *P. paniculata.* 'Anja' purplish-red, 'Hilda' white with a purple eye.

P. bifida (Gp 1) Mat-forming, looser than most in the group, flowers in clusters, very variable, white to deep lilac. In rich well-drained soil some forms seem strong enough to be used as a border edging, notably 'Blue form', 'Colvin's White' pure white, 'Petticoat' pink, and 'Starbrite' pale blue, compact.

P. carolina (Gp 3) Spreading clump, stems upright and procumbent, leaves glossy, lanceolate, flowers pink to purple, in very large heads over a long period in summer. 'Bill Baker' ✷ Outstanding cultivar, 40–50 cm (16–20 in) high, masses of deep pink, white eyed flowers for months. 'Magnificence' narrower heads of darker pink flowers. 'Miss Lingard' 🏆 similar but white. They flourish in sun or in partial shade, given reasonable moisture.

110 *Phlox carolina* 'Bill Baker' & *Centaurea montana alba*

P.* 'Chattahoochee'** *See* ***P. divaricata
P.* 'Charles Ricardo'** *See* ***P. divaricata
P. divaricata 🏆 (Gp 2) Similar to *P. adsurgens*, to 30 cm (1 ft), spreading more widely, flowers in longer stemmed umbels, violet-blue, usually with a darker eye and notched petals. Susp. laphamii Longer-tubed lilac flowers, petals rounded. Both grow well in moist shade and flower over a long period in late spring and early summer. They tend to exhaust the soil after two or three years, and should be replanted. 'Blue Dreams' strong-growing, flowers scented, lavender-blue, 'Charles Ricardo' pale lavender, 'Chattahoochee' 🏆 very distinct, compact, flowers deep lilac with reddish-purple eye, not always easy to please but it has flourished for several years in rich well-drained soil in partial shade 'Clouds of Perfume' pale lavender, scented, 'Dirigo Ice' strong-growing, large very pale flowers, 'Fuller's White' ✷ upright clump to 30 cm (1 ft), flowers pure white in a long succession. Slugs love it!

111 *Phlox divaricata* 'Chattahoochee'

P. douglasii (Gp 1) Low cushion, densely leafy prostrate stems, masses of white, lavender, or pink flowers in heads of 1–3, in late spring and early summer. One of the two main species of cushion phlox giving rise to a great range of cultivars usually seen as wall plants or on the rock garden, but making very colourful edging to any sunny border with reasonable drainage.

The following are among the most popular cultivars of *P. douglasii* but there is some muddling with those of *P. subulata*. Although I have allocated them to one or other species, look under both for any particular plant. 'Apollo' good-sized violet pink. 'Boothman's variety' 🏆 an old favourite, lavender with deep blue central zone, 'Concorde' deep bluish crimson flowers with greyish eye. 'Crackerjack' 🏆 superb recent hybrid, compact, brilliant magenta flowers in great abundance, 'Eva' and 'Galaxy' compact growers, the former lavender, the latter darker violet, 'Iceberg' 🏆 and 'Ice Mountain' excellent whites, the former slightly flushed palest violet. 'Kelly's Eye' 🏆 a superb outstandingly floriferous recent cultivar, pale pink with a deep reddish eye, 'Red Admiral' 🏆 deep crimson, excellent, 'Rose Cushion' very compact, rose-pink, deeper than the pale silvery pink of 'Rose Queen', 'Violet Queen' very compact, unusually dark violet flowers, 'Waterloo' older cultivar, purplish-pink.
P. maculata (Gp3) A little shorter than the *P. paniculata* cultivars but similar in habit, attractive and disease-free, flower heads of a very different shape, long and cylindrical. Two common cultivars 'Alpha' ✷ deep pink with a dark centre, and 'Omega' ✷ white with a small lilac eye.
P. nivalis (Gp1) Like *P. subulata*, generally more compact, flowers purple to pink. Three cultivars have enough vigour to be used in the same way as other Gp1 plants. 'Camla' the most upright, pale pink, 'Jill Alexander' pure white, 'Nivea' deeper pink.
P. pilosa ✷ (Gp3) Resembling *P. carolina*, leaves lanceolate, on spreading stems to 50 cm (20 in), flowers pink to purple in large loose heads at mid-summer. Plants I have grown have had clear pink flowers with a paler eye, over a long season, invaluable for the middle of a border in rich soil.

112 *Phlox* 'Millstream Jupiter'

P.* x *procumbens (syn. *P. amoena* hort.) (***P. stolonifera*** x ***P. subulata***) (Gp1/2) Mat-forming, to 12 cm (4.7 in), generally looser and taller than *P. subulata*, flowers purple, 'Rosea' deep pink. 'Millstream' deep pink, white centre and reddish eye, an outstanding plant that flourishes in partial shade.

P.* x *rugellii (***P. amoena*** x ***P. subulata***) (Gp1) Loose mat, 12 cm (4.7 in), flowers purplish-blue in clusters.

P. stolonifera (Gp2) Similar to *P. divaricata*, to 25 cm (10 in), leaves hairy, ovate, flowers lavender to violet or white in flattish heads on stiffly upright stems, in late spring. 'Ariane' the best pure white, well rounded flowers. 'Blue Ridge' 🏆 popular for many years, clear lavender-blue, 'Pink Ridge' and 'White Ridge' similar except in colour. All excellent in good humus-rich soil that never dries out, in partial shade.

P. subulata (Gp1) The classic cushion phlox, rarely seen in its wild form but with a very large number of cultivars, some of them undoubtedly derived from other species. The following are some of the best.

Variety	Flowers	Remarks
'Alexanders Surprise'	Large, salmon pink	
'Amazing Grace' ✸	Pink, white eye	Vigorous, one of the best
'Apple Blossom'	Purplish pink, dark eye	
'Atropurpurea'	Small, reddish-purple	Vigorous
'Betty'	Large, deep pink	
'Bonita'	Large purplish lilac	
'Daisy Hill'	Bright pink	Vigorous
'G.F. Wilson'	Large, pale lavender	A vigorous old hybrid
'Greencourt Purple'	Pinkish purple, dark eye	
'McDaniel's Cushion' 🏆	Bright reddish-pink	Vigorous. One of the best
'Maidens Blush'	Pink, red eye	
'Marjorie'	Rose pink	
'May Snow'	Pure white	
'Oakington Blue Eyes'	Deep lavender	
'Red Wings' 🏆	Rose red with darker eye	Vigorous
'Samson'	Large, salmon pink, red eye	
'Scarlet Flame'	Large, carmine-red	
'Tamaongalei'	White, streaked reddish-pink	Good new cultivar
'Temiskaming'	Dark magenta	Reliable old cultivar
'Vivid'	Clear pink	Very compact
'White Delight'	Pure white	Vigorous

Phuopsis

P. stylosa One species, mat-forming, rhizomatous, herbaceous, semi-prostrate branching stems, whorls of narrow pointed pale green leaves that are strongly and not pleasantly aromatic, dense rounded heads of 2 cm (0.8 in) long tubular pink flowers for several weeks in summer. Easily grown and attractive apart from the smell, covering the ground well in any sunny position. It can be propagated from cuttings. Turkey–Iran.

Physostegia (*Labiatae*) (Obedient Plant)

Twelve species of upright-growing, vigorously spreading perennials, with lanceolate toothed leaves, and narrow, upright, often branching spikes of broadly tubular, pink to purple, or white flowers, with two spreading lips, on short pedicels which remain in position if moved, hence the common name. They are very vigorous and can spread widely in moist rich soil, but are shorter and less invasive if dry.

P. virginiana Generally too tall for consideration, but a few cultivars are shorter, 'Galadriel' only 40–50 cm (16–20 in), purplish-pink, 'Summer Snow' creamy buds opening to pure white, 'Vivid' deep reddish-pink.

Phyteuma (*Campanulaceae*)

Genus of some 40 species, mainly clump-forming rosetted perennials growing from a taproot, the leaves lanceolate to ovate, usually toothed, with dense terminal heads or spikes of intriguing blue, purple or white flowers in summer, with very narrow incurving petals often joined at the tip until the pollen is shed. They vary greatly in height and only the taller species are suitable for the border, preferably well-drained and

partially shaded. They can be propagated by seed or by division, but their tap-rooted habit makes the latter hazardous, and plants should be established when young.
P. betonicifolium Stems to 40 cm (16 in), leaves narrow, toothed, long-stalked, 4 cm (1.6 in) long, oval, deep blue spikes. Italy.
P. charmelii Very similar to *P. scheuzeri*, but leaves pale green. S.W. Europe.
P. japonicum Rhizomatous, large ovate leaves, branching spikes of deep blue flowers in late summer to 50 cm (20 in). It is relatively untried in gardens. Japan, Korea.
P. nigrum Clump-forming to 60 cm (2 ft), leaves oval, basal, oval spikes of deep purplish-blue flowers. One of the best for a shady site. C. Europe.
P. orbiculare Clump-forming, rosettes of toothed leaves of variable shape, upright stems to 30 cm (1 ft), dense globular heads of deep blue flowers. It is quite easy especially on limy soils. Native to Britain and most of Europe.
P. scheuzeri Similar to *P. orbiculare*, taller, leaves narrower, blue-green. Perhaps a little easier than the last. Alps, Apennines.

Pimpinella (*Umbelliferae*)

A large genus of generally unexciting umbellifers with one first-class exception.
***P. major* 'Rosea'** Clump-forming to 50 cm (20 in), leaves fern-like, spreading 'cow-parsley' heads of soft pink flowers. Its delicate colour makes it one of the most attractive umbellifers, and it is easily grown in humus-rich soil in partial shade or in full sun if moisture is adequate.

Plantago (*Plantaginaceae*)

P. major In a genus better known for its weeds than for any garden plants, the ornamental leaf forms of this rosette-forming species are sometimes grown in the border. 'Rubrifolia' has reasonably attractive purple-tinged leaves, but it can seed freely, and not everyone would want to grow it. The Rose Plantain 'Rosularis' is a curiosity in which the flower spikes are replaced by an 8 cm (3 in) wide rosette of green leaves, resembling a rose flower.

Platycodon (*Campanulaceae*)

P. grandiflorus ♕ The only species, a variable herbaceous clump-forming perennial, leaves ovate to lanceolate, blue-green, in whorls below and alternate above, on upright stems to 60 cm (2 ft), but often less, solitary or a few large blue or white flowers, opening from inflated balloon-like buds into broad bells to 6 cm (2.3 in) wide, with spreading pointed lobes, in late summer. It is a striking and easily-grown perennial, readily raised from seed, for a sunny or lightly shaded well-drained border. E. Asia.

Several varieties and cultivars have been named, varying in colour and height. Var. *albus* white, sometimes faintly flushed with blue. Var. *apoyama* very compact form to 25 cm (10 in), large blue, or rarely white flowers. Unless isolated carefully it will not come true from seed. Var. *mariesii* ♕ intermediate in size, rarely above 40 cm (16 in), generally flowering earlier, with dark flowers. There are several blue cultivars, including doubles like 'Hakone', mostly with self-explanatory names, also some pink and white-flowered plants. 'Perlemutterschale' (syn. 'Mother of Pearl') has large silvery pink flowers.

Pleurospermum (*Umbelliferae*)

A small genus of which only one is regularly seen in gardens.
P. brunonis Clump-forming to 60 cm (2 ft) but frequently less, leaves ferny, broad heads of typical umbellifer flowers of an unusually pure white. It is one of the most beautiful umbellifers for the border, and can be raised from seed. Himalayas.

113 *Pleurospermum brunonis*

Podophyllum (*Berberidaceae*) (May Apple)

Two or three species of unusual herbaceous woodland perennials, clump-forming with upright stems to 30 cm (1 ft), longer after flowering, bearing paired large palmate leaves, rounded in outline, and cup-shaped pink or white flowers, in early summer, followed by large dangling red fruits. They are exciting plants for flower, foliage, and fruit, which flourish in moist humus-rich soil in shade, excellent among rhododendrons and taller woodland perennials. They can be raised from freshly sown seed, or theoretically by division, but they are best left undisturbed.
P. hexandrum (syn. *P. emodi*) ✱ ☼ Large 3–5-lobed leaves to 25 cm (10 in) wide, heavily splashed with purple especially when they first unfurl, upward-facing pale pink or white anemone-like flowers with 6 petals and conspicuous yellow anthers. Himalayas. Var. *chinense* more deeply lobed leaves and deep pink flowers. 'Majus' an uncommon taller cultivar with larger well-marked leaves and larger fruits.
P. peltatum (May Apple) Leaves well-developed at flowering

time, often hiding the 8-petalled white flowers. It is a less striking plant.

Polemonium (*Polemoniaceae*) (Jacob's Ladder)

Genus of about 30 species of mainly clump-forming perennials with pinnate leaves and leafy upright stems bearing heads of tubular flowers with spreading lobes in shades of blue, or less often pink or white, in summer. They all have attractive leaves and usually excellent flowers, but a few species seed around with excessive abandon; the sterile hybrids are welcome! There are several tricky alpine species, excluded here, but most are easily grown and very colourful border plants for sun or partial shade, in any reasonably moist soil. The species are easily raised from seed, and the cultivars can be increased by division in spring.

P. boreale Clumps 20–30 cm (8–12 in) high, leaves mainly basal, downy, with up to 20 leaflets, heads of purplish-blue flowers. It is not very robust. Circumpolar.

P. brandegeei Clumps of dense rosettes of very sticky hairy pinnate leaves, heads of 6–10 long straw-coloured flowers on upright 20 cm (8 in) stems. It is an attractive yellow species but it needs well-drained soil. *P. pauciflorum* or *P. flavum* sometimes seem to be offered in its place. S. USA.

P. caeruleum Leafy perennial up to 1 m (3 ft) or more, but usually considerably less, with up to 30 leaflets, terminal clusters of many light blue or white (var. *album*) cup-shaped flowers with deep yellow stamens, with some axillary. It flourishes in most soils in sun or partial shade, and seeds itself around with abandon, excessively in my garden, so that it needs careful placing. A wild garden is ideal. W. USA. Var. *himalayanum* a superior plant, flowers very large and darker, it also seeds freely. 'Brise d'Anjou' remarkable new cultivar with every leaflet variegated with a clear-cut deep cream margin. It looks very striking but may be easier to place as a container plant than in the garden. It is probably best in some shade.

P. carneum ✱ Spreading clump to 40 cm (16 in), long sticky leaves with 10–20 leaflets, loose branching sprays of comparatively large pale peach-coloured saucer-shaped flowers, over a long period around mid-summer. A delightful plant which never seeds excessively, and does well in partial shade. W. USA. 'Apricot Delight' seems to be very similar but somewhat stronger in growth.

114 *Polemonium carneum*

P. cashmerianum Like a small dainty *P. caeruleum*, to 40 cm (16 in), flowers blue.

P. flavum (syn. *P. foliosissimum* var. *flavum*) Similar to *P. pauciflorum* and sometimes offered in its place, smaller more wishy-washy flowers. S. USA.

P. foliosissimum Differs from *P. coeruleum* in very narrow pointed leaflets, and more purplish flowers on very leafy stems. It is more attractive in leaf and seems less troublesome in its seeding. W. USA.

***P.* 'Lambrook Mauve'** 🏆 (*P. carneum* x *P. reptans*) A delightful hybrid similar in habit to *P. carneum* but with soft mauve flowers. It is one of the finest low-growing polemoniums.

P. pauciflorum Clump-forming, usually more upright than *P. carneum*, leaves sticky, 30–40 cm (12–16 in) stems bearing clusters of very long-tubed creamy-yellow flowers with spreading lobes. reddish-flushed on the tubes and the reverse of the lobes. Another excellent easily-grown species in sun or shade. S. USA.

P. pulcherrimum Very variable 5–30 cm (2–12 in), clump-forming, flowers bell-shaped, blue with yellow throats. The larger forms from lower altitudes are reasonably easy to grow. W. USA.

P. reptans Spreading clump-former to 30 cm (1 ft), widely spaced leaflets and clusters of good blue funnel-shaped flowers on arching stems. It is a good low-growing species with several cultivars: 'Blue Pearl' one of the best blues, 'Pink Beauty' almost identical to 'Lambrook Mauve' which is a better name, unless stocks are muddled.

P.* x *richardsonii (Possibly *P. caeruleum* x *P. reptans*) Like a good form of *P. reptans* with extra-large sky-blue flowers, a real asset to the front of the border.

***P.* 'Sapphire'** Of uncertain origin, clump-forming to 40 cm (16 in), abundant small light blue flowers in early summer.

P. yezoense Uncommon, clump-forming to 40 cm (16 in), with loose heads of blue flowers. Japan.

Polygala (*Polygalaceae*)

A large genus of annuals and perennials, many of them shrubby, of which only a few are sufficiently hardy to be considered for the edge of a border or among shrubs. These are attractive low sub-shrubs with small leaves and pea-like flowers, the petals forming a keel and two spreading wings. They grow best in sun or light shade in well-drained soil, but are not always easy to please. They can be propagated by cuttings in early summer.

P. calcarea Tricky British lime-loving native, forming a mat to 5 cm (2 in) high, small deep green leaves, upright spikes of brilliant deep blue flowers in early summer. W. Europe. 'Lillet' ✱ easier to grow and more floriferous. Given good drainage it could be used as a sunny border edging.

P. chamaebuxus Suckering sub-shrub to 15 cm (6 in), leaves thick, glossy, ovate, heads of a few flowers in late spring or early summer, with yellow or white keels and bright yellow wings which turn reddish or brown with age. Var. *grandiflora* (syn. var.

purpurea, var. *rhodoptera*) larger flowers with deep rosy-purple sepals. These seem to grow best in partial shade in humus-rich soil, for example among small ericaceous shrubs, or woodland bulbs. W. Europe.

Polygonatum (*Liliaceae/ Convallariaceae*) (Solomon's Seal)

About 30 species of rhizomatous perennials, often spreading vigorously, typically with long arching stems bearing prominently veined parallel leaves with pendulous cylindrical flowers in their axils, that are most frequently white with greenish tips. They are sometimes followed by fleshy fruits.

Their beautiful growth habit makes them among the most striking perennials for woodland conditions, growing among large trees and shrubs or the largest woodland perennials, lilies etc. Some can take over a lot of ground with a dense carpet of rhizomes, and will even tolerate fairly dry conditions, and the less vigorous species can be used on a smaller scale among smaller shrubs and perennials.

They can be devastated by sawfly larvae, which look like grey caterpillars and appear every June in my garden. They are easily killed by insecticides, but unless caught quickly can defoliate every polygonatum in a garden, irrespective of species. They can be propagated by division, or by seed, which is a much slower process. I have included the taller species as their height varies considerably with conditions.

P. biflorum Stems arching, to 1 m (3 ft) or more, leaves alternate, broad, flowers axillary, greenish-white, fruits black. One of the less invasive species for its large size, with an uncommon 'dwarf form'. N. Am.

P. curvistylum Upright purplish stems to 60 cm (2 ft), leaves long, narrow, flowers axillary, pink, darker purple within, in long-petioled clusters. An uncommon species that has not so far proved invasive. China.

P. falcatum Sometimes confused with *P. humile*, a taller plant to 70 cm (28 in), leaves lanceolate to ovate, flowers white, green tipped, in nodding clusters. 'Variegatum' ✱ ☼ an exquisite variegated form, with a very narrow band of cream round the margin of each leaf. Japan, Korea.

115 *Polygonatum falcatum* 'Variegatum'

P. geminiflorum Uncommon, to 50 cm (20 in), stems mottled, flowers creamy-white with green tips, nodding in pairs, fruits red. Kashmir.

P. graminifolium 10 cm (4 in), leaves very narrow, flowers purple. A tiny rarity from China, that is relatively untried but does not seem difficult.

P. hirtum 45 cm (1.5 ft) Leaves oval to elliptic, flowers green-tipped, white, in small clusters. It is a vigorous grower and should not be planted among small plants. E. Europe–Turkey.

P. hookeri Very low-growing carpeter, 5 cm (2 in), leaves paired, narrow, flowers solitary, occasionally two, upright-facing, deep pink. Said to grow best in full sun, but I have been quite successful with it in partial shade, among low shrubs. Himalayas–China.

P. humile Dwarf running species, 15 cm (6 in), leaves alternate, lanceolate, flowers one or two, greenish-cream, in the upper leaf axils. It has been erroneously called *P. falcatum*. Although quite small it can spread widely in good conditions, so its company needs to be chosen carefully. China-Japan.

116 *Polygonatum humile*

P. x hybridum (*P. multiflorum* x *P. odoratum*) 🏆 The commonest Solomon's Seal, to 1 m (3 ft), often confused with *P. multiflorum*, arching stems with alternate leaves held horizontally, flowers white, green-tipped, in pendent clusters beneath them. A magnificent shade-lover that will even tolerate dryish soils and can build up into very large clumps. 'Striatum' (see plate 42) lower-growing, with leaves streaked with cream, a popular variegated plant but less elegant than *P. falcatum* 'Variegatum'.

P. multiflorum Very like the last but usually shorter, flowers narrower in smaller clusters. Europe–Siberia.

P. odoratum Very similar to *P.* x *hybridum* but shorter, with angled stems, leaves broader, flowers longer, in clusters of 1–3. 'Flore Pleno' 🏆 dainty double flowers. Europe–Asia.

P. roseum Rare. To 70 cm (28 in), leaves narrow, opposite and whorled towards the tips, flowers axillary, small, 1–3,

pink. An attractive but little tried species.
P. stewartianum Upright to 60 cm (2 ft), leaves in whorls, flowers in clusters in the axils, small, pink. An interesting plant different in habit and colour from most species, but easy in the same conditions.
P. verticillatum Similar to the last but with greeny white flowers.

Polygonum See *Persicaria*

Potentilla (*Rosaceae*)

About 500 species of shrubs and perennials, the latter very variable in habit, from small cushions to spreading mats to upright clumps, usually with deeply divided leaves and 5-petalled saucer-shaped flowers, yellow, white, pink, or red, or combinations of these colours A few are only suitable for the alpine house or rock garden, and I have excluded these together with the many shrubs.

Most of those described are easily-grown in a sunny border. Several of the low spreaders seem rather leafy for the amount of flower, and some are invasive. The 'garden hybrids' and taller perennials are colourful plants for the front or middle of the border around mid-summer, but they are sometimes short-lived, unless propagated regularly. The species can be propagated by seed or in many cases by division or cuttings of young shoots, the method of choice for the cultivars.
P. alba Clump with low spreading branches, to 25 cm (10 in), leaves palmate, silver-hairy, flowers white, 2 cm (0.8 in) across, in abundant clusters, early summer. Makes a good edging in well-drained soil. C–E. Europe
P. anserina A dangerously invasive plant to be avoided, in spite of its attractive leaves.
P. atrosanguinea Clump to 40 cm (16 in), often much less, leaves ternate, leaflets rounded, often silver-hairy, flowers in loose clusters, deep to bright red or yellow, in summer. Var. *argyrophylla* (var. *leucochroa*) more compact, leaves very silver, flowers red or yellow. From Himalayan collected seed I have grown tall plants with green leaves and deep blood red flowers, and compact plants with beautifully silver-hairy leaves and red or yellow flowers. These with others are the parents of the garden hybrids. Himalayas.

117 *Potentilla atrosanguinea red & Bupleurum species*

P. aurea Like *P. alba* in habit, but leaves green, flowers deep yellow, dark eyed, in mid-summer. S. Europe.
P. crantzii Like *P. aurea*, more upright and compact, flowers in loose heads deep yellow, orange at the base. A variable sometimes over-leafy plant. Europe.
P. cuneata Low running sub-shrub, leaves ternate, green, flowers bright yellow variable in size. A quite attractive mat while in flower. Himalayas.
P. eriocarpa Like *P. cuneata*, leaves paler green, deeper lobed, flowers larger and later. China.
Hybrids: A range of medium-sized perennials with long branching stems, dark green toothed leaves, and loose heads of brilliantly coloured flowers, making a fine splash of colour in the summer border, for several weeks. They should be cut back after flowering. The following are readily available: 'Etna' semi-double, deep red, margined yellow, 'Flamenco' and 'Gibson's Scarlet' vivid single red, 'Gloire de Nancy' orange and red combined, 'Monsieur Rouillard' double, deep red margined yellow, 'William Rollison' semi-double deep orange, centre yellow, 'Yellow Queen' double, yellow, dark eyed.
P. x hopwoodiana (*P. nepalensis* x *P. recta*) 45 cm (1.5 ft) Spreading, flowers pink with darker rose centre and pale margin, in loose clusters. One of the most beautiful and reasonably long-lived.
P. megalantha (syn *P. fragiformis*) Compact clump to 20 cm (8 in), leaves trifoliate, silky-hairy especially beneath, flowers large, dark yellow, in small clusters, mid-summer onwards. Useful for the border edge. Japan.
P. nepalensis Similar to *P. atrosanguinea*, to 50 cm (20 in), leaves 5-lobed, toothed, flowers red or orange, in open heads on upright branching stems. Himalayas. 'Miss Willmott' deep reddish-pink, 'Roxana' orange-pink with red eye. All are excellent border plants.
P. neumanniana (Syn. *P. tabernaemontana*) Spreading mat, to 20 cm (8 in), leaves 5–7–lobed, toothed, hairy beneath, flowers small, yellow, in large clusters. An easy carpeter. Europe.
P. recta Upright clump to 50 cm (20 in), leaves green, toothed, flowers in loose sprays, bright deep yellow in 'Warrenii'. 'Pallida' flowers soft primrose, a delightful colour that makes it invaluable in mid-summer. They are easy perennials that will seed around freely. Europe.

118 *Potentilla recta pallida & Lythrum salicaria 'Firecandle'*

P. reptans Low, invasive carpeter with yellow flowers. Probably not worth growing.
P. rupestris Clump to 60 cm (2 ft), leaves pinnate, toothed, flowers white in loose heads, mid- to late summer. Not in the first rank. S. France.
P. thurberi Clump to 70 cm (28 in), leaves digitate, toothed, flowers reddish-purple in loose heads. Rarely grown. S. US–Mexico.
P.* x *tonguei (*P. anglica* x *P. nepalensis*) 🏆 Low spreading mat, leaves 3–5-lobed, toothed, flowers in loose sprays, orange-yellow with dark red centre. One of the best low-growing species, long-lived with a long flowering season.

Pratia (*Campanulaceae/Lobeliaceae*)

Closely allied to Lobelia, and included in it by some botanists. A few flat carpeters from Australasia that spread widely in good soil, with small toothed rounded leaves, and small lobelia-like flowers, white or blue, in summer. Although only an inch or so high they are very floriferous and can be invasive, so they are better used in the border or among shrubs, than on the rock garden. They can be propagated by division at any time.
P. angulata Flowers white with violet veining. Runs rapidly in warm moist gardens, but will not survive below -7 °C (-20 °F). 'Treadwellii' larger, more rampant. 'Tim Rees' leaves purple-backed, more vigorous and more tender.
P. pedunculata Similar with clear light blue flowers. It is probably more invasive, and less likely to be curbed by frost, but it makes a fine carpet of blue if space can be found for it. 'County Park' flowers darker blue, fragrant. 'Tom Stone' flowers paler blue, vigorous.

Primula (*Primulaceae*)

A very large and popular genus of perennials, divided by botanists into a number of Sections, which are useful to gardeners as their members usually share similar cultural requirements. They include a few greenhouse plants, many small and sometimes difficult 'alpines' with special requirements, and the somewhat specialized auriculas, many of which need to be grown under glass. I have excluded these as being 'difficult' in the open garden, and I have also, with some doubts, excluded the huge range of 'primroses' and 'polyanthus', on the grounds that they are frequently available as seed strains, and that in most gardens they are only satisfactory if they are frequently divided and replanted.

I have concentrated mainly on the species and cultivars of four Sections; the Cortusoides Section are woodlanders for rich woodsy soil in partial shade, the Denticulata Section with typical globular flower heads, easy in heavy moist soil, the Proliferae Section contains the moisture-loving candelabra primulas, the Sikkimensis Section mainly moisture-loving species with cowslip-like heads. They are abbreviated below to (C), (D), (P), and (S). Most of these are good perennials flourishing in reasonably moist partly shaded borders or in woodland in humus-rich soil, where drifts of them look magnificent among shrubs, woodland bulbs and perennials, such as meconopsis, polygonatums and lilies. Most of the latter two sections thrive in moister conditions, for example as pond marginal plants or in permanently damp woodland, where they will tolerate full sun.

Most primulas are easily raised from seed, especially if it is sown as soon as ripe and kept cool during the winter, when it will germinate in spring. Many seem to germinate more quickly in bottom heat but the seedlings will then need care under glass. Many species will build up into substantial clumps that can be divided in early spring. Except where stated all those described are from E. Asia, particularly the Himalayas and China.
P. alpicola (S) 15–40 cm (6–16 in), leaves narrowly oval, flowers fragrant in umbels, mainly nodding, funnel-shaped, farinose, white, cream, yellow, or purple. Var. *luna* flowers yellow, var. alba white, var. violacea pink to purple. Easy in good rich soil, moist but not wet.
P. aurantiaca (S) Like *P. bulleyana*, but leaves darker green, mid-rib purple, stems dark purple without meal, flowers deep brownish orange. A beautiful species but less strong-growing.
P. beesiana (syn. *P. bulleyana* subsp. *beesiana*) (S) Like *P. bulleyana*, but flowers deep rose, with yellow eye.
P.* x *bulleesiana (*P. bulleyana x P. beesiana*) (S) Flowers yellow, orange, pink, to purple.
P. bulleyana 🏆 (S) Like *P. prolifera*, but leaves with a purple mid-rib, stems and calyces white-mealy, buds red, flowers golden-yellow. One of the best yellow candelabras.
P. burmanica (S) Like *P. bulleyana*, but non-mealy, flowers purple, eye orange.
P. chionantha *Nivalis* 🏆 To 40 cm (16 in), leaves farinose, flowers white, fragrant in 1-4 whorls. The easiest of the Nivalis section, needing (S) conditions.
P. chungensis (S) Like *P. bulleyana*, but leaf more coarsely toothed, mid-rib green.
P. cockburniana (S) Dainty plant to 20 cm (8 in), leaves obovate, stem white-mealy, flowers in 1–3 whorls of 3–8, bright orange-red. A pretty but very short-lived plant easily kept going from seed.
P. cortusoides (C) To 40 cm (16 in) or less, leaves pale green, crinkled margin irregularly lobed and toothed, flowers in umbels of 2–12, slightly nodding or horizontal, flat-faced, rose, petals notched, eye yellow. Easy in humus-rich soil.
P. denticulata 🏆 (D) Robust clump-former, usually 20–40 cm (8–16 in), leaves obovate, finely toothed, flowers in dense globular heads in shades of pink to purple, pale to deep lavender, red and white. One of the most popular primulas flourishing in rich, reasonably moist soil, but tolerant of a range of conditions, very colourful en masse at the edge of a border or among shrubs. Although some named cultivars are available, it is most readily grown from 'seed strains' in a great range of colours.

P. florindae ♕ (S) To 80 cm (30 in) or more, leaves oval, cordate base, flowers bell-shaped, nodding, yellow, in very large umbels. Similar to *P. sikkimensis* on the grand scale, and needs even wetter conditions

P. heucherifolia (C) Usually confused with *P. polyneura*, but leaves rounded, flowers deep reddish-purple, nodding, in one-sided umbel, on 30 cm (1 ft) stems.

P. ioessa (S) Similar to *P. alpicola*, but smaller, flowers comparatively large, cream or lilac, in smaller umbels. It tends to be shorter-lived than others of the section.

***P.* 'Inshriach Hybrids'** (S) A robust strain of very bright shades of yellow, orange, pink and red.

***P.* 'Inverewe'** ♕ (S) Robust, flowers bright orange red.

119 *Primula* 'Inverewe'

P. japonica ♕ (S) To 40 cm (16 in), leaves pale green coarsely toothed, stems efarinose, green or reddish, flowers in 3–10 whorls, reddish-purple, or sometimes white or pink, eye dark. Very easy and does not need very wet conditions. 'Miller's Crimson' robust, flowers dark red. 'Postford White' ✱ vigorous, flowers large, white with yellow eye. A magnificent easily grown plant that comes true from seed.

120 *Primula* 'Postford White'

P. jesoana (C) Often confused with *P. polyneura*, very like *P. kisoana* but more slender and taller, leaves more deeply lobed. Probably less easy.

***P.* 'Johanna'** Section *Farinosae*/*Orephlomis* (*P. warshenewskiana* x *P. clarkei*) Two small 'alpine species', much more robust than either. Similar to *P. rosea* but needing woodland rather than wet conditions.

P. kisoana (C) Spreading rhizomatous species to 20 cm (8 in), leaves kidney-shaped, hairy, shallowly lobed, flowers 2–8 in umbels, rose with darker eye, or white, petals deeply notched. *P. k. alba* ✱ exceptionally beautiful. These are not difficult in good rich woodland soil.

P. poissonii (S) To 40 cm (16 in), leaves bluish-green, oblanceolate, stems green, flowers deep pinkish-purple, eye yellow or white, in 2–6 whorls. A recent reintroduction from China, it seems fairly easy.

P. polyneura (C) Variable to 40 cm (16 in), usually less, strongly clump-forming, leaves dark green, hairy especially beneath, deeply lobed, stems hairy, flowers in umbels of 2–12, pale pink to deep purple or red, greenish-yellow eye, notched petals. The easiest of the section, an excellent garden plant for woodland conditions.

P. prolifera (syn. *P. helodoxa*) (P) To 60 cm (2 ft), leaves oblanceolate, deep green, stems without meal, flowers slightly pendant, short-stalked in 1–7 whorls, bright yellow. Easy.

P. pulverulenta ♕ (S) To 80 cm (30 in), leaves oblanceolate, irregularly toothed, mid-rib whitish, stem very white-mealy, flowers in large whorls, deep reddish-purple with dark eye. The most vigorous and perennial of the candelabras and superb with its white stems. 'Bartley

Hybrids' are similar but in varying shades of pink to purple with pale or dark eyes.
P. rosea ♕ Section *Farinosae*/*Oreophlomis* Vigorous clump-former, leaves glossy, oval, flowers large in umbels, vivid rose with yellow eye, in late spring. A wonderful marginal plant enjoying wet heavy soils, it looks splendid with calthas, lysichitons and other bog plants, before the candelabra primulas. 'Grandiflora' is the best, largest-flowered cultivar.
P. secundiflora ✱ (S) or (P) To 40 cm (16 in), leaves smooth, narrowly oblanceolate, stems green, flowers deep purple, pendant in a one-sided cluster on white-mealy stalks, rarely in 2–3 whorls. A very beautiful species, easy in humus-rich soil, needing only moderately damp soil.
P. sieboldii ♕ (C) Spreading rhizomatous, to 20 cm (8 in), pale green, hairy, oval, margins wavy, bluntly toothed, flowers large, variable in shades of pink to purple or white (var. *alba*), eye white, petals usually notched or frilled, in umbels of 2–10. Several cultivars have been named, including 'Snowflake' good white with unnotched petals, 'Geisha Girl' pink with fringed petals. They are excellent easy plants that deserves more popularity, planted in the shade of rhododendrons and other woodland shrubs.

121 *Primula sieboldii*

P. sikkimensis (S) To 40 cm (16 in), leaves oblanceolate, flowers narrowly tubular in large pendent clusters, cream to yellow. Easy in wet situations.
P. vialii ♕ Section *Muscarioides* Clump-forming, to 40 cm (16 in), leaves lanceolate, hairy, toothed, flowers in a dense cylindrical spikes, deep lavender from scarlet buds, giving a red-hot poker appearance, vivid red above and blue below. It is a unique easy but short-lived plant, forming perennial multiple crowns in good conditions, but always worth growing from seed as a biennial to replace the losses.

122 *Primula vialii*

P. waltonii Like *P. alpicola* but with purple flowers. The true plant is rare in gardens.
P. wilsonii Like *P. poissonii*, but taller with smaller red to purple flowers.

Prunella (*Labiatae*)

Genus of a few low creeping European perennials of varying leaf shape, with short dense spikes of tubular flowers, pink to purple or white, 2-lipped, the upper erect, the lower spreading, in whorls amid bracts, in summer. They make useful colourful ground cover for the front of a border or among shrubs, flowering over many weeks. They can easily be propagated by division.
P. grandiflora Spreading carpet 20–30 cm (8–12 in) high of oval, shallowly toothed or entire leaves, with dense spikes to 4 cm (1.6 in) long of deep violet-purple flowers. Several named cultivars with larger flower spikes include 'Alba' and 'White Loveliness' white, 'Loveliness' ♕ pale violet-blue, 'Pink Loveliness' a clear soft pink, 'Rotkappchen' ('Red Cap') carmine. They are of equal merit, easy in any soils, and moderately spreading in good conditions.
P. laciniata Similar to *P. grandiflora*, leaves deeply cut, flowers cream, rarely flushed pink.
P. vulgaris Similar in habit to *P. grandiflora*, flowers much smaller, deep purple, probably more invasive.

Pterocephalus (*Dipsacaceae*)

A few perennials, closely allied to *Scabiosa*, but having bristly fruiting calyces, only one seen regularly in gardens. They can be raised from seed, or cuttings in early summer.
P. hookeri Rare Himalayan–Chinese species, 20–30 cm (8–12 in), leaves basal, oblanceolate, pinnately lobed or entire, flower heads rounded, solitary, to 4 cm (1.6 in) wide, cream or very pale pink, with conspicuous dark anthers. A promising species, recently more widely available from collected seed.

P. perennis (syn. *P. parnassi*) Mat or cushion to 10 cm (4 in), leaves grey-downy, spathulate, toothed, flower heads solitary, 3–4 cm (1.2–1.6 in) wide, deep pink to purple, in late summer. Attractive for a wall or edge of a border in well-drained soil, it resents excessive winter wet. Europe.

Pulmonaria (*Boraginaceae*)

Genus of some 14 spreading rhizomatous low perennials, from Europe or western Russia, many with leaves marked with white, and heads of funnel-shaped flowers with spreading lobes, in shades of pink to purple, blue, or white, in spring. They are invaluable as ground cover with beautiful leaves and abundant flowers early in the year. They grow best in rich moist soil with abundant humus in partial or full shade, but tolerate full sun with sufficient moisture. They are ideal growing among shrubs where their flowers combine well with vigorous woodland bulbs such as *Anemone nemorosa* and *A. ranunculoides* forms, and with hellebores and cardamines, and those with well-marked leaves remain attractive for most of the year.

They are best increased by division, as seedlings are likely to vary greatly.

P. affinis Leaves ovate, pointed, spotted and blotched white, flowers deep blue from red buds. A rarity, but probably not difficult.

P. angustifolia 🏆 (See plate 23) Low spreader, leaves, long, narrow, unspotted, flowers deep blue in dense heads. One of the lowest and most spreading with very good flowers, fully making up for the 'ordinary' leaves. 'Alba' white, 'Azurea' deeper blue, possibly taller, 'Blaues Meer' leaves larger, flowers darker, more robust, 'Munstead Blue' has larger leaves and reddish-violet flowers that become blue later.

***P.* 'Barfield Regalia'** Very large, leaves long, narrow, almost unmarked, stems to 45 cm (1.5 ft), flowers large, dark blue after opening pink. A very vigorous plant needing space.

***P.* 'Beth's Blue'** To 30 cm (1 ft), leaves ovate, green with white streaks and blotches, flowers in open heads, deep blue from red buds. Rarely grown.

***P.* 'Beth's Pink'** Leaves ovate, broad, flowers blotched white and pale green, flowers coral.

***P.* 'Blue Crown'** Leaves narrow, dark green, sparsely spotted, stems reddish, flowers dark violet-blue.

***P.* 'Blue Ensign'** Leaves long, narrow, dark green unmarked, flowers dark violet-blue in compact heads. Excellent vigorous plant.

***P.* 'Glacier'** Low spreader, leaves long-petioled, sparsely spotted light green, flowers pale pink becoming white.

***P.* 'Lewis Palmer'** (syn. 'Highdown') Tall, leaves long, narrow, dark green heavily blotched greenish-white, flowers dark blue in large dense heads. One of the most vigorous and colourful.

P. longifolia ✸ ☼ Dense clump. Leaves mainly upright, long and narrow, dark green vividly white-spotted, flowers bright blue from dark calyces. First-class foliage and excellent colour. 'Bertram Anderson' especially well-marked leaves and bright flowers, but less robust. 'Dordogne' more heavily marked or almost entirely silver.

***P.* 'Mary Mottram'** Basal leaves very large, silver with green rim, stem leaves brightly white spotted, flowers reddish with violet centre, becoming bluer.

***P.* 'Mawson's Blue'** Low sparse spreader, leaves narrow dark green, flowers deep blue on flopping stems

P. mollis Leaves large, downy, unspotted, flowers large, violet-blue in dense heads. 'Royal Blue' more vigorous with large deep violet-blue flowers, but muddy pink-tinged plants may masquerade as it.

***P.* 'Mournful Purple'** Leaves should be dark green, blotched pale green, flowers deep purple in drooping clusters.

***P.* 'Mrs Kittle'** Compact, leaves white-spotted, flowers very pale pink becoming pale lavender.

***P.* 'Nurnberg'** Vigorous, low spreader, leaves light green, spotted bright white, flowers in compact heads, pink streaked violet from red buds.

P. officinalis Low spreading clump, leaves cordate, bristly, spotted pale green or whitish, flowers in compact clusters, deep pink in bud, then pink, finally violet-blue. The commonest species, but not the best for leaf or flower colour. Several improved cultivars: 'Alba' white, some pink on the tube, 'Blue Mist' and 'Bowles Blue' possibly the same, leaves as type, moderately marked white and pale green, flowers pale blue, early, 'Cambridge Blue Group' variable well-spotted, flowers light blue, 'Sissinghurst White' AGM very vigorous, leaves spotted, flowers white from pale pink buds, 'White Wings' compact, leaves sparsely pale-spotted, flowers white with pink eye.

***P.* 'Roy Davidson'** Compact, leaves long, narrow, heavily white-spotted, flowers pale blue to violet in dense heads.

P. rubra 🏆 Vigorous spreader, leaves large, pale green unspotted, very hairy, flowers pinkish-red in large open heads, very early. First-rate vigorous ground cover, the flowers keeping their colour unchanged. 'Albocorralata' less vigorous, leaves paler, flowers small, white, on shorter stems, 'Ann' leaves spotted, flowers coral pink, veined and chequered white, 'Barfield Pink' very similar to the last, deeper in colour, with smaller pale areas, less vigorous and floriferous, 'Barfield Ruby' vigorous, similar to *P. rubra* but flowers larger, 'Bowles Red' like *P. rubra*, but leaves faintly spotted, flowers more orange in tone, 'David Ward' leaves grey-green variegated with cream margins, flowers pale coral, best in shade, 'Redstart' very vigorous, flowers slightly larger on upright stems.

123 *Pulmonaria rubra*

P. saccharata Vigorous clump-former, leaves large with variable white spots and blotches, sometimes almost completely covering the blade, flowers pink in bud changing to reddish-violet. The flowers are disappointing but the leaves can be excellent in some forms: 'Alba' leaf spots paler, flowers white from pink buds, 'Argentea Group' ♀ leaves in the best forms entirely silvery-white, narrowly margined green, one of the best for foliage, 'Dora Bielefeld' vigorous, leaves palely spotted, flowers clear pink eventually violet, better flower colour than most, 'Fruhlingshimmel' leaves brightly spotted, flowers pale blue with darker eye, 'Leopard' leaves dark green brightly spotted and blotched white, flowers reddish-pink on upright stems, 'Mrs Moon' not very distinct, usually with leaves spotted pale green, flowers pink to violet, 'Pink Dawn' compact, leaves blotched pale whitish-green, edge waved, flowers large deep pink becoming violet, 'Reginald Kaye' vigorous, leaves almost covered with white blotches, flowers reddish in bud opening to violet with red tube, good flowers.
***P.* 'Smoky Blue'** Recent cultivar, leaves spotted silver, flowers smoky-blue with pale veining.
P. vallarsae Similar to *P. mollis*, downy leaves smaller, wavy-edged, heavily blotched, flowers violet. 'Margery Fish' the form usually grown, dense carpeter, leaves whitish grey with green spotted margin, flowers reddish-pink maturing violet.
***P.* 'Weetwood Blue'** Compact grower, leaves long, narrow, dark green, unspotted, flowers rich blue from dark purple buds.

Pulsatilla (*Ranunculaceae*)

A genus of exquisitely beautiful perennials, ideally suited to the rock garden, with some needing special care. They have very large, usually hairy, bell-shaped flowers with a conspicuous boss of yellow stamens, pendent or upward or outward-facing, in shades of pink to purple, pale to deep lavender, or white. The pasque flowers, *P. vulgaris* and its closest relatives can be relied on to do well in the front of a normal border with reasonable drainage in a sunny position. They are easy to raise from seed and a large colony can be a magnificent sight, not only in flower but carrying their large fluffy seed heads, iridescent against the light, often for several weeks.
P. halleri Similar to *P. vulgaris*, to 15 cm (6 in), leaves 3–5 pinnate, finely divided, very hairy, leaflets, flowers before the leaves, bells less deep, lilac to purple. *P. h. alba* flowers pure white. Subsp. *grandis* flowers before the leaves, very silver-hairy, golden in the rare 'Budapest'. Subsp. *slavica* leaves with three leaflets, flowers very large, lilac. All are very fine and not too difficult. E. Europe.
P. pratensis Similar to *P. vulgaris* but leaves much more divided, flowers with the leaves, nodding, deep purple in subsp. *nigricans*, reddish, or greenish-yellow, petals recurved. Uncommon but easy. C. Europe.
P. vulgaris ♀ To 18 cm (7 in), leaves pinnate, leaflets 7–9 with narrow lobes, not hairy, flowers deeply campanulate, pale to dark purple or lilac blue, reddish, or white, with the leaves. Plants are usually grown from seed and vary in colour and also in the quality and substance of the flowers. If possible select them in flower. *P.* v. *alba* can be magnificent with very large white flowers, but they can be squinny. Var. *rubra* has deep red flowers, 'Rode Klokke' deep red, 'Barton's Pink' and 'Eva Constance' paler pink. The named cultivars are not always reliable as they should only be propagated from root cuttings, and this is difficult.

124 *Pulsatilla vulgaris* mixed

R

Ranunculus (*Ranunculaceae*)

A large genus including many useful perennials and many noxious weeds. They vary enormously in size and habit from tiny and sometimes difficult alpines, through spreading carpeters to large clump-formers. They usually have divided leaves and all have more or less typical buttercup flowers in shades of yellow, white, or orange to red, solitary or in large loose heads. Exclusion of the many small species needing special care, of the invasive weeds, and of the tallest perennials, leaves us a selection of good perennials, generally easy to grow, especially in moist humus-rich soils.

Most of the species can be raised from seed which should be sown as soon as ripe or even when still a little green, without storage, or the stronger growing can be divided in early spring.

R. aconitifolius Clump-forming to 60 cm (2 ft), leaves 3–5-lobed, toothed, flowers 2 cm (0.8 in) wide, white tinged pink on the back, in large loose heads on branching stems, in late spring. 'Flore Pleno' 🏆 the Fair Maids of France, similar, flowers exquisite, tightly double pure white. Beautiful perennials for partial shade, or full sun if the soil remains moist.

R. bulbosus The double form of the bulbous buttercup, to 30 cm (1 ft), is worth growing for its fully double bright golden-yellow flowers.

R. constantinopolus Spreading clump-former to 60 cm (2 ft), leaves downy, 3-lobed, deeply toothed, flowers in loose heads, 3 to many, bright yellow. 'Plenus' the variety usually grown, beautiful green-centred fully double yellow flowers.

R. cortusifolius Clump-forming, to 80 cm (30 in), glossy leathery leaves, large, rounded, base cordate, shallowly lobed, flowers in large loose heads, bright yellow. A magnificent buttercup for moist shade, but only hardy to -5 °C (23 °F).

R. creticus Similar to the last on a smaller scale, rare in gardens.

R. ficaria (The Lesser Celandine) A beautiful almost ineradicatable menace in gardens with its small clusters of tuberous roots which spread rapidly, but with many better-behaved named cultivars, Generally they make a low dense spreading carpet to 15 cm (6 in) of rounded glossy cordate leaves sometimes with dark markings, appearing in earliest spring and disappearing in early summer, with abundant buttercup flowers in shades of yellow, orange, or white, single or double. They are very colourful accompanying spring bulbs and early woodland perennials between shrubs, and are easy in partial or full shade, especially in moist soil. They can be divided in spring as soon as the leaves appear.

The following is a selection of the best and most readily available: 'Albus' (var. *albus*) leaves with dark mark, flowers yellowish fading quickly to white, 'Aurantiacus' (var. *aurantiacus* 'Cupreus') leaves marked with silver and brownish, flowers deep coppery-orange, 'Brambling' leaves silver-grey with purple markings, flowers very small, yellow, 'Brazen Hussy' ✱ ☼ leaves chocolate, flowers deep yellow, a wonderful colour combination. Although said to seed back to the type in my experience this rarely happens. 'Collarette' leaves with dark streak, flowers double yellow, outer petals normal with anemone centre, 'Crawshaw Cream' similar to 'Brazen Hussy' but with creamy-white flowers, a promising newcomer, 'Double Bronze' leaves unmarked, flowers large, double yellow with bronze backs, 'Double Mud' similar to the last, cream with bronze backs, 'E.A. Bowles' double anemone-centred yellow, 'Flore Pleno' (var. *flore-pleno*) double yellow with green reverse, 'Green Petal' double with green petals irregularly streaked yellow, 'Lemon Queen' pale yellow single with bronze reverse, 'Major' very large version of the type, can be invasive, 'Randall's White' leaves unmarked, creamy-white, backed purple, 'Salmon' White' similar but leaves with a dark streak.

R. gramineus 🏆 Clump to 40 cm (16 in), leaves narrowly lanceolate, glaucous greenish-blue, flowers in loose heads on slender stems, large glossy yellow in early summer. A magnificent buttercup of unusual habit, for well-drained soil. 'Pardal' ✱ is a fine new selection larger in all its parts.

125 *Ranunculus gramineus* 'Pardal'

R. montanus A small alpine species but the cultivar 'Molten Gold' is an easy low carpeter with comparatively large golden-yellow flowers on 12 cm (4.7 in) stems.

R. platanifolius Similar to *R. aconitifolius*, but taller with larger flowers. Rarely seen in gardens.

R. repens A dangerous spreading weed, but its double-flowered variety is somewhat less invasive, making a spreading carpet.

Ranzania (*Berberidaceae*)

R. japonica ✱ The only species, a Japanese woodland herbaceous perennial to 40 cm (16 in), leaves 3-lobed in pairs at the top of the stem, flowers in loose clusters of 1-several, widely bell-shaped, the petals recurving at the tips, pale lavender, occasionally followed by white fruits. The flowers appear in early spring before or with the leaves, the stems then lengthen rapidly to its full height. It is a charming but uncommon plant for moist humus-rich soil, a good associate for woodland bulbs like *Anemone nemorosa* forms, erythroniums and trilliums.

Ratibida (*Compositae*)

Uncommonly grown genus of biennials and perennials from the American prairies.

R. columnifera The only species seen in gardens, a short-lived perennial to 70 cm (28 in), occasionally more, leaves hairy, pinnately lobed, flowers large with narrow recurving petals and a strikingly long central brown column. Although supposedly perennial I find it short-lived, but the unusual flowers are a 'talking-point' and it is easily raised from seed.

Rehmannia (*Scrophulariaceae*)

Genus of a few Chinaese perennials and biennials, of which only two are widely grown in gardens. They are clump-forming plants to about 40 cm (16 in), with lobed or toothed leaves and large streptocarpus-like flowers with a spotted throat and broad lower lip, in summer. They are spectacularly beautiful plants with striking flowers, but are not fully hardy They can be raised from seed or increased by cuttings or division. I find that they run gently underground and rooted offsets can be potted and overwintered under glass as a precaution, although they survive our mildest winters.

R. glutinosa 🏆 To 60 cm (2 ft), often less, leaves obovate, sticky, hairy, coarsely toothed, flowers solitary on branched stems, yellow, or purple with yellow throat, dark-spotted within. Probably the hardiest species.

126 *Rehmannia glutinosa*

R. elata (*R. angulata* hort.) Similar to *R. glutinosa* but usually taller, leaves pinnately lobed, hairy, flowers semi-nodding in loose leafy racemes, rose-pink, throat yellow, red spotted.

Reineckia (*Liliaceae/ Convallariaceae*)

R. carnea The only species, a spreading rhizomatous perennial with leaves in tufts, glossy light green, long and narrow, flowers small, pink, with spreading lobes, in short dense spikes in late summer. Reminiscent of the liriopes in growth, the foliage is pleasing in a shady place, but the flowers are sparsely produced. It can be increased by division.

Rhazia *See* ***Amsonia***

Rheum (*Polygonaceae*)

A genus of mainly large perennials with magnificent foliage and stout spikes of small flowers in summer. Most are too tall to consider here, but there are a few uncommon smaller species. They can be raised from seed or by division.

R. alexandrae ✱ An astonishing plant that should probably be too tall, but in less than ideal conditions it makes a clump of glossy cordate dark green leaves to 25 cm (10 in) long, with upright stems bearing a flower spike entirely hidden in large overlapping greeny-white bracts, giving an effect reminiscent of a handkerchief tree at ground level. It does not seem easy to please but I have flowered it quite well in moist soil in full sun. China.

R. moorcroftiana Similar to *R. spiciforme* but taller to 60 cm (2 ft). Himalayas.

R. nobile Currently being grown from recent seed collections. It is similar to *R. alexandrae* but likely to be larger, and more striking, with a reputation for difficulty. China.

R. spiciforme To 30 cm (1 ft), rosettes of cordate leaves, becoming reddish, flower spikes green, becoming red in seed. Himalayas.

Rhodanthemum (*Compositae*)

Previously in *Chrysanthemum* and *Leucanthemum*, they are still more likely to be found offered as one of these. They are alpine perennials for well-drained soil, but the one described is worth considering for the front of a sunny border. It is easily increased by cuttings.

R. hosmariense 🏆 Semi-shrubby mound-forming perennial with fine silver filigree foliage and large yellow-eyed daisies over a very long season in spring and summer. It always looks good as a silver foliage plant, and the large flowers enhance its beauty.

127 *Rhodanthemum hosmariense* & *Erysimum cheiri* 'Harpur Crewe'

Rhodiola (*Crassulaceae*)

About 7 herbaceous perennials, closely allied to Sedum, and often included in it, clump-forming with stiff upright leafy stems, leaves very fleshy, glaucous, ovate, toothed,

and flowers in dense domed heads in summer. They are easy in well-drained soil in full sun, and more striking than most sedums. They can be raised from seed or cuttings.
R. heterodonta (syn. *Sedum heterodontum*) To 30 cm (1 ft), leaves alternate, oval, toothed, flowers in dense heads, greenish-yellow tinged with pink, from conspicuous deep red buds. Most striking in bud.
R. rosea (syn. *Sedum roseum*) To 30 cm (1 ft), stems very leafy with sessile, rounded, toothed leaves, flowers in larger heads, yellowish orange. One of the more appealing 'sedums'.

Rohdea (*Liliaceae/ Convallariaceae*)

R. japonica The only species generally grown, a slowly-spreading rhizomatous perennial, clumps of dark leathery lanceolate leaves in two ranks, to 30 cm (1 ft), flowers widely bell-shaped, greenish-cream, in short spikes on 10 cm (4 in) stems, followed by red fleshy fruits. The flowers tend to be hidden, but the leaves are attractive in a shady place. It can be grown from seed, or by division. E. Asia.

Romanzoffia (*Hydrophyllaceae*)

Small perennials usually grown on the rock garden, but also suitable for the margin of a shady bed of moist humus-rich soil. They form dense mounds of very dark green rounded or kidney-shaped leaves, smothered in clusters of small white saxifrage-like flowers in spring or early summer. They are attractive little plants that combine well with other low woodlanders like anemones, hellebores, trilliums etc. They can be increased by seed or by division. N. Am.
R. sitchensis (syn. *R. suksdorfii*) Mound to 20 cm (8 in), leaves kidney-shaped, shallowly lobed, flowers white, yellow in the throat, in branched clusters.
R. tracyi Similar but more compact, with underground tubers, spring-flowering, dying down soon after flowering.
R. unalaschensis Intermediate in size, flowering in early summer.

Roscoea (*Zinziberaceae*)

Genus of about 17 species of herbaceous perennials from the Himalaya and China, with fleshy roots, clumps of lanceolate leaves which clasp the stem, and big flowers with a large erect middle petal and two smaller lateral petals, and a broad, often notched or bilobed, lower lip, yellow or in shades of pink to purple, in summer. It is remarkable that they are not more popular. Their large flowers have an air of orchid-like exoticism, yet they are easy to grow in reasonably moist humus-rich soil in partial shade, or in full sun if they receive sufficient moisture. They may be raised from seed sown fresh, or by division.

There is some confusion in the nomenclature, which may be sorted out as the result of work on recent seed introductions from China.
R. alpina Small species to 20 cm (8 in), leaves to 12 cm (4.7 in), partly developed at flowering, flowers solitary, pink to purple, upper petal to 2 cm (0.8 in), lip to 2.5 cm (1 in).
R. auriculata To 40 cm (16 in), leaves to 25 cm (10 in), 'eared' at the base, flowers solitary, bright purple, upper petal to 3.5 cm (1.4 in), lip to 4.5 cm (1.8 in), late summer.
R. 'Beesiana' Like *R. auriculata*, but flowers yellow streaked purple, or occasionally pure yellow. An easy plant, probably *R. auriculata* × *R. cautleiodes*.
R. cautleoides 🏆 To 30 cm (1 ft), leaves 10–30 cm (4–12 in), flowers 1–3 open together, a little smaller than the last and bright yellow in the type. 'Grandiflora' stronger with larger flowers. 'Kew Beauty' ✸ a fine form with larger soft primrose flowers. Beautiful easy plants, varying considerably in height, and in flower size.

128 *Roscoea cautleyoides* 'Kew Beauty'

R. humeana 🏆 To 35 cm (14 in), leaves broader, to 25 cm (10 in), flowers opening several together, usually pinkish-purple, larger than in typical *R. cautleiodes*, with a deeply bilobed lip. One of the best in the garden.

129 *Roscoea humeana*

R. procera (syn. *R. purpurea*) ✱ To 45 cm (1.5 ft), leaves to 25 cm (10 in), flowers solitary at one time, deep purple, usually the largest of the genus. A superb plant, contrasting well with *R. cautleoides*.
R. purpurea *See* ***R. procera***
R. scillifolia To 40 cm (16 in), leaves shorter and narrower, flowers 1-2 open, smaller, lip narrower.

Rudbeckia (*Compositae*)

Genus of annuals and mainly tall herbaceous perennials with upright branching stems bearing large yellow daisy flowers with a conspicuous central almost black cone. They are among the most important yellow perennials for late summer, but the majority must be excluded as too tall. They are best propagated by division or cuttings. The following are fairly compact, and their strong yellow contrasts well with the deep reddish-purple of the taller origanums and *Verbena bonariensis*.
R. fulgida var. ***deamii*** 🏆 Clumps to 60 cm (2 ft), leaves ovate, hairy, toothed, flowers abundant, 5 cm (2 in) wide, deep yellow. A superb plant for every border. 'Goldsturm' 🏆 is similar with larger flowers. 'Goldquelle' 🏆 is probably derived from the tall *R. laciniata*, with leaves divided into narrow lobes, only to 70 cm (28 in), and large double flowers.

Ruta (*Rutaceae*)

Aromatic perennials usually grown in the herb garden, but their domes of attractive glaucous or variegated foliage, with a haze of tiny yellow flowers in summer, make them useful in the mixed border. They frequently cause severe skin reactions in sensitive people, who should avoid growing them or at least avoid the cutting back that they need after flowering or after a hard winter. They can be propagated by cuttings or seed.
R. graveolens The Common Rue is the species usually grown, with its more ornamental cultivars. A rounded dome of glaucous 2–3-pinnate leaves, with small narrow lobes, and loose heads of small greenish-yellow flowers for several weeks. 'Jackman's Blue' 🏆 has more glaucous blue foliage. In 'Variegata' the leaves are irregularly margined with cream.

Salvia (*Labiatae*)

A huge genus of annuals, biennials, perennials and shrubs, varying greatly in size and in habit, but generally having clusters or spikes of bright tubular 2-lipped flowers in summer, the upper lip arching forward over the lower. Many are tender, or on the borderline of hardiness, and many are too tall to consider here. I have also excluded a few small and difficult species which resent wet conditions in the open and some shrubby species like *S. greggi* and *S. microphylla*, too large unless heavily pruned.

Their requirements vary but generally they are easy plants for a sunny position, and they can be raised from seed or very easily from cuttings. The less hardy do best in well-drained soil, and as they include many of the most beautiful, they should be propagated regularly and cuttings overwintered under glass as a precaution. They are excellent as patio plants in containers.
S. aethiopis Similar to *S. argentea* but shorter and leaves a little less downy. For similar conditions. Europe–W. Asia.
S. argentea 🏆 Rosettes of large white-woolly rounded leaves with pyramids of white or yellowish flowers in summer. It is a superb foliage plant for hot dry positions but often dies after flowering. Med.
S. blancoana Mound to 40 cm (16 in) of prostrate stems with silver-grey leaves, flowers bluish-mauve, widely spaced in slender spikes. Med.
S. blepharophylla Semi-shrub, stems spreading with small glossy leaves, flowers red in short spikes.
S. buchananii 🏆 Semi-shrub to 40 cm (16 in), leaves glossy dark green, purplish backed, stems reddish, flowers large, hairy, deep purplish-red, in short spikes. One of the most striking species for warm gardens, probably only hardy to -5 °C (23 °F). Mexico.
S. bulleyana Clump-forming to 70 cm (28 in), leaves oval, coarse, large spikes of deep yellow flowers with brownish purple on the lower lip. An easy and hardy plant in light shade. China.
S. candidissima Similar to *S. argentea*, leaves smaller, less hairy, flower spikes shorter, less branched. E. Europe–Turkey.
S. discolor Semi-shrub, to 40 cm (16 in) or more, stems and narrow leaves intensely white-downy and sticky, flowers almost black in loose spikes, protruding a little from large white bracts. A dramatic plant with perhaps the blackest flowers of any, but decidedly tender except in near-frost-free gardens. Peru.
S. farinacea Clump-forming to 40 cm (16 in), leaves lanceolate on stiffly upright stems which become bright blue towards flowering, flowers in tall spikes, brilliant blue. 'Alba' flowers white. S. USA. Mexico. 'Victoria' 🏆 flowers deep blue on more branched stems. Brilliant for large groups or bedding, easily raised from seed as annuals, but perennial in warm gardens.
S. forsskaolii Clump-forming to 70 cm (28 in), leaves large hairy, flowers large, violet with white lip, in long branched spikes. S.E. Europe, W. Asia.
S. gesnerifolia Semi-shrubby to 60 cm (2 ft), leaves ovate, flowers large, scarlet, in short spikes. Mexico.
S. greggii* x *S. lycioides ✱ Lower than the shrubby *S. greggii*, with more spreading denser growth, and deepest violet flowers. Hardy to about -7 °C (20 °F). S. USA, Mexico.
S. hians ✱ Clump-forming to 60 cm (2 ft), but often less, leaves ovate, abundant, flowers large in broad spikes, darkest blue with white on the lip. An excellent perennial for rich but well-drained soil in sun or part shade. I find it is sometimes short-lived.
S. juriscii To 30 cm (1 ft), stems branched, white-woolly, semi-prostrate, leaves finely divided into linear lobes, flowers

small but abundant in branching heads, pale violet-blue. An attractive plant for the front of a border in well-drained soil. Yugoslavia.
S. lavandulifolia Like *S. officinalis*, but compact to 30 cm (1 ft), leaves smaller, grey, flowers deep lavender from reddish calyces. S. Europe.
S. leucantha 🏆 Shrubby to 1 m (3 ft), usually much less except in very warm gardens, stems white-woolly, leaves narrow, white-backed, flowers large, white, from hairy pale violet calyces. One of the most beautiful but only winter-hardy in very warm gardens. S. USA. Mexico.
S. lyrata Upright rosetted perennial to 50 cm (20 in), leaves entire or divided, ovate, flowers purplish-blue in moderately dense spikes. Reasonably hardy. USA.
S. multicaulis Mat-forming , upright stems to 40 cm (16 in), leaves grey-green, crinkled, flowers in upright spikes, with very large reddish-purple calyces concealing small whitish flowers. An unusual and beautiful small species.
S. nemorosa Hardy clump-former to 80 cm (30 in) or more, densely branching with narrow simple leaves, flowers in erect spikes deep blue with purple calyces. The cultivars, possibly hybrids, are probably superior: 'Amethyst' looser spike of pinkish-blue flowers for most of summer, 'Lubeca' and 'East Friesland' more compact and equally floriferous and deeply coloured, the latter considerably taller, 'Plumosa' reduced flowers and very large purple bracts, ornamental throughout the summer. All these are easily grown and hardy, ideal as contrast to the ubiquitous yellow daisies.
S. officinalis (Common Sage) A hardy evergreen bushy species with aromatic grey-green woolly leaves and short spikes of pale lavender flowers. It can be grown as a moderately ornamental foliage plant, and some of its cultivars are an improvement although less hardy: 'Albiflora' flowers white, 'Aurea', 'Kew Gold', and 'Icterina' 🏆 golden foliage, 'Berggarten' larger broader leaves, 'Purpurascens Group' reddish-purple leaves, an attractive foliage plant, as are its form 'Purpurascens Variegata' and 'Tricolor' with purple-tinged grey-green leaves margined with cream.
S. patens 🏆 Upright clumps from fleshy roots, leaves ovate on hairy stems, flowers very large, paired in long spikes, brilliant bright blue. A wonderful plant for its fine colour, only hardy in near frost-free gardens, but worth lifting and storing dry like dahlias in winter. Mexico. 'Cambridge Blue' 🏆 equally fine with pale blue flowers, 'Chilcombe' pinkish-blue flowers, 'Guanojuato' ✱ a huge form with much larger flowers, but equally tender, 'Oxford Blue' and 'Royal Blue' in differing shades of blue, 'White Trophy' (syn. *Alba*) a good large-flowered white.
S. potentillifolia ✱ A low mound of spreading stems to 30 cm (1 ft), obovate, grey-green, downy toothed leaves, a long succession of short spikes of clear blue flowers with white on the lips. A very promising newcomer, beautiful in foliage and flower, hardy to -8 °C, possibly lower.
S. pratensis Tall hardy clump-former with spikes of rich dark blue flowers. 'Haematodes Group' 🏆 a better plant, more compact with reddish stems and abundant spikes of paler lavender-blue flowers, 'Lapis Lazuli' more compact with leaves tinged red, flowers pink from purple calyces. These are excellent easy perennials.
S. przewalskii Spreading mound of procumbent branching stems to 50 cm (20 in), leaves heart-shaped, flowers hairy, pinkish-purple in loose spikes. A recent introduction from China has attractive soft grey-violet flowers, and is very hardy.
S. ringens Semi-woody clump to 50 cm (20 in), leaves pinnately divided, flowers lilac-blue, nodding, in loose spikes. An uncommon but very attractive and quite hardy species. Balkans.
S. roemeriana Low mound of branching stems with dark green kidney-shaped veined leaves and short spikes of deep scarlet flowers. A beautiful species, only hardy in warm gardens but easily raised from seed.
S. sinaloensis Similar to *S. roemeriana* but with dark blue flowers.
S. x superba (*S. nemorosa* x *S. villicaulis*) 🏆 A rather tall spreading perennial to 80 cm (30 in) or more, leaves lanceolate, fine dark violet-blue flower spikes throughout late summer, especially if it is cut back after its first flush. A very hardy plan, ideal to contrast with achilleas and yellow daisies.
S. x sylvestris (*S. pratensis x S. nemorosa*) Variable perennial similar to *S. x superba* with several cultivars. Generally rather tall for consideration in good conditions, but fine easy hardy plant with leafy stems and abundant spikes of deep blue flowers. The following are usually under 80 cm (30 in) high: 'Blauhugel' dwarf cultivar with clear blue flowers, 'Blaukonigin' (Blue Queen) compact with deeper violet flowers, 'Mainacht' low-growing with very dark flowers, 'Rose Queen' leaves grey-green, flowers pale pink from reddish calyces.
S. transsylvanica Bushy to 40 cm (16 in), leaves broad, flowers purple with white on the lip in tall spikes. An easy plant similar to *S. officinalis*.
S. verbenaca Upright clump to 70 cm (28 in), leaves pinnately lobed in rosettes, flowers deep lavender, rather small in widely spaced whorls. Europe–W. Asia.
S. verticillata Upright clump to 80 cm (30 in), leaves oval, heart-shaped, toothed, flowers purplish-blue in dense whorls. Europe–W. Asia. 'Alba' has white flowers. 'Purple Rain' an excellent recent cultivar with spikes of an unusual soft reddish-purple shade, the tips nodding. They are easy hardy perennials.

Sanguinaria (*Papaveraceae*)

S. canadensis ✱ The only species, a spreading rhizomatous hardy perennial from N. American woodland, to 20 cm (8 in). The rhizomes ooze red sap when cut, hence the name Bloodroot. Leaves rounded, heart-shaped, bluish grey-green, divided into 7 lobes with waved edges, folded beneath the flowers at first but opening wide on lengthening petioles after flowering. Flowers pure white, 3 cm (1.2 in) wide, anemone-like, with 7-10 petals, and conspicuous golden stamens in spring. A supremely beautiful plant, but the flowers are fleeting. It grows and increases well in moist woodland soil and can be increased by division in early spring. 'Plena' 🏆 is more widely grown, with exquisite fully double flowers, which last a little longer. 'Pink Form' a rarity with leaves faintly flushed with pinkish-purple, flowers also faintly but distinctly flushed mauve especially on opening.

130 *Sanguinaria canadensis*

Sanguisorba (*Rosaceae*)

Small genus of spreading clump-forming perennials, with pinnate toothed leaves, and flowers in late summer in dense bottlebrush spikes, often curved, on branching wiry stems, in shades of pink to purple or white. They are valuable for attractive leaves and flowers, easily grown except in dry soils and may spread widely. They can be increased by division in autumn or spring. Most of the commoner species are too tall to consider but the following are generally under 75 cm (2.5 ft).

S. albiflora (syn. *S. obtusa* var. *albiflora*) Similar to *S. obtusa* but with paler leaves and white flowers. Japan.

S. hakusanensis Clumps to 60 cm (2 ft), leaves pinnate, leaflets ovate, toothed, flowers deep rose-pink in elegant curved spikes. One of the most beautiful.

S. obtusa Similar but more compact with greyish-green crowded leaflets.

S. officinalis 'Tanna' A lower growing form of the Great Burnet, with abundant short crimson-purple spikes.

Santolina (*Compositae*)

The Lavender Cottons are a small genus of aromatic shrubby perennials, mainly with finely divided silvery leaves, and rounded heads of small disc flowers in shades of white to yellow in summer. They are excellent silver foliage plants in mild gardens, and they all benefit from being cut back hard if they become straggly. Grow in well-drained soil in a hot position, as they resent excessive moisture especially in winter. They can be raised from cuttings during spring or summer.

S. chamaecyparissus 🏆 To 50 cm (20 in), upright or spreading, stems white, leaves finely divided into linear white-woolly leaflets, flowers deep yellow. Med. A variable plant with several cultivars and varieties usually more intensely silver: 'Lambrook Silver' an excellent cultivar with very silver leaves, 'Lemon Queen' a low mound with paler flowers, var. *nana* 🏆 a very neat compact dwarf, 'Pretty Carol' to 40 cm (16 in) with soft grey leaves, 'Small-Ness' ✸ an excellent compact cultivar with silver-grey finely divided leaves and lemon-yellow flowers, 'Weston' only 15 cm (6 in), very silver.

S. elegans Mound to 20 cm (8 in), intensely silvery white, flowers very pale just above the leaves. Spain.

S. pinnata To 70 cm (28 in), leaves grey-green, pinnate, flowers off-white. Subsp. *neapolitana* has more silver leaves and bright yellow flowers.

S. rosmarinifolia (syn. *S. virens*) Similar in habit to *S. chamaecyparissus* but leaves deep green, and flowers bright yellow. Less attractive as a foliage plant but the yellow button flowers are effective. 'Primrose Gem' 🏆 has more finely divided leaves and primrose-yellow flowers.

131 *Santolina rosmarinifolia*

Saponaria (*Caryophyllaceae*)

Some 30 annuals, biennials and perennials, with simple opposite leaves and small to medium flowers with 5 spreading petals generally in shades of pink or white. The perennials vary from tight cushions for the rock garden to invasive perennials to be avoided anywhere except perhaps in the wild garden. I have excluded the smaller cushions, but there are a number of reasonably strong cushion-formers that will do well at the edge of a sunny border. Most can be propagated by cuttings or division, or the species can be raised from seed.

***S.* 'Bressingham'** A low mound of hairy leaves on reddish to 10 cm (4 in) with dense clusters of rich pink flowers. One of the best for edging.

***S.* x *lempergii* 'Max Frei'** ✱ Clump-forming to 40 cm (16 in) with abundant loose sprays of pale pink flowers over a long season from mid-summer. An excellent border plant with campanulas and origanums.

132 *Saponaria x lempergii* 'Max Frei' & *Origanum laevigatum* 'Herrenhausen'

S. ocymoides 🏆 Low, wide-spreading carpeter with small hairy leaves completely covered in small pink flowers in early summer. A very easy plant that can occupy considerable space. 'Rubra Compacta' 🏆 A superior compact plant with darker flowers.
S. officinalis (Bouncing Bet) Beware! It is too invasive for most borders with brittle red-tinged rhizomes, but very attractive in the wild garden, given sufficient space, with its large heads of single or double pale pink flowers. Several cultivars have been named but they are almost equally dangerous when established: 'Alba Plena' double white, 'Dazzler' pink, with leaves cream-variegated, 'Rosea Plena' and 'Rubra Plena' flowers double rose-pink, and reddish fading to pink.
S.* x *olivana 🏆 A beautiful low mat-former for well-drained soil. It is slow to get going but soundly perennial.

Satureja (*Labiatae*)

Mainly low aromatic shrubby perennials including Savory, with small leaves and short heads of 2-lipped flowers resembling those of thyme, white or in shades of pink to lilac late in the season. They are used as culinary herbs but are also suitable for the front of a sunny border in well-drained soil. They can be propagated by cuttings in early summer.
S. coerulea 🏆 Shrubby to 25 cm (10 in) with small linear leaves and dense spikes of bluish-violet flowers. Not widely grown.
S. montana (Winter Savory) Variable, generally densely shrubby to 40 cm (16 in) with small hairy leaves and leafy spikes of white to pale purple flowers. Subsp. *illyrica* is a better garden plant, more compact with deeper coloured flowers.
S. spicigera Low mat-former with small linear leaves and spikes of whorled white flowers.

Saxifraga (*Saxifragaceae*)

A genus of great importance to the rock gardener, but with comparatively few plants suitable in size and vigour for the border. These are mainly easy shade-lovers, and in addition to the taller species I have included a selection of the 'Mossy saxifrages' which are very low-growing but can make ample and colourful mats in a shady situation in front of shrubs or among other woodland perennials. They are of mixed parentage and I have listed them together rather than under their cultivar names. The plants described are very variable in growth habit and flower but the majority grow best in reasonably moist but well-drained soil in partial shade. Most can be raised from seed or their rosettes can be rooted as cuttings.
S.* x *arendsii *See* **'Mossy hybrids'**
S. cortusifolia Clump-forming to 25 cm (10 in), leaves to 8 cm (3 in) wide, kidney-shaped, deeply lobed, white flowers with two long, narrow petals and three short and clawed, in large loose heads in autumn. 'Dwarf form' smaller in all its parts. Excellent plants for their attractive leaves and late flowering, in a moist humus-rich shady border. Japan.
S. cuneifolia Mat-forming with 4 cm (1.6 in) wide rosettes of spathulate leaves and small heads of white flowers, yellow at the base. Var. *capillipes* smaller with purple-spotted flowers. They are easy low carpeters for a partially shady position, resembling miniature editions of London Pride. S. Europe.
S. cuscutiformis Clump-forming to 25 cm (10 in) with rounded toothed leaves, bronze-tinged and netted with conspicuous white veins, and red runners that form new rosettes which then root down. Flowers white, 2 cm (0.8 in) long, the upper two petals shorter than the lower, in loose panicles. The leaves are particularly beautiful but the plant is only fully hardy in warm gardens, where it appreciates partial shade. China.

S. fortunei 🏆 Variable, clump-forming, leaves similar to *S. cortusifolia*, but with deep reddish backs and an increasingly deep red suffusion of the whole leaf as the season progresses. The flowers in autumn are quite large, pure white with the lower one or two petals toothed and much larger than the upper. China, Japan, Korea. Var. *incisilobatum* has more deeply lobed leaves. 'Mt Nachi' has much smaller copper-tinged leaves. 'Rubrifolia' and 'Wada' ✱ ☼ have even more beautiful leaves heavily suffused with red throughout the season. These are all most attractive plants for a moist shady position.
S. geranioides Loosely cushion-forming to 20 cm (8 in), leaves broad, kidney-shaped, divided deeply into pointed segments, flowers bell-shaped, white in loose heads. An attractive plant for the edge of a shady border. S.W. Europe.
S. granulata Clump-forming, leaves kidney-shaped, 2 cm (0.8 in) wide, lobed, with axillary bulbils, flowers quite large, creamy-white, in large sprays. 'Plena' Fair Maids of France has larger double flowers. These are easily grown shade lovers, that increase freely by their bulbils, even becoming naturalized in moist gardens. Europe.
***S.* 'Mossy hybrids'** Low mossy carpets of deep green rosettes smothered in flowers in a range of colours from white to deep red. They are excellent as edging to a shady border, in front of shrubs and larger shade-loving perennials. There a large number of them and the following is a selection of the best: 'Ballawley Guardsman' crimson-scarlet, 'Bob Hawkins' ☼ beautiful silver-variegated leaves, flowers white, fairly slow-growing, 'Cloth of Gold' gold-variegated, not very vigorous, 'Dubarry' tall deep crimson, vigorous, 'Elf' a miniature, carmine, 'Fairy' compact, white, late, 'Four Winds' medium tall deep crimson, 'Gaiety' deep pink, early, compact grower, 'Hi-Ace' compact, white variegated, flowers white, 'James Bremmer' tall, large white, vigorous, but rather loose, 'Pearly King' compact, white, 'Peter Pan' compact, crimson, 'Pixie' very small, pinkish red. 'Sanguinea Superba' deep crimson, 'Schwefelblute' ('Flowers of Sulphur') pale primrose, spreading, 'Sprite' medium-short deep rose, 'Triumph' compact, very fine deep red. 'White Pixie' very compact, white, 'Winston Churchill' large clear pink.
S. rotundifolia Loose clumps of rosettes of rounded, coarsely-toothed hairy leaves to 5 cm (2 in) wide, 30–50 cm (12–20 in) stems bearing heads of small white stars in summer, the petals sometimes marked with yellow and red. Subsp. *chrysospleniifolia* very similar, with hairy-margined leaves.
S. stolonifera (Mother of Thousands) Loose clumps of rosettes of kidney-shaped or rounded hairy leaves to 8 cm (3 in) wide, reddish on the reverse and veined silver, with long reddish stolons producing new rosettes. Stems to 40 cm (16 in) bear loose sprays of small white flowers with two long and three short petals. An interesting foliage plant popular as a house plant, and only hardy in milder gardens, where it will spread extensively in shade. China, Japan.
S. umbrosa Very similar to *S.* x *urbium* and often confused with it, less robust with shorter petioles. Pyrenees.

S.* x *urbium London Pride 🏆 A spreading carpet of loose rosettes of narrow spathulate leaves, reddish beneath, and sticky stems to 30 cm (1 ft) bearing loose heads of red-centred white flowers. A very easily grown and popular plant that thrives in deep or partial shade and makes an attractive edging to a shady border, although too coarse to mix with the more delicate woodlanders. 'Aureo-punctata' has golden-variegated leaves, 'Primuloides' (*S. umbrosa* var. *primuloides*) 🏆 much more compact with smaller leaves, 'Clarence Elliott' 🏆 and 'Walter Ingwersen' very similar selections with red stems and pink flowers.
S.* x *wallacei An uncommon Mossy hybrid of uncertain origin with very large dark green rosettes and heads of outstandingly large flowers to 3 cm (1.2 in) wide.

Scabiosa (*Dipsacaceae*)

Genus of 70-80 species of annuals and perennials, the latter mainly within our size limits, and making an important contribution to the summer garden. They are clump-forming with entire or pinnate leaves, and flowers of typical domed shape, solitary or in loose branching heads, in shades of blue, pink, or occasionally yellow.

They are easily grown in well-drained soil, preferably limy, in full sun, but resent excessive winter wet in stodgy soil. Their long flowering season makes them ideal plants for the front or middle of the border. The many cultivars of *S. caucasica* are best divided every two or three years, and will continue flowering for longer if they are dead-headed. The species can be raised from seed, but the cultivars should be propagated by division.
***S.* 'Butterfly Blue'** ✱ Mound-forming to 25 cm (10 in), leaves grey-green, deeply lobed, flowers deep lavender, 4 cm (1.6 in) wide, in long succession. First-rate, with a very long season.

133 *Scabiosa* 'Butterfly Blue'

S. caucasica Leaves grey-green, the basal leaves simple, lanceolate, the stem leaves pinnately lobed, flowers large lavender-blue in branching heads over many weeks, the most popular species with many cultivars: var. *alba* flowers white with a hint of green, 'Bressingham White' larger-flowered white, 'Clive Greaves' flowers very large and plentiful, pale blue, 'Fama' flowers large, bright blue, 'Floral Queen' tall, flowers pale blue, 'Goldingensis' flowers large, deep lavender, 'Miss Willmott' tall and vigorous, flowers cream, 'Moorheim Blue' flowers dark blue, 'Perfecta' flowers large, blue, with fringed margin, 'Perfecta Alba' similar, pure white, 'Staefa' tall, blue.
S. columbaria Clump-forming to 50 cm (20 in), with much branched wiry stems, leaves grey-green, hairy, deeply lobed on the stems, flowers to 4 cm (1.6 in) wide, lavender. 'Nana' more compact. Var. *ocholeuca* (*S. ochroleuca*) very similar with pale yellow flowers. These are beautiful compact plants, but sometimes prove short-lived.
S. farinosa A dense clump to 25 cm (10 in) of dark green remarkably glossy spathulate lobed leaves, and short-stemmed pale lavender flowers intermittently throughout the summer. A very attractive and unusual scabious, but it appears to be more tender than most. It is easily propagated from cuttings.
S. graminifolia Cushion to 30 cm (1 ft), leaves grass-like, grey, hairy, flowers to 4 cm (1.6 in) wide, pale lavender or pink. An attractive dwarf for the edge of a border.
S. lucida Resembling *S. columbaria*, but flower stems unbranched, flowers reddish-purple.
S. 'Pink Mist' Very similar to 'Butterfly Blue' but with pink flowers.
S. rumelica *See* ***Knautia macedonica***

Schizostylis (*Iridaceae*)

One species of spreading rhizomatous perennial with several cultivars, with broad grassy light green leaves and one-sided spikes of 4–8 large 6-petalled flowers with narrow tubes and spreading lobes, in long succession in autumn. Grown in rich moist soil it spreads quickly and flowers freely, but it is intolerant of drought and quickly exhausts the soil and stops flowering, unless dug up and replanted in fresh soil frequently. At its best it is invaluable for providing late colour, and the flowers are excellent for cutting. It is propagated by division.
S. coccinea The type has deep scarlet flowers, var. *alba* white. Of numerous cultivars the following are most readily available: 'Cardinal' vigorous, flowers large deep red, 'Jennifer' large soft pink, 'Maiden's Blush' soft pink, 'Major' very large-flowered scarlet, 'Mrs Hegarty' an old favourite, small pink, 'November Cheer' vigorous, flowers deep pink, late, 'Pallida' very large, palest pink, 'Professor Barnard' medium, dusky red, 'Salmon Charm' salmon-pink. 'Sunrise' large pink, an outstandingly vigorous cultivar, 'Tambara' smaller rose flowers, 'Viscountess Byng' an old cultivar with deep red flowers, late, 'Zeal Salmon' large salmon-pink.

134 *Schizostylis* 'Sunrise'

Scopolia (*Solonaceae*)

A few poisonous perennials, of which one is worth growing in the garden in a shady place among shrubs. It can be propagated by division or from seed.
S. carniolica Spreading rhizomatous plant to 50 cm (20 in), with simple alternate leaves which become large and coarse after flowering, flowers bell-shaped, nodding, among the leaves, usually brown outside and green within, sometimes all yellowish-green, in late spring. Quite attractive until it becomes over-leafy after flowering.

Scrophularia (*Scrophulariaceae*)

A genus of coarse perennials with insignificant flowers, the only one grown regularly being worth a place in the border for its excellent variegated foliage. It can be propagated by division or by cuttings of young growths.
S. auriculata (syn. *S. aquatica*) Clump-forming to 70 cm (28 in), with opposite ovate leaves and sprays of very small dark reddish-brown flowers in summer. 'Variegata' has beautiful leaves edged with white.

Scutellaria (*Labiatae*)

Some 300 perennials and sub-shrubs, some low mat-formers, others upright clump-formers, with 2-lipped flowers, the upper hood-like, the lower often drooping, variable in colour, in summer. The smaller species may be sufficiently strong growing to use as a border edging, especially in well-drained soil. They can be propagated by cuttings of young growth or by seed.
S. alpina Low carpeter to 25 cm (10 in), leaves to 3 cm (1.2 in) ovate, toothed, flowers in short spikes, purple, lower lip white. Sufficiently floriferous to make a splash of colour at the margin of a border. Europe.
S. altissima Upright clump to 70 cm (28 in), leaves narrowly ovate, cordate, to 10 cm (4 in) long, very small flowers paired in long slender spikes, blue, occasionally yellow, with white lower lip. Quite attractive and seeds around freely. S.E. Europe, Russia.
S. baicalensis Low cushion to 30 cm (1 ft), with hairy lanceolate leaves and one-sided spikes of large flowers with

dark purplish-blue upper lip and paler blue lower. E. Asia.
S. galericulata Spreading clump to 50 cm (20 in), leaves ovate to 5 cm (2 in) long, flowers in leafy spikes, blue-violet or occasionally pink. N. Europe, N. Asia.
S. hastifolia Like *S. galericulata*, but with hastate (with 2 lobes at the base) leaves and larger flowers. Europe, Asia.
S. incana ✱ Upright clump to 70 cm (28 in), possibly more, with coarsely-toothed ovate leaves and one-sided spikes of large greyish-blue flowers from grey hairy buds, in late summer. An exceptionally beautiful perennial for late summer. USA.

135 *Scutellaria incana*

S. indica var. ***parvifolia*** (var. *japonica*) Semi-prostrate cushion of hairy stems to 30 cm (1 ft), leaves ovate, toothed, flowers in dense terminal spikes, pale purple, rarely white. Easily grown. Japan.
S. orientalis Low spreader to 30 cm (1 ft), leaves grey-green, deeply lobed, long upright flowers in dense clusters, pale yellow, in summer. An attractive carpeter for full sun. Europe, Asia.
S. pontica More prostrate than *S. orientalis*, with reddish-purple flowers. Turkey, Caucasus.
S. prostrata Similar to *S. pontica* with yellow flowers, the upper lip suffused purple. Himalayas.
S. scordiifolia Similar to *S. orientalis* with dark green toothed leaves and bluish-violet flowers. A vigorous carpeter which can spread widely. Korea.

Sedum (*Crassulaceae*)

A large genus containing a galaxy of perennials of widely differing habit, but usually with thick succulent leaves and small starry or bell-shaped flowers in dense heads or spikes, mainly in mid-summer to autumn. There are small cushion plants for the rock garden, widely spreading mats suitable for edging, but including some excessively invasive plants, plants of shrubby habit, and clump-forming plants suitable for general border use. The latter include some of the finest late-flowering perennials which are also excellent foliage plants. They may generally be propagated by seed or by cuttings.

In this very large genus I have picked out a selection of the best species and cultivars for the border, mainly from experience in my own garden, and excluding the smallest-growers and the most invasive. They are easy plants for well-drained soil in full sun except where stated.
S. aizoon Clump-forming to 40 cm (16 in), with oblong, toothed, green leaves on unbranched upright stems, terminating in flat-heads of starry deep yellow flowers. 'Euphorbioides' (syn. *aurantiaca*) more compact with reddish stems and deeper golden flowers. E. Asia.
S. alboroseum Usually seen as 'Medio-variegatum', upright to 30 cm (1 ft), leaves bluish-green, elliptic, with a central cream blotch, flowers greenish-white and pale pink in flat-heads. China, Japan.
S. anacampseros Mat-forming to 25 cm (10 in), with branching very leafy stems, leaves glaucous, rounded, sessile, flowers in dense rounded heads, purple. An attractive foliage plant.
S. 'Autumn Joy' (Herbstfreude) 🏆 Clump-forming to 50 cm (20 in), rounded leaves blue-green, toothed, flowers in broad flat-heads, deep pink darkening to coppery red with age. A splendid plant akin to *S. spectabile*, with striking leaves and a long season of flower.

136 *Sedum* 'Autumn Joy'

S. cauticolum Clump-forming to 15 cm (6 in), leaves rounded, glaucous, purple-margined, on reddish stems, flowers in dense heads, deep reddish-pink. Like a small earlier-flowering *S. sieboldii*.
S. hidakanum ✱ Compact mound to 20 cm (8 in) of small purple-tinged bluish leaves, smothered in late summer with heads of rose-pink stars for several weeks. A beautiful easy plant of doubtful name, possibly referable to *S. pluricaule*.
S. kamtschaticum 🏆 Loose mat to 20 cm (8 in), leaves glossy light green, sessile, spathulate, toothed, flowers deep orange-yellow stars in loose heads. Var. *ellacombei* 🏆 a lower more spreading mat with obovate leaves and smaller and paler flower heads, Var. *floriferum* 'Weihenstephaner Gold' 🏆 a vigorous low carpet with deep yellow flowers, 'Variegatum' 🏆 leaves broadly margined with yellow, and darker flowers. It is a magnificent slow-growing foliage plant.
S. middendorfianum Like a small form of *S. kamtschaticum* with linear leaves. N.E. Asia.
S. pluricaule Mat-former to 10 cm (4 in), with small purplish grey rounded leaves, and masses of pink flowers in autumn. E. Asia.
S. populifolium Upright sub-shrub to 25 cm (10 in), dark green leaves cordate, broad, coarsely toothed, flowers pale pink in large branching heads. An attractive rather slow-growing species. C. Asia.
S. 'Ruby Glow' 🏆 (*S. cauticolum* x *S. telephium*) Sprawling mat of branching stems with bluish-grey leaves, and masses of deep reddish-purple flowers in late summer. One of the most colourful low-growing sedums.
S. sieboldii clumps of arching stems to 20 cm (8 in), with toothed rounded leaves with purple margins, in threes, and rounded pink heads late autumn. 'Medio-variegatum' 🏆 leaf centre blotched with cream, a good foliage plant which sometimes reverts.
S. spathulifolium Low mat-former to 6 cm (2.3 in) with dense rosettes of grey-green spathulate leaves and many flat-heads of yellow flowers, with several cultivars varying in foliage colour: 'Aureum' leaves tinged golden, deepening during the summer, 'Cape Blanco' 🏆 leaves with a silvery white bloom, compact and hardy, 'Majus' is larger in all its parts, var. *pruinosum* larger than the type, leaves with a whitish bloom, 'Purpureum' 🏆 large purple leaves, 'Roseum' has pink-tinged leaves. All these make colourful mats at the edge of a border.
S. spectabile 🏆 Variable clump-former with upright stems to 40 cm (16 in), bearing fleshy, pale glaucous grey-green, sparsely toothed leaves, and large flat-heads of pale pink flowers in late summer to autumn. An invaluable plant, with several cultivars varying in foliage and flower colour. All are very attractive to butterflies. 'Album' flowers pure white, 'Brilliant' 🏆 deeper pink, 'Iceberg' white, often with a faint pink tinge detracting from the cool effect, 'Meteor' carmine, vigorous, 'September Glow' purplish-red, tall, 'Stardust' paler green leaves and white flowers, making a good cool contrast to the dark red cultivars.
S. spurium Creeping mat to 5 cm (2 in), leaves obovate dark green, flowers pink in flat-heads. It makes fair deep green low ground cover, tolerant of some shade, with more exciting cultivars: var. *album* differs only in its white flowers, 'Atropurpureum' purple leaves, deep red flowers, 'Coccineum' leaves flushed red, flowers reddish-purple, 'Erdblut' leaves green, margined red, flowers carmine, 'Fuldaglut' leaves and flowers darker than the last, 'Green Mantle' leaves green, flowers very pale pink, 'Purpureum' and 'Purpurteppich' ('Purple Carpet') purple leaves, very large in the latter, and dark reddish-purple flowers, 'Schorbuser Blut' ('Dragon's Blood') more compact, small bright reddish leaves and purple flower, 'Variegatum' ('Tricolor') narrower leaves edged with cream, and pale pink flowers, a very bright carpeter.
S. telephium Rhizomatous with upright or procumbent stems to 40 cm (16 in), usually less, furnished with glossy light green toothed oblong leaves, and pale pink flowers in large flat-heads. Subsp. *maximum* leaves green, very thick, more rounded, clasping the stem, flower heads greenish cream, rarely pink, a substantial plant that seems to seed around freely. *S. m.* 'Atropureum', usually more stiffly upright, very deep purple glossy leaves and reddish-pink flower heads, 'Morchen' ✱ ☼ similar, very upright, darkest purple leaves and flowers, a fine plant which looks best in a group planted closely, 'Munstead Red' leaves bronze-purple, flowers red, subsp. *ruprechtii* ✱ similar to subsp. *maximum*, but somewhat smaller; leaves bluish-green, flowers very abundant in terminal flat-heads with smaller heads in all the leaf axillae, greenish-yellow. From a brief experience it seems outstanding.

137 *Sedum telephium maximum*

S. 'Vera Jameson' ♕ Low mound of spreading stems to 20 cm (8 in), leaves rounded, reddish-purple, flowers pale pink. A lovely hybrid.

138 *Sedum* 'Vera Jameson'

Semiaquilegia (*Ranunculaceae*)

Small genus closely allied to Aquilegia, with similar lobed leaves and with attractive spurless flowers in early summer. They are easy in well-drained soil in a sunny position, but are usually short-lived. They are easily raised from seed, which usually comes true.

S. adoxoides (syn. *Aquilegia adoxoides*) To 30 cm (1 ft), leaves 3-lobed with 2–3 leaflets, flowers white or pale pink nodding, on branching stems.

S. ecalcarata (*Aquilegia ecalcarata*) To 30 cm (1 ft), leaves more divided, generally with more reddish-purple flowers. A beautiful and dainty plant for grouping in the front of a border.

Senecio (*Compositae*)

A huge genus recently subdivided, with many of the most widely grown species in Brachyglottis, These are generally shrubby and I have excluded them, together with several very tall species, and others that need glass protection in winter. The remainder are very diverse and are described individually.

S. abrotanifolius rhizomatous clump-former to 40 cm (16 in), leaves bi-pinnately divided, glossy green, daisy flowers to 4 cm (1.6 in) wide, orange-yellow striped brown, in late summer. An uncommon but striking plant.

S. cineraria Semi-shrubby to 40 cm (16 in), leaves deeply lobed or pinnate, grey above, white-downy beneath, flowers small, dark yellow, in loose heads. A first class foliage plant with some 'improved' cultivars. They are often raised annually from seed or cuttings, but are perennial in mild gardens. 'Ramparts' good deeply divided silvery white leaves. 'White Diamond' ♕ an established favourite with silver-grey leaves.

S. leucosyachys See ***S. viravira***

S. pulcher ✱ Rosette-forming to 40 cm (16 in), leaves glossy dark green, to 20 cm (8 in), elliptic to lanceolate, toothed, flowers in loose heads, brilliant magenta with yellow centre, in autumn. Remarkable for its colour and late season, it is only hardy in mild gardens and needs rich but well-drained soil.

139 *Senecio pulcher*

S. viravira (*S. leucostachys*) ♕ Low mound of spreading stems with deeply divided white-tomentose leaves and insignificant flowers. A superb white-foliage plant that will wander into its neighbours, making a striking contrast to the purple leaves of the darker cultivars of *Sedum telephium*. Only hardy in mild gardens but great for containers.

Serratula (*Compositae*)

Several herbaceous perennials, of which only one is widely grown.

S. seoanei (syn. *S. shawii*) ✱ Clump-forming to 30 cm (1 ft), leaves lanceolate, coarsely toothed or pinnate, flowers centaurea-like on branching stems, deep purplish-pink, in late summer to autumn. Beautiful late flowerer for a very well-drained sunny border. It can be grown from seed, or offsets rooted as cuttings.

S. tinctoria Rarely grown, it resembles a larger version of *S. seoanii*.

Seseli (*Umbelliferae*)

A rare genus in gardens, with attractive finely divided glaucous or silvery foliage and typical large umbels of small flowers, usually white but sometimes pink to red, in summer. *S. montanum* which frequently has red flowers, and *S. gummiferum* with silvery leaves and extra large white umbels, are among the smaller and more perennial species, occasionally available.

Sidalcea (*Malvaceae*)

A genus of a few annuals and perennials, of which two American species are widely grown and have been hybridized extensively. They are clump-forming with lobed or divided leaves, and stiffly upright stems to 1 m (3 ft) bearing dense spikes of mallow flowers in summer, white or in shades of pink to deep purple. They grow best in light well-drained soils in full sun and are excellent easy plants for providing shades of pink in the middle of the border. They should be cut back after flowering to encourage further late flowers. They can be propagated by division or the species by seed.
S. candida To 80 cm (30 in) with 2.5 cm (1 in) wide white flowers with blue anthers.
S. malviflora Generally taller with larger pink flowers in single or branching spikes. This species and many of its hybrids are too tall for consideration here but the following cultivars are usually within our limits: 'Loveliness' delightful soft silky pink, 'Oberon' more compact, flowers rose-pink, 'Puck' one of the lowest-growing, clear pink.

Silene (*Caryophyllaceae*) (Campion, Catchfly)

A large genus of annuals and perennials, varying greatly from low-growing alpine species needing special care, to a few easy plants of small to medium size, in bushy or upright clumps. Generally they have simple, entire leaves and long-tubed flowers with spreading petals, often with an inflated calyx, in shades from white through pink to red. They are easily grown in a sunny border in well-drained soil, and some are suitable for the wild garden. They may be raised from seed or the cultivars increased by division or cuttings.
S. asterias Uncommon, erect clump-former to 70 cm (28 in), rosettes of small leaves and clusters of deep purple flowers.
S. dioica Our native Red Campion is only suitable for the shady wild garden as it seeds too freely, but several cultivars are better garden plants: 'Flore Pleno' fairly compact with double deep pink flowers, 'Graham's Delight' a tall plant with cream-variegated leaves, 'Minikin' ('Compacta') only attains 30 cm (1 ft), flowers medium pink, 'Richmond' flowers deep rose-pink, 'Rosea Plena' similar to 'Flore Pleno' flowers paler.
S. fimbriata (syn. *S. multifida*) Rare, upright clump-forming, very leafy hairy stems and clusters of a few large white flowers with inflated calyces. Excellent in shade.
S. nutans Clump-forming to 30 cm (1 ft), small lanceolate leaves and erect branching hairy stems bearing masses of narrow-petalled creamy-white flowers with purplish calyces. An attractive soundly perennial species, rarely seen.
S. schafta 🏆 Bushy habit to 25 cm (10 in), small leaves on branching semi-prostrate stems and masses of deep rose-pink flowers for several weeks in autumn. A long-lived plant, vigorous enough for the border with good drainage. 'Shell Pink' ✱ a recently arrived cultivar of a delightful shade of soft shell pink, of similar vigour to the type.
S. uniflora (syn. *S. maritima*) (See plate 58) Mat-forming to 15 cm (6 in), leaves very glaucous 2 cm (0.8 in) long, lanceolate, flowers solitary to 4, white with pale greenish inflated calyces. It has a reputation for seeding excessively which I do not find well-deserved. It makes a startling contrast in my garden to the black-eyed magenta *Geranium subcaulescens*. The cultivars are certainly well-behaved: 'Druett's Variegated' leaves well-margined with cream, attractive, 'Robin Whitebreast' more compact with double white flowers, 'Rosea' pale pink single flowers, 'Silver Lining' leaves narrowly margined with white.

Sisyrinchium (*Iridaceae*)

A genus of some 100 species, mainly clump-forming herbaceous perennials, with dense fibrous roots or short rhizomes, grassy or sword-shaped leaves, and wiry stems bearing a succession of flowers, usually 2 to 8, from starry to bell-shaped, from buds protected by 2 or more spathes. They include a few species to be avoided, with very small flowers which seed excessively, and a number of very beautiful small to medium plants suitable for the front of a border. Many are only suitable for the rock garden or alpine house, and I have selected those which seem to grow and increase well enough to plant in a mixed bed in sun or light shade, preferably in soil that never dries out. They can be raised from seed, and most are very easy to increase by division in spring.

There seems to be considerable confusion in the naming of species in cultivation.
S. angustifolium (syn. *S. graminoides*) (The Blue-eyed Grass) Probably best avoided except in the wild garden, to 30 cm (1 ft) high, leaves narrow, branching stems, rather small yellow-eyed blue flowers with a remarkable propensity for seeding around.
S. arenarium Said to resemble a poor form of *S. striatum*, but the plant I grow, supplied by several nurseries, is a delightful plant resembling *S. bellum* but with pale creamy-yellow flowers.
S. atlanticum Like a slender *S. idahoense* with smaller violet-blue flowers.
S. bellum ometimes included in *S. idahoense* To 40 cm (16 in) but generally much smaller, a spreading clump of slightly glaucous leaves with clusters of 2.5 cm (1 in) wide, deep blue, occasionally white flowers, an inch or two above them on branched stems. It is an attractive plant to use as edging to a border, easily increased by division.

140 *Sisyrinchium bellum* (*S. idahoense*)

***S.* 'Biscutella'** Similar to *S. angustifolium* but flowers in an intriguing dusky mixture of yellow and brownish-purple. It seeds around gently and without much variation.
***S.* 'Californian Skies'** Similar to *S. bellum*, to 20 cm (8 in), flowers large deep blue. A very reliable plant with a long flowering season.
S. californiacum (syn. *S. brachypus*) Variable, usually to 20 cm (8 in), flowers deep yellow often with darker veining. Plants under the name *S. brachypus* are generally dwarfer. They are quite attractive but seed rather too freely.
S. depauperatum (*S. junceum* ssp. *depauperatum*) resembles *S. angustifolium* in habit, broader leaves and creamy-white flowers, with dark purplish-black centres and a delicate dark central vein. I find it very free-seeding in well-drained soil, but it looks good in a reasonable-sized clump.
***S.* 'E.K. Balls'** Leaves fan-shaped, flowers deep mauve in abundant sprays.
S. filifolium (syn. *Olsynium filifolium*) Allied to *S. junceum* and sometimes included in it. Like *S. angustifolum* in habit, with large open-bell-shaped flowers to 3 cm (1.2 in) wide, white with violet veining. A beautiful but rarely seen species, perhaps best on the rock garden.
S. idahoense Confused with *S. bellum*, and considered by botanists to be close to *S. angustifolium* (syn. *S. graminoides*), unbranched stems, large deep blue flowers with a yellow eye. In my experience with plants grown from collected seed it is taller and even more robust than the plants in cultivation of *S. bellum*, which may be a dwarf form of it.
S. macounii, usually grown as its white variety *S. macounii* 'Album' ✱ is thought to be a dwarf form of *S. idahoense*. A very fine low clump-former that thrives in sun in moist soil or in partial shade. None of these seed around for me.
S. macrocarpum ✱ Clump-forming to 20 cm (8 in), leaves broad, greyish-green, flowers to 3 cm (1.2 in) wide, deep yellow with a brown line towards the base. Possibly the largest-flowered species, and a fine plant, but more tender than most. It has survived recent winters to -7 °C (20 °C).
***S.* 'Mrs Spivey'** Floriferous, pure white.
***S.* 'Pole Star'** Pure white, long-flowering.
***S.* 'Quaint and Queer'** Very like *S.* 'Biscutella', a sombre mixture of yellow, brown, and purple.
S. striatum The largest, clump-forming to 60 cm (2 ft), with fans of broad iris-like leaves, and spikes of 2 cm (0.8 in) wide mid-yellow flowers with brownish veining in summer. 'Aunt May' (syn. *Variegatum*) ✱ leaves margined with a broad cream stripe, one of the brightest variegated plants for the front of the border.

Smilacina (*Liliaceae/ Convallariaceae*)

A few woodland rhizomatous perennials closely allied to Polygonatum with similar leaves on arching stems terminating in large clusters of small, usually white flower, followed sometimes by conspicuous fruits. Only two are widely grown. They are beautiful easy plants that can spread widely in moist humus-rich soil in shade. They can be propagated by seed sown fresh, or by division.
S. racemosa 🏆 Spreading clump 60–90 cm (2–3 ft) high, with Solomon's Seal-like leaves and long dense fluffy heads of small creamy-white flowers in late spring. Less spreading and more desirable than the larger polygonatums.
S. stellata Lower-growing, leaves fewer and more glaucous, flowers starry in loose spikes.

Solidago (*Compositae*)

Genus Of about 100 species of very hardy clump-forming herbaceous perennials mainly from N. America, of varying habit, with simple, usually toothed leaves, and large heads or spikes of small bright yellow flowers in summer. The larger Golden Rods can be invasive and are not perhaps in the first rank of border plants, but some of the smaller cultivars and species described here are of some value for their mid- to late summer blooming. They are very easy to grow even in poor soils, and can be propagated by division. Several will have a second flowering period if they are cut back after the first flowers are over. They can cause asthma in susceptible people.

Cultivars: 'Crown of Rays' to 60 cm (2 ft), upright, flowers in large flat branching heads, one of the finest cultivars, 'Cloth of Gold' to 40 cm (16 in), vigorous, flowers in dense deep yellow heads, 'Golden Baby' and 'Golden Dwarf' good compact dwarfs, 'Golden Falls' taller to 70 cm (28 in), upright growth, deep yellow, 'Goldenmosa' 🏆 to 70 cm (28 in), bushy, very large mid-yellow flower heads, one of the best, Laurin 30 cm (1 ft), deep gold, 'Queenie' (Golden Thumb) to 30 cm (1 ft), leaves variegated with gold, 'Tom Thumb' compact dwarf with short dense yellow spikes.
S. cutleri Dense clump to 30 cm (1 ft), leaves spathulate-ovate, flowers golden-yellow in short dense spikes in late summer. A good easy dwarf.
S. decumbens (*S. spathulata* var. *nana*) Clump-forming to 20 cm (8 in), stems reddish, Flowers in dense somewhat globular heads.
S. flexicaulis A tall species with short clusters of yellow

flowers, rarely seen except in its variegated form 'Variegata' shorter, with leaves spotted with deep yellow.
S. virgaurea A tall species except in its compact form 'Nana' to 45 cm (1.5 ft) with dense yellow spikes.

X ***Solidaster*** (*Aster* x *Solidago*) (*Compositae*)

Similar to Solidago but with less vigour and more charm.
S. luteus Clump-forming to 80 cm (30 in), rarely more, leaves narrow, sparsely toothed, large branching sprays of yellow flowers. 'Lenore' a superior cultivar slightly shorter, with flowers of a soft shade of pale yellow.

Sphaeralcea (*Malvaceae*)

Genus containing a few semi-woody perennials, mainly from Southern N. America, with variable, usually deeply lobed, greyish leaves and saucer-shaped, mallow flowers in shades of pink to red. They are excellent for warmer gardens, the spreading species covering a considerable area in the course of a season and mingling with other surrounding plants, with their main flowering period in late summer, but continuing for weeks. They seem to be hardy in very well-drained soil to -7 °C (20 °F), and are easily propagated from cuttings so that plants can be overwintered under glass as a precaution. The following are species currently readily available, but their names seem somewhat confused and their descriptions are based on my experience in the garden of nursery material.
S. fendleri ✱ Low spreading mat of branching stems to 30 cm (1 ft) high and 1 m (3 ft) or more wide, 3–5-lobed grey-green triangular leaves, masses of beautiful soft pale pink flowers with deep purple centres, from mid-summer to autumn, especially in a hot season. *S. f.* var. *venusta*, sometimes offered as 'upright form' has similar flowers but is upright in habit, attaining 1 m (3 ft) or more.

141 *Sphaeralcea fendleri*

S. miniata Compact, shrubby to 60 cm (2 ft), leaves shallowly 3–5-lobed, light green, on hairy stems, flowers a little smaller, resembling those of *S. munroana*.
S. munroana Similar to *S. fendleri* but flowers deeper in colour with a tinge of salmon.

Stachys (*Labiatae*)

A large genus containing a few mainly low-growing garden-worthy perennials, some with fine silver-grey foliage and insignificant flowers, others with striking upright spikes of whorled 2-lipped flowers in summer. They are very easy, especially in well-drained soil, and they can be propagated by division.
S. byzantina (Lamb's Tongue) ✿ A spreading carpet of rosettes of fine white-woolly leaves to 10 cm (4 in) long, with short spikes of small whorled flowers among white bracts. It is a superb foliage plant but the flower spikes detract from it, and non-flowering cultivars are available: 'Big Ears' exceptionally large leaves and taller spikes of purple flowers, 'Cotton Balls' no true flowers but spikes of round woolly clusters of buds, 'Primrose Heron' golden tinted leaves, especially in spring, 'Silver Carpet' an old favourite making a vigorous silver carpet, unadorned by flowers.
S. citrina Low mat to 20 cm (8 in), leaves grey-green, rounded, flowers in short clusters, pale yellow. Needs excellent drainage.
S. coccinea Clump-forming, light green, toothed, ovate leaves and whorls of large flowers in an unusual shade of deep reddish salmon for a long time in summer. It is a striking plant but seems to be tender below -4 °C (25 °F). It is easily grown from cuttings and rapidly makes a sizeable plant.
S. discolor Clump-forming to 30 cm (1 ft), leaves deeply toothed, very hairy, white beneath, flowers pink among white-woolly bracts.
S. macrantha ✱ Spreading mound of dark green, hairy, shallowly toothed leaves, and abundant spikes of large rose-purple flowers in summer. One of the most colourful species for foreground planting. 'Nivea' white, 'Robusta' 🏆 larger and very vigorous, early-flowering, 'Rosea' good soft pink, 'Superba' 🏆 flowers larger and darker.

142 *Stachys macrantha*

S. monieri Clump-forming with rosettes of dark green, ovate, crinkled leaves, and widely spaced whorls of deep pink or white flowers.
S. officinalis (Wood Betony) Like *S. macrantha* but spreading more widely, with shorter spikes of smaller purple flowers. 'Alba' and 'Rosea Superba' have larger white and pink flowers. Suitable for the wild garden in sun or shade.

Stokesia (*Compositae*)

S. laevis ✱ The only species, clump-forming to 60 cm (2 ft), semi-prostrate to erect branched stems from rosettes of lanceolate leaves to 20 cm (8 in) long, and fine centaurea-like flowers with frilly rays, typically lavender-blue, in a long succession in late summer. C. USA. 'Alba' pure white, 'Blue Star' larger flowers, 'Wyoming' darker blue. Excellent plants for near the front of the border, and good for picking. The species can be raised from seed and the cultivars by division or cuttings of young shoots.

143 *Stokesia laevis* 'Alba'

Streptopus (*Liliaceae*/*Convallariaceae*)

A small genus of very beautiful woodland plants closely allied to Polygonatum, with similar arching stems bearing alternate leaves held horizontally, and hanging tubular flowers followed by large pendent fruits. They need moist humus-rich soil in shade, but are less vigorous than the larger polygonatums.
S. amplexicaulis Stems to 80 cm (30 in), leaves lanceolate clasping the stems, glaucous bluish on the reverse, paired flowers small, greenish-white, with recurving petals, in mid-summer, followed by conspicuous red fruits. N. temperate areas.
S. roseus Similar to *S. amplexicaulis*, to 40 cm (16 in) only, leaves sessile, green, flowers solitary, rose-pink, much more effective, fruits red. N.E. USA.
S. simplex Resembling *S. amplexicaulis* but usually lower, with larger pure white flowers with less reflexed petals. Himalayas–China.

Stylophorum (*Papaveraceae*)

Celandine Poppies, three species of very attractive woodlanders with lobed leaves and branching heads of good-sized bright yellow poppies over a long period in summer. They are easily grown in shade with reasonable moisture, and can brighten dark areas among shrubs. They are often short-lived, but are very easy to raise from seed.
S. diphyllum Clump to 40 cm (16 in). Leaves pinnately lobed, with 5–7 bluntly toothed lobes, flowers saucer-shaped, 5 cm (2 in) (2in) across, throughout the summer. I find it self-sows gently.
S. lasiocarpum To 45 cm (1.5 ft), leaves with up to 10 small leaflets, the terminal one much larger, flowers somewhat paler. A shorter-lived plant that usually self-sows with abandon.

Succisa (*Dipsacaceae*)

S. pratensis (Devil's Bit Scabious) The only species, a clump-forming perennial, to 70 cm (28 in), leaves elliptic to lanceolate, narrower on the stems, stems branching widely, many globular 2–3 cm (0.8–1.2 in) wide scabious-like heads of pale violet, occasionally white or pink, in late summer. Easily grown in moist soil, but not very spectacular in the border.

Sutera (*Scrophulariaceae*)

A genus of mainly sub-shrubby perennials from S. Africa, a few of which have been seen in gardens recently. They seem easy in sunny, well-drained soils, and are probably hardy to -7 °C (20 °F).
S. pristisepala Low spreading cushion to 60 cm (2 ft) with tiny grey pinnate, hairy leaves, and short loose spikes of tiny, pinkish-lavender, diascia-like flowers, with a yellow spot in the throat. It is an attractive plant for foliage and flowers.

Swertia (*Gentianaceae*)

A few annuals and perennials rarely seen in gardens, but occasionally available from seed collections to the Himalayas and E. Asia, they resemble the more robust gentians with upright spikes of similar flowers in subdued colours, usually greeny white. They need the same conditions in the garden.

S. kingii Clump-forming to 60 cm (2 ft), flowers as described. The only species readily available in Britain.

Symphyandra (*Campanulaceae*)

A genus of very attractive short-lived campanula-like perennials, with large pendent bell-shaped flowers. They are usually biennial or monocarpic in the garden, but I have included them as they generally remain as a colony by self-seeding, and are a great asset to the summer garden. They are easy in a sunny border, and are readily raised from seed.

S. armena Stems to 30 cm (1 ft) upright and spreading, leaves hairy, ovate, lobed, flowers to 2 cm (0.8 in), hairy, white, in heads of 2–6.

S. hofmannii Stems to 50 cm (20 in), stiffly upright and branching, leaves ovate-lanceolate, toothed, flowers 3 cm (1.2 in), creamy-white, at the branch tips. A striking plant with a long season in summer.

S. ossetica Similar to *S. hoffmanii* but to 40 cm (16 in), with narrower pale blue flowers.

S. pendula Similar to *S. armena*, with longer creamy-white flowers in short spikes.

S. wanneri Similar in habit to *S. hofmannii*, but with abundant leafy spikes of narrow violet-blue flowers over a long period. A striking species which usually self-sows.

S. zanzegura Stems spreading and branched with rounded, toothed, hairy leaves, and loose sprays of pale lavender flowers. It self-sows freely.

Symphytum (*Boraginaceae*)

The Comfreys are a genus of mainly coarse spreading perennials, most of them invasive to some degree. Their coarse dense foliage subdues weeds and they make useful ground cover in difficult places or the wild garden, in sun or partial shade. Only a few are suitable for the border. I have been selective in choosing some of the best small-growing of these. They can be propagated by division, or the species by seed.

S. caucasicum Spreading clump to 70 cm (28 in), with typical hairy borage-like leaves and and loose clusters of good blue flowers, opening pinkish. Although one of the best for colour it is too invasive for a small border. 'Eminence' is a better coloured and somewhat less invasive cultivar.

S. ibericum (syn. *S. grandiflorum*) Very invasive with coarse leaves and wishy-washy cream flowers from reddish buds. Various cultivars are available, of clearer colour, for example 'Hidcote Blue' and 'Hidcote Pink'. 'Hidcote Variegated' has cream-splashed leaves but is liable to revert.

***S.* 'Rubrum'** Of doubtful hybrid origin, resembles a less invasive *S. ibericum* with clusters of deep red nodding flowers in summer.

S.* x *uplandicum (*S. asperum* x *S. officinale*) Generally too tall for consideration here, but 'Variegatum' 🏆 with fine cream-margined leaves may just be suitable, an excellent foliage plant with the usual poor flowers. They can be removed!

Synthyris (*Scrophulariaceae*)

Genus of several woodland or alpine species from N. America, the latter needing special care. They have basal, lobed or dissected leaves and upright dense spikes of tubular blue flowers in spring. The woodlanders are easy in humus-rich soil in partial or full shade with adequate moisture, and are very attractive companions to the woodland bulbs like Anemone nemorosa and erythroniums and trilliums. They can be raised from seed or divided, but the latter is best avoided.

S. missurica ✱ Clumps to 30 cm (1 ft), of rounded, shallowly toothed dark green leaves and upright spikes of deep lilac flowers in long succession from early to late spring. A delightful long-lived plant.

144 *Synthyris missurica*

S. reniformis Similar to *S. missurica* but shorter, with fewer-flowered racemes of larger lilac flowers.

S. stellata Very similar to the last and possibly confused with it in gardens.

T

Tanacetum (*Compositae*)

Some 70 species of annuals and perennials, the latter including many plants previously know as Chrysanthemum and Pyrethrum, and often to be found under these names in catalogues. They are usually woody-based, upright or bushy, with finely divided usually aromatic leaves, and flowers either discoid without rays or typically chrysanthemum-like. They vary in habit from low-growing silver-foliage plants to upright clump-forming 'pyrethrums' and are mainly easy to grow in full sun and well-drained soil. Propagation is usually by division or by cuttings.

I have excluded the species used primarily as herbs, and the few taller species.

T. argenteum (syn. *Chrysanthemum argenteum*)
Mat-forming, stems and leaves intensely silver, leaves

deeply 5–7–lobed, flowers white, button-like in dense heads. An excellent low silver mat for a hot dry well-drained site in mild gardens.
T. coccineum (syn. *Pyrethrum coccineum*) Popular border perennials under their old name with many cultivars, clump-forming to 70 cm (28 in), with pinnately divided green leaves and large single or semi-double daisy flowers in a range of pinks, reds, or white, in early summer. They are easily grown in sun or light shade, and make a fine splash of colour in the middle of the border, but they usually need staking and should be divided regularly every two or three years and replanted in fresh soil. Some of the best cultivars include: 'Alfred' dark red double, 'Brenda' 🏆 deep rose-pink single, 'Eileen May Robinson' 🏆 an excellent single pink, 'Evenglow' rich scarlet, 'James Kelway' 🏆 deep scarlet single, 'Queen Mary' double pink.
T. densum ☼ Mat-forming to 20 cm (8 in), leaves finely divided, silver, flowers tiny, in dense heads, yellow. A beautiful ferny-leaved silver foliage plant needing very well-drained soil. *T. d.* Subsp. *amani* (syn. *T. haradjanii*, *Chrysanthemum haradjanii*) ☼ is even better, leaves more finely cut and smaller.
T. parthenium (syn. *Chrysanthemum parthenium*) (Feverfew) 60 cm (2 ft) Spreading, clump-forming perennial, leaves divided, pale green, aromatic, flowers small white, in dense heads, in summer. Probably best in the herb garden as it seeds excessively and is difficult to dead-head completely. 'Aureum' more attractive foliage plant, leaves bright yellow, but it also seeds excessively. I have given it up, but the wild garden might suit it. 'Double White' and 'Sissinghurst White' (syn. *Rowallane*) double flowers, the latter larger, 'White Bonnet' similar but with large single rayed flowers. These spread by rhizomes rather than seed, and are worth growing, given sufficient space.

Tanakaea (*Saxifragaceae*)

T. radicans The only species, a slowly spreading evergreen rhizomatous perennial to 25 cm (10 in), leaves leathery, dark green, coarsely toothed, flowers tiny, greenish-white in loose arching panicles in summer. It is a beautiful small woodlander for humus-rich soil in moist shade. Japan, China.

Telekia (*Compositae*)

Two species of robust herbaceous perennials, of which *T. speciosa* is too large.
T. speciosissima (syn. *Buphthalmum speciosissimum*) To 40 cm (16 in), leaves large, ovate-oblong, toothed, flowers to 7 cm (2.8 in) wide, solitary on stiff upright stems, deep yellow, in late summer. It is a good yellow daisy that thrives on moist soil in light shade. N. Italy.

Tellima (*Saxifragaceae*)

T. grandiflora The sole species, rhizomatous clump-forming, leaves rounded, hairy, shallowly lobed or toothed, flowers very small greenish-white bells in long, narrow upright spikes, in summer. It makes dense ground cover and is often recommended for this, but it is one of the freest seeding of all plants, and is to my mind a rather boring menace. The cultivar 'Rubra' (syn. 'Purpurea') has reddish-tinged flowers and is slightly more attractive but still a menace. W., N. Am.

Tetragonolobus (*Leguminosae*) *See* **Lotus**

Teucrium (*Labiatae*)

Some 100 species of perennials, mainly Mediterranean, usually mat-forming or sub shrubby, often aromatic, with simple or lobed leaves, and typical labiate flowers, tubular with a broad lower lip. Some species have attractive grey or silver leaves but few are spectacular. They are easy, especially in very well-drained soil in full sun. They can be propagated by seed or by cuttings.
T. ackermannii *See* ***T. polium***
T. chamaedrys Variable, spreading carpet to 25 cm (10 in), leaves deep green flowers in loose spikes, pinkish-purple. A more vigorous species for border edging.
T. hircanicum Clump-forming to 40 cm (16 in), grey-green, ovate-lanceolate, toothed, flowers in long dense spikes, reddish-purple, in late summer.
T. montanum Mat-forming, leaves narrow, hairy, flowers creamy-white in short spikes.
T. polium Mat-forming to 25 cm (10 in), leaves narrow, grey-hairy, flowers small, white, yellow, or reddish, in dense heads. Subsp. *aureum* is more attractive with whiter leaves and bright greenish-yellow flowers in more substantial heads.
T. pyrenaicum Low mat-forming, leaves grey-green, rounded, flowers larger than most, cream, with small reddish upper lip.
T. scorodonia Spreading, rhizomatous to 30 cm (1 ft), leaves crinkly, usually hairy, flowers in short one-sided spikes, greenish-yellow. A moderately attractive foliage plant, especially in its more widely grown cultivars, 'Crispum' leaves very crinkled, frilly-edged, 'Crispum Marginatum' similar but leaves margined with white.
T. subspinosum Low densely branching spiny shrublet to 15 cm (6 in), leaves small grey, hairy, flowers deep reddish-purple in the upper leaf axils. Makes a beautiful low cushion, but can be persistently wrecked by cats, which lie on it or tear it to pieces.

Thalictrum (*Ranunculaceae*)

Genus of some 85 perennials, clump-forming and sometimes spreading widely, with beautiful aquilegia-like leaves, and usually loose heads of many small fluffy flowers in summer, which lack petals but have prominent clusters of stamens and in some species colourful sepals. They vary greatly in habit from low slowly-spreading clumps for the rock garden to tall invasive colonizers best in the wild garden. They all combine exceptionally dainty flowers with beautiful, usually glaucous leaves. Generally they thrive best in humus-rich soil in light shade, with reasonable moisture. They can be propagated by seed sown as fresh as possible, or by division, but the more delicate species seem to resent root disturbance.

I have reluctantly excluded many fine plants that usually exceed 75 cm (2.5 ft), but I have included most of the available smaller species, suitable for the front of shady borders.

T. alpinum Rhizomatous slow spreader to 15 cm (6 in), leaves with 10–20 rounded leaflets, flowers small, sepals greenish flushed pink, filaments pale purple with yellow anthers. Rarely grown, with good foliage but somewhat insignificant flowers. Circumpolar.

T. ichangense (syn *T. coreanum*) Low slowly spreading clump, leaves biternate, leaflets to 3 cm (1.2 in) wide, flowers pale purple with prominent stamens. Uncommon but only slightly less attractive than *T. kiusianum*. China.

T. isopyroides Clump-formng to 20 cm (8 in), leaves with many very glaucous leaflets, flowers small, purplish-brown. Better foliage than flowers. W. Asia.

T. kiusianum ✱ Slowly spreading clump to 15 cm (6 in), leaves biternate, leaflets to 1.5 cm (0.6 in) wide, purple-tinged, flowers pinkish-purple with very prominent stamens. One of the most exquisite small woodlanders. Japan.

T. minus Very invasive colonizer, usually 30–50 cm (12–20 in), leaves with many green leaflets, occasionally glaucous, flowers many, small, in loose heads, sepals greenish, stamens yellow. Although attractive I think this is a plant to avoid except where it can have plenty of space to itself. Subsp. *adiantifolium* has even better adiantium-like leaves, and may be less invasive. Subsp. *olympicum* (syn. Subsp. *saxatile*) is certainly smaller and better-behaved. Europe, N. Africa, Asia.

T. orientale ✱ Small clump-forming to 25 cm (10 in) but usually less, leaflets few, toothed, flowers comparatively large and few in loose heads, lilac, rarely white. An exceptionally lovely plant, but not particularly easy. It seems to do best in rich but very well-drained peaty soil. Propagation is difficult because it resents disturbance and rarely sets good seed. Greece, Turkey.

145 *Thalictrum orientale*

T. tuberosum ✱ Tuberous-rooted clump-former to 30 cm (1 ft), resembling the last but with larger leaves, and much larger cream flowers. Very beautiful and probably easier than *T. orientale*. S.W. Europe.

146 *Thalictrum tuberosum*

Thermopsis (*Leguminosae*)

Genus of some 20 hardy perennials, mainly from USA, clump-forming or running, with attractive 3-lobed silvery-green leaves and upright spikes of large lupin-like yellow flowers in summer. They are most attractive plants that deserve to be more widely grown, but some are decidedly invasive and should be avoided in borders. They are easily grown in any reasonable soil in sun and can be propagated by seed or division.

I have included all those likely to be available although they may be a little tall in ideal conditions. There seems to be confusion in their synonymity.

T. caroliniana *See* ***T. villosa***

T. lanceolata Rhizomatous spreading clump, to 40 cm (16 in), with almost sessile silvery leaves, and dense terminal spikes of flowers. Possibly too invasive for the border. E. Asia.

T. lupinoides (syn. *T. fabacea*) Similar to *T. lanceolata* and apparently confused with it, but taller to 90 cm (3 ft), with leaves on long petioles, and axillary flower spikes. Distinctly invasive. E. Asia.

T. mollis ✱ Clump-forming to 80 cm (30 in), with silvery-green leaves and fine upright spikes of soft yellow flowers. A first-rate non-invasive border plant, that looks good with dark strains of aquilegia, or similar deep purples or violets.

147 *Thermopsis mollis*

T. montana Running rhizomatous plant with scattered upright leafy stems and bright yellow flower-spikes. Definitely invasive, and probably best avoided.
T. villosa (syn *T. caroliniana*) Very similar to *T. mollis* with hairier leaves, and an equally good plant.

Thymus (*Labiatae*)

About 300 species of aromatic perennials mainly from around the Mediterranean, with a large number of cultivars, of low bushy or mat-forming habit, with small oval to linear leaves, sometimes coloured or variegated, and dense heads of tubular flowers amid leaf-like bracts, sometimes brightly coloured, in summer. They are generally very floriferous, making broad carpets of colour, in shades of pink to purple or white, excellent as a border edging. Some are colourful foliage plants. The more bushy varieties should be cut back hard after flowering to prevent them becoming straggly. They vary in hardiness and all need a sunny position in well-drained soil. They can be propagated by cuttings or the mat-formers by division.

In view of the large number of plants available I have excluded those better with the protection of a cold greenhouse.

T. caespititius compact mat, to 7 cm (2.8 in) in flower, flowers purplish-pink to white in short spikes.
T. camphoratus Spreading bush to 30 cm (1 ft), flowers white in rounded heads.
T. capitatus Compact bush, flowers purplish-pink. Very floriferous in nature, but needs a warm garden.
T. carnosus Cushion to 15 cm (6 in), leaves white to pale pink in short spikes.
T. x citriodorus Bushy to 20 cm (8 in), leaves narrow, lemon-scented, flower spikes pale lilac. Several excellent cultivars with more interesting leaves: 'Archers Gold', 'Aureus' 🏆 and 'Bertram Anderson' 🏆 all with deep yellow leaves, 'Argenteus' and 'Silver Queen' 🏆 leaves edged white, giving a silver effect, 'Doone Valley' flat mat, very dark green leaves flecked with gold, 'Golden King' and 'Golden Queen' gold-variegated, the former a more upright bush.
T. comosus Mat-forming, flowers in larger spikes.
T. doerfleri Mat-forming with very hairy leaves and purple flowers. 'Bressingham Pink' an improved cultivar with soft pink flowers.
T. herba-barona Low cushion to 15 cm (6 in), leaves caraway-scented, flowers in short spikes, pale purple.
T. leucotrichus Mat or low cushion to 6 cm (2.3 in), leaves downy, flowers purple amid purplish bracts. Slightly tender.
T. longicaulis loose mound to 10 cm (4 in), flowers pale to deep purple, variable.
T. mastichina ✱ ☼ Bushy to 20 cm (8 in), leaves silvery, flowers long, white, in abundant round heads. One of the most striking species that deserves to be grown more widely.

148 *Thymus mastichina*

T. neiceffii small bush, leaves linear, flowers soft pink.
T. pallasianum Low cushion to 15 cm (6 in), flowers pale pink with pinkish calyces.
T. polytrichus Mat-forming, leaves linear to ovate, usually hairy, flowers typically purple with purple-tinged bracts. Many popular improved hybrids and cultivars, more often found under *T. serpyllum*, of which the following are among the most distinct: 'Albus' pure white, 'Annie Hall' low, pale pink, 'Coccineus' 🏆 dark green, flowers dark red, 'Coccineus Major' larger-growing, 'Elfin' a compact mound with tiny leaves, 'Goldstream' dark leaves flecked with yellow, dark flowers, 'Minor' small-growing pink, 'Pink Chintz' 🏆 leaves hairy, flowers salmon-pink, 'Porlock' low cushion, pink, 'Rainbow Falls' leaves golden-variegated, flowers pale purple, 'Ruby Glow' leaves dark, flowers dark red, 'Russetings' leaves bronze-tinged, flowers purple, 'September' late-flowering pink, 'Snowdrift' good white,

'Vey' compact-growing salmon-pink.
T. pseudolanuginosus Mat-forming, leaves very hairy grey, flowers pale pink.
T. puleginoides Mat-forming, strongly aromatic, flowers purple in short spikes.
T. richardii Loose mat to 12 cm (4.7 in), leaves ovate, flowers purple in short spikes, subsp. *nitidus* (*T. nitidus*) narrower leaves and paler flowers.
T. serpyllum Similar to *T. polytrichus*, but probably rarely grown. Its many cultivars in catalogues are correctly referable to *T. polytrichus.*
T. vulgaris The commonest culinary thyme, bushy, leaves narrow grey-green, flowers pale to deep purple. Some more garden-worthy cultivars are 'Aureus' with gold variegated leaves, 'Erectus' more upright-growing, 'Silver Posie' silver-variegated, with paler lilac flowers.

Tiarella (*Saxifragaceae*)

A small genus of woodland perennials, spreading by stolons or clump-forming, with lobed leaves sometimes with bronze markings, and spikes of small flowers with narrow petals and prominent stamens. With their attractive leaves that sometimes colour in autumn, and dainty flowers, they are beautiful easily grown plants for moist shade, among shrubs or in the front of a border. They can be propagated by division or by seed.
T. cordifolia 🏆 Stoloniferous, to 25 cm (10 in), leaves broadly 5-lobed, toothed, sparsely hairy, usually stained with purple along the veins, flowers in dense spikes, white from pinkish buds, in late spring. A quietly attractive plant that can spread widely in good conditions. Recently some particularly beautiful cultivars and hybrids with even more ornamental leaves have been introduced, mainly from the USA: 'Eco Red Heart' ✸ ✿ leaves red-centred, flowers pink, 'Filigree Lace' a hybrid with *T. trifoliata*, leaves more deeply lobed, 'Glossy' exceptionally glossy leaves, white flowers, 'Laird of Skye' leaves deeply lobed, heavily mottled purple, 'Slick Rock' a mat of much smaller star-shaped leaves and white flowers.

149 *Tiarella cordifolia* 'Eco Red Heart'

T. polyphylla Similar in habit to *T. cordifolia*, leaves shallowly 5-lobed, hairy, flowers in loose spikes, nodding pink or white, from pink buds, in summer. 'Pink form' leaves strongly tinged with purple, flowers pink.
T. trifoliata Clump-forming, to 30 cm (1 ft), leaves trifoliate, leaflets 2–3-lobed, hairy, flowers white in spikes, in summer.
T. wherryi 🏆 Clump-forming, leaves longer than wide, 3-lobed, sharply toothed and pointed, tinged with purple, flowers in fairly dense spikes, pink-tinged especially in bud. One of the most appealing, but less strong-growing. 'Bronze Beauty' even better with an overall bronze suffusion.

Tolmiea (*Saxifragaceae*)

T. menziesii (Piggyback Plant) The only species, related to *Heuchera*, growing in similar woodland conditions, clump-forming to 50 cm (20 in), leaves shallowly palmately lobed, very hairy, on long petioles, flowers in one-sided spikes, greenish-purple. Interesting in its habit of forming plantlets along the leaf veins, and with fairly ornamental leaves, it is worth a place in a shady bed among shrubs.

Trachystemon (*Boraginaceae*)

T. orientalis The only species cultivated, a coarse shade-loving perennial close to *Brunnera* and rather tall in good conditions, with rough hairy leaves and loose heads of purplish-blue flowers.

Tradescantia (*Commelinaceae*) Spiderwort

Some 70 species of low spreading perennials, to 60 cm (2 ft), many only suitable for the greenhouse, but several useful hybrids and cultivars for the border, with dense clumps of iris-like leaves, and terminal or axillary clusters of flowers with three equal widely open petals arising from twin bracts, in summer. The plants always seem a little leafy for the number of flowers at any one time, but they have a good range of colours and are easily grown in sun or light shade. They can be propagated by division in spring.
T.* x *andersoniana (syn. *T. virginiana*) Most of the hardy plants available come into this complex. All have glossy linear-lanceolate leaves to 30 cm (1 ft) long from a dense branching rhizomatous rootstock, and single flowers as described or occasionally double: 'Alba' white single' Blue Stone' blue, 'Caerulea Plena' double blue, 'Innocence' pure white, 'Iris Pritchard' white faintly tinged blue, 'Isis' 🏆 deep blue, 'J.C. Weguelin' 🏆 pale blue, 'Karminglut' reddish-carmine, 'Osprey' 🏆 pure white with a bluish centre, 'Pauline' pale pink, 'Purewell Giant' deep reddish-purple, 'Purple Dome' purple, 'Valour' purplish-red, 'Zwanenburg Blue' large-flowered, pure blue.

Tricyrtis (*Liliaceae*/*Convallariaceae*) (Toad Lilies)

Some 15 species of clump-forming perennials, mainly

from Japan and Taiwan, with erect or semi-prostrate stems, alternate narrow pointed leaves, and axillary or terminal flowers in heads or solitary, from mid-summer to autumn. In most species the six petals are widely spreading, often heavily spotted, with a centre protruding well above the petals, composed of a very large 3-lobed stigma and six long filaments with large anthers. The very unusual flower shape and heavy spotting of most species make this a most attractive genus for the garden. They are easily grown in rich moist soil in light to heavy shade, among shrubs or in a shady border, combining well with the late-flowering anemones and *Cyclamen hederifolium*. They can be grown from seed sown as fresh as possible, or by division in spring.

T. flava To 30 cm (1 ft), leaves with darker blotching, flowers axillary, yellow with red spotting and a yellow eye. Uncommon but not difficult.

T. formosana 🏆 To 60 cm (2 ft), leaves glossy dark green to 12 cm (4.7 in), stems upright, branching, flowers in loose terminal clusters, white, spotted purplish-pink. *T. formosana* var. *stolonifera* ('Stolonifera Group') spreading more widely at the root, usually more purple. An excellent easy species.

T. hirta ✱ To 80 cm (30 in), without stolons, leaves downy, pale green, flowers axillary, larger than *T. formosana*, white, heavily spotted purple. Other cultivars usually referred to this species include 'Alba' unspotted greenish-white flowers with pink stamens, 'Lilac Towers' to 60 cm (2 ft), lilac flowers all the way up attractively arching stems, 'Miyazaki' similar in habit to the last but taller, white flowers spotted lilac, 'Variegata' similar, leaves yellow-edged, 'White Towers' ✱ a beautiful plant, like 'Lilac Towers' but pure white. All are excellent plants in a shady bed.

T. latifolia To 60 cm (2 ft), upright, leaves broad, dark-blotched, flowers yellow with purple spotting, in the upper leaf axils, soon after mid-summer.

T. macrantha To 30 cm (1 ft), stems prostrate or low-arching, brown-hairy, leaves ovate to 10 cm (4 in), flowers large, bell-shaped, yellow spotted purple within, in the upper leaf axils. Subsp. *macranthopsis* has longer stems, narrower leaves, and paler flowers. Although most attractive and unusual, their prostrate habit and large nodding flowers make these difficult to grow well. They are best planted to hang downwards so that their flowers will not be spoilt by the weather.

T. macropoda Upright to 70 cm (28 in), leaves broad, flowers in terminal clusters, white spotted with purplish-pink.

T. ohsumiensis Resembling *T. flava*, stems very leafy, flowers larger, to 5 cm (2 in) wide, pale yellow with reddish spots. An easy species that tolerates sun as long as it is moist.

T. perfoliata Low arching habit, stems to 50 cm (20 in), glossy leaves clasping the stems, flowers resembling *T. flava*, but upright-facing with white anthers.

***T.* 'Sinonome'** ('Shimone') Stoloniferous, late flowering, flowers white with reddish-purple spotting. An easy new cultivar.

Trientalis (*Primulaceae*)

4 species of rhizomatous perennials of which two are occasionally available, with a whorl of simple leaves on upright stems, and starry flowers on slender pedicels in the leaf axils. They are charming, but rarely grown plants, needing woodland conditions with rich acid soil, in which they can spread widely if suited. They can be grown from fresh seed.

T. borealis (syn. *T. americana*) To 25 cm (10 in), leaves lanceolate, pointed, to 10 cm (4 in) long, flowers white, 1.5 cm (0.6 in) wide, in summer.

T. europaea To 20 cm (8 in), leaves obovate, to 6 cm (2.3 in), flowers to 1.8 cm wide, white sometimes flushed pink. Var. *rosea* has flowers more convincingly pink.

Trifolium (*Leguminosae*) (Clover)

The clovers are a large genus of mainly invasive perennials unsuitable for the garden, except for the small *T. uniflorum*, more suitable for the rock garden, and some cultivars of the invasive species which are worth considering for their attractive leaves. They mainly have typical trifoliate leaves and clover-like heads of small pea flowers. They may be propagated by division.

T. pratense The red clover. 'Susan Smith' less invasive, attractive leaves netted with gold veining.

T. repens The invasive white clover. 'Aureum' has large golden-veined leaflets, and can be too vigorous, 'Purpurascens' has 4 dark maroon leaflets, less dramatic than 'Purpurascens Quadrifolia' in which the leaflets have a well-defined green margin, 'Wheatfen' 3 purple leaflets with no green margin, less strong-growing.

T. rubens A striking but somewhat invasive clover, with exceptionally large spike-like of deep reddish-pink flowers.

Trollius (*Ranunculaceae*)

The Globe flowers are a genus of about 20 species of herbaceous perennials with clumps or rosettes of lobed or divided leaves, and branching stems bearing single large, or almost globular double buttercup flowers, with large sepals and a cluster of small petals, in shades of white, deep yellow, or orange, in late spring and early summer. They are mainly from Eastern Asia, except *T. europaeus*. They are very beautiful, and are generally easy to grow given rich soil and plenty of moisture at all times, making excellent plants for pond margins or in moist borders, in sun or light shade, associating splendidly with the earlier candelabra primulas. They can be propagated by division in spring or autumn or by seed sown as fresh as possible.

I have included most of the species and cultivars available although a few may be a little large in ideal conditions.

T. acaulis To 25 cm (10 in), leaves 5-lobed, toothed, solitary

flowers deep yellow, single, to 5 cm (2 in) across, on leafy stems, opening before the leaves are fully developed. A delightful dwarf.
T. asiaticus To 60 cm (2 ft), similar to *T. europaeus* and sometimes confused with it, the leaflets finely lobed and toothed, and flowers bowl-shaped, deep yellow to orange.
T. chinensis A tall species, leaves 5-lobed, finely toothed, flowers golden-yellow, cup-shaped with a central cluster of long protruding petals.
T. x cultorum Hybrids of *T. asiaticus, T. chinensis*, and *T. europaeus*, sometimes to be found under those species, clump-forming to 80 cm (30 in) or occasionally more, with lobed leaves and variable flowers: 'Alabaster' ✱ flowers soft yellowish cream, one of the most attractive, 'Canary Bird' lemon yellow, 'Earliest of All' very early, deep yellow, 'Fire Globe' globular deep orange, 'Golden Queen' 🏆 large, globular, orange, 'Goldquelle' 🏆 late-flowering deep yellow, 'Helios' early, deep yellow, 'Lemon Queen' large, pale yellow, 'Orange Princess' 🏆 very tall plant, orange, 'Pritchard's Giant' similar to the last, 'Superbus' late, pale yellow 🏆.
T. europaeus To 70 cm (28 in), similar to *T. asiaticus* and sometimes confused with it, a larger plant, leaflets deeply toothed, flowers paler lemon-yellow. An easy and beautiful plant for the garden.
T. pumilus Similar to *T. acaulis*, leaves all basal, flowers smaller, with darker exterior to the sepals.
T. yunnanensis To 60 cm (2 ft), leaves deeply 3–5-lobed, flowers large, opening flat, deep yellow, with a central cluster of 1 cm (0.4 in) long petals with deeper orange tips.

Tulbaghia (*Liliaceae/Alliaceae*)

A small genus of clump-forming rhizomatous or bulbous perennials from S. Africa, to 60 cm (2 ft), with narrow garlic-scented, often glaucous, onion-like leaves, and abundant umbels of long-tubed starry flowers, sometimes with an obvious central corona, on upright slender stems in late summer and autumn. They are popularly looked on as greenhouse plants but are much more hardy than is generally recognized; the most widely grown *T. violacea* has flourished and increased for many years in a sunny bed in well-drained soil in my garden. They are beautiful late-flowering plants, their only fault being the very unpleasant smell of the foliage if bruised in any way. They can be grown from seed or divided in spring.
T. cepacea Included in *T. violacea* by some authorities, under this name I grow a very similar and equally hardy plant with soft purplish-pink flowers.
T. cominsii Small species to 25 cm (10 in), with umbels of white flowers with a little purple staining on the tube and a purple eye. Early experience suggests it is worthy of trial in the open garden.
T. natalensis To 30 cm (1 ft), but often less in the garden, it has green grassy leaves, and white flowers with a conspicuous central orange corona. This has proved as hardy as *T. violacea*.
T. violacea ✱ To 60 cm (2 ft), dense clumps of onion-like grey-green leaves and large umbels of pale pinkish-violet flowers carried well above them. *T.* v. *pallida* is similar with very pale violet flowers.

150 *Tulbaghia violacea*

U

Umbilicus (*Crassulaceae*)

A small genus of succulent-leaved perennials, of which the native Penny Wort is the only one regularly grown in gardens.
U. rupestris (Penny Wort) Small clumps of round succulent leaves with a central depression and spike of greenish-white tubular flowers on stems to 40 cm (16 in). Its interesting leaves make it worth growing, especially as a wall plant, in any well-drained soil in sun or partial shade.

Urospermum (*Compositae*)

U. dalechampii The only perennial species, spreading clump-former to 40 cm (16 in), hairy prostrate or arching stems, grey-green, simple or pinnatifid, dandelion-like leaves, and 5 cm (2 in) wide, lemon-yellow, semi-double daisy flowers in summer. It makes an attractive spreading mound, with flowers of a pleasing shade of yellow, and is easy in well-drained soil in full sun. It can be raised from seed, or rooted stems can be detached in spring. Med.

Uvularia (*Liliaceae/Convallariaceae*)

A small genus of N. American woodland plants, rhizomatous perennials with simple alternate leaves on thin upright stems and long pendent, pale or deep yellow bell-shaped flowers, often with twisted petals (petals), in spring. They are most elegant plants for moist humus-rich soil, preferably acid, in full or partial shade, ideal for growing among shade-loving shrubs, in the company of trilliums and erythroniums. They can be propagated from fresh seed or possibly by division of established clumps, although these are better left undisturbed.

U. caroliniana Usually to 20 cm (8 in), downy stems, bright green oval leaves, and slender pale yellow flowers. It runs quite freely in good conditions.

U. grandiflora 🏆 The most robust and widely grown, to 60 cm (2 ft), leaves oval clasping the stem, 5 cm (2 in) long deep yellow pendent flowers with attractively twisted petals. One of the most beautiful of all woodlanders. *U.* v. *pallida* ✱ is offered by nurseries, and has pale primrose flowers.

151 *Uvularia grandiflora pallida*

U. perfoliata Similar to *U. grandiflora*, but usually a little shorter with smaller pale yellow flowers.

U. sessilifolia Similar to *U. caroliniana*, but without any pubescence, and with leaves glaucous or paler beneath.

V

Valeriana (*Valerianaceae*)

A large genus of shrubs and perennials, several of which are widely grown. They have opposite simple, or divided leaves, and dense clusters of small tubular flowers, white or in shades of pink. *V. officinalis* and some other species are too tall to consider here, but there are few low-growing species suitable for the front of the border, in well-drained soil in a sunny position. They are sometimes short-lived.

V. arizonica Mound to 30 cm (1 ft), basal leaves long-stalked, ovate, simple or pinnately lobed, flowers in dense heads, white or pink. S. USA.

V. montana Creeping mat to 40 cm (16 in), leaves ovate, usually simple, flowers in rounded heads, pink, white, or lilac. S. Europe.

V. saxatilis similar to *V. montana* with oblanceolate leaves and looser clusters of white flowers. S. Europe.

Vancouveria (*Berberidaceae*)

Three species of creeping rhizomatous perennials from N.W. America, resembling epimediums, with similar biternate divided leaves and sprays of dainty nodding flowers. They are easily grown in reasonably moist shady beds, making useful ground cover among shrubs. They can be raised from seed sown fresh, or by division.

V. chrysantha (syn. *V. hexandra* var. *aurea*) Similar to *V. hexandra*, but leaves evergreen and flowers yellow.

V. hexandra To 30 cm (1 ft), leaves deciduous, with 5–9 leaflets, flowers white in large loose sprays. An easy plant that can spread widely in good moist soil, but is less invasive in dry conditions.

V. planipetala Similar to *V. hexandra*, but leaves more leathery, evergreen, and darker, and white flowers tinged with lavender.

Verbascum (*Scrophulariaceae*)

A large genus of mainly biennials with a few perennials and shrubs, typically with attractive large rosettes of green or more often grey to white leaves, and striking upright spikes of flowers, most often in shades of yellow. Many are tall plants and I have excluded all the useful biennials, which have considerable impact in the border or wild garden. The following are the smaller perennial species. A few need special treatment, particularly as wall plants, but generally they are easy in well-drained soil in full sun. They are propagated by seed, or the named cultivars can be grown from root cuttings.

V. chaixii Clumps of green rosettes of hairy, ovate, shallowly toothed leaves, stems sometimes branched, to 80 cm (30 in) but frequently less, flowers yellow with purple filaments. Europe. 'Album' similar with dense spikes of white flowers with purple eyes. Very attractive plants which seed freely and come true.

152 *Verbascum chaixii* 'Album'

V. dumulosum ✱ Sub-shrubby to 20 cm (8 in), white-felted leaves and short spikes of large yellow flowers with some red in the centre. A beautiful plant with almost white leaves and attractive flowers in early summer. It will not thrive in damp gardens unless planted on its side in a wall, the ideal site in which it seems to be a good perennial. Turkey.
***V.* 'Golden Wings'** (syn. *Celsioverbascum* 'Golden Wings') Rounded sub-shrub, small green toothed leaves, short spikes of yellow flowers with deep orange anthers. Easier to grow than *V. dumulosum*, in well-drained soil.
***V.* 'Helen Johnson'** ✱ A remarkably perennial cultivar that can attain 1 m (3 ft) in height, but I find is usually around 60 cm (2 ft), with grey-green downy leaves and long spikes of peach-coloured flowers all through the summer.
***V.* 'Letitia'** (*V. dumulosum* x *V. spinosum*) Rounded sub-shrub to 25 cm (10 in), small grey-green leaves, very abundant spikes of comparatively large flowers over a long period. Another shrublet needing particularly good drainage.
V. pestallozae Very similar to *V. dumulosum*, but with brownish hairs, more difficult and uncommon, but worth trying as a wall plant. Turkey.

Verbena (*Verbenaceae*)

A large genus of annuals, perennials and subshrubs, many of which are of borderline hardiness, but are widely used as container plants on patios, or as 'fillers' in the border. This particularly applies to the low spreading cultivars which flower all through the summer and have a happy knack of scrambling through other plants. They make spreading carpets of branching stems with small toothed or lobed leaves and dense flat-heads of small flowers in summer. Some of these will survive mild winters in Britain and are invaluable perennials in warmer climates. They are easily propagated from cuttings throughout the summer.
V. corymbosa Spreading rhizomatous species to 70 cm (28 in), with long, branching, upright and prostrate stems, ovate leaves, and flat-heads of pale purple flowers. This is remarkably hardy and can cover a lot of ground. S. Am.
V.* x *hybrida There are many complex hybrids in the group, generally making low mats of leafy branching stems, smothered with an endless succession of flattish heads of flowers in shades of pink to purple or white. They vary in hardiness and should be propagated regularly and young plants overwintered under glass. 'La France' ✱ lavender-blue, is the most vigorous and hardy, but the following are some of the most popular, 'Aveyron' bright pink, vigorous, 'Carousel' purple and white striped, 'Gravetye' pale purple, low mat-forming, 'Hidcote Purple' an excellent deep bluish-purple, 'Huntsman' vivid red, 'Lawrence Johnston' 🏆 vivid scarlet, 'Loveliness' excellent deep lavender, 'Silver Ann' 🏆 a striking combination of pale and deep pink, 'Sissinghurst' 🏆 reddish-pink, vigorous, 'White Knight' and 'White Cascade' white.

153 *Verbena* 'Hidcote Purple' & *V. peruviana* 'Alba'

V. peruviana (syn. *V. chamaedrifolia*) A low mat with small leaves and deep crimson flower heads. 'Alba' similar in habit, flowers pure white.
V. rigida Clump-forming with rigid, upright or spreading, branching stems, with sessile toothed leaves, and terminal heads of deep purple flowers. S. Am.
V. tenera Similar to *V. peruviana*, with purple flower heads in late summer. In 'Mahonettii' the petals are conspicuously margined in white.
V. tenuisecta Similar to *V. tenera* but flowers variable in colour from white to shades of blue to purple.

Veronica (*Scrophulariaceae*)

A large genus of mainly perennial herbs, variable in habit, from small-leaved mats of low to medium height, to larger-leaved upright-growing clump formers, some of which are near to our height limit. The flowers are usually 4-petalled, small in dense terminal spikes, or larger, solitary, in the leaf axils, in a range of colours from white to pink to pure deep blue, usually in summer. The mat and cushion-forming plants are excellent as foreground planting in the border, where they will provide carpets of colour for several weeks. The taller species and cultivars make substantial clumps with striking flower spikes in the middle of the border. They are generally easy to grow in a sunny situation, as long as drainage is reasonably good. They can be propagated by division in autumn or spring, or the species can be raised from seed.
V. armena Low mound to 15 cm (6 in), leaves small, divided, flowers deep blue in 2–5 cm (0.8–2 in) spikes. An easy small-growing cushion. W. Russia.
V. austriaca Clump-forming to 30 cm (1 ft), with erect and semi-erect stems, leaves variable, usually narrow and divided, flower spikes bright blue, often paired. C. Europe–W. Asia. 'Ionian Skies' ✸ mat-forming, very floriferous, pale blue. Subsp. *teucrium* similar but more upright-growing, with several cultivars. S. Europe. 'Blue Fountain' to 60 cm (2 ft), bright blue, 'Crater Lake Blue' 🏆 (see plate 1) compact to 30 cm (1 ft), bright blue, 'Kapitan' gentian blue, 'Royal Blue' 🏆 50 cm (20 in) bushy, deep blue, 'Shirley Blue' 🏆 25 , cm (10 in) bright blue. All are excellent plants to provide genuine blue colour in the front of the summer border, easily increased by cuttings or division.

154 *Veronica austriaca* 'Ionian Skies' & *Lupinus varicolor*

V. beccabunga Spreading mat with prostrate rooting stems, thick glossy ovate leaves, and axillary spikes of pale to mid-blue flowers. It thrives in pond margins or other very wet conditions.
V. caucasica Clump to 25 cm (10 in), finely cut leaves, loose spikes of small white flowers veined with blue.
V. chamaedrys (Germander Speedwell) Spreading rhizomatous mat, with upright and prostrate stems, leaves lanceolate or ovate, simple, paired spikes of bright blue flowers with a white eye in late summer. It can become invasive. Europe, Siberia. 'Miffy Brute' (Variegata) is similar but with leaves beautifully margined with cream.
V. cinerea 🏆 Low mat, narrow white-felted leaves, deep blue flowers with white eyes. A very attractive species for well-drained soil.
V. exaltata Similar to *V. longifolia* but earlier flowering, hairy toothed leaves and narrow pale blue spikes.
V. fruticans Sub-shrubby mound to 20 cm (8 in), leaves narrow, shallowly toothed, flowers deep blue with a reddish eye, 1.5 cm (0.6 in) in diameter in short dense spikes. Reliable for the border front. W. Europe.
V. fruticulosa Similar to the last with wider leaves and pink flowers. S.W. Europe
V. gentianoides 🏆 Carpets of rosettes of glossy dark green oval to lanceolate leaves, and upright leafy stems to 30–40 cm (12–16 in), with long terminal spikes of pale to deep blue flowers, usually with darker blue veining. A fine species making a spreading mat of good foliage with very attractive flowers. There are several good cultivars; 'Alba' white faintly tinged blue, 'Nana' compact, to 10 cm (4 in), pale blue flowers, 'Tissington White' narrower leaves, flowers white with greyish veining. 'Variegata' ✸ ☼ leaves boldly margined with cream, an excellent foliage plant with attractive flowers.

155 *Veronica gentianoides*

V. liwanensis Low mound to 15 cm (6 in), leaves lanceolate to ovate, flowers comparatively large, mid-blue. In large spikes. W. Russia.

V. longifolia Tall upright clumps to 80 cm (30 in) but often less, leaves narrow, whorled or opposite, dense terminal spikes of pale lavender flowers. Europe. There are several cultivars; 'Alba' tall, white, 'Blauer Sommer' and 'Blaureisin' vigorous bright blue, the latter more bushy, 'Rosea' pale pink, 'Schneereisin' long spikes, deep blue. All are good plants for the middle of the border.

V. nummularia Mat-forming with small broad leaves and heads of blue or pink flowers. S.W. Europe.

V. oltensis Similar to *V. liwanensis* but leaves shorter and pinnately divided.

V. pectinata Mat to 15 cm (6 in), leaves hairy, toothed, flowers deep blue in dense erect spikes, terminal and axillary. An easy and reliable carpet of blue. Balkans, Asia Minor.

V. peduncularis Mat-forming, prostrate rooting stems, leaves small, toothed, tinged with purple, flowers in loose clusters, pale blue to white. 'Georgia Blue' ✸ a superb recent introduction, a wide spreading mat of purple-tinged leaves, smothered in abundant deep blue flowers in spring and early summer, and occasionally later. W. Asia.

156 *Veronica peduncularis* 'Georgia Blue'

V. prostrata (syn. *V. rupestris*) Mat-forming to 15 cm (6 in), leaves ovate, hairy, toothed, dark green, flowers very variable blue to pink in dense upright spikes, early to late summer. Europe. One of the best carpeters with several cultivars; 'Alba' white, 'Blauspiegel' bright blue, 'Blue Sheen' pale blue, 'Lodden Blue' bright blue, 'Mrs Holt' a good soft pink, 'Nana' compact-growing, bright blue, 'Rosea' pale pink, 'Silver Queen' silvery blue, 'Spode Blue' deep blue, 'Trehane' leaves golden, flowers blue, an unusual combination, probably best in light shade to avoid burning.

V. reptans Dense low mat with small rounded leaves and short spikes of 3–6 pink flowers. Frequently found in lists as *V. repens*. S.W. Europe.

V. saturejoides Low mat-forming with oblanceolate hairy leaves, and spikes of bright blue flowers with reddish eyes. Balkans.

V. schmidtiana Low cushion to 20 cm (8 in), deeply toothed or divided leaves, loose spikes of many purplish-blue flowers with darker veining in late summer. Japan. 'Nana' more compact flowers purer blue, 'Nana Rosea' similar, pink flowers. All are easy front-of-the-border plants.

V. spicata Dense clump of 5 cm (2 in) long, narrow downy leaves, with long upright spikes to 40 cm (16 in) of good blue flowers. Europe. Subsp. *incana* (syn *V. incana*) 🏆 outstanding plant with white-felted leaves and stems and clear blue flowers. There are several excellent cultivars, first class plants for the front to middle of the border: 'Alba' pure white, 'Barcarolle' (Baccarole) rose-pink, 'Blue Fox' tall, deep blue, Erika compact, deep pink, 'Heidikind' short deep reddish-pink, 'Icicle' white, 'Red Fox' deep reddish-pink, 'Romiley Purple' deep reddish-purple, 'Saraband' silver-grey leaves, deep violet-blue, 'Silver Carpet' 15 cm (6 in), leaves silver-grey, dark blue, 'Wendy' looser habit, grey leaves, blue.

V. telephiifolia Dense mat of small, rounded leaves, flowers pale blue in dense spikes. Caucasus.

V. wormskjoldii (syn. *V. stelleri*) Clump-forming with erect stems to 15 cm (6 in) bearing deep blue flower spikes. N. Am.

Vinca (*Apocynaceae*) (Periwinkle)

Six species of trailing evergreen perennials, with dark green, entire, opposite leaves, and funnel-shaped flowers with spreading petals in the leaf axils, on long shoots that root at the nodes and spread widely, making dense ground cover in most soils, but generally too invasive to associate with small perennials. Take care in their positioning as they are difficult to remove when well established. They can be increased by division or by cuttings.

V. difformis Resembling *V. major*, it is the most tender and early-flowering species with pale blue flowers. It is not widely grown, and is less invasive.

V. herbacea Rarely grown herbaceous species, otherwise similar to *V. difformis*.

V. major The most rampant and invasive species, with dark green, ovate, hairy-margineed leaves and soft violet-blue flowers. *V. m. alba* similar, white, subsp. *hirsuta* narrower leaves with hairy petioles. There are several cultivars, of which the following are some of the most popular: 'Jason Hill' leaves dark green with pointed lobes, dark violet with a white eye, 'Maculata' leaves with a central yellow blotch, pale blue, 'Oxyloba' (var. *oxyloba*) narrower pointed leaves, dark violet, 'Reticulata' leaves veined with yellow early in the season, 'Variegata' 🏆 robust, leaves strikingly margined with cream. It is an excellent foliage plant especially for cutting.

V. minor Similar in habit to *V. major* but with slightly more slender shoots and smaller leaves and flowers. It is possibly less invasive but can cover a lot of ground. *F. alba* has pure white flowers. There are many cultivars of which the following are readily available; 'Alba Variegata' leaves margined yellow, white, 'Argenteovariegata' 🏆 leaves cream-variegated, blue, 'Atropurpurea' 🏆 deep reddish-purple, 'Aureovariegata' leaves yellow-variegated, 'Azurea Flore Pleno' 🏆 double blue, 'Burgundy' reddish-purple, 'Gertrude Jekyll' 🏆 leaves small, small white from pink buds, 'Gruner Teppich' robust leafy ground cover with few flowers, 'La Grave' 🏆 large violet-blue, 'Multiplex' double reddish-purple, 'Silver Service' leaves narrow, white-variegated, double blue.

Viola (*Violaceae*)

A large and complicated genus with many species, including the ever-popular pansies violas and violettas with a huge range of named cultivars. Many of the species are too small or difficult to consider as border perennials, and a comparatively small proportion of the cultivars make reliably perennial plants without constant propagation and care. Gardeners interested in these can see and choose a remarkable selection at specialist nurseries and on their exhibits. In the descriptions below I have concentrated on the more robust and perennial species and a small personal selection of some cultivars that I have found reliable in the garden. These grow best in rich but well-drained soil in partial shade along the edge of borders or among shrubs. Some will thrive in full sun as long as they never become too dry.

The species can be grown from fresh seed preferably sown as soon as ripe, and they and the named cultivars can be increased by cuttings taken during summer, early enough for them to become well established before winter.

V. 'Belmont Blue' ('Boughton Blue') ✱ Pale lavender with darker veining. A superb vigorous perennial, close to *V. cornuta*.

V. bertolonii Close to *V. gracilis*, pale violet, reasonably easy in well-drained soil, seeding itself around moderately. S. Europe.

V. biflora Small with bright yellow flowers veined with brown in the centre, often in pairs. Runs about in deep shade. N. hemisphere.

V. 'Bowles Black' Small almost black flowers, seeds around freely.

V. 'Coeur d'Alsace' Small plant with small rose-pink flowers.

V. cornuta 🏆 (See plate 36) Robust mat with pale violet flowers all through the summer. Several named forms and many hybrids. The best of all for the garden, superb fully perennial plants for the front of borders in sun or shade, frequently self-sowing freely, and tending to scramble into other plants. S. Europe. 'Alba Group' equally valuable and easy, pure white, coming true from seed. 'Lilacina Group' similar soft lilac, 'Minor' much more compact, about half the size of the type, it grows equally well but frequently hybridizes with the type, producing progeny of gradually increasing size. 'Minor Alba' is the white form. 'Purpurea Group' and 'Rosea' are similar, purple and pink respectively.

157 *Viola cornuta* 'Lilacina' & *Centaurea maritima alba*

158 *Viola cornuta* 'Minor' blue & white

V. corsica A rare but easy plant with large deep lavender pansy flowers, maintaining itself well in well-drained soil by self-sowing almost to excess. Corsica.

V. cucullata (syn. *V. obliqua*) clumps of comparatively large rounded glossy leaves and pale violet flowers with a darker violet veined centre. Easy in a shady place, but close to and

possibly confused with *V. soraria* and *V. septentrionalis*. N. Am.
V. dissecta Small clumps of pinnately divided leaves and white flowers with bluish-purple veining. *V. d. chaerophylloides f. eizanensis* (syn. *V. eizanensis*) is similar with larger leaves and pink flowers. Both grow well in shade. Japan.
V. elatior ✱ Upright bushy to 30 cm (1 ft), leaves lanceolate, toothed, flowers pale lavender with deeper veining in the throat, axillary in long succession. The only easy shrubby violet, seeds freely in shade or full sun. C. Europe–W. Asia.
V. 'Freckles' *See* ***V. sororia***
V. gracilis Similar to *V. bertolonii* and needing good drainage. Balkans
***V.* 'Haslemere'** *See* **'Nellie Britton'**
V. hederacea Mat-forming with prostrate rooting stems, bearing small rounded leaves and scattered blue and white flowers with the upper petals pointing back. It has a reputation for tenderness but has survived many winters in my garden in a warm sheltered spot. S. Australia.
***V.* 'Huntercombe Purple'** 🏆 Robust mat, flowers elongated, deep violet-purple with a pale eye.
***V.* 'Irish Molly'** Vigorous, flowers golden-bronze, darker above.
***V.* 'Jackanapes'** 🏆 Strong-growing, flowers brownish-purple above, deep golden-yellow below, with dark central veining.

159 *Viola* 'Jackanapes'

V. labradorica *See* ***V. riviniana***
***V.* 'Little David'** Vigorous, flowers pale cream, a little darker than 'Moonlight'.
***V.* 'Maggie Mott'** Taller-growing, flowers mauve with cream centre.
***V.* 'Martin'** Deep bluish-violet, centre cream.
***V.* 'Molly Sanderson'** Like 'Bowles Black with much larger flowers. It is spectacular but does not seem as strong as one would wish.'
***V.* 'Moonlight'** 🏆 Similar to 'Little David' with larger flowers.
***V.* 'Nellie Britton'** ('Haslemere') Resembling *V. cornuta* with reddish-mauve darker-veined flowers.
V. papilionacea Close to *V. sororia* and should probably be included in it, similar to *V. cucullata* with longer hairless leaves which may conceal the flowers, violet with a white centre. More commonly grown as 'Albiflora' (*V. priceana*) white with blue veining. Their naming is muddled but they are all easy plants in moist shade. N. Am.
V. pedatifida Small clumps of finely divided leaves, deep violet flowers in long succession. Another very freely seeding species. N. Am.
V. riviniana The Wood violet is rosette-forming with many laterals that root down, forming an extensive carpet, and small dark violet flowers. Usually grown in the form 'Purpurea' with deep purple leaves, one of the most popular violas under the name *V. labradorica* 'Purpurea'. Although the leaves and flowers are attractive it can be quite invasive in good soils. Europe.
V. septentrionalis Similar to *V. papilionacea*, with coarsely toothed leaves and flowers varying from pale lavender to deep lilac, white-bearded in the throat. N. Am.
V. sororia Similar to *V. papilionacea* and probably including it, with hairy leaves, and violet flowers with a white eye. 'Freckles' ✱ should probably be included here, an intriguing reliable plant with white flowers heavily freckled with blue spots. N. Am.
V. tricolor (The Wild Pansy) A freely seeding plant in well-drained soil, with small flowers varying between blue and yellow or bicoloured with the upper petals blue and lower yellow or white. Although so small it often seeds so freely that it maintains a carpet. Europe.
V. yezoensis Slowly spreading rhizomatous mat, leaves ovate, bluntly-toothed, flowers white striped purple. Japan.

W

Wahlenbergia
(*Campanulaceae*)

A genus of annuals and perennials resembling campanulas, mainly from Australasia and S. Africa. Most are too small to consider here, but there are one or two species that are worth considering for the border, clump-forming perennials with narrow lanceolate leaves, and loose sprays of lavender bell-shaped flowers on slender branching stems, over a remarkably long time in summer. They are of borderline hardiness, but *W. ceracea* has survived several mild winters in my garden. It is easily raised from seed, and indeed produces abundant self-sown seedlings.

W. ceracea As described above, and similar to the next. S. Australia.
W. undulata Descriptions of this plant are very similar to the above but it is taller with slightly larger flowers. Excellent for mild gardens and worth considering as an 'annual' in colder situations.

Waldsteinia (*Rosaceae*)

A small genus of creeping rhizomatous perennials with glossy, semi-evergreen, strawberry-like leaves, and solitary or clustered yellow flowers with five spreading petals, in summer. They make fair carpeting plants for sun or shade but do not flower as freely as one might wish.
W. fragarioides 15 cm (6 in) Clump of toothed 3-lobed leaves, clusters of yellow flowers 1-2 cm across in early summer.
W. geoides Similar, with 5-lobed coarsely toothed leaves, and 20 cm (8 in) stems.
W. ternata The only widely grown species, making an extensive mat of 3-lobed leaves, with 20 cm (8 in) stems bearing loose sprays of 1.5 cm (0.6 in) wide bright yellow flowers. A vigorous ground cover which will grow in quite dry shade.

Z

Zaluzianskya (*Scrophulariaceae*)

A genus of a few S. African annuals and perennials, the few in cultivation having sticky, aromatic, toothed leaves and plentiful loose sprays of white flowers with deep crimson on the reverse. They are doubtfully hardy, only surviving the mildest winters in Britain, but easily propagated from cuttings and rapidly making substantial cushions from overwintered cuttings. They are very attractive plants for warm gardens, with their remarkable crimson buds opening to pure white flowers.
Z. katerinae The plant I have under this name is as described, making a 20 cm (8 in) high mound of grey-green leaves and flowering for several months.
Z. ovata This is very similar. I suspect they are in fact identical, with one misnamed.

Zauschneria (*Onagraceae*)

A genus of probably four species of sub-shrubby or mat-forming perennials from S. USA, placed by some botanists in Epilobium, and by others into one species *Z. californica*. They have small undivided leaves, usually grey-green and downy, and loose heads or spikes of long tubular flower with four spreading lobes, normally vivid orange red, in late summer to autumn. They are quite easy in well-drained soil in the hottest place available and are brilliant plants for late colour. They can be in creased from cuttings, and may set viable seed in a hot summer.

160 *Zauschneria* 'Dublin' & *Lobelia laxiflora*

Z. californica Upright bushy species with grey-green leaves, and 3–4 cm (1.2–1.6 in) long flowers. Subsp. *latifolia* (syn. *Z. arizonica*) a larger plant with wider leaves, in my experience is less free-flowering. 'Albiflora' ✱ valuable white-flowered form which contrasts well with any of the others. 'Dublin' 🏆 small bright green leaves and darker red flowers. It is probably the hardiest. 'Olbrich Silver' ✱ a remarkable form with white-felted leaves contrasting brilliantly with its large red flowers. It is relatively untried and may not survive much winter wet. 'Solidarity Pink' pleasing soft pink flowers, but less easy to grow and flower well.
Z. cana (syn. *Z. microphylla*) Upright clump with tiny grey leaves and long slender flowers. Usually seen as 'Cedric Morris' ✱ ☼ a robust form that thrives in a warm sheltered place.
Z. garrettii Similar to *Z. californica*, lower-growing, grey-green ovate leaves, similar flowers. It quickly forms a broad mound and flowers well.
Z. septentrionalis ✱ Recently introduced, a splendid low mat-forming species, with broadly lanceolate leaves, silvery-grey when dry but becoming greener in wet periods, typical vivid red flowers.

Appendix 1

Genera Containing Shade-loving Plants

Adonis
Anemone
Anemonella
Anemonopsis
Asarum
Astilbe
Astrantia
Borago
Boykinia
Calceolaria
Caltha
Cardamine
Chelidonium
Clintonia
Codonopsis
Corydalis
Deinanthe
Dicentra
Digitalis
Diphylleia
Disporopsis
Eomecon
Gentiana
Gillenia
Glaucidium
Hacquetia
Helleborus
Helonias
Heloniopsis
Hepatica
Heuchera
Heucherella
Hosta
Hylomecon
Iris
Jeffersonia
Jovellana
Kirengoshoma
Liriope
Lithophragma
Luzuriaga
Meconopsis
Meehania
Mertensia
Mimulus
Mitella
Omphalodes
Ophiopogon
Ourisia
Oxalis
Paris
Patrinia
Persicaria
Philesia
Phlox
Podophyllum
Polygonatum
Primula
Pteridophyllum
Ranunculus
Ranzania
Rehmannia
Reineckia
Rohdea
Romanzoffia
Roscoea
Sanguinaria
Saxifraga
Stylophorum
Tanakaea
Thalictrum
Tiarella
Tolmiea
Tricyrtis
Trientalis
Tripetelaia
Trollius
Uvularia
Viola

Appendix 2

Specialist Societies

The Specialist Societies have excellent publications with information about small perennials, as well as extensive seed lists.

Alpine Garden Society
AGS Centre, Avon Bank,
Pershore
Worcs WR10 3JP

North American Rock Garden Society
PO Box 67
Millwood
NY 10546
USA

Scottish Rock Garden Club
Groomís Cottage
Kirklands
Ancrum
Jedburgh
TD8 6UJ UK

The Hardy Plant Society
Little Orchard
Great Comberton
Nr Pershore
Worcs WR10 3DP

Hardy Plant Society Mid-Atlantic Group
49 Green Valley Rd
Wallingford
PA 19086
USA

British Hosta & Hemerocallis Society
Cleave House
Sticklepath
Okehampton
Devon EX20 2NN

American Hemerocallis Society
1454 Rebel Drive
Jackson
Mississipi 39211
USA

American Hosta Society
7802 NE 63rd Street
Vancouver
WA 98662
USA

British Iris Society
The Old Mill House
Shurton Stoquersey
Somerset
TA5 1QC

American Iris Society
8426 Vine valley Drive
Sun Valley
CA 91352
USA

American Penstemon Society
1569 South Holland Court
Lakewood
CO 80232
USA

Further Reading

Alpine Garden Society Encyclopedia of Alpines (1993). 2 vols.
Bird, R. *Border Pinks* (1994). Batsford.
Cobb, J.L.S. (1989) *Meconopsis.* Helm and Timber Press
Grey-Wilson, C. (1993). *Poppies.* Batsford.
Grey-Wilson, C. (1997). *Cyclamen.* Batsford.
Harkness, B.E. (1993). *Seedlist Handbook.* Batsford.
Jelitto & Schacht *Hardy Herbaceous Perennials* (1990). 2 vols. Batsford.
Köhlein, F. (1991). *Gentians.* Helm and Timber Press
Mathew, B. (1997). *Growing Bulbs.* Batsford.
Mathew, B. (1989). *Hellebores.* Alpine Garden Society.
Philips, R. & Rix, M. *Hardy Perennials* (1991). 2 vols. Pan.
Rice, G. *Hardy Perennials* (1995). Viking.
Rice, G. & Strangman, E. (1993). *Hellebores, The Gardener's Guide.* David & Charles.
Richards, J. (1993). *Primula.* Batsford.
Royal Horticultural Society A–Z Encyclopedia of Garden Plants (1996).
New Royal Horticultural Society Dictionary of Gardening (1992) 4 vols.
Stuart Thomas, G. (1982). *Perennial Garden Plants.* Dent.
Turner, R., (1995). *Euphorbias.* Batsford.
Yeo, P.F. *Hardy Geraniums* (1985). Batsford.